JIMMY DURANTE

JIMMY DURANTE

His Show Business Career

with an annotated
filmography and discography

by DAVID BAKISH

McFarland & Company, Inc., Publishers
Jefferson, North Carolina, and London

Frontispiece: Durante in a 1953 publicity shot for *The Colgate Comedy Hour*.

British Library Cataloguing-in-Publication data are available

Library of Congress Cataloguing-in-Publication Data

Bakish, David.
    Jimmy Durante : his show business career, with an annotated
filmography and discography / by David Bakish.
        p.   cm.
    Filmography: p.
    Discography: p.
    Includes bibliographical references (p.) and index. ∞
    ISBN 0-89950-968-1 (lib. bdg. : 50# alk. paper)
        1. Durante, Jimmy.   2. Entertainers—United States—Biography.
I. Title.
PN2287.D87B35   1995
792.7'028'092—dc20
    [B]   94-32141
                                                                          CIP

Manufactured in the United States of America

McFarland & Company, Inc., Publishers
Box 611, Jefferson, North Carolina 28640

For Linda,
her love and sense of humor.

To the memory of
my contralto aunt,
Louise Mitrani,
who always started each day
with a song.

And for Corey,
a sweet Yorkie who would love
to sink her teeth
into this book.

CONTENTS

ACKNOWLEDGMENTS

This study of Jimmy Durante's show business career is indebted to Gene Fowler's *Schnozzola* (1951), as well as to published comments by Bob Hope and many others; to interviews Durante himself gave for radio, television, and the print media; and to Durante associates and relatives who consented to interviews. Unlike earlier books on Durante, this study is carefully documented and carries appendices that should be valuable to later researchers and biographers. It should be noted that the wealth of conflicting information and incomplete recollections from Durante's friends and associates makes some errors of fact and omission inevitable. I hope other researchers will find Durante important and interesting enough to follow up and improve upon my work.

Most people whom I asked to share memories of Jimmy Durante were generous in their cooperation. Even before this project had taken shape, Dave Stryker, a trombonist at the Alamo Club in the early days, relived what he could recall; later, Sally Gappell, the widow of another trombonist at the Alamo, Moe Gappell, shared her memories. Although Margie Durante, Jimmy's widow, chose not to contribute, Jimmy's nephew Julie Romano, his wife, and children were most cordial. Marion Romano, the widow of Julie's brother Bobby, helped. Another nephew, Albert J. Durante, Jr., recalled the earliest days in New York.

Friends and associates of Durante in show business made my research easier: the late Garry Moore, Phil Cohan, Candy Candido, the late Jackie Barnett, Alan Young, the three children of Jack Roth (Margie Sexton, Eileen Euler, and the late Marty Roth), George Finley, Betty Jane Howarth, Wanda Smith, Vega Maddux, Sonny King, Ethel Bradley (sister of Durante housekeeper Maggie Arnold), Judge Abraham Lincoln Marovitz, Robert Golden (stepson of Eddie Jackson), Charles Isaacs, Jack Elinson, and Robert E. Rhodes, professor of journalism.

Since this book places its primary focus on understanding and laying out the elements of a career rather than on the personal life that is the focus of a traditional biography, most interview questions pertained to how

Durante used his material and how he interrelated with others in show business.

A greater effort was made to interview people with knowledge of the nightclub, radio, and television segments of Durante's career than of the less successful movie segment. I did view 37 of the 38 films in which Durante appeared, missing only the obscure Italian film *Il giudizio universale* directed by De Sica, and did read books by or about the actors, directors, and producers with whom Durante worked.

People who located records, cassettes, books, clippings, photographs, sheet music, and other helpful material include members of Record Research Associates, New York: Eric Anderson, Jerry Valburn, Dan Singer, Henry E. Schmidt, Len Kunstadt, Bob Lippet, David Weiner, and Lloyd Rauch (who put me in touch with Durante trombonist Dave Stryker). Others who offered helpful material were Tom J. Stuto, Ken Mills, Ray A. Gain, Jess Rand, Stuart Jay Weiss, Charles Stumpf, Sam "Trombone" Komoroff, Anthony DiFlorio III, John Newton, Steve Ramm, Ernie Harburg, Fred Carl, and David Inman (author of *The TV Encyclopedia*, 1991). Brian Rust, Mark Berresford, Charles Garrod, and Lawrence Gushee, professor of music, responded to discographical inquiries.

A number of important archives provided valuable information, including the New York Public Library at Lincoln Center, especially the Billy Rose Collection; the Cinema-Television Library of the University of Southern California, with special thanks to Ned Comstock, archives assistant, and Leith Adams, archivist, Warner Bros. Collection; the Theater Arts Library, the University of California at Los Angeles, with special thanks to its head, Brigitte J. Kueppers, and public services librarian Raymond Soto; the Rudy Vallee Collection, Thousand Oaks Library, Thousand Oaks, California, with special thanks to Henry K. Mattoon, archivist; SPERDVAC (the Society to Preserve and Encourage Radio Drama, Variety and Comedy), California; the Radio Historical Association of Colorado; Warner Bros. Archives, William Seymour Theater Collection, Princeton University Library; Martin Halperin, member of Pacific Pioneer Broadcasters; MGM Project, Catalogue Division, American Film Institute, Los Angeles, with thanks to Pat Hanson and David Parket; Motion Picture, Broadcasting and Recorded Sound Division, Library of Congress, with thanks to Madeline F. Matz, research librarian; Museum of Television and Radio, New York; Theater Department, Museum of the City of New York; Film Stills Archive, Museum of Modern Art, New York; Theater Collection, Free Library of Philadelphia.

I am grateful to the NBC Legal Department, which with the help of Ken Burr and Marcy Kinoo-Smith gave permission to quote extensively from an NBC Monitor Radio interview with Durante; to Professor Herman

Harvey, for providing a videotape of a televised interview he conducted with Durante, a transcript, and comments on what it was like to meet the comedian for a serious discussion; to Playbill, Inc., for permission to reprint the title page from its *Red, Hot and Blue!* Broadway program; to CPP/Belwin, which with the help of Len Perry gave permission to reprint lyrics from "You Gotta Start Off Each Day with a Song"; to the Museum of the City of New York, which provided two prints that originally appeared in *Collier's* magazine, and gave permission to republish them; to the Museum of Modern Art for providing one print for inclusion in my book; to Frank Driggs for providing one jazz picture. All other photographs are from my personal collection.

My thanks also go to the people who tried to help me place my book, particularly to Shana Alexander, Stanley Meyer, Patricia K. Meyer, and Marv Kaye.

Medgar Evers College, City University of New York, made the early days of my research easier by granting me a sabbatical from my position as professor of English and humanities.

My deepest gratitude goes to David Goldenberg, former president of the International Association of Jazz Record Collectors, a fan of vaudeville and radio, a close and generous friend who encouraged me from the beginning; to my dear friend Mort Savada, a renowned 78rpm jazz and pop record dealer with an encyclopedic knowledge; to Len Selk, a Benny Goodman scholar and friend who volunteered to read an early draft of my manuscript with a most critical eye; and to my wife Linda Kaplan Bakish who not only read my early and later drafts, but who endured my long hours incommunicado at the computer and even longer hours "on vacation" at research centers and interviewees' homes.

Finally, I am grateful to my parents, Sephardic immigrants from Bulgaria who brought me into the world on the Lower East Side of New York in 1937, and to my kid sister Reina, who takes pride in my writing despite our sibling rivalry.

DAVID BAKISH
New York
July 1994

INTRODUCTION

A look at the life and career of Jimmy Durante carries us through much of American popular culture in the twentieth century. There is Durante growing up on the culturally diverse Lower East Side, coming of age during the development of ragtime and jazz in gangster-dominated nightclubs. There is Durante in the carnival atmosphere of vaudeville, working on Broadway with extravagantly talented producers, in the Hollywood of the early days of sound movies, and among the exciting multitude of comedians on national radio. There is Durante with excellent nightclub-like variety shows in the golden years of early network television. There is, too, the Durante who shone most brightly for over fifty years: the master of nightclubs around the country, stretching from New York to Los Angeles, Las Vegas to Chicago, Detroit, Miami, and San Juan.

Practically everything in American culture has changed greatly in the hundred years since his birth in 1893, but the spirit of Jimmy Durante is still with us. Many Christmas seasons bring us Durante's inimitable voice narrating the animated story of *Frosty the Snowman*. As he sings the familiar title song, he is the gentle ghost of the Christmas spirit.

Sleepless in Seattle, a 1993 romantic comedy starring Tom Hanks and Meg Ryan, begins with Durante's recording of "As Time Goes By" and ends with his version of "Make Someone Happy." The viewers' mood is set by Durante's excellent evocation of gentle and enduring love. In the 1991 film comedy *City Slickers*, starring Billy Crystal, the soundtrack includes Jimmy Durante singing "Young at Heart." Crystal and two friends have arrived at a ranch to drive cattle and try to rediscover some honest roots of their confused middle-aged lives. Durante's song offers a counterpoint to the slickness that has obscured the roots of many Americans.

My Stepmother Is an Alien (1988), produced and directed by Richard Benjamin, is a science-fiction comedy and love story starring Dan Aykroyd as an M.I.T. scientist in contact with another galaxy. Kim Basinger is Celeste, the beautiful but bizarre emissary from space with whom Aykroyd falls in love. As the scientist tries to convey to Celeste all that is unpretentious, genuine, and good in ordinary life, much is made of Jimmy Durante as an example of the best that earthlings have produced, an embodiment of the qualities that must not be lost.

In the film's concluding hologram, Durante fades from view speaking his signature line of farewell, "Good night, Mrs. Calabash, wherever you are." Perhaps a new generation will rediscover Jimmy Durante—his talent, his generous spirit, his appeal to something within us that transcends shallow materialism.

Chapter 1

OVERVIEW OF A CAREER

Unique among entertainers, Jimmy Durante was not, to put it charitably, handsome. His big nose became his most famous trademark, about which the jokes were endless and endlessly amusing, like Jack Benny's reputed stinginess, Harpo Marx's pocketful of silverware, or Gracie Allen's relatives. He was called *Il Naso*—The Nose—in his childhood, Schnozzle professionally in the 1930s, Schnozzola or The Schnoz later.

Jimmy can be seen in a widely published toddler picture wearing a frilly brocade dress. Everyone, including the adult Jimmy, knew how homely he was, even as a baby. Yet he was to turn the tears of childhood into the poetic laughter of a comic Cyrano de Bergerac. Cole Porter's classic song "You're the Top," written for the 1934 musical *Anything Goes*, immortalizes Jimmy's nose. In typically witty lyrics that pay tribute to everything that can be considered the best and finest in the world, Cole Porter lists Mahatma Gandhi, Napoleon brandy; a Waldorf salad, a Berlin ballad; Fred Astaire, Camembert; a Dutch Master, Mrs. Astor; and rhymes *Inferno*'s Dante with "the nose on the great Durante."[1]

His second most talked about trademark was his show-closing, "Good night Mrs. Calabash, wherever you are." Visually, his closing ranks among the most effective of any on television. As the music for "Goodnight, Goodnight" (written by chief songwriter Jackie Barnett and Durante) began, he put on his hat and coat. Retreating from one spotlight to another, he ended the song and added his radio show adieu, "Good night, folks. And good night, Mrs. Calabash, wherever you are." When Durante is mentioned today, people still ask, "Who was Mrs. Calabash?"

Durante's third trademark was his mangling of the English language, making him the perfect foil for impeccable elocutionists such as John Barrymore and Arthur Treacher as well as for "Spanglish" spitfires like Lupe Velez and Carmen Miranda. He liked to combine his verbal misfires with courtly French phrases like "parlez-moi d'amour,"[2] all the while dressed in gentleman's top hat and tails. As he would so often say, singing with overwhelming politeness, "I'm Jimmy, the Well Dressed Man."

3

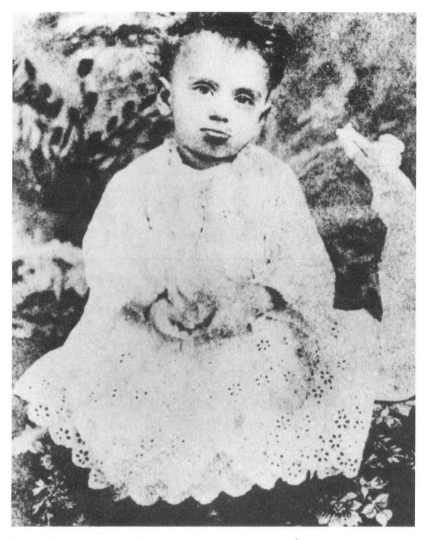

James Francis Durante as a toddler. Circa 1895. (Museum of the City of New York, The Theater Collection.)

All his career Jimmy showed in his performance material a respect for the refined speech and manners of educated and wealthy people, mixed with amusement at what looked so often like pretense or affectation. It was always a case of the street kid looking at the dandy, of the grade school dropout fencing with unwieldy weapons.

Perhaps most unusual about Durante was the total absence of enemies in both his personal and professional lives. In his dealings with mobsters and messeigneurs, he seemed to brighten the lives of all. Durante's great talent for the piano, for singing, for strutting, and for writing songs was matched by an equal talent for generosity to family, friends, audiences, strangers, children, charities, church groups, synogogues, and even gangsters and prostitutes who asked his help. He condemned no one, antagonized no one. The meanest of gossip magazines and newspaper columns rarely printed an unkind word about Durante.

In his mind, Durante was all his career part of a vaudeville act— Clayton, Jackson, and Durante—whose successful formula should not be changed. Over the years he continued to rely heavily on songs, interrupting himself with gags and stories, then returning to more of the songs and more interruptions. Like Eddie Cantor, he jumped around the stage in displays of high energy. Like the Marx Brothers, he broke up stage furniture and made dignified society matrons and gentlemen the butt of much humor. He used the same material—songs and gags and favorite mispronunciations—over and over with fans who expected repeat performances.

Some of these songs he wrote himself: "Inka Dinka Doo," "I'm Jimmy, the Well Dressed Man," "So I Ups to Him," and "You Gotta Start Off Each Day with a Song," among many others. Durante had a way of delivering songs that many tried, in jesting tribute, to copy. "When I sing a song, it's ruint forever!" said Jimmy. Al Jolson, Bing Crosby, and Frank Sinatra loved to sing duets with Durante, especially "You Gotta Start Off Each Day with a Song." Even opera greats such as Helen Traubel sang that song with him—all to their willing disadvantage.

When his personal success exceeded that of the Clayton, Jackson, and Durante team and only he was offered an MGM contract, he kept his partners on the payroll. Lou Clayton became his business manager, the tough, hard-pushing key to making Durante as big a star as he became. Eddie Jackson became part of many nightclub engagements and of the television show on which Durante captured the ambiance of vaudeville and his short-lived speakeasy of the 1920s, the Club Durant. When Clayton died in 1950, Durante was so upset he almost left show business instead of moving on to television for the next important step in his career. For years he kept Lou Clayton's pajamas and slippers by the side of his own bed.

In time, his material changed slightly: as he got older, he sang more sentimental songs mixed in with the old standbys. With Jackie Barnett producing, the old razz-ma-tazz alternated with songs of age like the Kurt Weill-Maxwell Anderson "September Song" or Cliff Friend and Jack Reynolds' "Old Man Time."

This star of vaudeville, the Broadway stage, Hollywood pictures, radio, television, recordings, and nightclubs never demanded star treatment. When MGM offered him a five-year contract in 1931, he moved from a modest home in Flushing, Queens (New York City), to bigger but still modest homes in areas of Los Angeles including, later, Beverly Hills. He remained in southern California for the rest of his life, except when in residence for business at the Astor Hotel in New York. At the Beverly Hills home, he did have a pool where his pals hung out, but he never put up a gate and fence to limit access to the house. He never refused autographs. He waved to fans as they called out to him when he drove his big convertible. The whole world knew him simply as "Jimmy," their Jimmy. His two wives, Jeanne, who died in 1943, and Margie, who survives him, were troubled by the lack of privacy and all the traveling he had to do, but Jimmy never closed the door to his many friends nor to his adoring public.

Jimmy's humor was rough-hewn yet gentle and innocent. His was always a family-oriented act, good for children as well as for adults. In an early 1960s television interview, Jimmy Durante indicated that he preferred performing for the working people. "That's America, the working class. I'd rather work for the working class that is America than go to the biggest affair out here in California and work for producers and anyone in the craft."[3]

In his book written with Pete Martin, *Have Tux, Will Travel* (1954), Bob Hope concisely analyzed the comic styles of many of his fellow stars. Durante, Hope said, "plays an obvious mug who can't handle big words, but who can handle a lot of laughs. He's got a happy personality and he makes you think he's having more fun than anybody else."[4]

Phil Cohan, Durante's radio show director and producer in the 1940s, observed that Jimmy Durante was not deliberately funny, not really a comic, but rather a "character." "You know, I never heard Jimmy tell a joke, in all the years. He loved to hear other people tell a joke."[5] Garry Moore, Durante's popular co-host on that radio show, said, "I don't think Durante made up a joke in his life, for himself. But he was very shrewd about what worked for him and what didn't. When we writers were sitting around talking, and someone would come up with a joke, Durante would laugh at it, and say, 'Yeah, but that ain't for me.'"[6]

Garry Moore thought people appreciate Durante for the wrong reasons: he pointed to what Robert Benchley, the humorist, remarked, that there ought to be an association, a *small* association, of people who appreciate Durante for the right reasons. Sure he was funny, and he was comical looking, but also there was an innate gentlemanliness about him, a certain nobility. If you only laughed at him because he had a big nose and talked in a rough voice and used malapropisms, that was not appreciating him for the right reasons. There was a certain extra quality about Durante—the audience didn't even know that was why they liked him so much.[7]

Chapter 2

BEGINNINGS AND FAMILY ROOTS

Durante grew up where he was born, on Manhattan's immigrant-filled Lower East Side. He was the youngest of four children. His father, Bartolomeo Durante, was a barber from Salerno, Italy. His mother, Rosa, also from Salerno, was a mail-order bride.

In his twenties, Bartolomeo had signed up as a day laborer and come to New York. Here he joined a construction crew building the Third Avenue El, a project the city authorized to begin in 1875, and completed in 1878.[1] Later, Bartolomeo also worked as a night watchman.[2]

An Italian woman who lived with her husband in the same Brooklyn boarding house as Bartolomeo, a Mrs. Lentino, saw the young man was homesick for Italy and lonely. She mentioned her sister still living in Salerno and asked if Bartolomeo wanted to write to her. He did. After a courtship by mail, he saved the money to pay passage for Rosa to become his wife. She is said to have arrived by ship on October 28, 1886, the same day the Statue of Liberty was unveiled on Bedloe's Island in New York Harbor.[3]

Bartolomeo opened a barbershop in Brooklyn. After the birth of their first two sons, Michael and Albert, and in 1891, their only daughter, Lilian, the family moved to Manhattan's Lower East Side. Bartolomeo took over a barbershop at 112 Cherry Street. The family lived at the rear in a three-room apartment on the ground floor with the entrance at 90 Catherine Street.[4] Nearby were South Street, the ships in the East River, Chinatown, and the Brooklyn and Manhattan bridges.

Jacob Riis, the nineteenth-century Danish immigrant, graphically described slum conditions on the Lower East Side in his landmark books *How the Other Half Lives* (1890), *The Children of the Poor* (1892), and *The Battle with the Slum* (1902), reinforced by the many flash photographs he took inside the tenements. In this area, overcrowded with the poorest European immigrants and their large families, Riis observed as many as six children sleeping in one bed. In one double tenement a police count

7

showed 297 tenants, 45 under the age of five, plus three peddlers sleeping in the muddy basement. All endured the hot stale air of summer, flocking to the streets and fire escapes for relief, and the insufficient heating during cold winters, sleeping bundled in their street clothes to keep warm.

Despite conditions of great poverty and high death rates among young children, this Lower East Side nurtured many great people, especially in the arts: the sculptor Jacob Epstein, composers Irving Berlin and George Gershwin, lyricist Ira Gershwin, comedians Joseph Weber and Lew Fields, Willie and Eugene Howard, Eddie Cantor, Fanny Brice, George Jessel, and George Burns.

Pointing to the family and community spirit that enriched the difficult lives of Lower East Siders, Durante told a television interviewer, "My dad made a good livin'. I wasn't born in poverty—not rich, but he owned a barbershop and he just made a good livin'. I used to work after school sellin' papers.... We were born in the back of the barbershop, three rooms, you know, where the facilities were out in the yard, and if there was anyone sick in your house you'd find the whole neighborhood up there washin' the dishes, cookin' for ya and dis and dat. But today you're lucky [if] you know your own neighbor. You haven't got that family spirit. [There were] very few shootings and killings—fathers killin' their children and [a] mother leavin' her child on the doorstep."[5]

When Bartolomeo and Rosa's youngest child, James Francis, was born in 1893, he was delivered by an Italian midwife and baptized by a local priest.[6] Before too long the Durante family moved upstairs to a larger apartment, and in 1903, when James Francis was ten, they moved again, to nearby No. 1 Catherine Slip.

Jimmy was given a nickname by other Italian immigrants and children on the street: "Naso," Italian for "nose." Durante was to say years later, "My nose made me a shriekin' violet ... I'd go home and cry.... I made up my mind never to hurt anybody else, no matter what. I never made jokes about anybody's big ears, cross eyes, or their stutterin'."

After school at P.S. 114, Jimmy sold newspapers and was known not only for his big nose but also for having the loudest voice among newsboys. It was said that the mayor of New York sent out for a paper when Jimmy's voice shook City Hall.

Jimmy began piano lessons with Professor Fiori, a short, mustached, authoritarian Italian, chosen by his father. Bartolomeo and Rosa thought Jimmy should study classical music. He was given works like "Poet and Peasant" and "La Paloma" to learn. Each lesson cost one dollar. But try as he did, his heart was not in it. He preferred playing the rags of Scott Joplin. As Durante told a radio audience in 1963, a tribute on his seventieth birthday, "it was quite an event when we got our piano. They had to hoist it up to the fourth floor and go in through the window. We were the aristocrats of that neighborhood: I think we were the only ones with a piano. And I had a lot of trouble with my professor. He wanted me to play 'Poet and Peasant,' and I wouldn't practice, and I wanted to be a great ragtime piano player."[7]

By the eighth grade Jimmy had dropped out of school to help support the family. Odd jobs included driving a one-horse coal wagon for three days and working at a wholesale hardware store on Chambers Street, where he earned $7.50 a week as head of the stockroom and one of the errand boys, until he was fired for representing the other boys in a request for higher pay.[8]

Jimmy's mother Rosa had a fiery temper. She was very proud and very intelligent, though uneducated. Rosa and her sister, Mrs. Palladino, had a rivalry. They both wanted their sons to play the piano. Mrs. Palladino's son, Arthur Palladino, was better at classical piano. When Angelo Fiori got tired of New York in the 1930s, he moved to California where he gave Bobby Romano, Rosa's grandson, piano lessons, with similar lack of results. None of his students became accomplished classical pianists.[9]

Jimmy's brother Michael, a young man, worked at the American Banknote Company on Broad Street, where he also got Jimmy work as a glass-washer and errand boy. In 1910 Michael got sick, and both he and Jimmy lost their jobs.[10] According to relatives, Michael later worked in the bookbinding business in New York. Jimmy's other brother, Albert J., became a policeman, working out of the Elizabeth Street Station on the Lower East Side before becoming a detective.[11] Albert died at Polyclinic Hospital after an abdominal operation April 18, 1934. A brief obituary appeared in *Variety*.[12]

Rosa's third child, Lilian, married Genaro Romano in New York City, December 18, 1910, at Transfiguration Church, Park Row and Mott Street. That marriage produced three sons. Genaro got sick (possibly a mental illness), causing much stress to the family. He went off to Italy to recuperate and stayed there. Lilian seemed glad to be rid of him. She owned a three-story apartment building, and with Jimmy's help she was able to manage.[13]

Jimmy bought a six-room frame house in Ridgewood, Queens, on the border with Brooklyn, shortly before his mother died of a blood clot in the brain, January 1, 1921. His father, sister Lilian, and her sons took up residence there. Bartolomeo was happy to give free haircuts to the local parish priests at Our Lady of the Miraculous Medal, on 60th Place, Ridgewood. He also derived pleasure from handing out money from Jimmy to children he encountered on the street.

Jimmy talked little about his family, with the exception of his mild-mannered father. There are photographs of Bartolomeo visiting Jimmy in Hollywood, sitting beside the pool, and reports that the old man, a proud barber, wanted to give Tarzan (Johnny Weissmuller) a haircut that he thought was much overdue. Jimmy himself was fond of telling how he once asked his father how he liked his son's movie performance, to which the old man replied, "Let's not get into an argument!"

Jimmy's father died on February 27, 1941, at the age of 92, at the Midtown Hospital on East 49th Street in Manhattan. Both *Variety* and *The New York Times* reported the death. Mentioned as his sole survivors were Jimmy Durante and Bartolomeo's daughter, Mrs. Lilian Romano, with whom Mr. Durante had lived at 61-54 Palmetto Street, Ridgewood, Queens.[14]

Within three years, 1941–43, Jimmy was to lose his father, his sister, and his wife Jeanne. The heartaches of childhood must have seemed small compared to these crises and the death of partner-manager Lou Clayton in 1950. It must have been hard to continue clowning for audiences, but Durante in time recreated a "family" of lifelong friends and associates. Although he never had any children of his own, he did very late in his life, at age 69, adopt a baby girl with his second wife.

Chapter 3

RAGTIME AND
NIGHTCLUBS

In 1908, at the age of 15, Jimmy was playing ragtime at neighborhood parties for 75 cents a night, as well as in Bowery clubs and between bouts at a prizefighting arena. Young Jimmy's first real professional job was playing piano in Coney Island. He began in 1910, after successfully trying out for the job by playing Scott Joplin's "Maple Leaf Rag," and went on to develop a local reputation as the best white jazz piano-player.

One history of the famous resort, entitled *Sodom by the Sea*, characterized Coney Island entertainment as "abounding in sentimentality and slapstick, for audiences consisting largely of urban yokels ... dens where sports and sophisticates were short-changed, insulted, jollied, swindled, drugged, slugged, robbed and occasionally murdered."[1] Drunk customers who still had money were sometimes given stale ginger ale and celery tonic instead of the champagne for which they were paying. Beginning in the 1870s, cabarets furnished the bulk of nighttime entertainment at Coney Island. One cabaret owner who later figured in Durante's early career was Carey Walsh. Walsh ran the Indiana House on Surf Avenue with Joe Gorman, a pickpocket. Walsh forced Gorman out and continued the establishment on his own. He would slip Mickey Finns into drinks for the hell of it; reportedly, he went into the rival Stauch's Restaurant, which claimed the largest dance floor in the world, and gave Mickey Finns to 25 American sailors "just for laughs." Louis Stauch offered a reward for finding the guilty party, but no one wanted to spoil a good joke.[2]

Early Coney Island pavilions perched on the sand within 200 to 300 yards of the high-water mark, and some had hotel accommodations, like Duffy's St. Nicholas Hotel.[3] Each spring the seaside resort would crank up its entertainment to supplement the attractive beach for working class sunbathers. A wall separated Coney Island from Sea Gate, its rich neighbor, preventing the hoi polloi from invading the domain of the elite, although many enjoyed the excitement of Coney Island's rough night life.[4]

Not least among the nighttime draws were the many Surf Avenue clubs that featured booze, loose women, ragtime bands, and singing waiters trying to get into show business. One of the earliest singing waiters to achieve success was Irving Berlin, born 1888 in Russia as Israel Baline.[5] Like Durante, he dropped out of school to help his family, and among many odd jobs worked a summer at Coney Island as a "straight" waiter at Stauch's and as a singing waiter at Perry's.

Izzy, as he was known, also worked as a singing waiter in a Chinatown saloon on Pell Street, the Pelham Cafe, run by a Russian Jew, Mike Salter, whom patrons called "Nigger Mike." The year was 1904, and Izzy was approaching 17. With the pianist at Pelham's, Izzy wrote a song "Marie, from Sunny Italy." The music was by pianist Mike Nicholson, with lyrics by Israel Baline. Perhaps because the name sounded "too Jewish," the sheet music published by Joseph W. Stern & Company contained the pseudonym "I. Berlin." For good luck, Izzy, now 19 years old, stuck with the new name, turning the "I" into "Irving."[6] Irving Berlin began pouring out a prolific stream of popular songs, reaching an early peak of popular and financial success in 1911 with "Alexander's Ragtime Band."[7]

In the spring and summer of 1910, a skinny, 5 foot, 7 inch, 17-year-old Jimmy Durante, played ragtime piano at Coney Island. The club, known variously as the College Inn or Diamond Tony's, was run by Antonio (Diamond Tony) Lento and was located on 15th Street, just off the main nightclub strip, Surf Avenue. Jimmy played every night from eight o'clock until the wee hours of the morning. His salary was $25 a week, which he got all in singles to impress his mother.

Prostitutes walking Surf Avenue rested at Jimmy's piano, finding him a sympathetic young man. Gene Fowler, Durante's biographer, writes about one of the women who had her drinks next to Jimmy's piano. Gladie was about 20 and a beautiful brunette. Jimmy fell for her, yearning to be her boyfriend. But every time he played the songs she liked, it only kindled her feelings for other men. Gladie would disappear for periods of time, returning to ask Jimmy for money to cover all her "emergencies." Once she wrote to Jimmy for money to help with an operation; she also wrote to Eddie Jackson asking $50. When Durante asked her on a long-distance phone call how much she needed, she upped the amount to $100. Although he knew he was being taken for a sucker, he told Gladie he would send her a check not only for the hundred she asked from him but also the 50 she asked from Jackson. Gladie's reply was "God bless you, Jimmy!"[8]

In the fall of 1910, Jimmy played piano at the Chatham Club on Doyers Street in Chinatown, five blocks from his home, then returned to Coney Island for the 1911 season, this time at Carey Walsh's place and with the new nickname "Ragtime Jimmy." Here he was often joined by singing waiters including Izzy Iskowitch, soon to be known as Eddie Cantor.

Cantor, a teenager, had started at Carey Walsh's with another boy, Joe Malitz. They worked as straight waiters for $3 apiece, less than one-third the amount earned by the singing waiters. When Malitz learned of the difference in salary, he quit. Cantor decided to stay and became a singing waiter.[9]

Cantor and Durante worked together just that one season. Cantor had already appeared in vaudeville, most recently in the act "Bedini & Arthur, Assisted by Eddie Cantor." In 1912, Cantor would join a vaudeville act produced by Gus Edwards, "Kid Kabaret," with George Jessel, Eddie Buzzel, Georgie Price, Leila Lee, and Gregory Kelly. The act brought in over $1,000 a week, considered very high for that day.

But at Coney Island, Cantor was hustling for tips with Durante. It wasn't long before they discovered a way to milk regular customers. Sentimental songs appealed to the tough audience the club drew, songs like New York Mayor Jimmy Walker's "Will You Love Me in December as You Do in May?," "I Wish I Had My Old Gal Back Again," "My Gal Sal," "The Ace in the Hole," and "All Aboard for Blanket Bay." One customer requested "Somebody Stole My Gal" so often that the musicians got sick and tired of it despite the sport's forking out $150 to $200 each time they met his request.[10]

Jimmy would memorize favorite songs of the richer customers and play them on the piano whenever a big tipper came in the door. Once a group of western tourists requested a song about a bluebird. Durante and Cantor didn't know what they were talking about so they faked it. When the westerners said that wasn't the song, Cantor, wide-eyed, asked, "Oh, are there two bluebirds?"[11]

Police raids of Coney Island cabarets had started about 1910, inspired by changing standards of public morality and the brawls resulting from heavy drinking and sex. Durante said, "You couldn't build a Sunday school out of those night spots. People knew they were tough joints, and if they gave 'em a play, had nobody but themselves to kick if they lost their shirts."[12] Prostitution was almost as big a problem as drinking, with girls flocking to Coney Island for each season, coming chiefly from Jersey City, Albany, and Boston.

By 1914 or 1915, Ragtime Jimmy had already played in about 20 joints all over New York. One of the rowdiest of these was Maxine's in Brooklyn, closed by the police. Said Jimmy, "Maxine's was so tough, that if you took off your hat, you was a sissy." There and elsewhere, Jimmy was surrounded by gamblers and mobsters who often gave him tips on betting the horses. Jimmy began a lifelong interest in horse racing, but was never a successful gambler. He wanted the winning horse so badly, he sometimes bet on four or five horses in the same race.[13]

In 1914 Jimmy got a job that would be important to his career and personal life. He began playing piano and soon was also in charge of hiring entertainment at the Alamo Club, also known as the Alamo Cafe, 253 West 125th Street. One of the best rathskellers in Harlem, with a large dance floor, it occupied the basement of the Hurtig and Seamon's burlesque house, catering to a white clientele. (In 1925, the place became the Swanee Club, a black nightclub that lasted until 1935.)[14] The girls from the burlesque shows dropped in after their work.[15] Durante said he got "$45 a week and tips for playing from 8 o'clock at night till I was subconscious."[16] He continued to play summers at Coney Island, first at the College Arms, then the College Inn, under the same management as the Alamo.[17] Both seasonal jobs would last the next seven or eight years.

By 1917, Chicago and New York were beginning to replace New Orleans as the base from which that great American artform, jazz, would grow. In that year, Storyville, the red-light district of New Orleans, had its brothels closed by order of the U.S. Navy. This brought unemployment to many jazz musicians, especially blacks, who decided to move north. By the end of the first world war, New Orleans was no longer the center of black and white jazz activity.

That same year, Jimmy went one night to one of the five Reisenweber's restaurants in New York, a small branch on Columbus Circle, to hear the hot new sensation, the Original Dixieland Jazz Band. It was an all-white group from New Orleans, led by Nick La Rocca. On their opening night, January 19, 1917, fresh from New Orleans and Chicago engagements, the management notice read, "Due to the expense of bringing the Original Dixie Land Jazz Band. We are Forced to Charge *a small sum of 25 cents per Person* during their Stay Only."[18] Durante was so impressed by the band that he invited them to play one night at the Alamo.

The Original Dixieland Jazz Band was a hit in New York, and less than two weeks later, January 30, made their recording debut for Columbia records, doing "Darktown Strutters' Ball" and "Indiana." But the company showed no interest in releasing the recording to the public or in doing more numbers, so the ODJB went to Columbia's chief competitor, Victor, where they recorded on February 26, 1917, "Livery Stable Blues" and "Dixie Jass Band One-Step" (Intro. "That Teasin' Rag"). This was the first of many records they would make for Victor. What had started as an imitation of black New Orleans sounds now became so popular that many other white jazz groups copied the ODJB. By way of saying thanks to the place that launched their big-time popularity, the ODJB named one of their recorded numbers "Reisenweber Rag" (Aeolian Vocalion, November 24, 1917).

Durante pursued his fascination with black music that had begun with hearing Scott Joplin's rags. He raved about this New Orleans jazz style. Through his friendship with New Orleans drummer Johnny Stein,

Durante's band at Alamo Club, New York City, circa 1917. Left to right: Johnny Stein, drums; Frank Lhotak, trombone; Frank Christian, cornet; Achille Baquet, clarinet; Jimmy Durante, piano. (Museum of the City of New York, The Theater Collection.)

Durante learned about a number of white New Orleans jazz musicians he might hire for the Alamo's five-piece band. Between 1915 and 1918, with Stein's help, Durante organized the Durante Original Jazz & Novelty Band and for recording in late 1918 and early 1919, the Original New Orleans Jazz Band.

Durante imported the best white ragtime players he could find. He got Johnny Stein (John Hountha Stein), drummer; Frank Christian, cornet; Frank Lhotak, trombone, from the midwest but playing in New Orleans; Achille Baquet, clarinet.[19] Baquet was, unknown to all, a light-skinned Creole Negro, the brother of George Baquet, the clarinetist with Freddie Keppard and the Creole Band,[20] important for having inspired jazzmen Jimmie Noone and Sidney Bechet (both also from New Orleans). Later, Alfred "Pantsy" Laine, Jack "Papa" Laine, Arnold Loyacano, Jack Loyacano, and Doc Behrendson, all from New Orleans, passed through Durante's Alamo band, as did Frank Cush (later with the California Ramblers) and Dave Stryker, neither from New Orleans.

Until as late as 1933, it was rare for black jazz musicians to play or record with white bands and still rarer for whites to work with black bands. Coleman Hawkins recorded with the white Mound City Blue Blowers on the Victor label in 1929 and on the Okeh label in 1931. White musicians Jack Teagarden, Joe Sullivan, and Eddie Lang recorded on the Okeh label with Louis Armstrong and his Orchestra in 1929. In November 1933, Billie Holiday made her recording debut with Benny Goodman (playing with a pick-up group, not his regular orchestra, which was formed a few months later). In February 1934, Benny Goodman and his Orchestra recorded some numbers with tenor saxophonist Coleman Hawkins. Additional

Durante's Jazz & Novelty Band, circa 1918. Left to right: Johnny Stein, drums; Achille Baquet, clarinet; Frank Christian, cornet; Frank Lhotak, trombone; Jimmy Durante, piano. (Frank Driggs Collection.)

important steps in racial integration occurred when Goodman hired Teddy Wilson in 1935, followed by his hiring of Lionel Hampton, Fletcher Henderson, Charlie Christian, and Cootie Williams, all in the years 1936–40.

When the popularity of radio began to cut into record sales, Columbia Records, a leading producer of jazz records, together with Okeh and Victor Records, was kept afloat by its increasing issue of "race" records in the 1920s, recordings by black musicians, including the extremely popular (especially with the black public) Bessie Smith, who did her first recordings in 1923. Many white performers and groups copied black singing and playing styles, often refining and removing the rough edges that made black music appealing in the first place.

Late in 1918, probably November, Jimmy Durante led his New Orleans Jazz Band in recording for the Okeh label. At studios in New York they recorded "Ole Miss" and "Ja Da" (Intro. "You'll Find Old Dixieland In France"). These numbers were redone in January 1919 for the Gennett label and again by Gennett about March of that year, under the name

Original New Orleans Jazz Band.[21] What we hear on these rare early jazz recordings, running about three minutes each, is a hot jazz band with exciting sounds. Behind the lead clarinet of Achille Baquet we have the strong driving piano of Jimmy Durante and the drums of Arnold Loyacano propelling the band.

In May 1920, Durante recorded with the Alamo band under the name Jimmy Durante's Jazz Band. They did "Why Cry Blues" for Gennett, the only side to be released under this group's name. Achille Baquet excelled at a crying and laughing clarinet lead, in ensemble with Frank Christian, cornet; possibly Dave Stryker, trombone; Johnny Stein, drums; Jimmy Durante, piano.[22] The instrumental was written by Durante and Baquet, one of Durante's first known compositions; the other was "The Symphony Jass Fox-Trot," co-written with Jefferson D. Loyacano. Both were copyrighted December 8, 1919. The latter was never recorded.[23]

Durante's work did not seem much hindered by the coming of Prohibition earlier that year, 1920. On January 16, the 18th Amendment to the Constitution, ratified by the necessary two-thirds of the states on January 16, 1919, went into effect all across the country. The prohibition of alcohol, a noble social experiment or an ill-conceived folly, resulted in increasingly violent organized crime feeding on popular resentment of individual rights lost. The places Durante and his group played became the shadowy speakeasies of the "roaring twenties," the unsavory surroundings for jazz not so far removed from the New Orleans brothels of the 1910s.

The year 1921 was marked by an outpouring of more jazz recordings with Durante at the piano and (often ignored by writers who discuss Durante's career) the first large batch of published songs from Durante as composer.

In 1921, Durante collaborated with the famous black jazz singer Mamie Smith and black composer Chris Smith on the song "Let's Agree to Disagree." For someone who loved Scott Joplin as a child and who admired the jazz of black New Orleans culture, it must have been a thrill to write and play music in that rich vein. That same year Durante wrote "Daddy, Your Mama Is Lonesome for You," with lyrics by Chris Smith and Bob Schafer (which Durante sold outright for $100); "I've Got My Habits On," lyrics by Smith and Schafer, a near-hit which earned Durante almost $1,500 in royalties; "Sweetness," with lyrics by Schafer and Dave Ringle; "I Didn't Start in to Love You," lyrics by Sam Coslow; "I'm on My Way to New Orleans," lyrics by Bartley Costello; and "One of Your Smiles," music by William Herries and Durante, lyrics by Costello and John J. Kenny.

Among these early songs, the biggest hit was "I've Got My Habits On," which was published by Goodman & Rose, Inc. The sheet music cover has a blackface sketch plus insert photo of white singer [Isabella]

Patricola, who recorded it on Victor, November 22, 1921. Several other performers and groups recorded the song: Bailey's Lucky Seven, with Durante the probable piano player, Gennett, December 1921; Joseph Samuels' Jazz Band, Okeh, c. October 29, 1921; [Ben] Selvin's Dance Orchestra, Vocalion, c. November 16, 1921; Bennie Krueger and his Orchestra, Brunswick, c. December 1921. In January 1922, the great black jazz piano player James P. Johnson recorded a solo version of the song for a QRS piano roll.

The success of "I've Got My Habits On" resulted in Durante signing a contract with Joe Davis as a staff composer for the Triangle Music Publishing Company.[24] "Let's Agree to Disagree" was published by Triangle. Davis was a white publisher who wanted to capture the "race" song sheet music market. Triangle handled mostly blues and popular songs written by blacks. In the 1930s he changed the name of the company he had founded in 1919 to Joe Davis, Inc. Among other minstrel pamphlets, Davis compiled and edited *Tip Top Entertainment and Minstrel Album* (1936) and *Georgia Minstrel and Entertainment Folio* (1940).

Chris Smith, song collaborator with Durante, started in show business with a black medicine show, and did a vaudeville act with Elmer Bowman.[25] Smith wrote many songs for top black talent of the day, not only for Mamie Smith but also for Bert Williams ("You're in the Right Church but the Wrong Pew," introduced at Broadway's Majestic Theatre in the production *Bandana Land*, February 3, 1908). Collaborating with Henry Troy and Clarence Williams, he wrote "Cake Walking Babies from Home" for Alberta Hunter. She recorded it for Gennett, December 1924, under the pseudonym Josephine Beatty, accompanied by Clarence Williams' Red Onion Jazz Babies, featuring Louis Armstrong on cornet and Sidney Bechet on clarinet/soprano sax. Smith's best-known song was "Ballin' the Jack," written with lyricist Jim Burris.

Perry Bradford, a songwriter, pianist-singer, and one of the few blacks publishing black music, recalls in his autobiography *Born with the Blues* (1965) that in 1923 Jimmy Durante and Eddie Jackson came to his Perry Bradford Music Publishing Company in the Gaiety Theater Building at 1547 Broadway to "get the Negro slant on how to do 'Stewin' the Rice,' a new dance. . . ." Chris Smith and Jim Burris were in the office at the time. In that same building were W.C. Handy's company, the Pace & Handy Music Company; the office of Bert Williams & Will Vodery; and a music publishing firm run by the black jazz pianist, leader, and composer, Clarence Williams, composer of "Royal Garden Blues," written with Spencer Williams (no relation), "Sugar Blues," "Gulf Coast Blues," and "I Ain't Gonna Give Nobody None of My Jelly Roll."[26]

Jazz recordings with Durante on piano continued to pour out through that productive year of 1921. Durante worked with several groups composed of much the same personnel chosen by Sam Lanin, prolific bandleader responsible for hiring many of the best white jazzmen early in their careers. By changing the names of the groups, Lanin could collect money from more small record labels. One of these groups was called Lanin's Southern Serenaders. Phil Napoleon, later to become a jazz luminary, was the trumpet player in the sextet, with Durante on piano and Jack Roth on drums. Roth would play with this and with increasingly more professional (quality) jazz groups until 1922, when he became Durante's long-time career drummer and part of his inner circle. The group, which also included Doc Behrendson on clarinet, Loring McMurray on alto sax, possibly Moe Gappell or Dave Stryker on trombone, recorded for the small, obscure label, Arto, "Memphis Blues" and "The St. Louis Blues." A month later, about August 1, 1921, they recorded for the larger Emerson label, "Shake It and Break It" and "Aunt Hagar's Children Blues." Other recordings followed for Pathe Actuelle, for Emerson, and for Banner. Durante made his last recording with this group around February 1922. When Lanin's Southern Serenaders next recorded in July 1922, Frank Signorelli had replaced Durante on the piano.

Overlapping this period with Lanin's Southern Serenaders were Lanin groups called Ladd's Black Aces and Bailey's Lucky Seven. Durante was their piano player. Ladd's Black Aces recorded for Gennett "Shake It and Break It" and "Aunt Hagar's Children Blues," August 1921, the same numbers many of the same musicians were recording for Emerson as Lanin's Southern Serenaders. Ladd's Black Aces continued recording with Durante through November 1921. Frank Signorelli took over the piano chores on the group's next date, about February 25, 1922.

Bailey's Lucky Seven, with Durante, recorded for Gennett, "How Many Times?" and "Wimmin (I Gotta Have 'Em, That's All)" in October 1921. Durante left the group at the end of the year, replaced by an unknown piano player and on some of the later sessions by Signorelli. Roth remained on drums until about 1924. Jazz heavyweights who played on later sessions, minus Durante, were Miff Mole, trombone, from October 1923 on, and Red Nichols, trumpet, from August 1924 on. The last recorded session was February 1926.

In April 1922, the Original Memphis Five, one of the most important early white jazz groups, made its first recording, "Gypsy Blues" and "My Honey's Lovin' Arms," for Arto. Jack Roth was the drummer on this and all other recording sessions through 1925. Other members of this group's first recording were Phil Napoleon, trumpet; Miff Mole, trombone; Jimmy Lytell, clarinet; Frank Signorelli, piano; later, Loring McMurray, alto sax and tenor sax; Charlie Panelli, trombone; and, in 1926, Red Nichols, trumpet.

The Original Memphis Five was named after W.C. Handy's "Memphis

Blues." Signorelli and Napoleon argued many years later over which of the two started the band. In *Variety*'s 18th anniversary issue, January 3, 1924, an ad was placed for Frank Signorelli, "organizer and manager of the Original Memphis Five (pianist)" and Phil Napoleon, cornetist of the Original Memphis Five. At the bottom of the Season's Greetings are the additional names of James Lytell, clarinet; Jack Roth, drums; Charles Pavely (sic), trombone. The OMF had first played together the summer of 1917 at the Harvard Inn, a Coney Island dance hall. When the band broke up, Signorelli and Lytell joined the more famous Original Dixieland Jazz Band; Napoleon and Mole joined Sam Lanin's orchestra at the Roseland Ballroom; and Jack Roth replaced Johnny Stein in Jimmy Durante's band.

It's clear that some of the jazzmen with whom Durante recorded from late 1918 to early 1922 went on to establish solid reputations in early white jazz. From other groups that had included Durante, they formed the very much respected Original Memphis Five and the Original Dixieland Jazz Band. Had Durante not teamed up with vaudeville performers Clayton and Jackson, would he have had the developing talent to become a major force as a jazz piano player? After his death, *Down Beat*, a leading jazz magazine, ran an obituary calling Durante a "jazz pioneer."[27]

Jazz critic Rudi Blesh believed that ragtime in white hands moved away from the originators like Scott Joplin and James Scott to the commercialism of Tin Pan Alley. An exception he found remarkable was Durante, who "was an inexplicable throwback to Negro ragtime.... Something in Jimmy made [him] feel rhythm as the Negroes do. Even today [1950] the ragtime lilt is still there—'I keep me attitude,' he says."[28]

Another major critic, Gunther Schuller, had praise for Achille Baquet's smooth clarinet in Durante's early band,[29] but criticized Durante's 1919 group recordings for not improvising. In comments made two decades later, Schuller lumped Durante groups with those of Ted Lewis and Earl Fuller, objecting to their playing "novelty 'cornball' tunes," commercially popular but not artistic, and was especially offended by "squealing, yelping clarinets." He refers to this style as "trash."[30]

In the 1920s, there was some confusion over what was or was not jazz, even as it evolved through its infancy. A lot of publicity surrounded Paul Whiteman's concert at Aeolian Hall, New York, February 12, 1924. It was billed months in advance as the first American jazz concert by "a symphonic syncopation band." In a talk with a *Variety* reporter, Paul Whiteman disclaimed the title given him, "King of Jazz." He said, "My conscience is supremely clear, for the truth is that I have never played jazz and neither, to my knowledge, has any member of my band." The concert would include "some of our 'coon-shouters'"[31] to show "the difference between syncopation and jazz."[32]

Whiteman admitted to playing syncopated rhythms, but certainly his early orchestra played from charts. Aside from a few band members, like trumpeter Henry Busse playing some improvised licks, they did little of the improvisation characteristic of jazz.

Whiteman's statement and his concert came less than four years before Bix Beiderbecke, the great white jazz cornet player, would first appear in Whiteman's band (late 1927). In 1926 Whiteman's book, called simply *Jazz*, was published.[33] He explained there the therapeutic value of jazz and declared his intention of devoting himself more to jazz in the future. In 1930, Universal Studio's color film, *King of Jazz*, was released, starring Paul Whiteman and his somewhat-more-jazzy orchestra.

Post-1927 Whiteman recording dates with Beiderbecke, incidentally, also included Roy Bargy, the pianist who was later to be Durante's music director, Bing Crosby, and jazz C-melody saxophonist Frankie Trumbauer. In November 1935, Durante himself would work with Whiteman in a Broadway show, *Jumbo*.

But even as Durante was developing his skills as pianist, composer, and nightclub entrepreneur, he met three people who would change his life: Eddie Jackson, Lou Clayton, and Maude Jeanne Olson.

About 1915, when he began booking acts, Durante had auditioned Eddie Jackson and his vaudeville partner at that time, Eddie Murray, but the Alamo had not hired them. In 1917, Jackson was hired, together with his current partner Dot Taylor, a blues singer. The duo did a shimmy dance act in vaudeville. Little did Durante know then how important Jackson would become to his own career.

Jackson was a Jewish kid from Brooklyn, with a vaudeville specialty that changed little in his lifetime: he was known as a high-silk-hat cakewalker and baritone. The minstrel-style song "Bill Bailey, Won't You Please Come Home" would be his signature duet with Durante, both strutting with hats held high. Often this number would be done as a trio, with third partner-to-be, Lou Clayton.

Born Louis Finkelstein in Brooklyn, Clayton, like Jackson, had been a vaudeville hoofer, a good soft-shoe dancer who earned a lot of money, promptly lost to high-stakes gambling. About 1920, he formed a brief partnership with ukelele-playing and singing Cliff Edwards, better known as Ukelele Ike. The program for B.F. Keith's Palace Theatre for the last week of January 1921, commencing with the Monday matinee, January 24, lists the act of Clayton and Edwards in "Don't Do That." Always temperamental, Clayton had a dressing-room quarrel and fistfight with his new partner, and the partnership was dissolved.[34] Clayton and Durante would not meet until 1923.

An aspiring singer, Maude Jeanne Olson, walked into the Club Alamo one day in 1918, lost. This young lady from Toledo, Ohio, had been looking

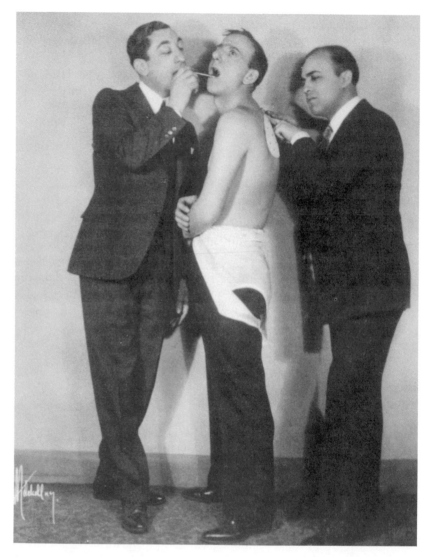

Clayton, Jackson, and Durante, circa 1929. Lou Clayton checks Jimmy's temperature while Eddie Jackson palpates his back.

for the nearby Ritz nightclub where she hoped to find work as a singer. She mistook the Alamo for the Ritz. Jimmy met her, liked her, and played the piano for her audition. She asked him, "Who told you you could play the piano?" To which, he says, he replied, "Them's the conditions that prevail,"[35] a response he would often use again.

Jeanne's family had moved from Toledo to Detroit when she was still

Jimmy and his first wife, Jeanne. 1930s.

a child. Her parents were divorced, and she was raised by her grand-
mother. She had one brother. All her life she remained close to both sides
of her family and her brother. A lyric soprano, she sang in Midwestern
vaudeville under the name of Maudie Jeanne. When she came to New
York early in 1918 she was trying to advance in show business. Says
Durante of those early days, "Sopranos and violins always seemed a little
bit sissy. We wanted noise, brasses and drums and piano." Brassy Jimmy
got along fine with this particular soprano.[36]

The year 1921 began on a sad personal note with the death of Jimmy's
mother on New Year's Day. The year, however, was to turn upbeat. On
June 19, 1921, in the Church of the Holy Innocents,[37] Jimmy Durante, a
rising jazz piano player, band leader, and composer, age 28, married the
girl who came into the Alamo to ask for a job and insulted his piano skills.[38]

The newlyweds rented a furnished room on 23rd Street, then a room
at 206 West 95th Street. The couple moved next to a much larger apartment on West 52nd Street where they took in drummer Jack Roth and his
new bride, Margie.[39]

At this time, Jimmy earned extra money by playing with his jazz group
on Sundays in Brooklyn. Before too long the couple could afford a larger
place in the suburbs. They bought an attractive three-bedroom house in
Flushing, Queens, at 29-05 162nd Street.[40] Jeanne, the aspiring singer,

became a housewife, a source of discontent in later years. Jimmy was insistent that she not continue a career of her own in show business.

In October 1921, Jimmy quit the Alamo. He applied for a piano job at Rector's and Reisenweber's, worked two weeks at a cafe under the Orpheum Theatre in Brooklyn, and tried for some jobs on Broadway. He was looking for a direction, for a change. Later he returned to the Alamo, quit again, and then worked as leader of a six-piece Dixieland band at the Nightingale, a cafe at 48th Street and Broadway. Eddie Jackson and Harry Harris sang as an act there. Frank Nolan, the headwaiter, later convinced Jimmy to open his own club.

Durante continued to have his compositions published in 1923. "Papa String Bean" had lyrics by Al Bernard. "I Ain't Never Had Nobody Crazy Over Me" had lyrics by Johnny Stein and Jack Roth, both drummers for Durante. Nick La Rocca, leader of the incipient ODJB, had performed in Stein's early New Orleans jazz group, Stein's Dixie Jass Band.

In 1923, cabaret owners were trying to cut the growing cost of live music. *Variety* reported that before Paul Whiteman's popularity the average salary for a cabaret band member was $60 a week; after Whiteman, $110 a week. These same musicians usually doubled in vaudeville, bringing up their income.[41] The cabaret owners were also worried about the many raids by federal prohibition agents. One raid against a downtown New York warehouse confiscated liquor valued at eight million dollars.[42] In the cabarets, a quart of champagne was selling for $25, and a quart of whiskey $24 to $28.[43]

Vaudeville in 1923 was going strong. Eddie Cantor was playing the Keith circuit's large houses. Other acts on the circuits included Burns and Allen and former burlesque comedian Bert Lahr. Roy Bargy and his Orchestra were playing at various big city theaters. And that spring the new boardwalk at Coney Island had its official opening.[44] Police were asking women not to go bare-legged on the beaches, but to wear stockings.[45] Before the summer season began, ads in *Variety* stated, "Freaks Wanted. Send photos. 20 weeks' work, no jumps. Address Steeple Side Show, H. and H. Wagner, 2644 East 23rd Street, Sheepshead Bay, N.Y."[46]

A minor social event of 1923 was the grand opening of the Club Durant. Engraved invitations went out.[47]

You are Cordially Invited to attend
the
Grand Opening
of the
Club Durant
232 West 58th Street
Three doors East of Broadway
on

Tuesday Evening, November 18th
Nineteen twenty-*four* [sic].

———

Entertainment Extraordinary
Featuring
Jackson and Harris
the Two Red Hot Syncopators
Rose Schall
and Broadway's Favorite
Jimmy Durante
and his Club Durant Orchestra

———

Mirth — Melody — Novelty

Maurice Zolotow gave a good description of the Club Durant in his book *No People Like Show People*. He says the place opened on January 22, 1923 (ten months before the Grand Opening, which he does not mention), and remained open about 18 months before being padlocked for liquor violations.[48] Black velvet covered the walls. The place seated 135, but the chairs did not arrive until the last minute on opening night because the delivery man was still waiting to be paid cash.[49]

The four partners were Frank Nolan, headwaiter from the Nightingale, Jimmy Durante, Eddie Jackson, and Harry Harris, each with a 25 percent interest. Durante had no money for his 25 percent share but was able to borrow it.[50]

The Club Durant, as one story goes, was to be Club Durante had the partners not run $100 short for the last letter in lights; another story was that the signmaker didn't know Durante's name ended with an "e."

The place became a popular speakeasy with Jackson and Durante, and a four-piece band—cornet, banjo, drums, and Jimmy or another musician on piano, with a postage-stamp size dance floor. Nolan handled the floor and Chinese food kitchen while Jackson, Harris, and Durante took care of the entertainment.

One guidebook of the day included the Club Durant in its coverage of supper clubs. "Self-expression in dancing is here the order of the night. This is the haunt of flaming youth, set to music. 'Top Hat' calls it 'competitive contortion.' The entertainment is familiar and easy going, also bright. Comedians wander among the tables, kidding their act, the audience and the world in general. There are winsome girlies, too, who run true to cabaret type in conformation, appointments and program. You can safely leave the Club Durant for the later part of your evening, as the closing hour is something no one ever mentions." The guide also lists the

Silver Slipper on 48th Street and Texas Guinan's club at 117 West 48th Street, the successor to her defunct El-Fey Club. "Padlocks may come and go. Texas, like love, laughs at locksmiths."[51]

It was at the Club Durant that Jimmy met Lou Clayton, soft-shoe dancer, tough guy, gambler, and with the ladies, a gentleman. Clayton had walked into the Club, and a mutual friend introduced them. As it turned out, Clayton knew Jimmy's brother Albert, a cop who had a beat near the Forsythe Baths, on the Lower East Side, where they met swimming and getting rubdowns.[52] Clayton soon bought out Harris' 25 percent interest, and the combination of Clayton, Jackson, and Durante got its start.

Durante himself told the story for NBC Monitor radio, February 9, 1963.

> We opened the Club Durant without Clayton. When we did open, I insisted on Jackson and a fellow by the name of Harris being partners. Now Clayton finally came up pretty near every night after we opened, and he used to get up on the floor and start dancin', and finally he bought Harris out. And then it became Clayton, Jackson and Durante. I played piano there with the four pieces. When I seen Clayton and Jackson walking around like bosses, we had a conference. I insisted on them hiring a piano player and let me walk around like a boss too. So we improvised on the floor and finally working together we got a routine every other week.... I wrote my own songs like "Did You Ever Have the Feeling" ... then "Jimmy, the Well-Dressed Man" and "Who Will Be with You When I'm Far Away" and "I Ups to Him (And He Ups to Me)" and "I Can Do Without Broadway (But Can Broadway Do Without Me?)" and a million songs. It was brought to an abrupt end one night when the doorman wouldn't let a couple of gentlemen in, and they asked for Durante. I had an awful habit in those days and I got it now. All a fellow has to do is come up and say "Hello, Jimmy," and I'll say "Hello," and I don't know who he is but I greet him pretty warmly. And this night I went down and the fellow ... said, "Jimmy, how are you? They wouldn't let me in." So I bawled the doorman out, I brought them upstairs, I bought them a drink, they bought me a drink. They put it in a little bottle and the next day we were padlocked.

The Club's credit at first was nonexistent. The cash did not flow until Broadway columnists caught on to the fun and spread the word. The first to pick up on this speakeasy was Sime Silverman, founder-publisher-editor of *Variety*. He trumpeted the therapeutic laugh value of Clayton, Jackson, and Durante, calling them the "Three Sawdust Bums" in his newspaper columns. Joining the chorus of approval were George S. Kaufman, Robert Benchley, Gilbert Seldes, Nunnally Johnson, and Charles MacArthur.

At the Club Durant the cover charge was $4 and a quart of illegal wine cost $25, very expensive in 1923 dollars. "Big shots" threw money around, like the guy who gave a waiter a hundred dollar bill for a bottle of Mumm's champagne, costing $29, telling the waiter to keep the change, or the guy who paid $500 for the singing of ten torch songs. Mobsters' guns were checked in the washroom, sometimes turned over to tough Lou Clayton himself, and literally kept on ice behind the bar, a good hiding place.[53] This exciting place, with interesting shows and interesting clientele, would swing until it closed at seven each morning.

Gangsters rarely created trouble, but the level of nervousness increased when the likes of Mad Dog Coll and Legs Diamond arrived to be entertained. One minor league gangster once told Jimmy that he brought some sunshine into the lives of the mob.

The summer after the Club Durant opened, Durante, with Clayton, Jackson, and their three wives, went to Coney Island looking for fall replacements. They heard a band play Jimmy's composition "I Ain't Never Had Nobody Crazy Over Me," liked the way it was handled, and hired Harry Donnelly, the seaside band's leader and pianist, and four of his musicians to join Jack Roth in the band. Donnelly was to remain with Durante until Jimmy went west to live in 1931.

In the mid 1920s, Jeanne was becoming nervous, was drinking too much, and was in ill health. She resented Lou Clayton's becoming Jimmy's business manager, and in later years would stop talking to Clayton altogether.[54] She would have liked his job for herself, especially since Jimmy did not want her to continue her singing career. And she resented her husband being away from home so much. He would return to suburban Flushing in the morning after working all night, eat breakfast, usually a couple of raw eggs, and go to sleep. When he woke in the afternoon, he would go right back to work again. She became fearful of being alone at night, fearful even to go to the bathroom, and she would call Jimmy at the Club for reassurance. Years later he would regret cutting off her career and not spending more time with her.[55]

After the Club Durant closed, Clayton, Jackson, and Durante opened the Dover Club. During their first season there the partners, according to Clayton, "started coming out with songs like 'I Can Do Without Broadway (But Can Broadway Do Without Me?),' 'Everybody Wants to Get into the Act,' 'Again You Turna,' and 'Broadway's a Phony.'"[56] The club closed in May 1926 but reopened that fall, with *Variety*'s Sime Silverman calling attention to the national reputation that the three were building on top of their considerable local fame.[57] The atmosphere of the Dover was recreated two decades later on Jimmy Durante's radio show.[58]

It was its wild, loud, physical quality that made the Clayton, Jackson, and Durante act so popular. It was the Ritz Brothers and the Marx Brothers set to razz-a-ma-tazz jazz and honky-tonk music. The biggest hit was Durante's song and stage-wrecking workout, "Wood," smashing everything in sight that was made of wood. The *pièce de résistance* was breaking up the stage piano and throwing its pieces into the orchestra. (Durante demonstrated the fine points of this demolition in a series of twelve photographs for *Life* magazine two decades later.)[59] The audience loved this musical mayhem in nightclubs from New York to Chicago to Detroit to Las Vegas to Los Angeles, coast to coast, year after year, decade after decade, briefly in vaudeville, on Broadway in *The New Yorkers* (1930), and on Durante's television variety shows, vaudeville reborn. Coupled with strutting to "Bill Bailey, Won't You Please Come Home," "Wood" was a burst of high-energy vaudeville.

From the Alamo to the Nightingale to the Club Durant to the Dover Club and other 1920s clubs, the pace quickened for Clayton, Jackson, and Durante in their appearances at New York nightclubs. Their fame spread by word of mouth like wildfire, something very fresh and different, an act that made you feel good, an act you would never forget.

They performed at many clubs, largely owned by gangsters. The Rendezvous Club was one of several owned by Frankie Marlow, who also managed prizefighters, owned horses, and was a high-stakes gambler. Marlow was also part owner of the Silver Slipper at Broadway and 48th Street, with Bill Duffy, a mobster, and Johnny Wilson, the prizefighter. Marlow himself was to be dramatically gunned down, gangster style, on the night of June 24, 1929.[60]

It was at the Rendezvous Club, Clayton reported, that, acting as Durante's business manager, he hired young singer Ethel Zimmerman, later known as Ethel Merman.[61] Merman said it was at Les Ambassadeurs (a later name for the same club), located above the Winter Garden Theatre, in 1929, that she appeared with Clayton, Jackson, and Durante, but not in any numbers with them.[62] Merman and Durante would later star on Broadway in Cole Porter's *Red, Hot and Blue!* (1936) and *Stars in Your Eyes* (1939).

The Rendezvous had been the Plantation, which was padlocked, changed hands several times, reopened in 1928 as the Rendezvous, was renamed Les Ambassadeurs, and folded again in February 1930. Les Ambassadeurs was one of the clubs owned by Marlow, with Larry Fay, and possibly with Durante having a share. Merman said she received $85 a week there and left the engagement because her tonsils, reputedly the biggest in show business, were inflamed.[63] Each week at Les Ambassadeurs Clayton, Jackson, and Durante received $2,700 (of the total $5,500 weekly Club expenses, with each of the 12 chorus girls receiving $50, the orchestra leader $140, 8 musicians in the band $100 each, 3 other "principals," $125, $90, and $75, plus waiters and others).[64]

In the fall of 1928, C,J&D performed at the notorious Silver Slipper, run by Big Bill Duffy. He and Owney Madden controlled several cafes, including the Cotton Club in Harlem where the great Duke Ellington had his band from December 4, 1927 to 1932. Owney Madden was also called "The Duke." Madden had come out of Sing Sing prison in 1923, sent up for taking part in a murder—a "bum rap," he claimed. Ten days after C,J&D opened, the Silver Slipper was closed by Prohibition agents.

When they closed at the Dover, early in 1927, Clayton, Jackson, and Durante were offered $3,000 a week by the Parody Club, where they performed in 1927 and again in 1929. It was a big windowless basement with luxurious upholstery, holding four hundred people, located on busy 48th Street, two doors west of Broadway. Also moving from the Dover were Leon the headwaiter, Jack Roth, and Harry Donnelly, together with the rest of the orchestra. Sime Silverman attended several nights a week. Some of the happenings on Mondays, Wednesdays, and Fridays were carried on radio station WMCA. What audiences might hear were, as one reviewer put it, "verbal slapstick and hokum, burlesque, parody, old jokes, and throwing hats," as well as songs like "Jimmy, the Well Dressed Man" and "Did You Ever Have the Feeling" (a very funny song about indecision, whether to go or to stay).[65] About the same time, February 18, 1927, Paul Whiteman's own Whiteman Club, at 48th Street and Broadway, had its grand opening, Durante taking over Whiteman's orchestra for a few minutes.[66]

Billy Rose, the songwriter turned big-time producer who would soon befriend Durante and hire him for his stage extravaganza *Jumbo*, opened his first nightclub in 1925. It was called the Backstage Club and was over a garage on 56th Street. More modest than his later ventures, it was financed by money from his first hit song "Barney Google" (1922). Helen Morgan sang on opening night, sitting on the piano because, with the crowd, there was no space to stand. A few days later the bodyguard of gangster Arnold Rothstein visited, saying he wanted 25 percent of the club. He threw a packet of big bills at Rose, assuring him protection from the cops and other mobsters. Billy refused. That night cops raided the place as Billy rushed to flush the booze. Billy changed his mind.[67]

Soon after this, Rose met Durante in the Silver Slipper, where C,J&D were performing, and the two became fast friends.[68]

Durante talked about his experiences with nightclubs to his journalist friend Jack Kofoed, and the result was the coauthored book *Night Clubs* (1931). Although it lacks specific dates, it contains valuable anecdotes about Durante and the period, plus rare photographs, including one of the Durante band at the Alamo, dated 1920. The book has a long preface by Kofoed, giving a history of New York nightclubs in the 1910s and 1920s, including the Tenderloin district between 14th Street and 34th Street, later extended to 42nd Street. The chapters that follow use the first person point of view for Durante's reminiscences, but the language is Kofoed's.

Durante here shows his sympathy for the hard-working, honest majority of chorus girls, coatroom attendants, and cigarette girls who aren't allowed to keep their tips, as well as sympathy for hungry performers who must audition afternoons with tables stacked up and no audience.[69]

The heart of Jimmy Durante, the place where he was most at home over the span of a very long career, was in a nightclub setting. "The night life gets in your blood. You grow restless when the yellow bulbs begin to flicker along Broadway. You want to step. It may be a gift or it may be a disease, but it exists, and as long as it does exist, there will be night clubs of one sort or another. And as long as there are night clubs, and my legs and voice hold out, I suppose I shall be around them."[70]

Chapter 4

VAUDEVILLE
AND BROADWAY

The team of Clayton, Jackson, and Durante, already famous through word-of-mouth praise from nightclub fans, made its vaudeville debut in March 1927 at Loew's State, 48th Street and Broadway. With their song, dance, and comedy act, they were to join briefly but dramatically the long tradition that had been part of the American stage from the previous century.

The term "vaudeville" is an old one. A Théatre du Vaudeville opened in Paris in 1792. Farces and satirical songs were known as *pièces en vaudeville* and *comédies avec vaudeville*. By the mid–19th century the word "vaudeville" came to mean the variety stage on the European continent and the music hall in England.[1] The American variety show, inspired by visiting English performers, took root at about the same time as the distinctively American burlesque or "leg show" was developing.

In the United States vaudeville became family entertainment while burlesque, frowned upon by vaudevillians and their management, became adult entertainment, a mix of vulgar comics, "top bananas," sex jokes and sketches, and girls with as much anatomy on display as each town or city would permit. Two national circuits of burlesque shows were in business by the early 20th century, as well as resident companies. The most famous was Minsky's in New York.[2] Those who liked a little spice in their entertainment found Billy Minsky providing such striptease artists as Ann Corio, Gypsy Rose Lee, Margie Hart, Hinda Wassau, Georgia Sothern, and Carrie Finnell.

Like most strippers (with Gypsy Rose Lee a notable exception), many of the baggy-pants comics never went much beyond the burlesque stage. Phil Silvers, Bud Abbott and Lou Costello, and Bert Lahr were a few of the exceptions. Phil Silvers, after vaudeville with the Gus Edwards Revue and touring with the team of Morris and Campbell, was a third banana with Minsky Burlesque in 1934. He stayed with Minsky until 1939, becoming the best top banana in burlesque. After Silvers made his screen debut in *Tom, Dick and Harry* (RKO, 1940), he teamed with Durante for the 1941 Warner Bros. comedy *You're in the Army Now*.

By 1940, burlesque was all but gone, at least in New York, as Mayor Fiorello LaGuardia could not distinguish between sexy art and pornography.[3] On April 30, 1937, LaGuardia refused to renew the licenses for the six Minsky burlesque houses in New York and even banned the words "Minsky" and "burlesque" in theatrical advertising. In 1939, a Minsky show starring Phil Silvers opened in Toronto at the Canadian World Exposition. The show lost money. No significant revival of burlesque occurred until 1962 when Ann Corio opened the show *This Was Burlesque* off–Broadway and was a success.

The New York Dramatic Mirror reported in its issue of December 24, 1898, that Tony Pastor deserved much credit for making once-shady "variety, or vaudeville as it is now called" an acceptable popular entertainment for all classes and all ages.[4] In 1878, when Harrigan & Hart began staging three-act farces, the variety field was left largely to Tony Pastor. Pastor opened a new theater in New York's Tammany Hall building October 24, 1881, where it continued to run through the remainder of the century. Favorites with Pastor's audiences were Lillian Russell and Eugene, declared by Pastor to be the best female impersonator he had ever seen.

Continuous performances were begun by B.F. Keith in Boston, July 6, 1885, and F.F. Proctor in New York, January 9, 1893, at his 23rd Street Theatre. Admission to the first vaudeville bill at Proctor's Theatre on that date cost 15, 25, and 50 cents.[5]

The success of his 23rd Street Theatre encouraged Proctor, with Francis J. Schnugg, a real estate operator, to build a lavish theater on 58th Street near Third Avenue. Behind this theater he built an immense palm garden, which connected to the building with a hall of mirrors. The Pleasure Palace opened on Labor Day, September 2, 1895. One of the opening acts featured elephants, furnished by George Lockhart. (Much later, in 1935, Durante would appear in Billy Rose's lavish spectacle *Jumbo* at the Hippodrome, putting himself under the giant foot of Rosie the elephant.) The acts on the bill at the Pleasure Palace were accompanied by an all-girl orchestra. During the 1895-96 season, the great ethnic comedy team of Weber & Fields appeared there.

Next, B.F. Keith, with the aid of E.F. Albee, remodeled the Union Square Theater as a continuous vaudeville house, opening September 18, 1893. He liked to run a one-act play done by well-known legitimate stage actors as a feature of the bill. This helped draw a more refined audience and soon attracted quality actors. Keith also imported many European performers. Also secured for the Union Square Theater in the summer of 1895 was Lumière's cinematographe, an imported novelty that Keith would use as part of vaudeville bills until replaced by more developed American motion pictures with clearer images.[6]

Continuous performances often meant 10 A.M. to 10:30 P.M., something on stage at all times except for a two-hour interval. Prices late in the century were, typically, 10 cents for the balcony, 20 cents downstairs.[7] By 1918, when vaudeville played matinees and evenings rather than continuous performances, the prices had risen: matinees, 25 cents, 50 cents, and best seats 75 cents; evenings, best seats (entire lower floor), $1.00.

American vaudeville put on one stage singers, dancers, comics, dog acts, acrobats, and dramatic actors. It drew some of its acts from still earlier American popular culture entertainments such as minstrel shows, complete with blackface imitation of Negroes, from medicine shows, with circus-like patter minus the sales pitch, and from the circus itself, long a part of European street culture.

Among the greatest promoters of this type of popular entertainment were P.T. Barnum, the first major American entrepreneur to develop, publicize, and popularize circus acts, and B.F. Keith, who moved from circus acts to variety shows and developed the most sought-after vaudeville circuit coast to coast.

Looking at just one week's vaudeville headline attractions can give a sense of how much was going on across the country before the advent of sound pictures and national network radio forced an end to the heyday of vaudeville. *Variety*, the *Wall Street Journal* of show business performers, reported in its January 9, 1920 issue the bills for the week of January 12. On the Keith circuit, in New York City, at Keith's Colonial, the Marx Brothers were appearing; at Keith's Riverside, starring were the Leon Errol Company as well as comedian Joe Cook; at the Keith Royal, bandleader Ben Bernie; in Allentown, Pa., at the Keith Orpheum, the song team of Sissle & Blake (Noble Sissle and Eubie Blake); in Indianapolis, Ind., at B.F. Keith's, the singer Belle Baker; in Louisville, Ky., at B.F. Keith's, the comedy team of Olsen & Johnson; in Rochester, N.Y., at the Temple Theatre, singer Blossom Seeley's Company; in Troy, N.Y., at Proctor's, comedian and song-and-dance man Joe Laurie. Meanwhile on the Orpheum circuit that week, in Des Moines, Iowa, at the Orpheum Theatre, singer-comedian Phil Baker was appearing; in Memphis, at the Orpheum, comic Jimmy Savo's Company; in Oakland at the Orpheum, Gus Edwards' Company with his child performers; in Portland, Ore., at the Orpheum, singer Eva Taylor's Company (Eva Taylor was black, married to jazzman Clarence Williams). On the Pantages circuit that week we could find in Calgary, Canada, at the Pantages Theatre, Ted Shawn's Dancers; at the San Francisco Pantages, song-and-dance comedian Eddie Foy's Company; in Tacoma, Wash., at the Pantages, Yip Yip Yaphankers, named after the military base on Long Island that Irving Berlin wrote about.

Finally, in Waco, Texas, at the Orpheum, Stan and Mae Laurel (Stan in drag as an old biddy appeared with Mae Dahlberg, an Australian who would become his common-law wife), and on the same bill, interesting for its ethnic slur that passed as humor, "The 3 White Kuhns."

At the same time that vaudeville was still going strong, there was one circuit far removed from the others—T.O.B.A., Theatre Owners Booking Association, known as TOBY. It was the main outlet for black performers, kept by southern segregation laws from participating in some theaters. Known by its performers as "Tough On Black Asses," T.O.B.A. paid lower salaries and booked shabbier theaters. Its best theaters were the Regal Theatre in Baltimore, the Howard in Washington, the 81 in Atlanta, the Booker T. in St. Louis, the Monogram and the Grand in Chicago, the Lincoln, the Alhambra, and (much later) the Apollo in New York.[8] Not many crossed over to greater fame and fortune in mainstream theaters.

A few black performers did manage to play engagements on white circuits, like the aforementioned Eva Taylor. Comedian-singer Bert Williams was a big star who did so on occasion, between his *Ziegfeld Follies* engagements where he was the only Negro headliner, light-skinned and, ironically, wearing blackface. Others were Dusty Fletcher (comedian of "Open the Door Richard" fame); comedian Mantan Moreland; comedian Pigmeat Markham; Tim Moore (who later played the first colored Kingfish in the changing Amos 'n' Andy series); dancer Bill "Bojangles" Robinson; dancers Buck & Bubbles; songsters-composers Sissle & Blake; dancers The Nicholas Brothers.

Like jazz, treated as a lower form of music compared to its more educated, more upper class cousin, so-called classical music, vaudeville was treated as a lower form of performance compared to the "legitimate" stage. Like jazz musicians, vaudeville performers did not have the luxury of concert halls and theaters where a full season's work would keep them largely in the same city, in front of respectful audiences. Like jazz musicians, vaudeville performers were gypsies, traveling to different cities and towns every week, playing to inattentive audiences who paid little money, for booking agents who underpaid all but the biggest stars.

Playing Carnegie Hall was the dream not only of classical musicians but also of many jazzmen, who sought the same respectability for jazz that classical music enjoyed. Benny Goodman and his orchestra gave the first jazz concert there on January 16, 1938. Playing the Palace in New York, physically standing on Broadway, surrounded by the lights of "The Great White Way," was the dream of vaudevillians. Opened on March 24, 1913, at the corner of Broadway and 47th Street, the Palace was under the control of E.F. Albee, head of the Keith Circuit. It was to become Nirvana, the Promised Land, Redemption; an act appearing there successfully would find higher billing across the country in the better theaters on the circuit, and no more so-called "tank towns" with the poorest working conditions.

Every performer paid close attention to his or her position on the bill and the number of minutes given to the act. Typically the bill contained eight acts, and the star turn was slotted seventh. Audiences might arrive late and miss the first act or two; later acts might warm up or turn off the audience. After the star, the audience would walk out before the eighth act could finish what was viewed as anti-climactic. The Palace program for the week of August 9, 1930, contained this request: "TO OUR PATRONS—The last act on our bill is always interesting and generally the feature of our show, and, in justice to this act, the audience is requested to remain seated until it is finished. It is very discouraging to leave while the artists are doing their best to please those remaining seated, who are discommoded by having their attention distracted from the stage by people leaving." The closing act was Walter Davison's Louisville Loons, 12 Soloists Blended into a Super Specialty Band, with Harlan Christie and Cecelia Blair. That act followed the star of the night, George Jessel, in the number seven slot. Also on the bill, but not in the star's slot, were Bill Robinson and Adelaide Hall together in song and dance, the fifth act, just before intermission, and Burns and Allen in a sketch called "Lamb Chops," just before that, as the fourth act.

A much earlier example of a vaudeville bill, as it was reviewed in 1918, had the famous beauty Lillian Russell, singer, as its headliner. She had been a star for many years, appearing as a youngster with Tony Pastor's Company in 1880. Now she was at the top of her career, returning to the stage at B.F. Keith's Palace Theatre, New York, for the week ending November 3. Lillian Russell was seventh of eight acts, following hat spinners, a violin and accordion act, a comedy sketch, a French singing comedienne, eccentric dancing and "Jazz" music, and a singing comedian. After the star turn, the vaudeville bill ended with a telephone skit and burlesque boxing. Then the audience got a bonus, a Charlie Chaplin short, "Shoulder Arms," which ran 38 minutes. Lillian Russell's act lasted 29 minutes. The critic reported that Lillian Russell received a great reception, glorious in her handsome gown, which she changed later in her act for a U.S. Marine uniform, telling how she had helped the American boys in the war "over there."[9]

Many acts were not so glamorous. One reported in 1919 was "Don, The Educated Canine." He was known as the "leading dog inebriate on the stage." With his handler Officer Vokes at his side, Don was dressed in tuxedo, white bow tie, and white cuffs, seated at a nightclub table with beer bottles and a glass.[10]

Whatever the material, each act jealously guarded it, since the same material, with the same style of presentation, would, once successful, be used over and over in city after city and maybe for a whole career. *Variety* wrote periodically about the newspaper's "Protected Material Department." This department filed sealed envelopes it received, usually sent by registered mail. New acts especially were screened carefully to make sure they were not using material already registered by some other established act. The effort was serious and needed to eliminate "lifted material" from vaudeville houses. Cooperating circuits, managements, and agencies included, at least as of January 1919, Marcus Loew Circuit, Fox Circuit, Miles Circuit, Finn-Heiman Circuit, Bert Levey Circuit, Shea Circuit, Feiber-Shea Circuit, Aloz Circuit, Pantages Circuit, B.S. Moss Circuit, Gus Sun Circuit, Michigan Vaudeville Circuit.

At least one vaudeville performer would, in later years, make jokes about his stealing everyone else's material a central part of his *shtick*. He was "Mr. Television," Milton Berle, one of television's first big stars. In vaudeville in the late 1920s and 1930s, he "borrowed" from other comedians, believing that what counted was personality, not material.

Some of the great vaudeville stars should be mentioned, at least in passing. The word *shtick*, often used to refer to comic acts, is Yiddish; many of the early comedians were Jewish, born in New York City or immigrants who settled in the city. Many of the comedy acts, as was the tradition and fashion upon the vaudeville stage, used ethnic humor. The most common of these acts used dialect—Dutch (parodying German immigrants, mixing German and broken English), Irish (a brogue mixed with simulated heavy drinking and Irish cop brawling), and what were known as "coon" acts, white men in blackface playing Negroes with the ignorance, superstitions, speech, and mannerisms then stereotypically attached to Negroes.

Many "coon" songs, Negro culture as seen by whites, were published at the turn of the century and are now collectors' items. Among the most popular were Ernest Hogan's "All Coons Look Alike to Me" (1896), Joseph Howard and Ida Emerson's "Hello! Ma Baby" (1899), and Theodore Metz's "A Hot Time in the Old Town" (1896). One song from this period, "Bedelia," with words by William Jerome and music by Jean Schwartz, even sought to combine the coon song tradition with the Irish song tradition. It was advertised as "The Novelty Song of the Century" and "The Irish Coon Song Serenade" (Shapiro, Bernstein and Company, 1903).

Not all coon songs were sung by white performers in the minstrel tradition of blackface. Bert Williams, most famous for his heart-wrenching song of loneliness and isolation, "Nobody," recorded for Columbia Records in 1906, also recorded for Victor, "The Phrenologist Coon" and "The Ghost of a Coon" (both 1901). Less famous black performers also sang such songs.

Perhaps the greatest of the early comedy teams specializing in ethnic material was Weber & Fields (Joseph Weber and Lew Fields). Their comedy act was firmly established on the stage in the 1880s, using all forms of ethnic material, including songs in blackface. Later there was the team of Smith & Dale (Joe Smith and Charlie Dale). A modern Broadway comedy and movie, both by Neil Simon, *The Sunshine Boys*, tells part of the story of Smith & Dale, their arguments and their classic doctor routine, "Dr. Kronkite." Neither the show nor the movie relates Smith & Dale's participation in the Avon Comedy Four, where with Will Lester and Jack Coleman, once singing waiters at the Avon Cafe on 116th Street in New York, they did sketches with Hebrew and German dialects playing against a tough guy and an effeminate guy. At the same time, two real German immigrants, Jewish brothers who grew up on New York's Lower East Side, Willie and Eugene Howard, developed very funny dialect routines. In the 1930s Willie Howard made a series of short films, a few of them with Eugene, recreating vaudeville characterizations. Other shorts of the decade featured vaudeville routines of Smith & Dale, Moran & Mack (the Two Black Crows), Joe Cook, and Eddie Cantor.

Clayton, Jackson, and Durante, two Jews and one Italian, used hardly any ethnic material in their act. They did sing that old rousing song that goes back to the waning days of minstrel shows, "Bill Bailey, Won't You Please Come Home" (composed 1902 by Hughie Cannon), with Jackson briefly mimicking supposed Negro dialect. And as was fashionable in a day when Al Jolson, Eddie Leonard, Al Bernard (a friend of Durante), George Jessel, Eddie Cantor, and Sophie Tucker all sang "Mammy" songs (all but Tucker in blackface), Clayton, Jackson, and Durante performed, frequently, but never in blackface, one of many "Rastus" songs, "Rufus, Rastus, Johnson Brown (What You Goin' to Do When the Rent Comes 'Round)." The music to this song was composed by one of the best popular composers of the turn of the century, Harry Von Tilzer, with words by Andrew B. Sterling. Published in 1905 by Von Tilzer's own music publishing company, the sheet music depicts in cartoon two "coons," a black man and a black woman, both with the exaggerated lips of caricature.

Another Rastus song was "Rastus on Parade," composed in 1895 by Kerry Mills, the same man who composed "Meet Me in St. Louis." Such songs continue to be played today by traditional jazz bands, all white, seeking to recreate the fun of those ethnic songs without considering the racial realities that existed beyond the footlights. One of these groups, for example, the South Frisco Jazz Band, recorded in 1984 an album entitled *Jones Law Blues* (from a song by black jazzmen Bennie Moten and Count Basie), which included the number "When Rastus Plays His Old Kazoo," written by Sam Coslow and Sammy Fain, well-known composers, with Larry Spier (Stomp Off 1103, released in 1985). The sheet music to "When Erastus

Plays His Old Kazoo," published by Spier & Coslow in 1927, calls it "A Unique Novelty Song," the cover showing a Negro man in loud striped suit holding a kazoo to his huge white lips, looking like a minstrel in black-face.

One song that was recorded had a title so blatantly racist, one wonders today how it could ever have been approved for release: "They May Call You Hawaiian on Broadway (But You're Just a Plain Nigger to Me)." It was recorded in New York, 1917, by George O'Connor, a man who trained as a lawyer but became a comedian in minstrel shows in the 1890s. Brian Rust, the discographer of early jazz and popular music personalities, said O'Connor was a favorite entertainer of "successive Presidents of the U.S.A."[11] This song was recorded, not as one might suppose, on an obscure small label, but on Columbia Records (Columbia A2441).

The one great vaudeville comedian who remains very popular today with audiences of all ages is W.C. Fields. He started as a juggler with some comedy. By 1900, he was billed as an "Eccentric Juggler," and in 1904, he added the pool table to his repertoire of dexterous skills. In 1915, he made his first of many appearances in the *Ziegfeld Follies*, and the same year made his first film, a short entitled *Pool Sharks*. W.C. Fields had the opportunity and skills to do what no other vaudevillian did: transfer all his vaudeville routines to film. These routines were so visual that Fields was not a success on radio, except in his classic guest appearances on the Edgar Bergen–Charlie McCarthy Show, trading insults with the smart-aleck wooden dummy. He died in 1946 before having an opportunity to see if he could hold television audiences as well as theater audiences, or whether the television thirst for constantly new material would wear out his popularity the way it did Milton Berle's. On film, he is as funny to watch today as he ever was.

Another great vaudeville comedian was Buster Keaton. He was born October 4, 1895, to Joe and Myra Keaton. Joe was an eccentric dancer and acrobat; Myra, a dancer who played cornet. When Buster was just a few months old, his parents carried him on stage and from that time on he was part of the act. He became a permanent member of the act when in 1900 they were billed the Three Keatons. A brilliant knockabout in baggy pants, Buster was the best slapstick artist, doing stunts and taking falls that would have killed lesser men. In 1917, he left the act to enter silent films and became a star to rival Charlie Chaplin. In the 1930s, at a low point in his career, he would make three sound films with Jimmy Durante.

When Clayton, Jackson, and Durante opened their vaudeville act on the stage of Loew's State in 1927, they broke up the furniture, flinging pieces into the orchestra pit. Clayton danced, Jackson sang, and Durante played the piano. Then they all danced and sang and threw more objects, including the piano. Durante barked his hoarse Lower East Side mispronunciations while everyone interrupted, ad-libbing and hurling insults. They gave a typically frenetic, screwball performance, like two other vaudeville acts that would reach as far as Hollywood, the Marx Brothers and Ted Healy and His Stooges (later The Three Stooges). It was just like the team's nightclub performances.

Backed by Harry Donnelly's Parody Club Orchestra (really the Durante band from the nightclub where they were also now playing), the act was titled "Jest for a Laugh." Songs the zany trio used included "Yucatan," "I'm Going to Tell a Story," "The Noose," "She's Just a Cow," and "Jimmy, the Well Dressed Man." Most of these numbers were not to remain staples in Durante's repertoire, although he did tend to repeat some material over and over in career-long performances. What did stick for a full career was "Jimmy, the Well Dressed Man," a song emphasizing Durante's fascination with high culture and the satirization of it. He loved to dress up in elegant clothes for that number and, in the Broadway shows and films of the 1930s, for other elegant gentleman roles, and he loved to sing French phrases and mix it up with formidable opera sopranos.

At Loew's State, Durante would refer to someone in the orchestra as "Umbriago," meaning "drunkard" in Italian. "Here, folks, is Mr. Umbriago!" Durante would bellow at someone he would accuse of messing up a musical note. The word was becoming part of his act and by 1944, with help from Irving Caesar, would become a song to be identified with Durante as much as "Inka Dinka Doo."

Variety's Sime Silverman had already fallen under the spell of the Durante style that he saw in the nightclubs. He reviewed the Loew's State opening performance and loved it.[12] But not many other critics thought it was a smash.

That smash hit in vaudeville would come just over a year later, in April 1928, when Clayton, Jackson, and Durante, doubling from nightclub appearances, opened at the Palace. They were headliners making $3,000 a week and did the Palace's biggest business that season, breaking the house record for the year.[13] At the time, the Palace gross receipts for a week were down from an average of $28,000 to $20,000. The drop was attributable to the recent opening of the first talking picture, *The Jazz Singer*, at the nearby Warner Theatre, New York (October 6, 1927).

Vaudevillians who played the Palace in 1928 included comedians Jack Benny, George Jessel, Burns and Allen, Jimmy Savo, who specialized in pantomime sketches, Van and Schenck, the popular singing team that specialized in comedy dialect songs in Italian or Yiddish, Lou Holtz, great dialect comedian, and the humorously suggestive songstress, the "last of the red hot mommas," Sophie Tucker.

This success at the Palace led to a contract with Florenz Ziegfeld for

Clayton, Jackson, and Durante to appear in the Ziegfeld revue *Show Girl*, opening the summer of 1929.

In the interim, they played vaudeville engagements and continued to appear in nightclubs. When they left the Parody Club on May 30, 1928, the group played Keith-Albee circuit theaters in New York and Newark, New Jersey, then the Midwest, going to Cincinnati, Chicago, and Milwaukee. Chicago went especially well, but after Milwaukee a booking-agent friend persuaded them to do a week in Minneapolis. Here to their great surprise, they were a flop. Everything that had worked for them before fell flat. As Durante belted out "Jimmy, the Well Dressed Man," someone in the audience was heard to remark, "He doesn't look so well dressed." Burns and Allen, who stayed over after their own engagement to catch Clayton, Jackson, and Durante's opening night, were a pocket of isolated laughter in the silent audience.[14] Recovering from Minneapolis, which Durante always pronounced "Minneanapolis," the trio returned to New York's nightclubs.

On February 3, 1929, the team opened for a week on the bill of the E.F. Albee Theatre in Brooklyn. Next to last on the bill, in the headliners' spot, the trio did their act called "Just [not Jest, as before] for a Laugh." They were backed by Jimmy Durante's Orchestra.

On May 9, 1929, Clayton, Jackson, and Durante went into the New York studios of Columbia Records to make their only recording together, "Can Broadway Do Without Me?" and "So I Ups to Him." Backed by a studio orchestra, these two numbers were to be performed by the trio in that summer's Broadway musical, *Show Girl*.

Ziegfeld had an artist's eye for talent and what the public wanted to see, a sense at least as good as P.T. Barnum's, and he would go anywhere to find that talent. Among his greatest stars appearing in his Follies were Eddie Cantor, Will Rogers, Fanny Brice, W.C. Fields, Bert Williams (his only Negro star), and Marilyn Miller.

Theatergoers looked forward to each year's edition of the justly famous Ziegfeld Follies, which showcased not only vaudeville's greatest stars but also the world's most beautiful girls in musical numbers choreographed more lavishly than any show today could possibly afford. For a hint of Ziegfeld's elaborate staging, look at some of the 1930s Hollywood musicals choreographed by Busby Berkeley, especially *42nd Street* (1933), *Gold Diggers of 1933* (1933), *Footlight Parade* (1933), and *Gold Diggers of 1935* (1935). Also watch the production numbers in MGM's film biography, *The Great Ziegfeld* (1936).

Ziegfeld himself produced an early film about his Follies, *Glorifying the American Girl* (1929), filmed at the Astoria, New York, studios of Paramount Pictures. Directed by Millard Webb and John Harkrider, it was made in black and white but, as originally released, with some two-color

Technicolor sequences. It was an awkward film technically, especially as compared with what Berkeley would do just a few years later. The 75 "glorified beauties" look chunky by today's standards, and the dancers seem to stomp rather than move with delicacy and agility. But this film is an interesting look at Eddie Cantor and Helen Morgan and provides a glimpse of Ziegfeld as he walks into the theater with Billie Burke on opening night.

What plot there is concerns a talented dancer trying to get her big break in show business without giving in to a lecherous partner. She becomes a star but loses her boyfriend, who marries a girl without career ambitions. This plot would become archetypal. Mary Eaton plays the show girl, and Edward Crandall the boyfriend. Rudy Vallee sings "I'm Just a Vagabond Lover," Helen Morgan sings "What Wouldn't I Do for That Man," and Eddie Cantor appears in a still-funny vaudeville routine about a Lower East Side Jewish tailor trying to sell a suit.

By 1929, Ziegfeld had already produced twenty editions of the Follies, beginning in 1907. The first edition starred Nora Bayes, and a new edition appeared every subsequent year except 1926. The most recent edition, 1927, had starred Eddie Cantor, Irene Delroy, Ruth Etting, Dan Healy, and the Albertina Rasch Girls. Florenz would have just one more edition of the Follies after this, in 1931, starring Ruth Etting, Helen Morgan, Jack Pearl, and Harry Richman. The great impresario died in 1932 at the age of 65; his wife, actress Billie Burke, continued to produce the Follies for a few more editions, still drawing stars, including Fanny Brice, Bobby Clark, and Milton Berle.

Clayton, Jackson, and Durante were entering select company. *Show Girl* was not the Follies but it had the same high standards. For the duration of their act upon this august stage, this team pushed back the sophistication of the evening every night and let the decorum fly.

Show Girl opened at the Ziegfeld Theatre, 6th Avenue at 54th Street, Tuesday, July 2, 1929. The program cover featured Billie Burke, painted by the artist Hal Phyfe. The two-act show starred Ruby Keeler, the wife of Al Jolson, a rising star in her own right. Second billing went to Clayton, Jackson, and Durante. Also in the cast were Eddie Foy, Jr., and, dancing with the Albertina Rasch troupe, Harriet Hoctor. The music was written by George Gershwin, lyrics by Gus Kahn and Ira Gershwin, with special numbers by Vincent Youmans; the musicians were Duke Ellington and his Cotton Club Orchestra.

There were problems with the show. Ziegfeld had given George and Ira Gershwin only two weeks to write a score. To help them do this, Ziegfeld brought in Gus Kahn to help Ira with the lyrics, and Jimmy Durante was allowed to supply his own songs.[15] The book by William Anthony McGuire was based on a novel by J.P. McEvoy that had been popular the year before, a story about backstage life following an unknown to stardom. The novel was shaped in the form of telegrams and letters, and in the opinion of at least the *New York Times* reviewer, Brooks Atkinson, not easily adaptable to the Broadway stage.[16] The result was an uneven, though opulent, musical production, heavy and slow in spots, with awkward transitions between excellent parts.

Clayton, Jackson, and Durante sang "Can Broadway Do Without Me?" in Act I and later Durante (as Snozzle) joined with Barbara Newberry (as Sunshine) and Girls to perform "One Man." Shortly before the first act finale Clayton, Jackson, and Durante sang "Jimmy, the Well Dressed Man." In Act II the same madcap trio sang "Broadway, My Street," followed by "Snozzle" alone singing "I Ups to Him."

In Act II after Durante sang "I Ups to Him," Ruby Keeler sang what was to be the smash hit of the show, "Liza." Controversy would surround this number for many years to come because Al Jolson stood up from his seat and took over the song from his wife. Why? Was Keeler suffering stage fright on opening night? She denied this. Herbert G. Goldman in his biography, *Jolson*, details the background of this event.[17] Al, a seasoned stage performer, had given his young wife Ruby more advice than she could absorb, making her more tense than she would have been. This was to be the first time she was billed as the star, carrying the show, and not just any show but a big Ziegfeld production. "Liza" was intended to be a second-act minstrel number with loads of beautiful girls embroidering Ruby's dancing. The high point was to come when Frank McHugh sang the verse and Ruby, as Dixie Dugan, stepped into the spotlight to go into her dance. She had barely begun this when Jolson sitting in Row C on the aisle jumped up and launched into the song. This ensured the number becoming a sensation that in itself would attract audiences. So Jolson continued to jump up and sing "Liza" for a week after the opening. When he left, ticket sales went down.

On Monday, July 22, Ruby became ill and had to leave the show. When she attempted to resume her role that Saturday night, she collapsed after the first act. Dorothy Stone took over Ruby's role. Without Ruby Keeler or Al Jolson, the show lasted for only a few weeks more,[18] a total of 111 performances.[19]

Of Clayton, Jackson, and Durante's performance in *Show Girl* Brooks Atkinson wrote,

> How to fit so rhymeless a trio of nonsense fabricators into anything more formal than a night-club racket has kept the pundits sitting up nights. Their transformation into "Show Girl" is not altogether sublime.When they transport their act intact and careen around the piano, Jackson strutting, Clayton hoofing and Durante bowing to the orchestra and breaking out into feverish and raucous songs, they recapture the

excitement of their humors. Durante's sizzling energy can galvanize any audience. But . . . His spluttering, insane material does not melt gracefully into a musical comedy book. His personality, however, batters its way through all barriers.[20]

The problem of fitting Durante's basically nightclub approach, his greatest strength, into a Broadway story would also be a problem in motion pictures.

Cole Porter, the sophisticated composer from Yale University, class of 1913, recruited Clayton, Jackson, and Durante to appear in his new Broadway show, *The New Yorkers*. Billed as "A Sociological Musical Satire," it opened December 8, 1930, at the Broadway Theatre, directed by Monty Woolley. Porter and Woolley had in 1929 staged Porter's *Fifty Million Frenchmen*, which ran for 254 performances. Both musicals had books written by Herbert Fields. The earlier show had offered a tour of Paris; this show offered a tour of high and low life in Manhattan. The story peg is a socialite in love with a bootlegger. To soften the social criticism, writer Fields makes the whole story a dream. None of the cast was given star billing. Hope Williams played the socialite Alice Wentworth from Park Avenue, where, as a line from the play goes, "bad women walk good dogs"; Charles King played the bootlegger Al Spanish, who's also good at murder. Jimmy Durante played Jimmie Deegan, a gangster, and his cronies were Lou Clayton and Eddie Jackson as Cyril Gregory and Ronald Monahan. Scenes swing radically from the St. Pierre Plaza Roof to the Lounge at Sing Sing.

The most striking number in the show is "Love for Sale," a stark invitation from a prostitute to "pay the price for a trip to paradise." Kathryn Crawford sang this song on opening night, but she was soon replaced by Elizabeth Welch.

In Act I, Clayton, Jackson, and Durante follow the opening song number, "Go Into Your Dance," with Jimmy's own composition, "Hot Patatta" (that's "potato" in Durante lingo). Later they sing with Hope Williams "Venice," by Cole Porter. The next to last musical number of the act again features the trio, in Durante's "Money!"[21] And in the number that rings down the curtain on Act I, they launch into a number with hilarious impact—"Wood!"—used two years earlier in their engagement at the Palace. This is the most memorable of the four Durante-written song routines from nightclubs and vaudeville used in the show. Clayton, Jackson, and the whole cast accuse Durante of having a head made of wood. He answers that they've just paid him a compliment because America wouldn't exist without wood. Jimmy recites from a brochure or an ad put out by a lumber association, all the many products that come from wood. He then leads Clayton, Jackson, and the rest of the cast in throwing extravagant numbers of objects made of wood: "transforming the stage into a dumping ground . . . furniture, boxes, doors, pushcarts, barrels, canoes, barber poles, rickshaws, even an outhouse, plus from the orchestra pit, violins, a bass drum, and parts of a piano. All the while everyone is feverishly chanting 'Wood.'"[22] In Act II, Clayton, Jackson, and Durante sing Durante's composition "Data," but after "Wood!" who could remember much of anything else?

Three days after *The New Yorkers* opened, the Bank of the United States closed and the Depression deepened. Tickets sold for a top of $5.50. Costs were cut, but the show still lost money, and after struggling for 168 performances, it closed.[23]

After *The New Yorkers*, Durante, without his partners, was offered a five-year contract by MGM. He left for the coast with his wife Jeanne.

Jimmy Durante's first time on stage without Clayton and Jackson came in April 1932 when he brought to Pittsburgh what *Variety* reviewed as a new act. Playing a week there for $3,500, he was still able to play off the orchestra pit crew as his stooges with his lunatic humor of wreckage and mayhem.[24]

With his first Broadway appearance without Clayton and Jackson, he was now a star in his own right. He appeared in the Lew Brown and Ray Henderson musical revue *Strike Me Pink*, opening at the Majestic Theatre March 4, 1933, with his name above the title: Lupe Velez, Jimmy (Schnozzle) Durante, and Hope Williams. Durante was paid $3,000 per week and split his money with Clayton and Jackson out of a sense of loyalty to them.

At Paramount's Astoria studios, Durante had made *Roadhouse Nights* (1930) with Clayton and Jackson; in Hollywood, working for MGM, he had made *New Adventures of Get Rich Quick Wallingford* and *The Cuban Love Song* (both 1931); *The Passionate Plumber, The Wet Parade, Speak Easily*, and *Blondie of the Follies* (all released in 1932); *What! No Beer?* (released early 1933), *Hell Below* (which would be released shortly); and, for Paramount, *The Phantom President* (1932).

Durante had worked with Hope Williams in his last Broadway show, and he would soon appear in movies with Lupe Velez. Durante and Velez were a bigger hit than the show. Their mispronunciations of the English language and their compatible brands of craziness worked well, proven again soon after this in the films *Palooka* (UA/Reliance, 1934), *Hollywood Party* (MGM, 1934), and *Strictly Dynamite* (RKO, 1934).

In *Strike Me Pink*, a musical revue for the stage, Durante makes his first appearance by coming down the theater aisle fighting with the usher to let him go up on stage. Later he and Lupe play "children of nature" frolicking in Central Park. Before the opening night performance was over, Jimmy told the audience about partners Clayton and Jackson. They made a surprise appearance, to the delight of the audience, singing their old songs.[25]

This type of show was a far cry from what had started out on the road as a show with a left-wing political message. When the show played at the Shubert Theatre in Newark, New Jersey, the week of February 20, 1933, a flyer proclaimed it "The Greatest Revue Ever Produced." Surviving from the earlier version before extensive rewriting was the number "Home to Harlem" in Act I, sung by George Dewey Washington and the Singing Ensemble against scenes showing the Negro's progress from cottonfield cabin to prison chain gang to a Harlem nightclub. Most important to the show after the rewriting, apart from Durante and Velez, was the bold announcement in the program that the show featured "The Most Photographed Girls in the World (The Famous Poster Models), Dancing Chorus of 75, and Brown & Henderson Songs." The show ran only 105 performances.

On Thursday, May 11, 1933, Jimmy Durante appeared as a guest on Rudy Vallee's Fleischmann Hour radio show, NBC. In the fall he was for several months a substitute host on the Chase and Sanborn Coffee Hour, NBC, Sunday nights, replacing Eddie Cantor, and again all Sundays during the summer months. Then in the fall of 1935, NBC and Texaco had Durante take over the *Texaco Fire Chief* program from Ed Wynn.

In addition to making movies and radio appearances, Durante did a stage revue on a double bill with a first run movie. After completing the filming for *Hollywood Party*, Durante and co-star Polly Moran played the week of March 16, 1934, at the Capitol on Broadway together with Broadway comic Lou Holtz. The comedy on the Capitol screen was MGM's *The Show-Off*, based on George Kelly's stage play, starring Spencer Tracy and Madge Evans. While the movie received positive reviews, one journalist went so far as to suggest that the stage show deserved top billing, and another praised Durante's rough and tumble antics with the musicians. Lou Holtz was funny, waving a cane and doing impressions of a Jewish Swiss who yodels. Polly Moran was best left in films, not a stage presence.[26]

While Durante played the Capitol, two of his recently completed films also were on Broadway: *George White's Scandals* at the Radio City Music Hall and *Palooka* at the Rivoli.

His career busy on all fronts, Durante accepted a leading role in a new Broadway show that would be a big hit for him, Billy Rose's *Jumbo*. A circus show extravaganza by a producer seeking to emulate (if not surpass) P.T. Barnum and the great Ziegfeld, *Jumbo* was a musical story about Barnum's circus (recast as John Considine's Wonder Show). Billy Rose had married Ziegfeld star Fanny Brice in 1928 (the marriage was to be dissolved in 1938), and he would buy the Ziegfeld Theatre in 1942. He had contributed sketches and song lyrics for several other producers' revues, including Earl Carroll's and Florenz Ziegfeld's.

Those who follow composers and lyricists know how prolific Irving Berlin, George and Ira Gershwin, and Cole Porter were in the early decades of the 20th century, but many forget how prolific and successful Billy Rose was as a lyricist. They tend to remember him as a producer. His most famous song lyrics included many durable hits: "That Old Gang of Mine" (1923), "You've Got to See Mama Every Night (or You Can't See Mama at All)" (1923), "Barney Google" (1923), "Don't Bring Lulu" (1925), "Tonight You Belong to Me" (1926), "Clap Hands! Here Comes Charlie!" (1926), "Me and My Shadow" (1927), "Back in Your Own Back Yard" (1927), "If You Want the Rainbow (You Must Have the Rain)" (1928), "I'd Rather Be Blue Over You (Than Be Happy with Somebody Else)" (1928), "There's a Rainbow 'Round My Shoulder" (1928), "Here Comes the Showboat" (1929), "More Than You Know," (1929), "I've Got a Feeling I'm Falling" (1929), "Great Day" (1929), "Without a Song" (1929), "It Happened in Monterey" (1930), "It's Only a Paper Moon" (1933), "I Wanna Be Loved" (1933), "The Night is Young and You're So Beautiful" (1936).[27]

Despite this writing success, Billy Rose chose for the massive undertaking of *Jumbo* to wear only the hat of producer. The music and lyrics were entrusted to one of show business' greatest writing teams, Richard Rodgers and Lorenz Hart, still a few years away from their greatest successes (and for the diminutive Larry Hart, just a few years away from his premature death in 1943 at the age of 48). The libretto was by Ben Hecht and Charles MacArthur, admirers of Durante's nightclub work. Hecht had written the screenplay for Durante's first film, *Roadhouse Nights* (1930) and MacArthur the script for Durante's second film, *New Adventures of Get Rich Quick Wallingford* (1931). The production was staged by John Murray Anderson, and the book directed by George Abbott.

For this production, basically the recreation of a one-ring circus, the entire cavernous Hippodrome, opened in 1905 with 5,500 seats, was torn apart and rebuilt to resemble a circus tent. Billy Rose had said this was the only theater big enough to hold his show. He started rehearsals in the summer of 1935, before securing either theater or financial backing. The Hippodrome was past its peak, often dark for weeks on end, but the news that Billy Rose was interested in it raised its normal rent many times over. While reconstruction progressed, rehearsals took place all over the city, in a riding academy in Brooklyn, in a church on 48th Street, and on the stage of the Manhattan Opera House. As the costs rose beyond what Rose himself could afford, he brought in financiers John Hay Whitney, Bernard Baruch, and Herbert Bayard Swope. Rose had served Baruch as stenographer when Baruch was head of the War Industries Board. Whitney was a multimillionaire. Rose quipped, "*Jumbo* will make me or break Whitney."[28]

Jumbo opened at the refurbished Hippodrome, November 16, 1935. No star was as big as Durante except Rosie the elephant, and she *was* big. Paul Whiteman and his orchestra contributed mightily to the festivities, as did the beautiful girls, the wild animals, horseback riders, and aerial acrobats, but basically the show belonged to Jimmy and Rosie. They got along fine—they had to because the script called for Jimmy to put himself, prone, under the gigantic, suspended front foot of Rosie every performance. Rosie never put her foot down until told by her trainer to do so. She did, however, have a few accidents with her toilet training, requiring crewmen with buckets and shovels.

With massive publicity engendered by Billy Rose's skill as an entrepreneur extraordinaire, music and lyrics by Rodgers and Hart, Whiteman leading the music, and Durante bringing down the house with just one line (trying to hide the elephant from creditors with arms spread in response to the question, "Hey, where do you think you're going with that elephant?", he answers, "What elephant?"), the show had to be a hit, but it lost money in its run of 233 performances. It cost $280,000, a high sum for its day, and lost $160,000. It had been in rehearsal for six months and ran five months. *Jumbo* set a record for postponed opening dates—six times, which Rose explained by saying, "Rome wasn't built in a day." Gracie Allen quipped to reporter Ted Husing for newsreel coverage of opening night, "If it stays open as long as it stayed closed, it will be another Eddie Cantor show."[29]

After losing money on Broadway, *Jumbo* played a special engagement at the Texas Centennial, Fort Worth, July 18–September 1936. Durante did not continue with the show, replaced by Eddie Foy, Jr. Shortly after it opened in Fort Worth, the Durante role was eliminated, together with most of the plot.[30] *Variety* reported, "*Jumbo* Disintegrates Into 50-Cent Circus; Texas Date Another Flop, Ran Show $30,000 Further Into Red."[31]

The songs from *Jumbo* that passed into the mainstream of popular songs included "The Circus Is on Parade," "The Most Beautiful Girl in the World," "My Romance," and "Little Girl Blue." Except for the first, sung by the Razorbacks, and the last, sung by Gloria Grafton, these numbers were sung as duets by Donald Novis and Gloria Grafton. Another fine song, "There's a Small Hotel," was cut before the show's opening, to reappear in Rodgers & Hart's *On Your Toes* (1936) and in the movie version of their *Pal Joey* (1957, from a 1940 Broadway production).[32]

Durante was given one song to sing in each of the two acts of *Jumbo*: "Laugh," with A. Robins, and "Women," with Barbette, the Allan K. Foster Girls and Dancers. When Adolph Zukor made the newsreel "Broadway Highlights of 1936," it included an all-too-brief segment of Jimmy singing "Women."

Durante's next appearance on Broadway was in Cole Porter's *Red, Hot and Blue!*, opening at the Alvin Theatre, October 29, 1936. Since writing the score for *The New Yorkers*, Porter had written for Broadway *Gay Divorce* (1932), running 180 performances; *Anything Goes* (1934), his biggest hit show so far, running 420 performances; and *Jubilee* (1935), 169 performances. With many more good Broadway scores ahead of him, Cole Porter's biggest hit by far would come in 1948 with *Kiss Me, Kate*, which ran for 1,077 performances before going to London in 1951 for another 400 performances.

The book for *Red, Hot and Blue!* was written by Howard Lindsay and Russel Crouse; Vinton Freedley was the producer, and Howard Lindsay did the staging. What theater buffs probably remember most is the creative way in which a dispute over top billing was resolved. Lou Clayton argued that Jimmy Durante should have top billing, and Ethel Merman's agent argued she should. Bob Hope, who also starred, got third billing and did not fight to have his name listed higher. The dispute was resolved by crisscrossing Durante's and Merman's names on the program:

By permission of PLAYBILL®. PLAYBILL® is a registered trademark of PLAYBILL Incorporated, New York, NY.

Originally intended for the stars of *Anything Goes*, Ethel Merman, William Gaxton, and Victor Moore, *Red, Hot and Blue!* was to be a political satire on the order of George and Ira Gershwin's *Of Thee I Sing* (December 1931). Merman, a rich society matron, "Nails" O'Reilly Duquesne, holds a lottery for charity where members of the U.S. Senate buy

On Broadway in 1936 with Ethel Merman in *Red, Hot and Blue!*

tickets, hoping to cut the national debt. The winner is to be the one who discovers the whereabouts of the childhood sweetheart of Bob Hale (Bob Hope, in the role intended for William Gaxton), the wisecracking lawyer Merman's character loves. It's advertised that the girl sought once sat on a hot waffle iron and has a distinctive mark. To assist in the search, Nails gets several prisoners paroled from a low-security facility that coddles its inmates, Lark's Nest Prison. The leader of the parolees is "Policy" Pinkle (Jimmy Durante, in the role intended for Victor Moore). Durante enters, looking very stylish in stripes, holding a polo mallet to show he's captain of the prison team.[33] Nails overcomes Policy's reluctance to give up his prison bachelor suite, "three cells and dungeon,"[34] for a Park Avenue penthouse. Eventually the girl is found, but Bob Hale no longer loves her and does not have to marry her since the Supreme Court declares any lottery benefiting the American people unconstitutional.[35]

    This confused plot met the approval of J. Edgar Hoover, formidable chief of the Federal Bureau of Investigation, who attended opening night with his constant companion, Clyde Tolson. They were good friends of Merman since she met them at the Stork Club. Hoover told the *New York Post* that buried in all the show's nonsense there was "quite a lot of truth."[36]

The critics' reviews were lukewarm. The plot was found weak, the songs second-rate Cole Porter, but the show was a star turn for Merman, Durante, and Hope.

In Act I, Hope and Merman sing the hit song "It's De-Lovely." Merman wrote that Hope tried to upstage her in that number, pulling funny ad-lib movements, and she had to ask producer Freedley to "straighten him out."[37] "It's De-Lovely" was a masterpiece of alliteration on the letter "D."[38]

This clever song was followed by Durante in a song Cole Porter wrote specially for him, "A Little Skipper from Heaven Above." Merman herself says this was a show-stopper for Durante, the only musical number Durante was given in the whole show. A still bigger hit, however, was Durante's monologue when, as both District Attorney and prisoner, he sends himself to the electric chair. Despite the flap over top billing, Merman felt more kindly toward Durante than Hope. She wrote in her autobiography, "I'd go so far as to say that Durante was a dream. Sweet, good-natured Jimmy befriended anybody who asked. He was a pushover."

Merman's additional songs in Act I included "Down in the Depths, on the 90th Floor," which Merman would often perform in later years, "You've Got Something" with Bob Hope, and another chance for Merman to release her huge voice, "Ridin' High." In Act II Merman sang "You're a Bad Influence On Me" and the title song "Red, Hot and Blue."

The show had a modest run of 183 performances, producer Freedley closing its run April 10, 1937, and sending the company to Chicago. There it got the rave notices it missed in New York[39] but still lost money. It opened at Chicago's Grand Opera House on April 14, expected to run well into the summer, but because it could not meet its high operating expenses of $20,000 a week,[40] it was closed May 1, 1937.

Bob Hope recalls that while working with Durante in *Red, Hot and Blue!*, Jimmy took him to a benefit at a hotel banquet room in a rough neighborhood of Hackensack, New Jersey. The crowd was expecting Durante and loved him, yelling "Hey, Schnozzola! Hey, Jimmy!" After one number, Durante turned the show over to Hope, whom no one in the audience knew. Hope saw granite faces, all men, all tough. He did five or six minutes with not a peep from the audience, not one laugh, so he called for Durante. The crowd applauded and yelled loudly for Durante but no Jimmy. Hope ran to the doorman asking if he had seen Durante, and was told he went down the hall. So Hope returned to do a golf routine for four or five minutes, called again for Durante to save him, but no Jimmy. He excused himself and went looking again. He found Jimmy across the street, seated in his car with his piano player and driver Harry Donnelly. Jimmy was laughing hysterically at pulling a fast one. To Durante, leaving Hope holding the bag was the joke of the year. Later, with *Red, Hot and Blue!*

in Chicago, Hope ran the same routine on Durante at the Lake Shore Athletic Club annual charity show. Again Durante tried to sneak out after introducing Hope, but Hope saw him trying to leave and asked the audience to bring Durante back for his favorite number. Jimmy returned, and Hope snuck out to a cab. The next day Durante wrote on Hope's dressing room mirror, "You are a louse," and threw powder all over. To this recollection of Jimmy Durante, Hope adds, "But with all of his violent ideas of humor, he's bighearted, and he lives to be nice to people. I don't think he has an enemy. I've never heard of one."[41]

After *Red, Hot and Blue!* closed in Chicago, Durante immediately went to work at that city's Chez Paree nightclub.[42]

Durante's next Broadway appearance was in the musical comedy *Stars in Your Eyes*, opening at the Majestic Theatre, February 9, 1939. The book was by J.P. McEvoy, lyrics by Dorothy Fields, and music by Arthur Schwartz. The production was staged by Joshua Logan, with settings by Jo Mielziner. Ethel Merman and Jimmy Durante had their names above the title. This time there was no fight over billing: Merman's name was first. The cast also included ballerina Tamara Toumanova, Richard Carlson, and Mildred Natwick, plus Al Goodman and His Orchestra.

What started out as a satire on leftists trying to work with conservatives in Hollywood evolved during road tryouts in New Haven and Boston into no more than a trite love plot. In the original script, Durante was Bill, a union organizer, but as the show reached Broadway, he was Bill, an apolitical movie idea man.[43]

In Act I of *Stars in Your Eyes*, Durante sings "Self Made Man" and with Mildred Natwick "Terribly Attractive." Merman sings "This Is It," "A Lady Needs A Change," "Just A Little Bit More," and, with the ensemble, the Act I finale. In Act II, Durante sings with the ensemble "He's Goin' Home." Merman sings "I'll Pay the Check" and the reprise of "This Is It." Merman and Durante team up for an effective, funny duet, the evening's high point, just before the show's finale: "It's All Yours." Merman wrote, "'It's All Yours,' a duet with Durante ... was a rousing roll-'em-in-the-aisles show-stopper ... [with] the interpolation of some corny joke every time we got to 'It's all yours, everything you see.' At that point, Jimmy tossed hats or telephones or whatever and we threw in a joke ... then, on with the song."[44] This was the great Merman fitting into Durante's characteristic destruction of songs, his career-long style that kept audiences amused.

The interplay between the two stars, including their ad-libbing, was a stronger attraction than the weak book and less than top drawer Fields and Schwartz songs. The show, hoping to draw business from the 1939 New York World's Fair, opening that spring, lost audiences to other shows—Mike Todd's all-black *The Hot Mikado*, which opened at the

Broadhurst Theatre March 23, 1939, starring Bill Robinson, and Billy Rose's *Aquacade*, at the World's Fair. *Stars in Your Eyes* ran 127 performances.

Durante's last appearance on Broadway was in the musical *Keep Off the Grass*, which opened at the Broadhurst Theatre May 23, 1940. Presented by the Shuberts, the show had music by James McHugh and lyrics by Al Dubin, and choreography by George Balanchine. More a revue than a play, it starred, with their names above the title, Jimmy Durante, Ray Bolger, Jane Froman, and Ilka Chase. The cast also included Virginia O'Brien, Larry Adler, Jackie Gleason, Emmet Kelly, and Dodson's Monkeys.

The show had many doctors trying to fix it out of town. Much was changed between Boston and Broadway, but the material for the sketches wasn't very good and the songs were weak. Possibly the best number originally in the show was dropped out of town, the second act song, "Toscanini, Stokowski, and Me." Durante waved a conductor's baton and sang. When the show limped to Broadway, only Durante's singing and carrying on and Bolger's dancing kept the audience's interest. The show folded after only 44 performances.

In Act I, Durante plays Dr. Kildare in the sketch by writer Mort Lewis, "The Tree Doctor." Later he sings "A Fugitive From Esquire" (lyrics by Howard Dietz), a good Durante-style song he would record later in the decade for MGM. He performs this number as a gentleman with four valets: Hal Neiman, Sid Walker, Jackie Gleason, and Peanuts Bohn. Then Durante appears as quiz panel celebrity and writer Clifton Fadiman in the spoof "Misinformation, Please," a sketch written by Parke Levy and Alan Lipscott. He is also Franklyn Sr., in the skit "Life With Mother," also by Levy and Lipscott. After Larry Adler playing his harmonica, there is the takeoff on the 1939 smash-hit film *Gone with the Wind*, called "Rhett, Scarlett & Ashley," sung by Durante, Bolger, and Ilka Chase.

In Act II, Durante appears as a museum guide in "Museum Piece," by S. Jay Kaufman and Mort Lewis, with eight art lovers including Ilka Chase, Jackie Gleason, Peanuts Bohn, Robert Shackleton, Sid Walker, Emmet Kelly, Hal Neiman, and Saint Subber. Later Durante appears as the character McSwindle in a parody of a recent Olsen and Johnson Broadway hit, *Hellzapoppin!* (1938), called "Shakespeare's-A-Poppin," by Mort Lewis, featuring Ilka Chase as Juliet. Durante also appears as "Mulligan" in a sketch with Bolger and Gleason called "Hormones," written by Norman Panama and Melvin Frank.

The number that was dropped in Boston from the score of *Keep Off the Grass*, "Toscanini, Stokowski, and Me," would be used by Durante very effectively in his own act. To associate himself with classical conductors, classical musicians, and operatic stars brought Durante a touch of class to add to his more proletarian charm. He did write a symphony that he talked about on his radio show. He didn't call it "Rhapsody in Blue" or "Symphony No. 1," but "Inka Dinka Doo," and he joked about never getting beyond the first few bars.

Jimmy Durante never again appeared on the Broadway stage. What a pity none of his seven wonderful Broadway performances were preserved on film or recordings.

Chapter 5

MOVIES

Astoria: 1929–30

After Ziegfeld's 1929 revue, *Show Girl*, closed, Clayton, Jackson, and Durante were signed by Paramount Pictures to do a movie, *Roadhouse Nights*. Starring Helen Morgan, Charles Ruggles, and Fred Kohler; it was filmed at Paramount's New York studios, run by Walter Wanger in Astoria, Queens. The script, originally titled *The River Inn*, loosely derived from Dashiell Hammett's novel *Red Harvest* (1929), was written by Ben Hecht. Hecht and Wanger had caught Durante's act with his partners at the Parody Club. Wanger liked what he saw and gave orders to rewrite the part of Helen Morgan's accompanist for Durante.[1] Clayton, Jackson, and Durante were paid the handsome sum of $50,000 for very small parts in the film. Shooting their scenes took one month, November 1929. At the same time they continued other work, appearing twice daily at the Palace Theatre and nightly at the Silver Slipper nightclub.

What appeared as the finished product of *Roadhouse Nights*, released in February 1930, was a grade B gangster movie with just enough songs by Helen Morgan and Clayton, Jackson, and Durante to whet the appetites of fans for more. In a nightclub run by a mobster-bootlegger, played by Fred Kohler, the tuxedo-clad trio sings Durante's "Everything Is On the Up and Up," strutting with canes and hats in the air. They are backed by the Durante orchestra, personnel uncredited but consisting of piano player, banjo, drums, trumpet with mute, and two saxophones. Durante is Daffy, Clayton and Jackson are Moe and Joe.

Midway through their number someone from the audience throws an object at Daffy. When he comes off the stage he complains, "I'm through wid dis joint. . . . Nobody's gonna throw things at me and get away wid it. I'm an artist, not a nigger baby . . . even waitin' on the tables." At some point, "not a nigger baby" was deleted as racially offensive, awkwardly leaving an abruptness of sentence inflection.[2]

Helen Morgan, as the mobster's girlfriend Lola, sings with the

Durante orchestra. Still later, Jimmy sits at the piano and sings with Clayton and Jackson, Jimmy's own "Hello, Everybody, Folks." At the end of this number, Jimmy brags, with one of his most quotable and oft-repeated lines, "I've got a million of 'em, a million of 'em!" Helen Morgan has a second song with the Durante orchestra (but without Durante), "It Can't Go On Like This," which the band jazzes up after she finishes her slow, moody vocal.

The quality of Durante's star potential was already clear in this first motion picture. He was brash, unlettered, and unpretentious. He wrote songs the way he talked, cutting syllables and throwing grammar to the wolves. He remarked in an interview on the eve of the release of *Roadhouse Nights*, "Let them 'cawn't dawnce' people talk like that, I don't care. I say that 'ain't' is beautiful and I'm always going to say it. If I changed my talking now my career'd stop. Don't forget another thing. When we talk and it don't sound right to the ritzy people, why, all right. When they talk it don't sound natural to us, so we're even." He tells how he writes his songs, like "So I Ups to Him." "What do you think I'm going to say? 'So I Arises and Fight Him'?" "[Our language] is easier and it's spreading like wildflower.... Why should I learn four-syllable words when I know four one-syllable words.... Say, ain't 'ahchacha' a three-syllable word?"[3]

The First MGM Period: 1933–34

The New Yorkers closed on Broadway by the summer of 1931. When Jimmy moved later that year to Hollywood with Jeanne, it was with expectations of a still greater career, determined to hold on to Clayton and Jackson as part of his team off-screen. MGM was adamant in not wanting to preserve the team of Clayton, Jackson, and Durante. This career move meant leaving the Palace where he had scored a success as recently as May 1931 with what reviews called the farewell engagement of Clayton, Jackson, and Durante.

In the movies, Durante could not duplicate the success he enjoyed on Broadway in the 1930s and in other areas of show business. On radio, he was doing fairly well in the 1930s and would do better in the 1940s, and in 1950s television, he would be at the top. His nightclub performances were always popular. The movies, however, did not know what to do with him. Though many top writers adored him, few could write the kind of material needed to best utilize this strange new star's talent,[4] and those that might have succeeded were kept busy with writing for other stars. He didn't have writers assigned to his pictures who were as successfully tuned in to his needs as S. J. Perelman, George S. Kaufman, and Morris Ryskind were tuned in to the needs of other new arrivals from the Broadway and vaudeville stages, the Marx Brothers. The heads of movie studios, especially Louis B. Mayer at MGM, adored him but unintentionally abused and burned out his talents. Adorable, agreeable Jimmy was thrown into far too many uninspired pictures just to jazz them up for a few scenes.

Was it a mistake to deny Durante the successful formula of Clayton, Jackson, and Durante? Many writers and producers believed then as now that the talents of Clayton and Jackson were too severely limited: one was a soft-shoe dancer, the other a coon-song singer, neither able to read lines and play character parts. Was it a mistake for Durante to utilize Clayton as his business manager? As ferociously as Clayton handled Durante in the nightclub business, was he too inexperienced in the movie business to know how to get Durante better roles?

MGM, under its five-year contract with him, threw Durante into one picture after the other, films ranging from fairly good to dreadful. From mid-1931 through 1934, Durante made ten films for MGM, plus one while on loan to Paramount.

His first for MGM, *New Adventures of Get Rich Quick Wallingford*, opened at Loew's State in Los Angeles, October 8, 1931, at the Capitol in New York, October 9, a day later in Detroit, and soon at theaters across the country to generally very favorable reviews, excellent reviews for Durante himself.[5] Directed by Sam Wood, who directed the Marx Brothers in their two biggest hits at MGM, *A Night at the Opera* (1935) and *A Day at the Races* (1937), and scripted by Charles MacArthur, this was the first of George Randolph Chester's stories, written soon after the turn of the century for *Cosmopolitan* magazine, to be filmed as a talkie.[6]

William Haines plays Jimmy Wallingford, a smooth-talking hustler who convinces greedy and gullible tycoons to invest in his money-making schemes, while swindling them. He has the help of his cronies Schnozzle (Durante) and Blackie Daw (Ernest Torrence). The story is interesting for the ingenious ways Wallingford is able to gain the trust of supposedly shrewd men. Through love of a decent woman, Wallingford finally goes straight, giving up all swindles for a good marriage.

Durante is mildly amusing, but far too often repeats the same expressions with which he was identified early in his career: "I got a million of 'em, a million of 'em!" (used six times), and to a lesser degree, "How mortifyin'" and "He's putty in their hands." His best moment comes late in the film when he sits at the piano and sings a song he wrote and often used in his act, "Did You Ever Have the Feeling."[7] As he performs this funny song on the topic of indecision, whether to go or to stay, he repeatedly puts on his hat and takes it off again.

This was the first film in which the name "Schnozzle" was used, though advertising for the earlier Paramount film printed the term. Durante had already been called "Schnoz," a Yiddish term for "nose," in his early nightclub days, as well as "Schnozzola," an Italianate version of "Schnoz." After the 1930s, the term "Schnozzle" was not much used to refer to Durante, but many friends and reporters called him "the Schnoz."[8]

Durante's second picture for MGM was *The Cuban Love Song*, released late October 1931. He played the friend of the romantic lead, portrayed by opera singer Lawrence Tibbett, a U.S. Marine visiting Cuba before being shipped to the war in France. Lupe Velez plays the singer's Cuban girlfriend. Durante has the small role of O.O. (Oswald Obidiah) Jones, the Marine's friend—he's not given much to do—while Lupe Velez, who will work well with Durante in three upcoming films, has her scenes only with Tibbett.

While Tibbett sings the romantic "A Cuban Love Song," Durante gets nothing to sing except a few nondescript notes at the piano, and in one scene with a crying baby to use his expression, "hot,cha,cha!" Yet there is enough here to intimate that, with the right material, Durante could be teamed with an opera star in a funny contrast between a rough kid from the streets with a hoarse, jazzy voice and an aristocratic, cultured voice straight from the most exclusive music academies. But MGM never caught on to this comic possibility, not even in the 1940s when they threw Durante into the same musicals with Wagnerian singer Lauritz Melchior. Durante would show what hilarity could result from such a situation properly handled: he worked well with Helen Traubel on his television series, using her larger-than-Ethel Merman's tonsils, her matronly comportment, and her high society aura as effectively as the Marx Brothers used Margaret Dumont in their 1930s films.

Used properly, the pairing of Durante and Lupe Velez later became a fairly successful combination: Durante mispronouncing the English language and a spitfire Mexican actress-singer mangling the same language, the team doing comic duets and fractured patter. Durante and Velez were paired with some success in the Broadway revue *Strike Me Pink*, 1933, and in the movies *Palooka* (United Artists), *Hollywood Party* (MGM), and *Strictly Dynamite* (RKO), all released 1934. Another similar combination, Durante and the Portuguese-born Brazilian actress-singer Carmen Miranda, worked well on 1950s television.

The briefest but most hilarious pairing of Durante's 1930s films was his few minutes of work with Marion Davies in *Blondie of the Follies* (MGM, 1932), parodying the John Barrymore-Greta Garbo love scene from MGM's exquisite *Grand Hotel* (also 1932).

Three 1930s match-ups looked good on paper: Durante with Buster Keaton, with George M. Cohan, and with comedian Jack Pearl. All three combinations were less than successful.

In the 1930s, the full power of the Durante magic was captured only once in a leading role. In a short made for the federal government's National Recovery Act, "Give a Man a Job," Durante faces the camera and filmed audience in a number with the immediacy, energy, and poignancy of one of his nightclub appearances. The whole film, like the very effective parody of *Grand Hotel*, lasts only about three minutes. Could this power be effective over a feature of 70 or 80 minutes or longer? Yes, it could, with the proper mix of sentimentality, nightclub-type routines, piano ragtime, destruction of pianos, malapropisms, and a straight man or woman to work off. The star vehicles for Durante could have been endless. As it was, though the public loved him, his cinematic star dimmed. With the help of radio, television, and nightclubs, his reputation rebounded. MGM did not bury his career the way it did Buster Keaton's.

In the 1940s, the MGM publicity department had Durante measuring Lassie's canine nose to see if it was bigger than his own. Why not star Durante, not with Lassie, who was a dramatic star, but with some cute little vaudeville-trained poodle? Maybe even train a look-alike for Muggins, the springer spaniel he shared with Jeanne. With Margaret O'Brien in *Music for Millions* (MGM, 1944), the publicity department stills stressed Durante's comic importance to the film. This was misleading. He all-too-briefly relieved the overlong love story with humorous songs, including "Umbriago," based on one of Jimmy's many gags carried over from his 1930s radio show.

Earlier than his work with child star Margaret O'Brien, Durante was given the assignment of working with Shirley Temple in 20th Century Fox's *Little Miss Broadway* (1938). Publicity photos showed Durante strutting with little Shirley, both hats held high in a traditional Durante and Eddie Jackson strut. When the film was released, however, this scene was cut; Shirley's dance with George Murphy was kept in. Shirley danced so well with Bill "Bojangles" Robinson in other films that one may wonder why her studio or Lou Clayton did not think of pairing her with Clayton, Jackson, and Durante doing some strutting and soft shoe.

Durante's admiration for black musicians and collaboration with black composers in the late 1910s and early 1920s, as well as his own considerable skills on ragtime piano, could have been channeled into Hollywood films about that seminal period of jazz history, employing some of the then-still-living black and white musicians who would soon be lost to the world.

What Hollywood did to Bill Robinson, Lena Horne, Louis Armstrong, Billie Holiday, Paul Robeson, and other black stars was no less than a crime of prejudice and a failure of courage and imagination. Bill Robinson, for example, did have good tap numbers with Shirley Temple in four 20th Century Fox films (*The Little Colonel* and *The Littlest Rebel*, 1935; *Rebecca of Sunnybrook Farm* and *Just Around the Corner*, 1938), as well as specialty numbers in *Hooray for Love* (RKO, 1935), *The Big Broadcast of 1936* (Paramount, 1935), and a few other films. But aside from *Stormy Weather* (Columbia, 1943), he had no leading roles. Like most early film appearances by blacks, Robinson had to play servants or other grinning, cheerful fools, not as extreme a caricature as Stepin Fetchit roles, but still completely and insultingly stereotyped.

The only time major Hollywood studios made intelligent musicals starring black talent was 1943. That year Columbia made *Stormy Weather*, directed by Andrew L. Stone, starring Lena Horne and Bill Robinson, with Cab Calloway, Fats Waller, Dooley Wilson, and the Nicholas Brothers. The same year MGM made *Cabin in the Sky*, directed by Vincente Minnelli, his first of many fine musicals for MGM, starring Ethel Waters, Eddie "Rochester" Anderson, and Lena Horne, with John Bubbles (of Buck & Bubbles), Louis Armstrong, Rex Ingram, and Duke Ellington.

Paul Robeson, potentially a greater film actor than the groundbreaking Sidney Poitier many years later, was denied dramatic and musical roles altogether, not only because of the usual racial insensitivity but also because he was sympathetic to Communist Party ideology. After a stirring and dignified appearance in Universal's 1936 *Show Boat* singing "Ole Man River," he had to go to England to make poorly financed films.

Perhaps the greatest jazz singer of all time, Billie Holiday, was used as a maid in one obscure independent film, *New Orleans* (1947). Lena Horne, another excellent singer, found herself under contract at MGM, among all its great stars the only Negro, beautiful and light-skinned. Invariably MGM cast her only in cameo singing spots that could be excised from musicals when they played the South. She badly wanted to play the part of the mulatto Julie in MGM's 1951 remake of Kern and Hammerstein's *Show Boat*, a character woven integrally into the fabric of the story. MGM assigned the role to Ava Gardner, who used makeup to darken her face. (In the earlier *Show Boat*, Universal had also used a white actress as the mulatto Julie, singer Helen Morgan.)

MGM bragged that it had as many stars as there were in the heavens, but the studio took few chances, and lacking inspiration, undertook few intelligent experiments with creative scripts and casting.

MGM, like other major studios, was established and run by immigrant Jews or sons of immigrant Jews. By and large, Jews were liberal Democrats or socialists who supported the civil rights of oppressed minorities like themselves, seeking freedom of speech and freedom of opportunity for blacks as well as for themselves. These Hollywood pioneers, Marcus Loew, Adolph Zukor, William Fox, Carl Laemmle, Louis B. Mayer, the Warner Bros., and Harry Cohn, however, wanted to be "more American" than most mainstream patriotic groups.[9] They wanted no films about anti–Semitism or racism, and no decently financed film on such a topic was released until the late 1940s, after World War II had been fought, with blacks serving in segregated units and most of Europe's Jews killed in Nazi concentration camps. Even then, the prevailing philosophy was "If you want to send a message, use Western Union."

Durante seemed perfect for Hollywood's escapist entertainment. He was low-brow, non-intellectual, nonpolitical, a rough-spoken little guy who needed the paternal, authoritarian protection of a firm but loving studio head. Louis B. Mayer, powerful head of MGM, adored Jimmy, partly because Durante passed through some of the same hard knocks as a child that he had endured. Mayer was discriminated against as a child in St. John, New Brunswick, Canada, because he was a Jew, the son of a poor Russian immigrant father who had brought Louis to Canada at the age of three.[10] Durante was discriminated against because he was Italian and because he was so plain and clearly ethnic in appearance.

Mayer thought he was protecting Jimmy, not abusing his potential Hollywood career. Wanting to forget and bury his own roots, Mayer changed his birthday to the 4th of July[11] and became an arch conservative, a power in California's Republican Party. In seeking to avoid message films opposing anti–Semitism, racism, anti–Italian, anti–Irish, or anti–Chinese prejudice, Louis B. Mayer, heading the studio with the biggest stars and biggest budgets, was sending all Americans and the world of filmgoers a message: Americans live like Andy Hardy, white Protestants in small towns, in comfortable homes, with black servants. They sometimes go to nightclubs in the big city where they encounter Irish and Italian gangsters and an occasional sexy Spanish dancer who threatens but fails to tarnish the all-American standard of morality. Even 20th Century Fox's 1940 masterpiece of social criticism, John Ford's *The Grapes of Wrath*, based on John Steinbeck's biblical novel, depicted only the Depression plight of poor whites, not that of blacks, Hispanics, or other ethnic Americans.

Generations passed before Hollywood would begin to overcome racial and religious stereotypes and show America in a more realistic and three-dimensional light. But not before one last failure of courage—the studios' ignominious turning on the few courageous writers who had dared to tackle social problems in the 1930s—cooperating with the Congressional witch hunts that sought to find and destroy Communists and Communist sympathizers. Louis B. Mayer wholeheartedly joined in this attack on freedom of speech. Aside from Lena Horne, the only black nose in his stable of stars belonged to Lassie, and the only controversy about his stars involved alcoholism or marital infidelity.

One of MGM's few films of social significance in the 1930s was *The Wet Parade* (1932), an overlong but otherwise fairly good film about the prejudice between post–Civil War South and North, alcoholism in families on each side, and the moral confusion of Prohibition. Directed by Victor Fleming and based on an Upton Sinclair novel, the film stars Walter Huston, with Myrna Loy, Neil Hamilton, Lewis Stone, Dorothy Jordan, Robert Young, Jimmy Durante, and Wallace Ford. Durante plays a Treasury Department Prohibition agent, Abe Shilling. "Shilling's the name. Two bits in London, a quarter here. Ha! Ha! Ha! . . . I got a million of 'em, a million of 'em!" Durante helps Robert Young, the new prohibition agent who saw his own father destroyed by bootleg liquor. While the crusader is intense, Durante provides lighter moments, telling a few weak jokes and punctuating them with his own laughter and famous "Hot-cha-cha!"

In this film Durante's best scene occurs at a nightclub become speakeasy, disguised as a Count from the Bulgarian legation. He's Abe the prohibition agent wearing beard, tux, and diplomatic sash across his starched white shirt. The hostess, played by Myrna Loy, introduces this celebrity to the club's audience, saying he doesn't speak a word of English. Abe tears off his beard, announcing a raid: "In plain Bulgarian, this jernt is knocked over!"

Abe is shot trying to help his partner in a later scene and dies. With his last breath Abe tries to tell a gag. His last words are "I got a million of 'em, a million of 'em." Durante's various roles call for him to die in only two of his 38 feature films, at the end of *The Wet Parade*, and much more dramatically (and hilariously) in United Artists' *It's a Mad, Mad, Mad, Mad World* (1963) where, at the beginning of the frenetic film, he literally "kicks the bucket."

It may well be, as Preston Sturges showed in his greatest film, *Sullivan's Travels* (Paramount, 1941), that what hard-pressed Americans need most in difficult times is laughter, that film escapism is more necessary than crusading realism. Charles Chaplin did both, well folded into the same film, especially *The Gold Rush* (1925), *City Lights* (1931), *Modern Times* (1936), and *The Great Dictator* (1940). Other comedians, including Buster Keaton, Jimmy Durante, Laurel and Hardy, Harold Lloyd, and W.C. Fields, did best with pure escapism.

Durante and Keaton made three films together for MGM: *The Passionate Plumber* (1932), *Speak Easily* (1932), and *What! No Beer?* (1933). All were directed by Edward Sedgwick, Jr., who, like Keaton, had vaudeville experience. Including two silent films (*The Cameraman*, 1928, and *Spite Marriage*, 1929), Keaton was to make a total of eight films for MGM, all but one directed by Sedgwick. The best of these was *The Cameraman*, and MGM knew it. For many years, according to Keaton biographer Rudi Blesh, MGM used it as a training film for its younger comedians, considering the MGM machine approach to film-making more important than respect for individual differences in comedic talent.[12] In *The Cameraman* Keaton succeeded artistically because, despite MGM's efforts to force Keaton and director Sedgwick to stick to the scripts, Buster was able to insert some good improvised bits. He was far less successful in inserting similar bits into the three sound films with Durante. The plots got in the way, and inhibited his improvisations.

By all accounts, the teaming of Durante with Keaton was a mismatch. Durante was brash, loud, and knockabout in his style; Keaton was subtle, acrobatic, and visual. Everything Durante said was funny because of the way he said it; Keaton, on the other hand, was so accustomed to the pantomime of vaudeville and silent films that, in his monotone voice, he seemed unable to speak much of anything funny, dialogue not being a part of what he did so well.

Some writers have said that Louis B. Mayer wanted to destroy Keaton because he was difficult and demanding as well as an alcoholic. Keaton himself says in his autobiography, "I heard rumors that Mr. Mayer was planning to build [Jimmy Durante] up at my expense. This didn't worry me much, although I can't say I liked it. With my record of successful pictures, I felt I was a fixture at MGM. I couldn't imagine anyone there wanting to get rid of me."[13]

Blesh writes bluntly that MGM murdered Keaton's art after allowing him the freedom he needed to reach the high standard he had achieved in *The Cameraman*, which was also a commercial success. He was increasingly under the heavy heel of MGM, instead of MGM working to assist Keaton in continuing to do what he had done so well.[14] As the studio's bad judgment forced bad films on Keaton, he slipped; as he slipped, he drank.

Another Keaton biographer, Tom Dardis, feels that no one at MGM was out to destroy Keaton, that he destroyed his own career by "his worsening alcoholism and his inability to regain control over the *kind* of pictures in which he appeared."[15] Keaton always regretted giving up his own studio to make pictures at big, booming MGM. In his autobiography he calls this "the worst mistake of my life."[16] The studio was inexperienced in working with comics. When Keaton arrived, the only stars to have done any comedy were Marion Davies and Marie Dressler. He wanted to do a film with Dressler but was refused.

Lawrence Weingarten, Irving Thalberg's brother-in-law, was assigned to be Keaton's producer. Aside from working with Jackie Coogan in silent films, Weingarten at that point had no experience with comedy. (Later he would successfully produce two of the fine Spencer Tracy–Katherine Hepburn comedies, *Adam's Rib*, 1949, and *Pat and Mike*, 1952.) Thalberg, a widely respected young production executive, worked as artistic director under Mayer's management for 12 years, but he suffered a severe heart attack in December 1932 (less than two weeks after Buster's third film with

Durante, *What! No Beer?*, had gone into production) and went to Europe for some rest. About that same time, Keaton collapsed from a combination of alcohol abuse and a tough acrobatic trick he was trying to do.

Keaton attributed this renewal of excessive drinking to his divorce problems and his knowledge that the film he was working on, *What! No Beer?*, was "a 100 per cent turkey."[17] Before the film was finished, Mayer, with Thalberg apparently not disagreeing, decided to terminate Keaton's contract. When Thalberg returned from Europe, he found much of his power had been taken away. He died of pneumonia in 1936 at the age of 37.[18]

Buster Keaton was a good judge of what worked for him and what didn't. MGM was pushing him, a great film comedian, into terrible films and, helplessly out of control artistically and personally, into obscurity and ruin. He hated two pre-Durante films MGM required him to make, *Parlor, Bedroom and Bath* and *Sidewalks of New York* (both 1931). He knew these films had weak plots and were wrong for him.

Keaton was also correct about the damage MGM was doing to Jimmy Durante's budding film career, though he might have been wrong in the remedy. Like all others in Hollywood, Keaton could only guess at how best to use Durante's rather unusual talents. Keaton told Charles Samuels how hilarious Durante was as part of a vaudeville team, especially in its "Wood" number.

> But the moment he broke up the team at M-G-M's suggestion, Jimmy, depending almost entirely on his singing, piano playing, and priceless personality was unable ever to carry one successful picture. My guess is that without ingenious sight gags to work with he lacked the variety required of the star of a screen comedy running from seventy-five to ninety minutes....
>
> At any rate, as I see it, there was no way to mesh, match, or blend Durante's talents with mine. Yet Jimmy would have been great in the pictures that we did together if he had been allowed merely to do spots of comedy instead of playing a character all of the way through.
>
> However, he was very good in the one picture we made together that had quality. I think this was because the character he played was very much like the real Jimmy Durante. The picture was *Speak Easily*.[19]

The Passionate Plumber, the first of the three Keaton-Durante films, has Keaton's name above the title, with supporting cast headed by Durante, followed by Irene Purcell, Polly Moran, Gilbert Roland, and Mona Maris. The film was an adaptation of Jacques Deval's comedy *Her Cardboard Lover*. Set in Paris, the film has Buster playing Elmer Tuttle, a plumber from Yonkers, New York. He's used as a set-up "cardboard" lover to make a negligent lover jealous and more ardent. The lover is Tony Lagores, played by Gilbert Roland, the Mexican silent screen heart-throb and character actor in many sound films. This macho lover has another woman on the side, tempestuous Nina, played by Mona Maris, a Spanish tigress who curses like Lupe Velez.

Durante plays chauffeur to the rich French lady Patricia, played by Irene Purcell. Her maid is Albino, played by comedienne Polly Moran.

The Keaton character is challenged to a duel by the lady's lover, and Durante serves as the second. No one is hurt, but not much humor is squeezed from this potentially funny, if overused, kind of scene. Nor is there much humor or other interest in the uninvolving story.

Durante has precious few good lines. He asks at one point, "Don't I always stand at attention when they play the Mayonnaise?" Later he has a mildly funny line, or a clinker, depending upon your taste, "Did you ever hear about the garbage man's daughter? She inherited a swell dump." Keaton does not fare any better. He has a brief pantomime routine with three mothballs he drops on a roulette wheel. He also wrecks the rich lady's car, but nothing funny comes of this. Later, an alarm clock goes off and Buster grabs it, trying to turn it off. Someone else takes it from him before he can develop any comedy routine from this. Throughout this film, Keaton delivers lines as though he is reading them.

The Passionate Plumber was shot in nineteen days. When it opened in March 1932 at the Capitol Theatre, Broadway at 51st Street, an advertisement in the New York *Evening Graphic* read, "Today Broadway goes nerts! Loses its attitude! Schnozzle (Cupid) Durante gets hot!" An arrow reading "Greatest of all comedy casts!" points to photos of Durante and Polly Moran. Buster Keaton's name is printed above theirs, but he's given no photo in the ad. The stage show on the same bill at the Capitol, surely better than the movie, was headlined by the black dance team of Buck & Bubbles in "Dance Dreams."

Speak Easily worked much better by comparison. Keaton wasn't happy with the film, just less unhappy than with his prior three films for MGM. Keaton's name was again above the title and Durante's below. The film also featured Ruth Selwyn, Thelma Todd, and Sidney Toler.

Keaton plays Professor Post at Potts College. A lonely, unworldly bachelor, he gets a letter telling him he's inherited $750,000. He joyfully packs up and leaves for adventures unknown, meeting traveling actors who get him to invest his as-yet-uncollected fortune in their show. His college associates admit to sending a fake letter about an inheritance to get the professor out into the world, feeling that even if he spends his own savings of $4,000, it will have done him some good.

Durante is James "Jimmy" Dodge, the producer of the show. He plays a few notes at the piano for an all-girl chorus line. Buster watches. At the end of the rehearsal, the Durante character says, in typical Durantesque fashion, "It's a hit! It's stupendious!" Later Durante sings a few notes of his own song, "I Can Do Without Broadway (But Can Broadway Do Without Me?)" When he auditions one of his so-called original songs from the show for a theatrical producer, played by Sidney Toler, he launches into "Singin' in the Rain." "I wrote that this morning." Then he plays "Oh Susannah," which he also attempts to pass off as his own, saying it's a song he calls "Speak Easily." Honest Professor Post protests, "That's plagiarism."

Femme fatale actress Eleanor Espere, played by Thelma Todd, throws herself at the professor, smelling money and a leading role. She tells him she went to finishing school, then takes off her dress to show what she finished. She gets the teetotaler intoxicated with gin, mixing him a batch of Tom Collins, which he calls Thomas Collins. Keaton does a believable drunk routine complete with good pratfalls over the sofa.

Opening night of the show, the first act snowfall ballet number with Eleanor is wrecked by the professor's unplanned entrance. James enters to try to save the number. This proves to be the best moment, probably the only good moment Keaton and Durante were to have together in any of their three films. Durante does an awkward ballet while Keaton does pratfalls. Later, in the second act, Keaton again wrecks a number, this time improving it with a funny silent film routine, getting caught on a revolving hook. The exasperated director (Sidney Toler) shouts, "Shoot him! They'll think it's part of the show." Naturally, the show is a big hit.

What! No Beer? gave Durante equal billing with Keaton above the title, Keaton's name first. The rest of the cast included Roscoe Ates, Phyllis Barry, John Miljan, Edward Brophy, and Henry Armetta. As the film opens, it's election eve, with dry and wet rallies for and against Prohibition. Keaton is Elmer J. Butts, a taxidermist with a little money saved up. Durante is Jimmy Potts, barber and friend of Elmer. They vote at the local precinct against Prohibition, creating a disturbance at the polls that was intended to be funny, but which falls flat. In the next scene Jimmy is in his barbershop giving Elmer a shave. The radio announces the state-by-state results of the vote. As the final results come in from Alabama, the announcer says, "Alabama votes wet by a safe majority, 2 to 1." Keaton comments, "Why that's only three votes."

While gangsters are upset by the vote, Elmer comes up with the money for the two of them to buy an old brewery to start making beer. They enter the dark building, groping for the light. Keaton: "It's so dark here I can't see the nose before my face." Durante: "I don't have that trouble."

Making beer, Jimmy screams in his raspy voice while the Buster character is given too little pantomime or clever things to say. He's overshadowed by Durante in every scene. The brewing goes awry, and Jimmy throws up his hands at a flood of suds, giving us one of his famous expressions, "It's a

Jimmy Durante and Buster Keaton in *What! No Beer?*, **MGM 1932.**

dilemmia!" Buster's only sustained scene of pantomime is a sad rerun of a once-hilarious routine he had done in the silent feature *Seven Chances* (1925), with boulders chasing him down a mountainside. Now he reworks this, with dozens of beer barrels escaping a truck parked on a steep hill threatening to roll over him as he and the barrels careen down the hill.

What! No Beer? was the worst of the three Keaton-Durante films, but it was the biggest box office success. Its opening at the Capitol Theatre drew large audiences and made a fast profit. Reportedly, MGM, seeing the money this film made, wanted to rescind its firing of Keaton and sent out feelers to him, but Keaton, through Sedgwick, told both Mayer and Thalberg to go to hell.[20]

As Keaton and Durante approached completion of *What! No Beer?*, Keaton had gone to Thalberg with an idea for a parody of MGM's own all-star *Grand Hotel*, which was also nearing completion. He wanted to call it *Grand Mills Hotel*, an all-star parody, to be produced by himself and directed by Sedgwick and himself. He speaks in his autobiography with Samuels about casting Jimmy Durante in the role of the bogus count, played in *Grand Hotel* by John Barrymore, and instead of Greta Garbo as his love interest, the aging ballerina would be Marie Dressler. Polly Moran would play the role of the secretary that was played by Joan Crawford.

Oliver Hardy would play the powerful manufacturer that Wallace Beery played, seeking to make a deal with a firm controlled by Stan Laurel. Buster himself would take the Lionel Barrymore role of the dying worker who wants to see life before he goes: a fatal illness would be turned into a severe case of hiccups with only thirty years to live.[21] The studio did show some interest in Keaton's idea but not enough to relinquish control to him, and he refused to work again for MGM without regaining control.

Meanwhile MGM did throw Durante into a brief scene in *Blondie of the Follies* (1932) where he and Marion Davies do a hilarious parody of the *Grand Hotel* John Barrymore-Greta Garbo love scene. The bit lasts not much over three minutes and is by far the best scene in an otherwise weak drama with some music. Marion Davies shows a good comic touch, but the love scene might have been even better with Marie Dressler in Jimmy Durante's arms.[22]

The year 1933 saw MGM releasing not only *What! No Beer?* but also two films with Durante in small parts, *Hell Below* and *Broadway to Hollywood*, plus another film co-starring Durante, *Meet the Baron*. After *Hell Below*, it was initially expected that Durante would play a starring role in MGM's mixture of comedy and melodrama with the working title "The Rear Car," renamed "The Red Light," and released late July 1934, without Durante's participation, as *Murder in the Private Car*, starring Charles Ruggles.[23]

Hell Below, an action film about a submarine crew during World War I, with the pre-release title "Pig Boats," had scenes filmed in Hawaii. It stars Robert Montgomery and Walter Huston. Durante is a sailor who meets a girl with a nose like his while on shore leave. Later he boxes a kangaroo.

Broadway to Hollywood, a minor film about a vaudeville family making it in the movies, stars Alice Brady, Frank Morgan, and Jackie Cooper, as the Three Hacketts. Durante has a brief scene in the last quarter of the film with the often-heard line in show business that you should be good to people on your way up because they're the same people you meet on the way down. Mickey Rooney has a small role; there is one musical number by Nelson Eddy and another by vaudeville star Fay Templeton. Production numbers from a failed MGM project that was put together in 1929 as a revue but not released, *The March of Time*, were spliced in.[24]

In *Meet the Baron*, Durante had a starring role with Jack Pearl, both names above the title with Pearl's first. Jack Pearl at the time was a very popular radio comedian, with his own show built around his use of German dialect and the appropriation of ideas related to the humorous tall tales written by 18th century German cavalry officer Baron von Munchausen. Whenever Jack Pearl's Baron would have the veracity of his stories challenged, he would respond confidently, "Vas you dere, Sharlie?"

Although the popularity of Jack Pearl's Baron on radio faded rather quickly, the Hooper audience ratings for shows on the air January 1933 give Pearl a higher rating than most other comedy variety shows that season.[25] MGM sought to capitalize on this popularity while it was at its peak. Pearl's only starring role in films was *Meet the Baron*. Despite the presence of Durante, the inclusion of Ted Healy and his Stooges (The Three Stooges), highly competent producer, writers, and director, the film was terrible, especially its script. The story was by Herman J. Mankiewicz and Norman Krasna, screenplay by Allen Rivkin and P.J. Wolfson, dialogue by Arthur Kober and William K. Wells. It was directed by Walter Lang and produced by David O. Selznick.

The film opens with the Baron, accompanied by Durante, as his manager, Joseph McGoo, tramping through a fake African jungle in fake beards, with the Stooges and a bunch of natives, on safari. Before you can blink, the ship sails back to a cardboard New York harbor. There's a ticker tape parade for the Baron, a proclaimed hero. A group of Mae West imitators are among those giving their welcome, and the Statue of Liberty speaks her own welcome.

The Baron is to deliver a speech at Cuddle College, a girls' school. The announcement that he would come is made by the dean, played by Edna May Oliver. This leads to an insipid song with the Metro-Goldwyn Girls, enlivened a bit by the interpolation of "Ciribiribin." Durante as the Baron's manager checks the contract and monitors the Baron's speech to make sure the contract limit on the number of words is not exceeded. The Baron also gives a radio interview which features—like his own radio show if you listen to tapes of it today—badly dated humor, not-so-funny tall tales. One of the better comments goes, "My Aunt Sophie did 'lighthouse keeping.'"

Ted Healy and his Stooges, veterans of vaudeville, are handymen at the college. They play cards and smack each other around in their usual style, but they're not given much to do. The Dean says, "I'm the dean, dean." The Stooges reply with Rudyard Kipling's poem, "Oh, you're a better man than I am, Gunga Din." Coming from the masters of mayhem this is practically Noel Coward or Cole Porter sophistication.

ZaSu Pitts, as the maid in a hotel, has eyes for the Baron. When Durante is introduced to her, he comes on like a sledgehammer. Thinking he's being genteel, he asks, "How are ya, babe?" and grabs her by the shoulders. When she repulses his advance, he gives one of his favorite lines, "I know I'm not good looking, but what's my opinion against thousands of others?"

The rest of the film is all downhill. Durante is given no songs at all to alleviate the growing tangle of uninvolving confusion. It turns out the Baron is really an imposter, but a radio network likes him and offers a good

Jimmy Durante as Schnarzan, a parody of Tarzan, in *Hollywood Party*, MGM 1934.

contract to do a weekly show. He marries the maid and swears to her he'll never tell another lie: "If I ever tell another lie, may all our children be acrobats." The last scene is set in a maternity ward, with twin baby girls, acrobats, swinging on the light fixtures.

Meet the Baron had some of the kind of chaos that worked for the Marx Brothers, but it didn't work for Jack Pearl. If Durante had songs and more to do, and the Stooges had more routines, and the chorus girls were used in more than their one production number, the film might have worked. As it was, this was the worst film David O. Selznick would ever produce.[26]

The strangest but probably most enjoyable of Durante's early MGM films was *Hollywood Party* (1934). This was as chaotic as *Meet the Baron*, but somehow, without even a director credited, it worked, especially for Durante. It's far from a masterpiece, but it's also far from a disaster, though some critics would disagree. Any film with Durante as a parody of Tarzan cannot be dismissed as a trifle.

Hollywood Party was a mishmash, overloaded with comic misfires.[27] Still, this musical is amusing and the best showcase for Durante's talent that MGM was to give him before his final film for MGM, *Billy Rose's Jumbo* (1962). He was less misused and less underused. By the time MGM made *Jumbo*, Durante had mellowed into a father or grandfather figure and no longer had the same frenetic energy and edge of comic violence.

The 1934 film, although it does not have his name above the title, stars Jimmy Durante. In his dreams, he is The Great Schnarzan, a screen star who does Tarzan-like roles, and whose reputation is wilting because he needs new, fiercer lions for his movies. (Durante's co-star in this film, Lupe Velez, was at the time married to Johnny Weissmuller, who made more and better Tarzan movies than anyone else, beginning with *Tarzan the Ape Man*, MGM, 1932.) Continuing his dream, Durante throws a party. The Baron Munchausen (played again by Jack Pearl) was to be the guest of honor. He arrives at the party with lions to sell. A show business rival of the Great Schnarzan, Liondora (George Givot), gate-crashes the party in an effort to get the lions for himself.

There's some rough and tumble dialogue between the Durante character and his girlfriend, played by Lupe Velez, who is angry because she was not invited to the party. After she verbally lashes him on the phone in her Spanish-accented English, we see a photo of Jimmy on her nightstand: his shirt is torn and he has a black eye.

There are some production numbers with many girls, but they're fragmentary and don't work well despite a style reminiscent of Busby Berkeley. As Jimmy leads an all-girl chorus he yells one of Durante's well-known lines, "Wait a minute! Wait a minute!" (skipping the usual next line in his routine, "I work here too!") and launches into a song he wrote, "Hello, Hello, Hello" (used again in a variation for *Two Sisters from Boston*, MGM, 1946). Fake African warriors in headdresses with bones in noses enter, followed by the Baron in the arms of the gorilla Ping Pong, son of King Kong. The Baron renews the song, "Hello, Hello, Hello."

Ted Healy and the Three Stooges enter to have anthropology professors measure the Stooges' craniums for prehistoric characteristics. Durante sings his lively song "Reincarnation." Still dreamlike, a stream of unconsciousness takes us to the Garden of Eden where Durante is Adam and a freshly created Eve has a Durante nose ("I've been ribbed!" protests Adam), and to Paul Revere's famous ride to see Durante's nose on Paul's horse. When the horse is asked how many more miles he has to go, he replies with Durante's line, "I've got a million of 'em!" Durante then reprises "Reincarnation," intimating maybe he was the horse in a previous life.[28]

Laurel and Hardy arrive at the party to retrieve the lions they had sold to the Baron for a bad check. They do two routines they've done better elsewhere: the doorbell and unfriendly butler; raw eggs smashed into uncomfortable body parts.

One segment of the film, for no logical reason at all, introduces Mickey Mouse, who has a brief comic scene with Durante. Women at the party scream that there's a mouse in the room. Durante picks it up by the tail and is pleased to see it's Mickey. Mickey imitates Jimmy with "Hotcha-cha" and "how mortifyin'," as Disney momentarily lengthens the mouse's nose to resemble Durante's. Mickey Mouse sits at the piano, plucking a few notes. This brief black and white segment is abruptly followed by a totally unrelated color cartoon, "Hot Chocolate Soldiers," complete with opening title card listing words and music by Nacio Herb Brown and Arthur Freed, pictures by Walt Disney. The few times *Hollywood Party* appeared on television (Ted Turner's TNT Cable Network), it was without this five-minute cartoon and the introductory Mickey Mouse segment. The uncut version was released on an MGM-United Artists videocassette in 1992.

A curiosity for Durante fans is the film's conclusion: an unbilled walk-on by Jimmy's real wife, Jeanne. She wakes Jimmy from his dream and tells him they will be late for Lupe's party. This is Jeanne's only feature film appearance.[29]

Hollywood Party has the kind of crazed, frantic energy that was so much a part of Durante's knock-about stage presence in vaudeville and on Broadway, and that was missing from or not developed in other MGM films. A few additional glimpses of that energy came the same year in non–MGM films *Palooka* (United Artists/Reliance, 1934) and *Strictly Dynamite* (RKO, 1934), not coincidentally pairing Durante again with Lupe Velez. They had good chemistry together.

After 1934, Durante did not make another movie for MGM until 1944, when he was put in a string of MGM musicals beginning with *Two Girls and a Sailor*, in supporting roles.

Other Studios: 1932–42

At the same time that he was making movies for MGM in the 1930s, Durante made films for other studios. In 1932, he worked for Paramount on the much-awaited and generally disappointing sound film debut of the great George M. Cohan. Film credits on the screen are preceded by the proud notice, "Paramount presents the first appearance on the talking screen of that eminent stage star, playwright *and* composer, MR. GEORGE M. COHAN in THE PHANTOM PRESIDENT." Below the title, Claudette Colbert and Jimmy Durante have their names in smaller print and in still smaller print, Sidney Toler.

Cohan was accustomed to being recognized as a star and treated with respect. When he arrived in Hollywood to make this picture, he was treated rudely, challenged at Paramount's gates by security guards who admitted only the cars of "stars," and made to wait all day long for a few minutes of filming. One Cohan biographer writes that Cohan was told by Paramount studio head Jesse M. Lasky that he would be given not just the role but allowed to participate in the writing of the film's script, though this latter promise was not in writing. Cohan's arrival in Hollywood, however, coincided with a power struggle at Paramount, and Cohan's friends there lost. It was decided to honor Cohan's contract and just get the filming over with.[30] The film was released September 23, 1932, to good reviews.

Cohan told a dramatic critic and Broadway columnist for the New York *Sun*: "Those fellows didn't know anything about me. Lot of them had never heard of me and didn't care about being told. They treated me like a man from another world. On the level, kid, Hollywood to me represents the most amazing exhibition of incompetence and ego that you can find anywhere in the civilized world. From all I could make out the only people with any sense are the technical boys and the camera men."[31]

In the year of Cohan's death, 1942, Hal B. Wallis and William Cagney (James Cagney's brother) produced *Yankee Doodle Dandy* for Warner Bros., starring James Cagney as Cohan. An ailing Cohan attended a private showing and was visibly moved at this screen tribute.[32] It was perhaps the best show business biography ever filmed.

In *The Phantom President*, George M. Cohan plays a dual role, Doc Varney, a charismatic, traveling medicine man, and also, because he's a dead ringer for him, Theodore K. Blair, a lackluster presidential candidate whom the bosses decide needs to project a better public image. Claudette Colbert is the candidate's girlfriend Felicia Hammond, the late President's daughter. Durante is Curly, Doc Varney's sidekick. Sidney Toler is Professor Aikenhead, one of four political bosses.

For a comedy featuring songs by Rodgers and Hart as well as by George M. Cohan, the music is curiously unengaging. Cohan's "The

Country Needs a Man" and Rodgers and Hart's "Give Her a Kiss" were both written for this film and used here more than once. Cohan also brings in his patriotic songs "Maybe Someone Ought to Wave a Flag" and "You're a Grand Old Flag." Much of the film employs Rodgers and Hart singing-talking style dialogue, recitative that is rhymed, similar to their score for Al Jolson's *Hallelujah, I'm a Bum* (United Artists, 1933). Cohan's own songs also fall into this recitative style.

Probably the best scene for Cohan occurs early, about 15 minutes into the movie. Doc Varney puts on his medicine show in blackface. Sideman Curly in introducing him mentions minstrel man Eddie Leonard. Cohan sings "Someone Ought to Wave a Flag," and tap dances, in a brief number ending with many flags on a pole. He continues to sing about his medicines and points to Curly, his pal with the "schnozzola." Durante then sings about his "schnozzola," pointing to it, followed by a few bars of his own song, "As the Nose Blows," which he would use every week on his 1933 radio show when he replaced Eddie Cantor. At the piano, Curly sings-talks a story in typical Durante style, about all the illnesses he had before he took the Doc's medicine.

Curly tries to sneak into the political party's nominating convention carrying a sign he made, reading PENNISSIPPI. He's thrown out but gets in by collecting tickets at a door with its sign (Men's Room) covered by his hat. At the convention Varney as Blair sings "Government of the People," moving into "The Country Needs a Man," in the same manner as his medicine-man spiel, holding up a bottle. Curly sits at a piano, singing and doing patter. "Rhode Isles, Vermonters, Connecticuters, Massachusians, New Hampshians, and Mainiacs," Durante barks, and sings "Vote for Blair." Varney as Blair sings "You Are Men and Free Men," segueing into "You're a Grand Old Flag" for a few notes. Delegates throw the whole piano into the air, and it falls squarely on top of Durante.

When Varney tries to tell a national radio audience that he's a fraud, he's cut off the air. Durante has his best scene here as Curly trying to read the discarded speech prepared by the party bosses. Speaking to an empty room he perspires profusely trying to navigate the sea of big words. In frustration he throws the speech away and adds his own sentiments, "We have too many jackasses in the government now." He jumps into his own routine, often used by Durante on his radio shows over the years, "A depression is a hole, a hole is nuttin', and if you think I'm gonna stand here and talk about nuttin', you're crazy!"

Palooka might be considered Durante's best feature film. Not only does it highlight his comedic talents well, but it is also well written, for a good cast with well-defined roles. The film never fails to hold the audience's attention. Loosely based on Ham Fisher's comic strip, *Joe Palooka*, the screenplay was written by five people: Jack Jevne, Gertrude

George M. Cohan and Jimmy Durante in *The Phantom President*, Paramount 1932. Cohan as blackface medicine man, Durante his assistant.

Purcell, and Arthur Kober, with additional dialogue by Ben Ryan and Murray Roth. An Edward Small production, it was directed by Benjamin Stoloff, and released as a Reliance Picture by United Artists.

The opening scene shows a man lighting gas lamps in front of a theater where a banner proclaims "high class vaudeville," with six big acts, the headliner being Mayme Palooka (Marjorie Rambeau) and her American Beauty Chorus. Boxing champ Pete Palooka (Robert Armstrong) drops backstage for a good luck kiss from Mayme before his big fight. He plays with his baby boy, who he says already has a good corkscrew punch like his old man, "a real Palooka." Pete wins and goes out celebrating with girlfriends instead of coming back to his wife. Mayme appears, slugs a girlfriend, and walks out on her husband.

The scene shifts to many years later. Mayme is on a farm in New York, raising chickens for their eggs and selling preserves. Joe (Stuart Erwin) is grown up, a young man helping his mother. The mailman delivers a postcard from Pete, which Mayme calls a "semi-annual report," this time from Fiji, showing four bare-breasted native girls, and saying next port Rio.

Joe drives into town to place crates of eggs on a train. He sees an argument in another car and a big guy punching a little guy. Joe steps in and knocks out the big guy with one punch. The little guy turns out to be Knobby Walsh (Jimmy Durante), and the big guy, his best professional boxer. Knobby is impressed by Joe's punch and wants to sign him up, telling Joe, "It ain't healthy livin' in the country. Why, look at me. Raised on gasoline fumes and carbon monoxide. The picture of vigorous vitality." After signing up Joe to box, Knobby boards the train exulting, "I got the world by the elbow!," especially happy to discover that Joe is champion Pete Palooka's son. Soon after this, Joe leaves his mother and his girlfriend Anne.

Lupe Velez is Nina Madero, the opportunistic girlfriend of middleweight champion Al McSwatt, played by James Cagney's look-alike brother, William Cagney. When Joe loses his first fight, he's booked to fight McSwatt as a safe tune-up for the champ. The radio announces the fight, so Mayme finds out about it and sends a telegram to Joe: "FOR YOUR OWN GOOD I HOPE YOU GET YOUR BLOCK KNOCKED OFF WITH LOVE, MOTHER." McSwatt arrives at the fight drunk, having partied all night with Nina. The fight goes on after Knobby assures McSwatt's manager that Joe can't fight. In the first round, Knobby calls out to Joe to hit his opponent "in the la-bon-zah" (an Italianate creation Durante used regularly on his 1930s radio show). Joe unexpectedly scores a round one knockout and is the new champ. Fickle Nina wants Joe to be her new man.

At the Paradise Club where she works, Nina sings to Palooka, "Like Me a Little Bit Less (Love Me a Little Bit More)," a good song by Harold Adamson and Burton Lane, swinging her hips sexily to the music. McSwatt watches. The Gus Arnheim Orchestra strikes up an instrumental version of Durante's "Inka Dinka Doo," that shows how beautiful the melody really is, foreshadowing Durante's own introduction of the song (with its lyrics by Ben Ryan) later in the film.

Durante gets to play a good comic love scene with Velez. Trying to get his fighter away from her clutches, he throws himself at her. Looking at his profile in her mirror, he adjusts his bow tie, sighing with pride, "And they talk about Barrymore." He grabs Nina (Lupe) by the arm, then shoulders, leans her back on the bed, telling her, "Take a look at that profile. Don't dat do nuttin' to ya?" Nina responds, "Yeah!" and smacks him. Later she tells him he has a big nose. When no one is looking, he applies Miracle Reducing Cream in an effort to shrink it.

Nina transforms the new champ into a well-dressed dandy who takes her to fancy places and pays her many bills. They pose for a kissing commercial, endorsing Doctor Gray's Gargle, and Joe poses in long underwear swinging a golf club. Knobby meanwhile recruits bozos to lie down in fixed fights, and Joe believes he's become a great boxer. When a French valet helps Joe get dressed, replying obsequiously too many times "oui-oui," Knobby tells him, "Will you stop oui, oui-ing all over the joint?"

Jimmy Durante's best scene, among many good ones, occurs when he gets thrown out of the Paradise Club for drunkenly trying to sing. He wanders over to a music store with a piano in the window. He breaks the glass and goes to the piano. He moves a marble bust of a woman, "Slide over, sister," and with a bust of Beethoven in the background, begins to play what the Ben Ryan lyrics call "that swinging symphony," his masterpiece, "Inka Dinka Doo." He plays the whole song, without his usual interruptions of his own songs, until a cop cuts off the last note with "Get your Inky Dinky Doo out of here!" It's a memorable, sweet, wonderful scene, with the introduction of what might be the best melody Jimmy Durante ever wrote.

After Palooka and McSwatt argue at the Club and agree to a championship fight, Knobby is angry. "It's mutiny, that's what it is, mutiny!" he explodes, using another favorite Durante line. Later he says, "It's treason, that's what it is, a ca-tas-ta-stroke" [a word Durante used over and over but with varying pronunciations]. Despite Pete Palooka helping to train his son, the fight is lost. As a wise precaution, Knobby bet his $10,000 on McSwatt, while in the ring encouraging Joe to "hit his opponent in the la-bon-zah" and sweating a "de-lem-i-a."

Joe goes back to Anne. Pete goes back to sea, leaving Mayme again. Knobby sends his winnings to Joe, who opens Mayme's Palooka Inn. The last scene has Knobby, all dressed up, coming to visit the Inn. Now McSwatt's manager, he's with Nina, who is his wife. Durante and Velez show their baby—using trick photography the little tyke has Durante's face. "Say something to daddy." The baby spits out a Duranteism, "Hot-cha-cha-cha!" with a one-toothed smile. The orchestra strikes up a few closing notes of "Inka Dinka Doo."

Durante and Lupe Velez made one other film together the same year as *Palooka*, RKO's *Strictly Dynamite*. It is a much weaker film, although the Durante-Velez chemistry is still there. The director was Elliott Nugent.

Durante plays Moxie, star of a radio comedy show, "The Snuggy Huggy Corset Hour." Lupe Velez plays the singer on his show and his girlfriend. Both kill the English language. Durante also kills the French language, ordering breakfast in bed from a French menu in a fancy hotel. His barber comes to his room to shave him, but Durante shaves the barber, saying, "I used to be a barber on Mulberry Street." (Mulberry Street is on the Lower East Side of New York, where Jimmy Durante grew up with a barber father.) The Durante-Moxie character gets out of his silk pajamas and into an elegant three-piece suit complete with cane, hat, and cigar.

The story is slight and dull, intended as a satire of a radio comedy show. The title comes from a supposedly funny comedy writer Moxie hires for his show, who thinks he's good: "I'm strictly dynamite." This writer

Jimmy Durante and Lupe Velez, in *Strictly Dynamite*, RKO, 1934.

(played by Norman Foster) gives Moxie a philosophical treatise by Henri Bergson on a theory of humor. Moxie-Durante reads a few big words from that book. The high points of the film are Durante singing his own very good song "I'm Putty in Your Hands," which he inexplicably rarely used elsewhere in his routines, and his "Hot Patatta," sung for a nightclub audience. This second song was such a good crowd rouser that Durante recorded it for Brunswick. It was released on the flip side of "Inka Dinka Doo." Lupe Velez also sings effectively, especially "Oh Me, Oh My, Oh You," by Harold Adamson and Burton Lane. There is some additional music by the Mills Brothers.

That same year, 1934, saw the release of one more non–MGM film, *George White's Scandals*, and made on the MGM lot soon after *Hollywood Party*, *Student Tour*.

Durante was on loan to Fox Film Corporation, just over a year before it merged with Darryl F. Zanuck's 20th Century Pictures (May 29, 1935). He made a very charming appearance in *George White's Scandals*. It was a revue with good production numbers and a minimum of plot. George White created and directed it. He brought with him much stage experience, performing as a dancer on vaudeville circuits with his partner Ben Ryan, and during the early 1910s appearing in many stage musicals including, in 1915, *The Ziegfeld Follies*. Beginning in 1919, George White produced, directed, and collaborated in the writing of 13 editions of his Broadway revue called *George White's Scandals*, which appeared throughout the 1920s and 1930s.[33] For Fox he filmed the 1934 *George White's Scandals* and *George White's 1935 Scandals* (1935), and later for RKO, a third screen edition under the same title as the first, *George White's Scandals* (1945). He staged many other revues for Broadway and theater-restaurants including his own nightclub, the Great White Way. White appeared in his two *Scandals* for Fox, and as himself in the Warner Bros. film about George Gershwin, *Rhapsody in Blue* (1945).

Because the plot never gets in their way, performers who were at their best in vaudeville-type acts could shine in *George White's Scandals*. This movie, with no names above the title, starred, in the order of their credits, Rudy Vallee, Jimmy Durante, and in her screen debut, Alice Faye. Within what slim plot there is, Durante substitutes for Rudy Vallee when he does not appear in time to do a "Mammy" number in blackface. Durante applies blackface in his dressing room, then appears in a production number, "Cabin in the Cotton," which gives Durante a concluding line about "why darkies were born." This was Durante's only screen appearance in blackface. There's also a charming production number, "My Dog Loves Your Dog," written by Jack Yellen, Irving Caesar, and Ray Henderson, who did all the music for the show. Here Durante sings to his girlfriend, then Rudy Vallee sings to his, then Cliff Edwards, and Durante wraps up the song with a last refrain. After a fine production number starring Cliff Edwards doing "Henry VIII" and his six wives, Durante, Vallee, and Edwards join in a delightful production number, "Every Day Is Father's Day with Baby," each pushing his own baby's carriage.

As wonderful as Durante was in *George White's Scandals*, he was wasted in MGM's weak film *Student Tour*. Directed by Charles F. Riesner, it concerned a college sculling crew on a world tour being tutored aboard ship by the philosophy professor (Charles Butterworth) whose course they had failed. Durante plays Hank Merman, trainer of the crew. The love story with Maxine Doyle and Phil Regan and most songs are of so-what quality, as is the one song by Nelson Eddy in a cameo appearance. Midway, Durante does get to sing his own composition "I Say It with Music," and Betty Grable fans may spot her here in one of her pre-stardom bit roles as part of a gymnastics team on the ship.

What little amusement there is comes principally from the few interchanges between Butterworth and Durante. In one scene, they attend a masquerade party as, respectively, Napoleon and Cyrano de Bergerac, including a fake nose for Durante. Later in a slide lecture on India, Durante inadvertently leans in front of the projector, and the silhouette of his nose is projected on the screen. Butterworth with a long pointer stick tells the class, "This is the largest protuberance known to nature." The students laugh. "My mistake. That is not Mt. Everest."

Three years later, Columbia Pictures would make a somewhat better film about collegiates, *Start Cheering*, and give Durante more to do in it, though still not much.

In 1935, Durante's father, Bartolomeo, visited Hollywood. The dignified gentleman amused himself by barbering without charge the priests at the Cathedral Chapel in his son's parish and trying to give long-haired Tarzan, Johnny Weissmuller, a free haircut. Early that same year the first film Durante had made for Columbia Pictures, *Carnival*, was released, and in the fall he was opening on Broadway in *Jumbo*, as well as taking over the *Texaco Fire Chief* program from Ed Wynn on NBC radio Tuesday nights.

Carnival, directed by Walter Lang, stars Lee Tracy as Chick Thompson the puppeteer, with assistants Sally Eilers and Durante (as Fingers, so named because he's a skilled pickpocket). One puppet looks like Durante, who doesn't have much to do except serve as the caring and loyal friend of the puppeteer.

A stage tour of Great Britain was a high point for Durante in 1936. After *Jumbo* closed at the Hippodrome, he sailed on the French liner *Normandie* to do his nightclub routine at theaters in Dublin, Glasgow, Liverpool, Blackpool, and, beginning June 1, 1936, two weeks at the world-famous London Palladium, British pinnacle of show business success, like the Palace. Here Durante received top billing on a variety show as "The Great 'Schnozzola'" and "The Hollywood Lover." The bookings were handled by the William Morris Agency in consultation with Lou Clayton and brought Durante close to $5,000 a week for five weeks of vaudeville.

While in England, Durante appeared in the film *Land Without Music*, starring Richard Tauber, after Lou Clayton demanded and got double the offered $20,000.[34] For the second time, Durante made a film with an opera star, the first being *The Cuban Love Song* with Lawrence Tibbett. Durante, as Jonah J. Whistler, doesn't get the opportunity to sing or do much else, although he has second billing. It'a a good film for Tauber, one of Germany's most beloved singers. As Mario Carlini, a revolutionary singer in a land that bans music because its subjects are too busy singing to work at anything else, Tauber sings Oscar Straus' operetta music written for the screen.

The film was released in England by Capitol Films and two years later in the United States by World Pictures as *Forbidden Music* (cut from 80 minutes to 63 minutes and listing Durante's name above the title, Tauber's below the title). A decade later the film was reissued in the United States by Screen Guild Productions as *That's My Boy*, capitalizing on the expression Durante started using in 1943. For this reissue, posters prominently featured his head shot with the copy, "Spectacle! Music! Songs! Laughs! Capitol Films presents JIMMY DURANTE in THAT'S MY BOY (formerly 'Forbidden Music'). Set to glorious melody by Oscar Straus, featuring Richard Tauber, June Clyde, Diana Napier, Derrick de Marney. Directed by Walter Forde."[35]

After his British film, Durante shooed away the rest of his troupe and took a continental tour by himself, going to Paris, Monte Carlo, and San Remo. He also visited Salerno, curious to see his parents' roots. There he saw his brother-in-law, Genaro Romano, gave him money, and left.[36] It could not have been too enjoyable a visit, with the Fascist dictator Benito Mussolini solidifying his troops' invasion of Abyssinia (Ethiopia) that year and moving ever closer to Germany's evil Chancellor, Adolf Hitler.

Durante sailed back to New York from Naples on the S.S. *Conte di Savoia* in time to rehearse a new Broadway musical. Cole Porter's *Red, Hot and Blue!* opened October 29, 1936. Two weeks earlier, during the show's tryout in Boston, James M. Curley, Governor of Massachusetts, presented Jimmy with a medal for "excellence of entertainment." Jimmy, in return, gave his best wishes to Curley in his race for U.S. Senator.[37] In November, Durante appeared with Bill "Bojangles" Robinson and New York Mayor Fiorello La Guardia at the Municipal Lodging House of New York to help celebrate Thanksgiving Day with the homeless.

After *Red, Hot and Blue!* closed in 1937, Durante returned to Hollywood to make three more non–MGM movies: for Columbia, *Start Cheering*, and for 20th Century Fox, *Sally, Irene and Mary* and Shirley Temple's *Little Miss Broadway*, all released in 1938.

Start Cheering, directed by Albert S. Rogell, concerns a handsome movie idol who decides to attend college without publicity. However, because he played a football hero in his last film, he's called to repeat the role and win the big game for the college. The humor and music enliven the trite story. Gertrude Niesen sings some bouncy songs. The Three Stooges do one of their funnier routines. "Point to the right," Moe orders Larry and Curly. Since they're standing in a circle, each points a different direction, drawing a smack from Moe. There's a nice silent comedy turn, a specialty act, by Chaz Chase. He lights cigarettes with matches, then eats both, peels candy bars and eats the wrappers. Durante, although he gets top billing, is under-utilized as Willie Cumbatz, assistant to the star's manager. Still, what he does is fine. He gets to sing, not once but twice, "I'll Do the Strut-away in My Cutaway."

Once more, in *Sally, Irene and Mary*, Durante wasn't given much to do. He gets a chance to work with Fred Allen, but does not enter until half the film is over. He gets the opportunity to sing "Hot Patatta," which had first surfaced in *Strictly Dynamite*. The stars are Alice Faye and Tony

Martin. Again in *Little Miss Broadway* Durante is wasted. His best work is literally left on the cutting-room floor: a song-and-dance number was filmed with Shirley Temple and Durante, but for whatever reason, it was dropped.[38] Yet Fox was not above using that excised scene in a publicity photo. In the released film, the audience sees Shirley Temple hoofing with George Murphy. Durante has no songs. There is a brief early shot of him conducting a band labeled "Jimmy Clayton and his Jazz Band," but no jazz number.

The pace of movie-making slackened. Hollywood was losing its enthusiasm for Durante as they misused him and dried up his screen audience. He faced some hard financial times. Radio gave him some work, though he would not be very successful there until 1943 and after. He appeared a number of times on the Rudy Vallee radio show, originating from Radio City, New York. He was also back on Broadway for *Stars in Your Eyes*, beginning February 9, 1939, and that fall in a stage show at the Paramount Theatre in New York, on the bill with the Russ Morgan orchestra. *Variety* reported that Durante was in top form.[39] This was the first time he had given a nightclub or vaudeville act on Broadway since early 1938, when he appeared at Billy Rose's Casa Manana with a chorus line of tall, beautiful showgirls handpicked by Rose.

After *Keep Off the Grass* flopped on Broadway in the spring of 1940, Durante made his next film and his only western, *Melody Ranch*, starring singing cowboy Gene Autry. The title came from Autry's radio show on CBS. Republic Pictures went beyond its usual budget, spending close to $400,000.[40] With Gene Autry were Jimmy Durante and George "Gabby" Hayes, for comedy. "Gabby" Hayes was a staple in many Gene Autry and Roy Rogers westerns. Ann Miller provided pulchritude and tap dancing. Barton MacLane and Horace MacMahon were major bad guy character actors in this and many other movies. Adding good Western music back-up were Bob Wills and his Texas Playboys. Special music was written by Jule Styne.

For Jimmy, doing a western proved more amusing in retrospect than in the making. It was the first time he was ever on a horse, and he had to be lashed to the saddle. Biographer Gene Fowler reports Jimmy as saying, "I'd never rode a horse and the horse never had been rode. So we started out on even terms. It was a catastastroke!"[41]

Word reached newspapers that Gene Autry would have a kissing scene with Ann Miller. The mail from youngsters who were Autry fans was so heavy, objecting to their hero kissing anyone, that the scene was dropped. In place of romance, the youngsters got Jimmy Durante, whom Autry called "one of the great scene stealers of all time."[42] Autry says Durante couldn't read a script or remember lines, always ad-libbing, so there was nothing to do but let him go and try to answer with something that made some sense. Durante has a good scene in a courtroom, situated in the corrupt town of Torpedo, playing not only the defendant but also the prosecutor and defense counsel. The bad guy (Horace MacMahon) was on trial for horse-stealing. Durante as his lawyer, Cornelius J. Courtney, ad-libbed everything. With his client on the stand, Jimmy asked, "Whatcha name?" "Jupiter." "Ahhh, Choopiter. Choopiter, do you swear to tell the troot, the whole troot, and nuttin' but the troot, so help ya, God?" "I do." Durante throws up his hands. "Aaaggh, we done lost da case right dere." Autry thought the scene ad-libbed was funnier than the original script's dialogue.[43]

In a later scene of *Melody Ranch*, Durante sings "Vote for Autry" for sheriff, his only singing in the movie. Still later he explains to Autry, "So I ups to him," which would have been a cue for his song by that name, but Autry cuts him off before he can sing a note.

Durante was appearing in Earl Carroll's theater restaurant in Hollywood, when he got the news that his 92-year-old father was dying. He rushed back to New York and was with Bartolomeo when he died on February 27, 1941. Upon returning to Hollywood, he made two films for Warner Bros.: *You're in the Army Now* (1941), a co-starring role with Phil Silvers, and *The Man Who Came to Dinner* (1942), a minor role.

Warner Bros. tested 22 acting teams for the lead comedy roles in *You're in the Army Now*. They settled on Jimmy Durante and Phil Silvers, with their third star, Jane Wyman. Although Durante and Silvers had roles of equal importance, their salaries were not equal. The film's budget lists Durante's salary as $25,000, Silvers' a mere $3,734, and Jane Wyman's $7,500. Direction was by Lewis Seiler. Consideration was given to buying and using the title "Brother Rat in the Army," to capitalize on the popularity of earlier Warner Bros. films *Brother Rat* (1938) and *Brother Rat and a Baby* (1940), military academy comedies starring Priscilla Lane, Wayne Morris, Eddie Albert, Jane Bryan, Ronald Reagan, and Jane Wyman, but the idea was dropped.[44]

The script was poor, but there was some good comic rapport between Durante and Silvers, seasoned vaudeville troupers. They play Jeeper Smith and Breezy Jones, two salesmen for the Whirlaway Vacuum Cleaner Company who get tricked into joining the Army. As salesmen, they enter a rural home to make their sales pitch. Durante, as Jeeper, promptly sits at the piano to play and sing his own composition written for this film, "Vacuum Cleaner of the Day," reworked and retitled "If You Owned a Whirlaway." Silvers gives Durante a singing lesson right there, shaping Durante's mouth with his hands and slapping his face. This is a mildly amusing routine that was one of Silvers' trademarks. At the next house, they incur the wrath of an Army colonel (played by character actor Donald MacBride, a master of the slow burn similar to the Keystone Cops' Edgar

Jimmy Durante in drag, with Anthony Caruso, in *You're in the Army Now*, Warner Bros., 1941.

Kennedy), who has a sweet daughter (played by Jane Wyman). In their third attempt to make a sale, they sell a vacuum cleaner to an Army recruiter while inadvertently enlisting.

The rest of the movie is a boot camp comedy, fairly amusing but not nearly as funny as, for example, *Buck Privates* (Universal, 1941), which helped make stars of Abbott & Costello; *At War with the Army* (Paramount,

1951), which helped make stars of Martin & Lewis, or Phil Silvers' own CBS television series about a gambling wiseguy soldier, Sergeant Bilko. The brash con artist, Silvers, and the brash "what-hit-me?" innocent, Durante, might have made a very good combination with better material. The insipid story of *You're in the Army Now*, with Jane Wyman as a colonel's daughter and Regis Toomey as the singing captain who loves her, didn't help at all. One song Durante wrote himself for this movie, "I Am an Army Man," which he was supposed to sing, was either not filmed or cut before release.[45] Another song, "I'm Glad My Number Was Called," by George Kelly and Charlie Adler (writers represented by Lou Clayton, who arranged for them to be paid $1,250),[46] was sung by Regis Toomey and the Navy Blues Sextette, with separate choruses by Silvers on stage and Durante while squeezing lemons on kitchen patrol.

Durante has a better time of it, funnier moments, than Silvers. Jimmy dresses as a girl performing a French cabaret apache dance, where the male dancer (Anthony Caruso) smacks the woman and throws her across the dance floor, to escape an angry sergeant chasing him. Later some WACs tell him, when he tries to kiss them, that in Alaska people kiss by rubbing noses. He proclaims, "I'd be the Errol Flynn of that joint." Still later, at the colonel's house, Durante sits at the piano, strikes a few notes, and tells the colonel's daughter a story about a fellow asleep in the park with about 25 flies on his nose, too lazy to brush them off. A bee stings him on the nose, to which the fellow retorts, "There's gotta be a smart-aleck in the crowd. Everybody off!" Durante adds, "I'm glad it wasn't my nose. They'd a had a picnic."

The last scene of the movie is a less-funny and shorter version of the climax from Chaplin's *The Gold Rush*, where the Arctic winds carry a house to the very edge of a precipice. Here using an Army tank for pulling, Durante and Silvers haul the colonel's house to a new site by the side of a cliff (after letting it slip loose en route onto train tracks, another silent film routine). The cliff is eroded by misfired artillery shells, leaving the house teetering on the brink as people walk about inside. Use of this Chaplin material brought Warner Bros. a threat of a lawsuit.[47]

In *The Man Who Came to Dinner*, a good adaptation of the 1939 George S. Kaufman–Moss Hart play, Monty Woolley repeats his Broadway starring role as Sheridan Whiteside, supported in major roles by Bette Davis and Ann Sheridan. Because he was a Broadway star but not a movie star who could guarantee ticket sales, Woolley did not get the part until Warner Bros. had completed extensive testing of other actors, beginning February 24, 1941, among them Charles Laughton, Robert Benchley, John Barrymore, Frederic March, and finally, Woolley. Orson Welles also indicated his interest in the lead role.[48]

Several comedians were considered for the minor role of Banjo (a name perhaps derived from Eddie Cantor's big "banjo eyes"), originated on Broadway by David Burns. Harpo Marx was one possibility. He played the role in summer stock at the Bucks County Playhouse, New Hope, Pennsylvania, July 1941. Records indicate, however, that only Borah Minnevich, the harmonica player, and Durante were in the final tests for the role. After Durante tested, executive producer Hal B. Wallis sent a memo suggesting Durante be signed for the role, but not for more than $10,000. In a contract signed July 21, 1941, Durante was guaranteed $7,500 per week for two weeks, or $15,000.[49]

Banjo, friend of the unwelcome celebrity who is recuperating from a fall, enters about 25 minutes from the end of the film. Durante charges in against the current of sophisticated comedy with his loud, rambunctious conversation and high energy, and plays a few bars of "Did You Ever Have the Feeling." Composer Durante was paid the token sum of one dollar for permission to use this song.

After these films, Durante resumed a more active schedule of vaudeville engagements and personal appearances. He appeared in February 1942 at a war bond drive at Los Angeles' Victory House, where he was photographed with Marlene Dietrich. At the same time, he was offered eight weeks of vaudeville and asked Eddie Jackson to join him. Clayton could not appear to complete the old vaudeville team because he was recovering from an automobile accident. With Eddie Jackson, Jimmy did shows in Brooklyn, Boston, Hartford, Providence, and Pittsburgh. On March 27, 1942, Jimmy "Schnozzle" Durante, as he was billed, opened in person at the RKO Boston, sharing the stage with Ina Ray Hutton and her versatile "Playboys" Orchestra, plus other acts. On the screen, "all new thrills as the Monster stalks again!": *Ghost of Frankenstein*, with Sir Cedric Hardwicke, Lionel Atwill, Bela Lugosi, Lon Chaney, and Evelyn Ankers. Price of admission, 30 cents to 1 P.M. On April 29 of the following year, Durante began a two-week personal appearance on the stage of the Capitol Theatre, New York. Newspaper ads billed him as "Dignity's Most Persistent Enemy." On the same bill were Sonny Dunham and his orchestra, Harold Nicholas of the Nicholas Brothers, and Marta Eggerth, who was also in the Judy Garland and Van Heflin movie on the Capitol screen, *Presenting Lily Mars*. At the bottom of the ad was an inducement to support the war: "Buy A War Bond Here And Get Free Ticket To See Inside Jap Suicide Sub! Times Square, Saturday and Sunday, May 1 and 2."[50]

Return to MGM: 1944–48

As his radio career gained momentum, Durante was given a new MGM contract calling for fewer pictures than the earlier contract. Instead of two or three a year he would average one. He now appeared in a string of six for MGM, uninterrupted by pictures for any other studio: *Two Girls and a Sailor* (1944), *Music for Millions* (1944), *Two Sisters from Boston* (1946), *It Happened in Brooklyn* (1947), *This Time for Keeps* (1947), and *On an Island with You* (1948).

Durante also filmed scenes for the MGM music and comedy revue *Ziegfeld Follies* (1946) that were dropped along with many other fine scenes.[51] As much footage was left on the cutting room floor as appeared on the screen.[52]

Had MGM now learned how to handle Durante's special talents? The studio gave him better specialty numbers but no leading roles. It still had no tolerance for Durante's seeming inability to follow a script as written. When he pronounced the words correctly he put the emphasis differently every take, and the unamusing word he heard most often was "Cut!"

Amazingly, MGM tried to straighten out his English, instead of finding a way of working in a continuing part that preserved his charming and amusingly idiosyncratic English. The studio sent him to school. "So what happens? When I loin a little English, they puts me in a pitcher wid Cugat. Bein' around Cugie, I unloins everythin' I loined in the school. And den when I improves again, they sticks me in a pitcher wid Iturbi. That really is the end. Den comes the last straw. They throws me in wid Melacure [Melchior]. Wid him I forgot everything except how to say smorgasbord. Boy, it was a catastastroke. But, a very funny thing, you know. I get a few letters sometimes. They ask if I really mispronounce the words. But I don't do it deliberately." Durante says that sometimes he doesn't know why an audience is laughing, and he's told it's some word he's just mispronounced. Durante attributes to Clayton a line he was fond of using himself. "Listen, don't teach him how to pronounce 'em, because if he does, we're all outa work."[53]

While radio, not MGM or other studios, was responsible for rebuilding Durante's career from its low point, MGM helped by releasing many of his best songs on the MGM label, often as a tie-in with the release of new films in which those songs were presented, and Durante performed them on his 1940s radio program. As a sign of the resurgence of his career, *Time* magazine featured him on a 1944 cover, and *Newsweek* on a 1946 cover.

Specialty numbers for Durante were more elaborate now. In *Two Girls and a Sailor*, starring Van Johnson, June Allyson, and Gloria DeHaven, Durante was allowed to do his nightclub routines. Near the beginning, he does for the third time in a film his old go-stay routine, "Did You Ever Have the Feeling," worked together with "Who Will Be with You When I'm Far Away." Near the end, he gets to do "Inka Dinka Doo" and his go-stay routine again, and there's a sight gag involving Durante's own baby photograph, with other characters cringing at its sight.

There are, in this first MGM picture under Durante's new contract, so many other specialty numbers by other talented people that the usual love story doesn't get in the way of the variety. Lena Horne, Virginia O'Brien, and Helen Forrest are among those who get to sing, one number apiece. Jose Iturbi and his sister Amparo play at twin pianos. The Xavier Cugat and Harry James orchestras perform. And the best specialty number of all, for comedy, was Gracie Allen as a serious concert pianist performing with a symphony orchestra "Concerto for Index Finger." Directed by Richard Thorpe, the film was produced by the very capable Joe Pasternak, a master at light musical comedy.[54]

Pasternak also produced the next picture in which Durante appeared, *Music for Millions*, directed by Henry Koster. Margaret O'Brien won a special Academy Award for outstanding juvenile acting in this 1944 release. She plays a little girl comforting June Allyson, her pregnant big sister who's worried about her husband missing in the war. Allyson plays string bass in Iturbi's symphony orchestra. She gives birth to a baby with her husband's picture by her side as the camera cuts to the orchestra playing Handel's "Messiah."

A bit emotionally overwrought, this film was probably just right for American audiences mindful of the continuing war in the Pacific. Highlights that relieve the pathos are Durante's performance of "Toscanini, Iturbi and Me" (a variation on his "Toscanini, Stokowski and Me"), with his "Chidabee" interpolated, and later, "Umbriago," written by Irving Caesar expressly for this film.[55] The "Umbriago" number has Jack Roth on drums and Eddie Jackson taking the microphone from Durante to lead the audience in singing,[56] generating as much enthusiasm on the part of the soldiers and performers as a new national anthem.

Still another Joe Pasternak production featuring Durante was *Two Sisters from Boston*, directed by Henry Koster. This was a nice period piece from turn-of-the-century New York. It stars Kathryn Grayson, June Allyson, Lauritz Melchior, Jimmy Durante, and Peter Lawford. Sammy Fain and Ralph Freed wrote two songs for this film that were perfect for Durante's style, "G'wan Home, Your Mudder's Callin'" and "There Are Two Sides to Every Girl," but in the film the first is sung only as soft background music by a girls' chorus, and the second by Grayson. To have heard Durante sing these, the audience would have had to buy the Majestic label 78rpm record released the same year. Why was he not given these songs to sing in the film? Jimmy does get to sing his own "Hello, Hello, Hello," another version of a song he had presented in *Hollywood Party*. And he sings a duet with the romantic lead, Kathryn Grayson, "Down by the Ocean," also written by Fain and Freed. More interesting would have been a duet featuring Durante and operatic singer Lauritz Melchior, who sings a rousing aria from Wagner's *Die Meistersinger*.

It Happened in Brooklyn dragged when neither Durante nor a young Frank Sinatra was singing. Directed by Richard Whorf and produced by Jack Cummings, this is the 1940s film in which MGM came closest to actually giving Jimmy Durante a starring role. Much of the movie concerns the love interests and insecurities of the Frank Sinatra and Peter Lawford characters, each casting an eye toward sweet songstress Kathryn Grayson, while Durante plays the janitor at New Utrecht High School, Brooklyn.

The film is at its best, however, when the trio of Durante, Sinatra, and young Bobby Long perform "I Believe," a first-rate song by Sammy Cahn and Jule Styne. And Durante and Sinatra are simply great in the duet they do on Durante's material, "The Song's Gotta Come from the Heart," written by Cahn and Styne, who also wrote for Sinatra "Time After Time." Sinatra made a wonderful team with Durante, here and on radio and television, just as many years later he worked so well with other high-energy performers such as Sammy Davis, Jr., and Liza Minnelli.

Sinatra liked working with Durante so much that years later he wanted to make a movie about Durante's life. The 1960 project would fall through, though Sinatra, with Dean Martin and Bing Crosby, would perform routines of Clayton, Jackson, and Durante on a fall 1959 Sinatra television show.[57] Both Sinatra and Durante were Italian, both had warm personalities (Sinatra's fights with journalists and associates notwithstanding), both played well to live audiences on stage in theaters and nightclubs, and both loved to strut in old vaudeville routines. Though Sinatra was not part of the vaudeville tradition, he did well with Gene Kelly in MGM musicals that called for vaudeville song and dance: witness their performances together in *Anchors Aweigh* (1945), *Take Me Out to the Ball Game* (1948), and *On the Town* (1949). When Sinatra celebrated his 75th birthday in December 1990, he marked the occasion with a concert at the Meadowlands in Secaucus, New Jersey, and a CBS television program excerpted from tapes of the concert. On the televised special, he said working with Jimmy Durante was a pleasure because he was a "sweet man," and he recalled shooting a scene in which Jimmy had the line, "I must have overslept." Jimmy forgot his line and said, "I must have underslept." The slip-up was left in the movie.

Durante appeared in two Esther Williams movies, *This Time for Keeps* and *On an Island with You*, Jimmy's first color films. Backing MGM's only swimming star were, in the first of these movies, Lauritz Melchior, Jimmy Durante, Johnnie Johnston, and Xavier Cugat and his orchestra. Despite the capable team of Joe Pasternak, producer, and Richard Thorpe, director, the movie is hampered by a plot that is tiresome, the usual formula love mix-up, only slightly alleviated by the attractive scenery of the summer resort in Mackinac Island, Michigan.

The audience at *This Time for Keeps* wakes up when Esther is swimming in a water ballet with a bevy of showgirls, or when Jimmy, who plays her piano accompanist and family friend, Ferdi Farro, goes into his production numbers. The most dramatic and most lavish number MGM ever gave Durante occurs when, dressed in a white tuxedo, he sits at a white piano on a pedestal in the middle of Esther's swimming pool, surrounded by Esther and her girl chorus. Jimmy sings "Ten Per Cent Off," by Ralph Freed and Sammy Fain, as the piano rises and Esther and the girls do their synchronized swimming around him. Then he and the piano gradually sink into the pool. Late in the movie, Durante gets the opportunity to sing in its entirety his own composition, "I'm the Guy Who Found the Lost Chord," for an audience of showgirl swimmers gathered around his piano and, as in the old days of vaudeville and in nightclub appearances, he ends by tearing the piano apart piece by piece. Before the "sinking in pool" number, Jimmy does another of his compositions, "She's a Little Bit This and a Little Bit That," plus a few snatches of "Inka Dinka Doo."

The second of these Esther Williams movies, *On an Island with You*, with the team of Pasternak producing and Thorpe directing, has far weaker material to work with than *This Time for Keeps*, which at least had spectacular specialty numbers. Set in Hawaii, the formula romance story runs too long, sorting out who gets whom among the romantic principals: Esther Williams, Ricardo Montalban, Peter Lawford, and Cyd Charisse. Both Esther and Cyd use a modified version of blackface (brownface?) to play "more authentically" native girls. In this web of who-cares intrigue, Durante is especially welcome as a breath of fresh Lower East Side air. In the midst of Hollywood's version of a Pacific paradise you can almost hear Durante, as Knobby Walsh from his Joe Palooka film a decade before, shouting, "It ain't healthy livin' in the country. Why, look at me. Raised on gasoline fumes and carbon monoxide. The picture of vigorous vitality."

When Durante (as Buckley, business agent with a film company) tells band leader Xavier Cugat that he used to be a part of the vaudeville team Clayton, Jackson, and Buckley, Cugat lets him sit at the piano and sing to the nightclub audience "I Know Darn Well I Can Do Without Broadway (But Can Broadway Do Without Me?)," segueing into "I'm Taking Miss Mary to the Ball" (composed by Edward Heyman and Nacio Herb Brown). Much later, in the same nightclub, Durante sings in its entirety "I'll Do the Strut-away in My Cutaway." Also, he consoles Esther, who is having trouble with her romance, by singing several bars of "You Gotta Start Off Each Day with a Song." Esther's two water ballet numbers are below par in their choreography, and Cyd Charisse's talents are underutilized in two merely fair dance numbers.

Midway in his second contract with MGM, and with his radio career going well, Durante was invited to autograph the sidewalk at Grauman's Chinese Theatre where the signatures of Hollywood's greatest stars are on view. On October 31, 1945, Jimmy Durante left an imprint of his nose—actually the whole side of his face—and one hand in cement, writing, "Sid—Dis is my Schnozzle. Wish I Had a Million of 'Em. Jimmy Durante." Next to his space are the imprints of Roy Rogers and his horse Trigger (his horseshoe, not his nose).

Durante's career was reviving, although his personal life was in turmoil. In 1942, a year after losing his father, he lost his sister, and in 1943, his wife died. (More about this in the next chapter, "Radio.")

Later Films: 1950–63

With the end of his second five-year contract at MGM, and his attention turned to a television debut, Durante made two low-budget films for other studios, *The Great Rupert* (Eagle-Lion, 1950) and *The Milkman* (Universal, 1950), both of them in starring roles.

The Great Rupert was a feature directed by Irving Pichel for George Pal, Hungarian puppeteer who in Hollywood was known for his series of "Puppetoons" and adventure films using clever trick photography. Pal in 1943 won a special Academy Award "for the development of novel methods and techniques."[58]

The working title before release was "the Great Amendola," referring to its star, Jimmy Durante. But the title was changed to put the emphasis on George Pal's novelty, the squirrel named Rupert, partly played by a real squirrel and partly by a puppet. Like the many animal acts to appear in vaudeville—dogs, chimpanzees, birds, fleas—Rupert, in this story written by Laslo Vadnay, is a remarkable trained performer, dancing to concertina music played by his trainer Joe Mahoney (Chick Chandler). Because Joe is down on his luck, no vaudeville business in sight, he sets Rupert free in the park near the rented room he had to give up the day before Christmas. Durante as another old vaudevillian, The Great Amendola, a juggler and an acrobat, moves into that room with his wife (Queenie Smith) and attractive daughter (Terry Moore), although they too don't have the $32 for a month's rent.

This is a modest, sentimental movie, a small scale analog of Frank Capra's perennial Christmas season favorite *It's a Wonderful Life* (RKO, 1946). When things are darkest for the almost destitute Amendolas, the squirrel miraculously answers their prayers. Because the landlord (Frank Orth) lost money in the bank crash of 1929, he stashes his money away beneath his floor boards. The squirrel scratches that money into the apartment below as Amendola's wife prays for a Christmas tree and for a pair of shoes for her daughter (who falls in love with the landlord's son, played by Tom Drake).

Durante comes across in *The Great Rupert* as a very warm, gentle father and husband. He sings part of his composition "Take an L," a warm children's song of love and tenderness that Durante used on his radio show as early as 1934. Earlier, he sings "Jingle Bells" and brief snatches of "Christmas Comes but Once a Year," which he wrote with Harry Crane, assisted by Jules Buffano. Both were recorded by MGM. The first was coupled with "Bibbidi-Bobbidi-Boo (The Magic Song)," from Walt Disney's *Cinderella* (1950), recorded 1949. The Christmas song was recorded 1950, coupled with "Frosty the Snowman." And overlooked by all except careful viewers is the small role played by Candy Candido, a regular on Durante's late 40s radio and early 50s television shows.

For publicity, Jimmy was photographed seated at the piano with a live squirrel in Scottish kilts by his side, and on one of the film's lobby cards, Jimmy sat at the piano and the squirrel puppet sat at a miniature piano atop Jimmy's.[59]

Durante seems to have had a lot of fun making *The Milkman* with co-star Donald O'Connor. Produced by Ted Richmond for Universal-International, and directed by Charles Barton, this comedy has B-quality writing similar to scripts for Red Skelton movies, material beneath the ability of the comedians involved. Still, this is an enjoyable film for the obviously affectionate interaction of the two really likeable stars and for the original songs by Jackie Barnett and Sammy Fain. Durante, as Breezy, veteran milkman, sings at the piano "Nobody Wants My Money." O'Connor, bumbling son of a rival milk company owner, sings "The Early Morning Song." Both sing as duets, "It's Bigger Than Both of Us!" and "That's My Boy." On this last number in the film, Durante gets up from the piano and joins O'Connor, who has been tap dancing, for an old-fashioned, vintage Durante strut, hat in hand, razz-a-ma-tazz style.

Soon after *The Milkman* was completed, Durante's personal manager, partner, and closest friend in the whole world, Lou Clayton, died. Without his father, his sister, his wife, and now without Lou, he paused to examine his career. With the management of the prestigious William Morris Agency and Abe Lastfogel, he plunged into television and a faster pace of nightclub appearances. He made no more films for several years. He did an unbilled cameo with marvelous effect in a 1957 Bob Hope movie, made a wasted appearance in a 1960 all-star fiasco starring Cantinflas, had a brief but touching appearance in an Italian-language De Sica film released in Italy in 1961, and, after a last major film for MGM in 1962, played a brief but good part in a very entertaining 1963 all-star Stanley Kramer comedy chase movie.

Bob Hope made many excellent comedies. *Beau James* (Paramount, 1957) was one of them. It was based on the life of Jimmy Walker, Mayor of New York in the 1920s, as visualized in Gene Fowler's 1949 biography

Durante and Donald O'Connor duet, "That's My Boy," from *The Milkman*, **Universal, 1950.**

of the same name. Melville Shavelson directed this Hope film as well as coauthoring one of Bob Hope's several books, *Don't Shoot, It's Only Me* (1990), and wrote the book for a 1969 Broadway musical derived from Fowler's *Beau James*, called *Jimmy*, starring Frank Gorshin. In the 1957 film, Bob Hope plays debonair, cocky, colorful, high-living Jimmy Walker. The story is narrated by columnist Walter Winchell. Making unbilled guest appearances are Jack Benny, George Jessel, and Jimmy Durante. Durante does a great song and dance number, alone and with Hope, the old classic (1894) "Sidewalks of New York."[60] Durante here is as fresh and dynamic as he was in the 1930s NRA short, "Give a Man a Job," in fact even better, giving a taste of the excitement he could generate in vaudeville and nightclubs.

Durante appeared in two all-star extravaganzas. The first of these was *Pepe* (Columbia, 1960), starring the Mexican comedian Cantinflas. Filmed in widescreen Panavision, with special sequences in CinemaScope, it was a three-hour film directed by George Sidney, who also produced.

Pepe was a Mexican peasant whose horse that he groomed and loved dearly, Don Juan, was sold at auction to a Hollywood director, played by

Dan Dailey. The distraught Pepe goes to Hollywood to get help from the stars in getting the horse back, resold to producer Edward G. Robinson. The very talented Cantinflas shows great charm when he's not overwhelmed by the vastly overstuffed but photographically beautiful sausage that comprises this interminable parade of over 35 stars, most of whom do little more than distract attention from Cantinflas and add nothing to the flimsy plot. Durante's role (as himself) is minor, gambling at cards with Pepe at the Sands Hotel in Las Vegas. Pepe complains in Spanish that Durante was trying to peek at the cards with his nose. Sinatra stands next to his own portrait on the wall next to the cashier's window, telling Pepe that he's one of the Sands' owners. One high point lost in the blur of overabundance is a production number much later in the film, a song and dance routine with Cantinflas, Dan Dailey, and Maurice Chevalier doing Chevalier's song "Mimi."

Durante's appearance in another long picture was a better experience. *It's a Mad, Mad, Mad, Mad World* (United Artists, 1963), was filmed in Ultra Panavision 70, a form of Cinerama, and directed by Stanley Kramer, who also produced. The slapstick comedy runs three hours, a reasonably funny chase by many greedy characters to beat each other to money buried under a palm tree. Jimmy Durante sets in motion this chase by an all-star cast. He dies from injuries in a car crash, revealing with his last breath the location of the buried treasure. None of the ensuing bits of humor are quite as funny as Durante literally "kicking the bucket," dying and sending a bucket rolling down a hill.

One other small role for Durante was, curiously, in an Italian-language film made by Vittorio De Sica, *Il Giudizio Universale* (*The Last Judgment*). While Stanley Kramer's *It's a Mad, Mad, Mad, Mad World* was a comic commentary on human greed, with an all-star cast, De Sica's film was a serious parable on human corruption, with an all-star cast. In addition to prominent Italian actors such as Vittorio Gassman, Silvana Mangano, Alberto Sordi, and De Sica himself, it included such European and American actors as Fernandel, Ernest Borgnine, Akim Tamiroff, Anouk Aimée, Melina Mercouri, Jack Palance, and Jimmy Durante.

Filmed on location in Naples and at De Laurentiis Studios, February to June 1961, *The Last Judgment* was a co-production of Laurentiis-Standard (Paris). It was shown at the Venice Film Festival late that summer and released in Italy, October 26, 1961, by Dino De Laurentiis, who served as its distributor. It was released neither in England[61] nor in the United States. This most obscure and unknown of De Sica's many films was a project De Sica and his script writer Cesare Zavattini had wanted to do for several years.[62] They had worked together on *The Bicycle Thief* (1949), *Miracle in Milan* (1951), *Umberto D* (1952), *Two Women* (1961), and other outstanding films. De Sica stated in an Italian magazine interview that he

What elephant? Durante's biggest one-line joke both on stage in 1935 and here in *Billy Rose's Jumbo*, MGM, 1962.

had spent four years on this project, interrupted to film *Two Women*, and that *The Last Judgment* takes up again the style of *Miracle in Milan*.[63]

The Last Judgment presents a series of vignettes that reveal life in Naples before the Last Judgment, which a voice from heaven announces will begin at six P.M. At first, no one pays attention, preparing instead for a grand ball that evening. At six the Last Judgment begins, in alphabetical order, with the proceedings on television. Fearful people vow to repent, a big storm blows up, the Last Judgment is postponed. People forget their vows, return to their corrupt activities and prepare for the grand ball. The black and white film suddenly turns to bright color for the ball (De Sica's first use of color in any of his films).[64] Outside on the street, a man with a big nose (Durante) is disappointed because he didn't get a chance to ask God why he was given such a face. "I wonder what God would've lost, had He made my nose a little smaller?"[65] The film ends on a moral note.

Jimmy enjoyed his second trip to the land of his parents. Because he had not learned much Italian as a child, he thought some of the local merchants were welcoming him, the Italian-American star, by putting signs in their windows, "CHIUSO DURANTE . . . " (closed for something—lunch, repairs, vacation, or "durante" something else).

Durante's swan song for the movies (except for the small part in Stanley Kramer's 1963 all-star comedy) and his last major role was a return, appropriately, to one of his biggest triumphs on Broadway, *Jumbo*. Then (1935) still a young man in his early forties, in 1962, he was in his late sixties. He didn't have Billy Rose as producer this time, but he had Joe Pasternak, who, with director Charles Walter, knew how to turn this circus story into a movie. It had a script by Sidney Sheldon, derived from the 1935 material by Ben Hecht and Charles MacArthur, songs by Rodgers and Hart, and, interestingly low on the list of credits, Busby Berkeley as second unit director. Included were 15 circus acts in a film set in 1910, using widescreen Panavision.

The stars in *Billy Rose's Jumbo* are, all with their names above the title, Doris Day, Stephen Boyd, Jimmy Durante, and Martha Raye. Durante is Pop Wonder, co-owner of a circus with his daughter, played by Doris Day. They struggle to keep it free of creditors. The biggest laugh on Broadway and again in this filming comes when Durante tries to hide Jumbo, the star elephant, from the sheriff. The sheriff asks where he's going with that elephant. Durante holds his arms wide and asks, "What elephant?"

Durante joins with Doris Day and Martha Raye to sing "The Circus Is on Parade," sings solo the reprise of "The Most Beautiful Girl in the World" (earlier sung by Stephen Boyd), and joins in the finale, "Sawdust, Spangles and Dreams," with Doris, Stephen, Martha, and chorus.

Near the film's end, after Pop Wonder's circus is lost, Durante and Raye do an impromptu offstage Tambo & Bones minstrel routine (minus the blackface they might have worn a few decades earlier).

This circus film, released December 5, 1962, in time for Christmas trade, stands up well with other American circus films, including *The Greatest Show on Earth* (Paramount, 1952). However, with a high budget, *Jumbo* did not score big at the box office despite good reviews, offering proof to the suspicion that the heyday of MGM musicals was over.

Chapter 6

RADIO

Eddie Cantor gave Durante his first big break on radio in the fall of 1933. This old friend took several months off from his vastly popular radio show, *The Chase and Sanborn Coffee Hour*, to make a movie.

Radio was the place to be for vaudeville comedians like Cantor and Durante, performers with attention-getting voices and routines not too dependent on visual impact. Among other vaudeville comedians who succeeded hugely on radio was Jack Benny with his mastery of understatement, timing (particularly the pregnant pause), routines about his stinginess and violin playing, and insult humor directed at him by Mary Livingstone, Dennis Day, and Eddie "Rochester" Anderson. Fanny Brice gave up singing for a part as a spoiled little girl, Baby Snooks, played against Hanley Stafford as Daddy. Fred Allen, with the pinched voice and the rapier wit, and with his wife, Portland Hoffa, was surrounded by the neighborhood characters of Allen's Alley, supplemented by a very amusingly staged feud with Jack Benny as they visited each other's shows. Edgar Bergen had Charlie McCarthy, the smart-aleck puppet who hurled insults at the unseen moving lips of the ventriloquist, plus Mortimer Snerd as a less brilliant dummy. George Burns and Gracie Allen played George as the straight man and occasional singer of fast patter, Gracie as the hare-brained expert on confusion, with her hilarious letters to a never-seen brother in jail. The quality of comedy was so high as to qualify for the rubric, Golden Age of Comedy, a title that could also apply to the days of silent movies and the first years of television.

As radio audiences moved from crystal sets with earphones to super-heterodyne receivers with powerful speakers that allowed families to share the listening experience, the NBC and CBS networks grew apace with their commercial sponsors. The country's biggest comic stars were attracted to the potential of building a bigger career in front of an ever-growing national audience. Many Americans might not have the opportunity or the means to see vaudeville or Broadway shows. They might not see many movies and would never go near a nightclub. Radio would entertain

97

whole families at home for free, and they would buy the products sponsors advertised.

The growth of radio continued until television began to make a major impact on its audience. With television, the effect on comic performers was the opposite of radio. Comedians feared overexposure of their routines. It was thought that once an audience saw a routine on television, it could not be used again on stage or in vaudeville.

Network radio could be said to have started on December 6, 1923, when stations WEAF (New York), WCAP (Washington, DC), and WJAR (Providence, RI) were connected by special telephone wire. It was at WEAF, financed and built by AT&T, that many techniques of broadcasting and commercial sponsoring were developed.[1] Another station as important as WEAF was WJZ (New York), founded 1921, which that same year broadcast Vincent Lopez and his orchestra on a regular basis from the Pennsylvania Grill in New York, and broadcast the first stage show, Ed Wynn in *The Perfect Fool* on February 19, 1922. In the early 1930s, Ed Wynn would have a successful radio comedy series, *Texaco Fire Chief*, with his character remaining that of a perfect fool. Also on WJZ in these early days was another radio pioneer, Paul Whiteman and his Orchestra, doing his first broadcast about 1922.[2] Among the earliest voices on radio were "The Happiness Boys," Billy Jones and Ernie Hare, supplementing their comedy songs on recordings with the first real comedy series on radio (first on the air August 22, 1923). And on the first network hookup involving WEAF, WCAP, and WJAR, three cities got to hear political speeches and the first broadcast of a football match, the Army-Navy game.[3]

In the summer of 1924, the radio audience could hear the presidential nominating conventions of the Republicans in Cleveland and of the Democrats in New York's Madison Square Garden. Calvin Coolidge's inauguration, on March 4, 1925, was carried by 21 stations coast to coast by the AT&T network. NBC (the National Broadcasting Company) was established November 15, 1926, with WEAF, New York, as its flagship station and a group of 19 affiliated stations. In January 1927, this NBC network broadcast the Rose Bowl football game from California to the parts of the nation coast to coast that were wired.[4]

In 1928, the next presidential election year, NBC was split into the Red and the Blue networks (the Red network the more prestigious of the two), semi-independent, with the flagship station for the Red network WEAF, and the flagship station for the Blue network WJZ, both in New York. (In 1942, the Blue network was sold, and from the fall of that year became ABC, the American Broadcasting Company.) In 1929, CBS (the Columbia Broadcasting System) was founded by William S. Paley. CBS went on the air with 47 affiliated stations, WABC (later WCBS) in New York as its flagship station.[5]

The 1929 fall season was important for many reasons: the start of the Great Depression, many Hollywood musicals, a thriving Broadway musical stage which included Ziegfeld's *Show Girl* with Clayton, Jackson, and Durante in the cast, flourishing jazz clubs, and the first appearance of several new weekly radio shows. Paul Whiteman and his Orchestra debuted on CBS. *Amos 'n' Andy*, a five-days-a-week 15-minute show, began on NBC-Blue, starring blackface comedians Freeman Gosden ("Amos") and Charles Correll ("Andy"), following their vaudeville act of "Sam 'n' Henry" with a series that would run for more than 20 years, despite growing protests by the NAACP, which accused the show of reinforcing negative stereotypes. More in line with Stephin-Fetchit-style shuffling were the blackface minstrels Moran and Mack, made popular by their recordings for the Columbia label, 1927–29. They were the stars of *The Majestic Theater Hour*, beginning its second and last season on CBS. (Another blackface team with stereotyped racial material was billed as "Molasses 'n' January": they appeared in weekly comedy skits on *Captain Henry's Show Boat*, an hour variety show sponsored by Maxwell House, on NBC-Red for several seasons beginning the fall of 1932.) Also in the vein of ethnic humor, the Henry George program aired the fall of 1929 for its first of two seasons on CBS, billed as "negro comedy." Also making its first appearance that season was *The Rise of the Goldbergs* on NBC-Red, later just *The Goldbergs*, a family situation comedy, written by and starring Molly Berg as the character Molly Goldberg, played with Yiddish-inflected English. And that fall brought to NBC-Red the very successful crooner Rudy Vallee with his Connecticut Yankees orchestra in the enduring *Fleischmann Hour*.[6]

While the 1930-31 season brought no new important comedy variety radio shows, the 1931-32 season brought Eddie Cantor to NBC-Red for 60 minutes each Sunday, and Bing Crosby to CBS for a 15-minute program of songs five nights a week.

The 1932-33 season brought to radio the debuts of many comedy shows: Jack Benny and Burns and Allen on CBS; Ed Wynn, Fred Allen, Jack Pearl, and Ken Murray on NBC-Red; the Marx Brothers on the NBC-Blue network, their only season on radio; and a comedy drama, *The Easy Aces*, with Goodman and Jane Ace, a 15-minute show on CBS three times a week. *Amos 'n' Andy* continued on the NBC-Blue network with their 15-minute daily comedy drama for its fourth season. Eddie Cantor was on NBC-Red for a second season.

The 1933-34 season brought other comedy variety shows: George Jessel, Joe Penner, and Olsen & Johnson, on CBS; Phil Baker, Wheeler & Woolsey, and Will Rogers, on NBC-Blue. With the 1934-35 season came Bob Hope and Beatrice Lillie, separately, on NBC-Blue (Hope would switch to NBC-Red the following season); and Joe Cook, NBC-Red. The

1935-36 season brought *Fibber McGee and Molly*, with Marian and Jim Jordan, NBC-Blue network, and Jimmy Durante taking over Ed Wynn's *Texaco Fire Chief* program on NBC-Red as *Jumbo Fire Chief*, a tie-in with the Billy Rose Broadway extravaganza *Jumbo* that opened November 16, 1935.

In later seasons radio saw many other comedy shows appear. These included Jack Oakie for two seasons beginning on CBS the fall of 1936 (with Jimmy Durante appearing on Oakie's show its second season); Edgar Bergen and Charlie McCarthy, NBC-Red, 1937-38; Fanny Brice, after starring on *Ziegfeld Follies of the Air* the 1935-36 season, starred on *Good News* with Frank Morgan, NBC-Red, 1937-38, and in 1940 her Baby Snooks character emerged on *Maxwell House Coffee Time*; Milton Berle on NBC-Red, 1939-40; Red Skelton and *Duffy's Tavern* with Ed "Archie" Gardner, both debuting on NBC-Red, 1941-42; Abbott & Costello, NBC-Red, 1942-43; Joan Davis, NBC, 1943-44; Judy Canova and Groucho Marx, both on CBS, 1943-44 (Groucho's show cancelled after the season, but after he discovered the proper format, he was very successful later on radio and TV with *You Bet Your Life*, a quiz show beginning the 1947-48 season).

When Jimmy Durante went on the air for Eddie Cantor in the fall of 1933, Cantor was beginning his third season of a 60-minute comedy-variety show every Sunday night on NBC-Red, *The Chase and Sanborn Coffee Hour*. His was the most highly rated show on radio, as measured by the C.A.B. (Cooperative Analysis of Broadcasting, a ratings service that measured audiences at that time).

Audiences across the country tuned in to hear Cantor entertain them with sketches and songs and leave them with his closing theme, "(I'd Love to Spend) One Hour with You." But at the beginning of this season, Cantor was busy filming *Roman Scandals* for Samuel Goldwyn. Durante, a star in vaudeville and on Broadway, and a fledgling star in Hollywood, was still unknown to radio audiences. His only previous radio appearances had been as a guest on Ed Sullivan's 15-minute talk show, which premiered on CBS January 12, 1932, and on *The Rudy Vallee Show*, also popularly known as *The Fleischmann Hour*, the first major network variety hour, which debuted on NBC October 24, 1929. Durante's first of several guest appearances with Rudy Vallee came on May 11, 1933.

Jimmy Durante in 1933 was already 40 years old, but as brash and energetic as a youngster. It is interesting to see his comic personality evolve in front of the national audience without the visual effects that worked so well for him on stage.

The Chase and Sanborn Coffee Hour (Cantor's program) with Jimmy Durante as substitute host, was broadcast each week from a makeshift radio studio on the RKO lot in Hollywood. Each show would open with Rubinoff's Violin and Orchestra playing a soft, smooth number. Then

Durante would whisper an expression he used more in his early career than later, "Hot-cha-cha!," and sing an opening song he would discard before his own show of the 1940s, "As the Nose Blows (So the Nose Goes)."[7] He would chat with the announcer for a while and then sing one of his regular repertoire of songs, with interruptions for stories, gags, and comments, perhaps ending such commentary with another often-used expression he never did discard, "I got a million of 'em, a million of 'em!" And at some point in each show Ruth Etting would sing.

On the show for November 5, 1933, as an example of Durante's radio work at that time, he talks about a trip where he encountered cannibals, then to Spain, where he sings about the rain in Spain (long before Lerner and Loewe's "The Rain in Spain" for *My Fair Lady*), then to Venice to see "my father's paisans." Jimmy sings "I'm Jimmy, the Well Dressed Man." He mentions Al Smith, the New York politician who grew up like Jimmy on the Lower East Side. Then he introduces Ruth Etting.

As this same show continues, Durante talks about having started to write his symphony, "Inka Dinka Doo." There follows a sketch, "At the Circus," with Bosco the Trained Flea missing. The circus is in financial trouble; the sheriff arrives threatening cash or jail, demanding the flea. Jimmy asks if he'll take an elephant in exchange for the flea. When Bosco is found, Durante sings "Happy Days Are Here Again," a song trotted out for innumerable political conventions.

The show closes in the same way as all these early Durante shows, with Jimmy singing "Who Will Be with You When I'm Far Away," a song he would continue to use very often in the 1940s. He jokes a bit more, with another "I've got a million of 'em!" thrown in. He repeats a few bars of his opening song, "As the Nose Blows." The announcer tells the radio listeners to tune in again next week for Jimmy "Schnozzle" Durante.[8]

After November 12, 1933, Durante left the Cantor program, but returned as a summer replacement in July, remaining on the air through September 30, 1934, the last broadcast in the series. Ruth Etting was gone before summer, but Rubinoff continued.

On the July 15, 1934, show Rubinoff opens with an orchestral number, then Durante does "As the Nose Blows." He uses the word "Schnozzola" in this early reference to himself. There is a sketch of Durante as a bullfighter, speaking to the promoter called Pedro Antipasto. Sizing up his challenge in the ring, Jimmy uses an expression he would continue to use extensively, "It's a delemia!" Jimmy succeeds in throwing the bull as the crowd roars. He sings "The Bee and the Rose" about his bullfighting technique—in the 1940s, he would often use a variation on the bullfighting story as an interruption of one of his songs. He again uses "Hot-cha-cha!" between lines of the song. He segues into "East Wind (Blows from the West)," from an awful poem written by a New York neighbor (according to Fowler, a Mr. Bloomish),[9] now a song frequently used in these early shows but not in the 1940s. He does a "Hillbilly Durante" sketch, sings a few notes of "Alexander's Ragtime Band," and turns a Kentucky barn into a nightclub, moving the animals from the barn into the house. He sings the lyric, "I'd just sit still a thousand years." Playing Hillbilly Pappy, Jimmy sings "Give Me a Hillbilly Tune" with a melange of patter, working in bits of other songs, as his developing style was likely to do.

On this same show Durante does a sketch, "The Inka Dinka Doo Follies," which becomes a regular feature on these early shows. He is defendant and counsel for the defense, with the singer Madamoiselle Fifi suing Durante for breach of contract. He is found guilty of contempt of court. He's not bothered by this, saying only "Okay," and immediately launches into "Who Will Be with You When I'm Far Away," for a few bars, interrupting himself for a story punctuated again by the expression, "I've got a million of 'em!" Continuing with his closing, Durante again sings "As the Nose Blows," and says "Good night, folks. It's mutiny, that's what it is! Hot-cha-cha!"

In the July 22, 1934 show, Durante follows much the same approach. John McIntyre, identified as the Master of Ceremonies, says the show is from Hollywood as Rubinoff's orchestra plays smoothly in the background. Durante enters, calling himself "Schnozzola" and singing "As the Nose Blows," throwing in a "Hot-cha-cha!" He does a golf sketch, addressing the ball, and the ball answers. He sings "East Wind (Blows from the West)." Rubinoff has a number. Then Durante does an overlong sketch, "Haunted House," and later a prison sketch under his running segment "Inka Dinka Doo Follies." He sings "Prisoner's Song," then uses an Italian-sounding expression he often uses in these early shows but dropped in the 1940s, "Viva la Bonzah!," to suggest something like the arrival of the cavalry.

Again as Durante approaches the conclusion of the show, he sings "Who Will Be with You When I'm Far Away," interrupting himself for patter with his British-stuffy-sounding butler Meadows, a regular on the show, Colline Campbell, who sounds like Arthur Treacher. He finishes the show with "As the Nose Blows" and says "Goodnight folks." Behind announcer John McIntyre's closing reminder about next week and the station identification we can hear Durante loudly whispering, "Hot-cha-cha!"

On the show of July 29, 1934, Durante does a song that he will use often again in the 1940s, "Take a W," later to be titled "Take an L," recorded for MGM under the later title. On the show of August 5, 1934, Durante sings his compositions "She's a Little Bit This, and a Little Bit That" and "Hot Patatta," excellent songs for him and used to good purpose in the movies and on his 1940s radio show. On the show of August 12,

1934, Durante sings more of his own compositions, "A Dissa and a Datta," for a few notes, leading into "Hot Patatta," then into "Again You Turna" for a few notes, and back to "Hot Patatta." On the show of August 26, 1934, Durante opens not with "As the Nose Blows" but with one of his best compositions, the song with which he would start most of his later shows, radio and TV: "You Gotta Start Off Each Day with a Song."

On the show of September 16, 1934, Durante does a sketch, "Shooting at MGM Studios." No actress wants to play opposite him as he plays the role of a great lover. Only Rex the dog wants the part. So Durante goes to a plastic surgeon to fix his nose. "That doctor is quite a chiseler," he says. Now he's Jimmy "Casanova" Durante, the great lover. He has the mistaken notion he can woo women with the simple eloquence of just saying "Hot-cha-cha!" No one believes he's Durante, with a straight nose. He's arrested for impersonating Durante and forging a Durante check. But fortunately his nose swells back to normal, and people recognize him again. On this show he also does a sketch, "Wrestling Match," with dialogue similar to the lyrics of "So I Ups to Him," which Clayton, Jackson, and Durante recorded for Columbia. This leads into the song "Take the Wrist," a variation on "The Bee and the Rose."

On the show of September 23, 1934, after beginning with "You Got to Start Off Each Day with a Song," Durante does his famous "Wood" routine, which he had done on Broadway in Cole Porter's *The New Yorkers* (1930) and in his vaudeville and nightclub routine. He sings the song "Wood," telling the audience, "Wood made everything in this great country. So you paid me a compliment when you said my head was made of wood." If this had been visual on a stage, he would have proceeded to destroy all wood objects he could lay his hands on, but on radio he had to settle for the sound effects to suggest that destruction.

In the last show of the series, September 30, 1934, Rubinoff plays an orchestral suite, Durante reverts to opening with "As the Nose Blows." He talks about playing polo: he's not a good player, "with mallets toward none." He throws a Hollywood Party at his house. (His MGM film *Hollywood Party* had opened earlier in 1934.) He sings "Start Off Each Day with a Song." He engages in some Russian-dialect patter with Mischa from Minsk, working for Rubinoff, who imitates Durante's singing of "As the Nose Blows" in a Russian accent. Durante sings one of his favorite songs, which he recorded with Clayton and Jackson for Columbia, "I Can Do Without Broadway (But Can Broadway Do Without Me?)." Then he imitates minstrel man Eddie Leonard in a few notes of "Ida (Sweet as Apple Cider)," and Al Jolson in a few notes of "Mammy." Durante says he's using two knees to beat Jolson's going down on one knee for that song. After this business he returns to finish the original song about Broadway.

In closing the last show of the series Durante sings "Who Will Be with

You When I'm Far Away" and "As the Nose Blows." He thanks the audience, "I'm leavin' the air. Hope you let me come back again." He thanks
the orchestra and cast, mentioning each member of the cast by name, including Harry Donnelly, his personal piano accompanist who has been
with him ten years. He tells the audience, "Eddie Cantor will be here next
week, next Sunday. Auf wiedersehen till we meet again. Hot-cha-cha!"

Durante was off the air until the fall of 1935 when he appeared on
what had been Ed Wynn's show on NBC, retitled for him, *Jumbo Fire
Chief.* The idea was to promote Billy Rose's new, expensive show, *Jumbo.*
The half-hour radio show premiered Tuesday, October 29, 1935,
presented directly from the Hippodrome, where *Jumbo* was in preview performances before opening November 16.

The cast of *Jumbo* as heard over NBC in its radio premiere was headed
by Durante as Claudius B. Bowers (the B standing for "Brainy"); Arthur
Sinclair as John A. Considine, owner of the Wonder Show; Donald Novis
as Matt Mulligan, Jr., son of Considine's rival; A.P. Kaye as Mr. Jellico,
cockney circus worker; Gloria Grafton as Considine's daughter Mickey;
Adolph Deutsch, musical director, instead of Paul Whiteman. Durante as
press agent for the Considine show brags to a man who comes to put the
circus on the auction block for nonpayment of federal taxes, not knowing
he's a government agent. Brainy Bowers brags that the show is doing fine,
when it's really losing money, "stupendious . . . calossial . . . a real bon-
zai." He brags that President Roosevelt and he are fraternity brothers of
Sigma Chi. Durante sings a variation on the 1928 song, "Laugh, Clown,
Laugh," mentioning the operatic Pagliacci, but turning the song into a
story about being in a losing fight. The chorus sings "The Circus Is on
Parade." The radio audience is then invited to tune in next week for the
continuation.

The radio show continued on Tuesdays, the one day of the week the
Broadway show gave no performances, through March 3, 1936, after
which Eddie Duchin and his orchestra took over from Durante but continued to use the vocals of *Jumbo* cast members Gloria Grafton and
Donald Novis.

The spring of 1936 took Durante to Europe for a stage tour
culminating at the London Palladium and the making of a British film,
Land Without Music, with German operatic tenor Richard Tauber. And in
the fall Durante opened on Broadway in Cole Porter's *Red, Hot and Blue!.*
Although Durante did not appear on radio during the 1936-37 season, he
did see the publication of *Jimmy (Schnozzle) Durante's Jumbo Song Book,*
words and music of three of his best and most performed original compositions: "I'm Jimmy, That Well-Dressed Man"; "I Know Darn Well I Can
Do Without Broadway (Can Broadway Do Without Me?)"; "You Gotta
Start Off Each Day with a Song"; plus five other of his compositions he

rarely performed but with titles that would remain often-used expressions of his on radio and occasionally also in movies: "I Got a Million of 'Em"; "It's Mutiny!"; "Hot-Cha-Cha!"; "I'm Mortified"; "It's the Gypsy in Me!" The cartoon on the cover shows an elephant and Durante looking at each other with their noses crossing.[10] Of course the important interrupting stories that make each song distinctive, in Durante's inimitable style, are omitted from the pages. There are captioned photos from Durante movies and a page of "High Falutin' Philosophy" in the Durante style, with bons mots such as, "Never take your pet dog to a flea circus—he may bring the leading lady home with him!"

On January 18, 1938, Durante was a guest star on *The Jack Oakie College*, sponsored by Camel cigarettes on CBS from 1936 to 1938. Later, on July 14, 1938, Durante made his second guest appearance on *The Rudy Vallee Show* (*The Fleischmann Hour*), NBC. After the announcer's opening, Rudy Vallee begins by giving his usual greeting, "Hi-Ho, Everybody." He says Jimmy Durante has been "too long out of microphone range." Durante enters in the last 15 minutes of the hour-long show. After an introduction he sings "You Gotta Start Off Each Day with a Song," interrupting himself for just one gag, then finishes what is for him a short version of the song. Then he goes into his bit, "Some Senators phoned, want me to say a few encouraging words about the Depression. I looked in the dictionary. What's a depression? A dent. And what's a dent? I'm askin' ya, what's a dent? A dent is a hole. And what's a hole? A hole is nuttin'. And if you think I'm gonna stand here and talk about nuttin', you're crazy!"[11]

Durante worked well with Rudy Vallee, that debonair collegiate. Rudy had him back for a third guest spot February 23, 1939. This time Rudy introduces Durante early and plugs Jimmy's new Broadway show, *Stars in Your Eyes*. Durante again sings "You Gotta Start Off Each Day with a Song," interrupting himself for one joke, then finishing the song. In a sketch he talks about being in the Foreign Legion, being thrown by a camel, and encountering time bombs. He sings-talks "I've Never Wore White Linen Knickers ... What a Wonderful Liar I Am." He does not appear in part II of the show, where Shakespearean actress Judith Anderson is the featured guest.

Durante reported again to the Radio City studios of NBC for another guest appearance with Rudy Vallee for the show airing June 1, 1939.[12] Rudy notes, "In a few short weeks we'll celebrate our tenth anniversary on the air." Durante plays a few notes on the piano, saying, "Rudy, please don't interrupt me, I'm so-quil-er-i-zing [soliloquizing]." "Rudy, I'm dreamin' of the past, those calcium [halcyon] days." They do a sketch with Durante as an auto racer, "14-Cylinder Durante."

Among the types of people with whom Durante worked best were

Spanish spitfires—Lupe Velez in the movies and Carmen Miranda on radio and television. On the August 24, 1939, Rudy Vallee program both Jimmy and Carmen are guests, but they are not given any scenes to share, a missed opportunity. Carmen sings in Portuguese and does a comic routine with Lou Holtz, a good comedian from vaudeville who is a regular on the Vallee show. Durante appears in Act II—Rudy liked to divide his hour show into two acts—entering with a few notes of "You Gotta Start Off Each Day with a Song." Jimmy informs everyone he played the trumpet. He goes into one of his most widely used routines. Different instruments of the orchestra speak up, and to each Jimmy says, "That's not a trumpet." When some bass instrument obviously not a trumpet is played (a bassoon or tuba), he says, as an expert on the subject, "That's a trumpet!"

Durante's next guest appearance with Rudy Vallee occurred September 28, 1939, again with Carmen Miranda as a guest, and again she did her comedy stint with Lou Holtz, not with Durante. Jimmy enters early, singing again what was becoming his opening theme song, "You Gotta Start Off Each Day with a Song," with the usual interruptions. He takes part in a sketch about a football game at Wha-Hoo University, a name he wants to change to Harvard University. He uses the word he's mispronouncing more than any other word, "catastrophe," pronouncing it "catas-ta-stroke" as he describes his football experiences. He ends with the song often employed for his closing, "Who Will Be with You When I'm Far Away," interrupted by a quick joke, back to the song, then another joke, one he likes to tell about bumping into a stranger who demanded an "autopsy," and back to end the song.

In October 1939, after opening in the Broadway musical *Stars in Your Eyes* and guesting on the Vallee show, Durante appeared on the stage of the Paramount Theatre.

The year 1940 was busy, with the opening of the Gene Autry movie *Melody Ranch*, Durante playing a cowboy role, and the May opening on Broadway of the musical *Keep Off the Grass*, plus the preparations for the 1941 movie releases of *You're in the Army Now* and *The Man Who Came to Dinner*.

Jimmy's father died in New York February 27, 1941, leaving Lilian Romano, Jimmy's sister, as the only member of Jimmy's immediate family still alive, and she would die the next year.

Durante's next appearance on radio was a return to *The Rudy Vallee Show*, no longer sponsored by Fleischmann and Royal Gelatin but by Sealtest, now reduced to a half-hour show on NBC. Of all the Durante guest spots with Rudy Vallee, the March 13, 1941 spot was the best at showcasing Durante's ability to work well with aristocratic types. He was paired with the great Shakespearean actor John Barrymore, a regular on the Sealtest show. They did a funny boxing sketch together, what Rudy called an "unfolding pugilistic pageant, 'The Battle of the Century?'" The sketch runs almost the full half hour. Barrymore says, with perfect, if exaggerated, elocution, "Du-ran-te? You call that facial protuberance of yours a pro-file? Why if you stood with your head bowed, you'd look like a tripod!" Durante replies, "Barrymore, I'm ignorin' ya. And when I ignore a man, he's being ignored by a real ignoramus!"

Jimmy continues the show with his singing "You Gotta Start Off Each Day with a Song," interrupting for a joke, more of the song, another longer joke, his often-told story: "the bull ups to me . . . the bull's not satisfied, he demands an autopsy . . . Gene Autry enters incognito, sings 'Home on the Range,' I'm saved, and the moral is . . . 'You Gotta Start Off Each Day with a Song.'"

Durante and Barrymore plan to train Rudy as a prizefighter and then bet on his opponent, Homicide Hooligan. Rudy sings a song, then says he'll fight with a nose guard to protect his singing voice. During the fight, Durante is not only Rudy's trainer but also the ring announcer—that's very funny. Vallee wins because Durante hits Hooligan with the water bucket. Vallee agrees to enter the ring for one more fight, and Durante goes off to buy another water bucket.

By the 1940s, the national radio audience had grown enormously. In the 1930s, radio had eroded the isolation of small towns across America, making American culture less regionally focused. Now with anxieties about World War II, millions with common interests glued themselves to radios for news of the Japanese and the Germans and to comedy and variety shows for escape from their political tensions.

Many of these entertainment shows were rebroadcast to troops overseas by the Armed Forces Radio Service (AFRS), supplementing original programs aimed at the tastes of the G.I.'s. The most popular of the series was called *Command Performance*, shows released from March 1942 to 1949. Another popular series was *Mail Call*. A third series, *Jubilee*, was designed to appeal primarily to black troops, featuring mostly black entertainers and emceed by Ernie "Bubbles" Whitman, who was also the m.c. at the Apollo Theater in Harlem at the time. These shows were joined by large numbers of "V-discs," sent to service clubs, hospitals, and locations where troops would be spending time while not in combat or in training, plus sent to Armed Forces Radio Stations for use on AFRS broadcasts. Durante joined performers like Bob Hope and Bing Crosby and many, many more who donated their time and talent on these series, though he was not on any V-discs.

The next important year for Jimmy Durante's career, especially his radio career, was 1943, the year he met Garry Moore. But before that happened, the year began on a tragic personal note, with the death of his wife

Jeanne in Los Angeles on February 14, 1943. This was the week after Jimmy arrived in New York to guest-star on *The Camel Caravan* radio show for a third appearance and to perform at the Copacabana. Jeanne, age 52, had been ill for at least two years, an illness complicated by her alcoholism. She had felt alone every time Jimmy took his act on the road or made trips to New York, staying for long periods at Broadway's Astor Hotel and phoning home to see if she felt any better. It was widely believed in the entertainment business that Jimmy turned down many engagements during Jeanne's illness so as not to be away from her for too long a period of time. This caused him financial problems. His friend in Chicago, Judge Abraham Lincoln Marovitz, helped set up a trust fund for him similar to the help the Judge had given to another comedian friend, Joe E. Lewis.[13]

Later Jimmy would say in interviews that being away from Jeanne so much was one of his biggest regrets. Many believed Durante's "Good night, Mrs. Calabash," which was soon to become an integral part of his performances everywhere, was his way of paying homage to Jeanne. Her death came less than a year after his sister, Lilian Romano, died in Brooklyn, June 24, 1942. Although Jeanne was ailing at the time Lilian died, she flew from Hollywood for Lilian's funeral.

When Durante made a guest appearance on *The Camel Caravan* the night of February 26, 1943, he was on one segment of the hour-long show, near the end, and a young man unknown to him and to most of the audience appeared early in the show. This was Garry Moore. He described this meeting.

> When Jimmy and I met, I was a new kid in town, in New York. I was doing sustaining daytime radio, which is about as low as you can get and still be on the network. But there was a show on the air called *The Camel Comedy Caravan*. It was a terrible show, the thesis being that if one comedian was funny, then six comedians would be six times funnier. They had music on it, but then in the course of an hour they'd have four or five different comedians, which is almost an impossible thing because that means each guy had to top the guy ahead of him. They'd use someone who was a revered legend, then someone who was a new kid in town. On this particular night they had invited me . . . as the new kid in town . . . to do a five-minute monologue. And Durante had been out of circulation for quite some while, on national things, because of the illness of his wife Jeanne. We just happened to be on the same show. We both got lucky that night. It's like a baseball game. You may be Reggie Jackson but you can't be sure you'll get a hit when you get up there.[14]

Phil Cohan, the man who directed the show that night, saw the potential of pairing Durante and Moore. "I was doing a show called *Camel Caravan*. We booked Jimmy as a guest. He had been at MGM in the early days, then petered out. At the same time I booked Garry Moore. They didn't work together on the show. Jimmy did his spot, and Garry did his spot, and I wanted Garry to be an m.c."[15]

Garry Moore says,

> What happened was, I was on early. The idea was that you start low and build high. You always close with your biggest thing. . . . But I got lucky and I scored well with my stuff. And when it came to Durante, he also did extremely well. Camel was looking for a nighttime show. And somebody in the control room, who I imagine was Phil Cohan, said those two guys are such a contrast. Because I was maybe 27 at the time and Jimmy would have been 47. I was kind of young and brash, a little bit on the preppy side [complete with crewcut] . . . . And Jimmy was Jimmy. . . . The contrast between these two characters would make an interesting theme. Neither Jimmy nor I was particularly crazy about it, but a good spot in prime time was hard to come by. In fact I had never been in prime time. So they teamed us up. Durante had never heard of me, and he couldn't imagine why the hell they were teaming him up with somebody nobody had ever heard of. To me, I was from Baltimore, I had never seen Durante in his great heyday with Clayton, Jackson, and Durante. All I knew about him was "Inka Dinka Doo."[16]

Durante appeared once more as a guest on *The Camel Caravan,* without Garry Moore. The show that aired March 19, 1943, included singers Lanny Ross, Rudy Vallee, and Georgia Gibbs, pianist and band leader Roy Bargy, Xavier Cugat with his orchestra and chorus, and comedians Joan Davis, Lew Lehr, Herb Shriner, and Durante with straight man Jimmy Wallington. Durante jokes with Wallington and sings "Who Will Be with You When I'm Far Away" and "Did You Ever Have the Feeling."

Camel was also sponsoring *The Abbott & Costello Show,* and as luck would have it, Lou Costello got rheumatic fever, and Bud Abbott refused to go on alone. The agency had to get together a replacement show in ten days to go on the air March 25, 1943. The pressure was on Phil Cohan, who decided to put Durante and Moore into that slot. Phil tells the story that Durante had a suite on the fourth floor of the Astor, right on Broadway, a very important hotel in those days. A script meeting was to be held there. Durante was seated among the writers, as was Garry Moore. The phone rang, someone asking for Garry Moore. Durante, startled in his own suite, growled, "What? There ain't no Moore here!" He couldn't remember the name of the guy he'd be working with. It was typical Durante.[17]

At first the show was called the Moore-Durante Show, but Garry knew Durante was the real star so the name was changed to the Durante-Moore Show. Garry says,

Jimmy Durante breaks up Garry Moore on CBS radio show, 1940s.

Oddly enough, by contract, which was ridiculous, one week they were going to call us the Durante-Moore Show and then the next week they
would call it the Moore-Durante Show. To me that was silly because
number one, you ought to call it one or the other, and in addition to
which, I shouldn't even have gotten billing. It should have been called the
Durante Show. Because he was a big star, and I had realized that by
then. . . . I remember saying I shouldn't get equal billing with Durante,
and Durante was the one who insisted that we keep the equal billing. I

said okay then, let's call it the Durante-Moore Show because people are calling it the Durante-Moore Show anyhow. It was always announced on the air that way, but the public in general would say, "Did you hear the Durante Show last night?"

When Durante and Moore went on the air for the first time as a team, all the scripts show the announcer Howard Petrie introducing "The Camel Program with Garry Moore and Jimmy Durante," Garry Moore's name first. As late as October 1943, into the new season, the script still gave Garry Moore's name first.

Garry Moore did not realize just how kind and generous Durante would be to him. "To me he was kind of a washed up—you know, when you're 27 and the other guy is 47, you think of him as an old man. So why would I want to team up with this over-the-hill guy, but in any event, we decided to take a crack at it. For the first three or four months, I guess, we were kind of like two wrestlers in the ring circling each other waiting for one or the other to give the other a knee in the crotch. When it became apparent that that kind of thing wasn't going to happen, we began to relax with each other and eventually became very fond of each other."

Durante and Moore continued on the air substituting for Abbott & Costello for the rest of that spring and through the summer of 1943, from the March 25 premiere show through the show of September 30. When the new, 1943-44, season began in October, Abbott & Costello were still not ready to resume their show, and Durante and Moore had signed with Camel to have their own show. The consequence was back-breaking work doing two shows every week, Thursdays on NBC as the substitute show for Abbott & Costello and Fridays on CBS for their own new show, both 30 minutes, both for Camel cigarettes, and both done in California. In November, Abbott & Costello returned to Thursday nights, and sanity returned to the writers working double duty.

From the show's inception, Xavier Cugat and his orchestra provided the music, a carryover from the previous season's Camel show. Cugat didn't fit into the style of the program. Durante had roots in jazz and still had a jazz-like style, and director Phil Cohan was a big jazz fan and friend of Paul Whiteman, with whom Durante had worked well in *Jumbo*. They wanted someone who could play jazzy music rather than Latin American specialties. So Cugat was replaced before the September 9, 1943, show by Roy Bargy, pianist and concertmaster with Paul Whiteman's Orchestra for ten years, 1928–38. Bargy, born the year after Durante, was a highly experienced composer, arranger, and pianist and had recorded with many jazz groups besides Whiteman: the Benson Orchestra (which he directed for two years, 1920–22, as well as playing piano), Isham Jones and his Orchestra (1925), Bix Beiderbecke (1928), Red Nichols and his Big Ten (1930–31), Adrian [Rollini]'s Ramblers (1934), The Three T's (so named for three top jazzmen, Charlie and Jack Teagarden and Frank Trumbauer, in a jazz group of nine, 1936), Frankie Trumbauer and his Orchestra (1934–36). He now was to have stability and financial security as Durante's musical director, part of the loyal Durante family, until his retirement in 1963. (He died in Vista, California, January 16, 1974.)

Howard Petrie would remain with the Durante show from 1943 until the fall of 1948, when Verne Smith took over as announcer, but returned for the final 1949-50 season.

The female vocalists on the show were stars in their own right. The first and the last stayed the longest—Georgia Gibbs, whom Garry Moore nicknamed "Her Nibs, Miss Georgia Gibbs," and Peggy Lee. Her Nibs stayed from March 1943 through March 1945. She was followed by Marion Hutton, for only three shows in April 1945. Dale Evans took over from the last week of April 1945, through the end of the next season, June 7, 1946, except for the few weeks in June 1945, when Jeri Sullavan appeared. That fall Suzanne Ellers became the vocalist for the full 1946-47 season. Peggy Lee began the 1947-48 season, with Jo Stafford substituting for an ill Miss Lee in late October and early November, and finished the season for Rexall, June 23, 1948.

Each show started with some studio audience applause and Howard Petrie announcing Durante and Moore, sometimes as "The Nose and the Haircut." Then there was usually a phone call from Durante, stuck somewhere with a problem, asking Garry Moore's help. For example, on the show for March 3, 1944, the phone rings. "Hello, Junior? This is Jimmy." "Jimmy, for goodness sake where are ya?" "I'm in a phone booth, and my nose got stuck in the telephone." "Well, so what?" "So come and get me. Every time I sneeze, I dial Kansas City." Then Roy Bargy's orchestra, with Jack Roth on drums and Jules Buffano on piano, would strike up what had become Durante's theme song, "You Gotta Start Off Each Day with a Song." Jimmy would always interrupt this song at least twice before finishing it, so he could tell one or two stories.

All these interruptions sounded like ad-libbing, but in fact, all were recycled, written for him years before. Garry comments: "He had an encyclopedic memory and he would have a whole catalog of jokes that worked for him in the past. And one night he may sing eight bars and stop and do a couple of jokes and they might be different tonight than they would be the next night. But they would all be from the large stockpile of jokes."

During the show Garry would tell jokes and serve as Jimmy's straight man. They would do comedy sketches, mixed with Durante singing-talking-singing songs as no other performer could. Frequently Durante would yell at the band for a supposed infraction of his rules, "Wait a minute, wait a minute! I'm woikin' here too!" and throw everything but the whole piano at Jack Roth. Once in a while, Garry Moore would sit at the drums. "I play drums, very badly," says Garry. "He would have prop music on his piano, and he'd come running over to me. Say he'd come to the end of a phrase and I would go into sort of a drum hot lick thing, hitting all those cymbals and everything, and he'd grab the music off his piano and rushing over to me at the drums say, 'Show me in the music where it says BAROOMP, BAROOMP!'"[18]

For "serious relief," the female vocalist would deliver one or two "normal" songs. The show closed with Durante singing "Who Will Be with You When I'm Far Away." This song was also done with multiple interruptions. Then Durante would add the words, "Good night, Mr. Moore. Good night, everybody." Mrs. Calabash came later.

As long as Durante and Moore remained together for Camel, there were almost no guests on the show to supplement the regular cast: they weren't needed. Marlene Dietrich did appear on the Thursday night substitute show for Abbott & Costello, September 9, 1943, to plug U.S. Savings Bonds and do a western sketch with Durante and Moore. She does not sing, but regular Georgia Gibbs sings the new song "Shoo Shoo Baby (Your Papa's Off to the Seven Seas)."

Durante and Moore, with their regular and substitute shows, spent three months of the fall of 1943 broadcasting from Los Angeles so Durante could be on the set of the MGM film *Two Girls and a Sailor*, released in 1944. After a return to New York, the Camel show left again for Los Angeles the end of April 1944 to remain in California except for another trip to New York in March 1945.

Durante had as much trouble with spelling as he did with pronunciation. With Camel the band would start to play the song "C-A-M-E-L-S." The whole cast including Durante and Moore were expected to sing that commercial. Everyone else would be singing C-A-M-E-L-S, and Durante would be singing "C-L-E- and I'm, I'm, I'm." Usually no one corrected Jimmy because what he said was unintentionally funnier than what the writers wrote. Garry Moore remembers that once Jimmy said, "Junior, I'm on the horns of a di-leem-i-a." Garry said, "Jimmy, it isn't 'di-leem-i-a,' it's 'dilemma.'" To which Jimmy replied, "Go ahead, educate me and we'll all be outa woik." The writers did not have to write misspellings and mispronunciations into the scripts: if they wrote "catastrophe" correctly, it was certain Jimmy would say "ca-tas-ta-stroke." Later the writers would give Garry streams of big words to throw at Jimmy, real tongue-twisters, which Jimmy would breathlessly mangle.

There are many stories that illustrate how much of the time Jimmy did not know what he said was funny. When Durante first moved to Los Angeles from New York, he bought a house in what proved to be the part of town that was going downhill, guessing wrong on how the place was going to grow. It got to be a seedy neighborhood, although Jimmy was rarely there anyway. So some of his friends talked him into moving to a relatively small but nice house in Beverly Hills. Garry Moore remembers one of the fancy decorators over there talking with Durante. "Phil Cohan and I were there. The decorator was talking about choices of wallpaper with flowers on it and so forth, and he said, 'You see, Mr. Durante, what we want to do is bring the outdoors indoors.' So Durante says, 'If I want the outdoors indoors, I won't have an indoors, I'd have an outdoors.'"

After Jeanne's death, Jimmy lived alone. Once Maggie Arnold, his housekeeper,[19] went home for the day, he was exposed to whoever decided to ring his doorbell. So someone, maybe the police, convinced him to put a peephole in the front door. Jimmy was asked if he thought this would help his privacy. He answered, "Oh yeah, now when they come to the door and I say 'who's there?' and they say 'does Jimmy Durante live here?' and I sez 'there ain't no Durante here' and they goes away." Now with that voice, who wouldn't know it was Durante?[20]

In the yard behind his new house, Jimmy was persuaded to build a small pool. When he had a housewarming, people went in swimming. And, Garry remembers, "Durante did nothing but pace around the edge of the pool. If he saw somebody treading water or standing still holding on to the edge of the pool, he'd say, 'Keep movin', everybody keep movin'!' He was afraid someone was going to pee in the pool."

Once the esteemed music critic Deems Taylor came backstage at the radio studio, ostensibly to say hello to Garry Moore but in reality to be introduced to Durante. Garry said, "Jimmy, I'd like you to meet Deems Taylor." Jimmy, puzzled, replied, "*Whose* tailor?"[21]

Durante also had trouble remembering faces and names, but would never admit he had forgotten or was being hoodwinked by a stranger. This weakness had resulted in admitting Prohibition agents to the Club Durant many years before. At that time, his piano player, Harry Donnelly, would cue him when strangers approached, like, "Oh, Jimmy, look, here comes *George Brown*, or *John Philips*, or whatever." And Durante would say, "Hiya, George, haven't seen ya, how ya been?" Garry Moore recalls, "We used to laugh at Durante because he was the warmest man in the world, and he'd maybe meet [someone] twice, and he'd never remember your name, never. But he'd see you coming, and he'd see a look in your eye that you expected to be spoken to."

Certainly nobody who ever met Durante would forget him. Especially not an elephant when everyone knows an elephant never forgets. Well, somehow, according to Phil Cohan, someone told Jimmy that Rosie, the elephant he had worked with in *Jumbo*, was retired and living at a wildlife preserve near Hollywood, somewhere in the San Fernando Valley. So Jimmy hopped in a car with Garry Moore and drove out to the Valley. According to Garry, he was out in a car touring the Valley for whatever reason

Maggie Arnold (long-time housekeeper), Jimmy and Jeanne. 1930s.

he can't remember, and they happened to come across an animal farm that furnished animals for movies. "We got out, went in and looked around. And Durante was talking about the elephant that he worked with in *Jumbo* in New York. There was an elephant in a corral nearby. Durante said in the hearing of the trainer, 'I wonder what become of Rosie who I worked with in *Jumbo*.' And the trainer said, 'That's Rosie right over there.' And Durante, without thinking, turned around and went over and embraced the elephant's trunk and said, 'God love ya, Rosie!'" The elephant took one look at Durante and walked away.

The president of the company that sponsored the Durante-Moore Show, Justin Dart, never did understand this kind of humor. Garry remembers this: "He didn't think Durante was funny and he didn't think I was funny. But when they decided to go on the air and they were shopping around for shows, we were the only ones who were available, so he bought us. He'd come and sit in the front row during a show and the whole audience was dying laughing. He'd just sit there with a straight face, shaking his head."

Camel did not renew the Durante-Moore Show. The last installment it sponsored was March 30, 1945, broadcast from New York. The following Friday, April 6, the show continued but under the new sponsorship of Rexall Drugs. Instead of using a booking agent when Camel dropped the show, Durante, Moore, and Phil Cohan, according to Cohan, saved the commission by forming their own package. They became legal partners for the purpose of marketing the radio show. Lou Clayton was Jimmy's agent, and Jimmy used the William Morris Agency on some matters, but according to Garry Moore, when it came time to draw up a contract with Rexall, the Durante-Moore-Cohan crew met with the Philadelphia agency representing Rexall, N.W. Ayer, "a very gentlemanly outfit. We had known their lawyer and chief negotiator who was very much of a gentleman. So at negotiation time we didn't even take a lawyer. We didn't take anybody. We went and they had their lawyer. 'Okay, where do we start?' We said, 'Look, what's equitable? You obviously have been doing study on what you want to pay and we have a rough idea of an area of what our pay ought to be. We trust you to do what is fair and good.' And the lawyer's jaw just dropped. He made up a contract and we signed it, and it was equitable." According to Phil Cohan, it was decided to split the money from Rexall in a 3-2-1 arrangement: Jimmy was to get $3,000 a show, Garry $2,000, and Phil $1,000. When Garry left the show, Jimmy and Phil split Garry's percentage.

Now, under the sponsorship of Rexall, for the first time the show was officially called *The Jimmy Durante–Garry Moore Show*, with largely the same supporting cast, but with Marion Hutton the new vocalist, replaced after a few weeks by Dale Evans, then by Jeri Sullavan.

Through the remainder of the 1944-45 season, there were no more important changes in format. The last night of that season, June 29, 1945, had ended with a guest star, Ray Bolger, to help plug the Rexall summer shows in which he starred with his special guests, starting with Bing Crosby on the first show. It was announced that Roy Bargy and Howard Petrie would continue on the program. After all this, the June 29th show closed with the usual words from Durante, "Good night, everybody."

With the start of the 1945-46 season for Rexall, September 14, 1945, there was written into the script a new closing comment. After "Good night, Mr. Durante," "Good night, Mr. Moore," Moore says, "Good night, everybody," and Durante adds, "Good night, Mrs. Calabash." Almost every script hereafter includes that closing. Where the script omits Mrs. Calabash, Durante puts it in.[22]

The radio audience began to write letters asking, "Who is Mrs. Calabash?" For many years Durante would tell different stories to different people, convincing each one he was giving them the real low-down.

The real story, according to director Phil Cohan, is that Durante heard the NBC radio program on Sunday afternoons featuring the opera singer John Charles Thomas. He would close his show with "Good night, Mother." Durante thought that was lovely and told his program director in the drawing room of a train from Los Angeles to New York, "I wish I could do something like that." A few days later, in the CBS studios in New York, late at night, Durante's writers were struggling with a script. Garry Moore, who usually wrote much of his own material, was there. Durante had left sometime after midnight. It was the night before a show. Everyone was getting tired. The idea was thrown out that Jimmy would like a new ending for the show. They wanted a funny name, and tried several. Then Phil Cohan, out of nowhere, looked at his pipe, a calabash pipe, and suggested Calabash as a name. Said Cohan:

> Calabash sounded good, so we stuck it in for one night. The agency said it sounded pretty good. Then later on we figured we have a pretty good gimmick here.
>
> At the end of the season we thought we got all we can out of "Good night, Mrs. Calabash." What are we going to do? Then somebody came up with the idea of having a race horse. This was the time of *Harvey*, the invisible rabbit, with Jimmy Stewart. I thought Jimmy [Durante] could go to the phone and his race horse, called Mrs. Calabash, would talk to him. Jimmy's crazy about the races, you know. He used to own a horse. We all thought that was great. One night about one o'clock the phone rings. Jimmy called, saying, "I was doing a benefit at a monastery. I asked what do you think if I made Mrs. Calabash a race horse. They were horrified." That nixed it, Jimmy being a good Catholic. So we were stuck with it. We didn't know quite what to do with the end of the season. I had cards printed—we got mail. I had Connie our secretary write up a card saying, "Thank you for writing and inquiring about Mrs. Calabash. There are some things a gentleman doesn't talk about. Signed Jimmy Durante." So it went, on and on.
>
> When in TV it was dramatized, it made a bigger impression, with Jimmy walking off in a trenchcoat. That was not my idea, but the calabash was strictly me. And then they added on, "wherever you are," which added to the mystique.[23]

Adding a slightly variant spin to this story is Garry Moore's version.

Well, the original idea was, we had a character on the show which we had been using, an imaginary character called Umbriago.... [The Italianate word] Umbriago means drunkard and also sort of village idiot.... And for a long while, just Umbriago's name would get a laugh. Jimmy would say, "I was walking down Fifth Avenue—who do you think I bumps into? Umbriago." Big laugh before he even got to the joke. After awhile that laugh began to get a little smaller, so we decided we had to—in the coming season—we better do something to freshen things up.

Somebody came up with the idea of having Umbriago get married and that would give us another character to talk about, Mrs. Umbriago. And then every meeting for a long while was, who is Mrs. Umbriago? What type of person should she be? What kind of jokes? And we decided she should be kind of stout. When we were going to talk about this girl falling in love, what was her name going to be? And that's when everybody started throwing out all the obvious Italian names like Mrs. Pastafazool, and Durante would sit there and shake his head and say, "Nah, that ain't right." That's when Phil [Cohan], who was smoking his calabash pipe said, almost as an aside, "How about Mrs. Calabash?" And Durante didn't know that Phil's pipe was a calabash pipe. He thought Phil made that up. And he said, "That's it! I like that!"

Then what crossed us up was when it was decided that we would run a teaser campaign. This was all in the spring toward the end of the season. We would ... have Jimmy say "Good night, Mrs. Calabash," but we wanted him to say it in a kind of jaunty, not leering voice, but sort of a happy voice, "Good *night*, Mrs. Calabash." Instead of which he gave it a wistfulness. And rumors began to get around that this was somebody who was sick or the late Mrs. Durante ... rumors—none of them of a fun person. And then finally one night for no reason we've ever known, or at least that I've ever known, he added, "wherever you are," and he said it in such a heartbroken way that people immediately began to think, "Isn't that sweet." Well, there went the whole picture of a wife for Umbriago, because ... everybody had their own picture and their own version of who she was—I'm talking about listeners. So that's as far as we got with Mrs. Calabash but it served a tremendous purpose.[24]

A year or two later, Durante and Moore were traveling cross country by train. The writers on the show were still making jokes about who Mrs. Calabash was, picking up on what the radio listeners were asking. Moore says he picked up on this and walked into Durante's stateroom, and just being flippant asked, "Who's Mrs. Calabash?" "And he looked at me with great surprise and said, 'Ya mean ya don't know?' And hell, I was there when it was invented. I said, 'No, who is she?' He said, 'Jeanne.'" Durante in his mind had converted a gimmick used for an effective show closer into something real, with deep personal significance.

During the 1946-47 season, with almost all Durante-Moore shows originating from Los Angeles, an important new addition to the show was the orchestra bass fiddle player turned comedian, Candy Candido. Born John Candido, he had started out, like Durante, without much formal schooling but with good music lessons, playing gigs in New Orleans where he grew up, and had intentions of making a full career as a musician. Comedy was far from his mind. He recorded with Ted Fiorito's big band as Johnny Candido, then as Candy Candido, for at least a decade, beginning 1932 on Brunswick, then Decca. He recorded with Gene Austin in 1933-34 and again in 1937, on various labels. He recorded four numbers for Vocalion under the name Candy and Coco, in 1934; Coco being the nickname of Otto Heimal, guitarist, a quartet that also included Gene Austin on piano, and Monk Hazel on either drums or cornet. And he made a few records for Decca under his own name, Candy Candido and his Swingsters, and Candy Candido and His Candy Kids, in 1937, only one of the records ever released.[25]

Candy Candido had many inspired moments as second banana comedian with Durante's extended family, on radio and television, plus traveling with Durante to perform in nightclubs. He will always be remembered best for just one spoken bass line, "I'm feeling mighty low." This was invariably the punch line to a routine involving his speaking voice's six and a half octave range, enabling him to speak, not sing, in soprano, alto, tenor, and bass pitches. Candy tells how he came to join Durante: his first appearance on the radio show was November 1, 1946. He had been working for five years at the Florentine Gardens, a nightclub in Hollywood, doing a comedy routine called "The Shooting of Dangerous Dan McGraw," using many voices, including the line, "I'm feelin' mighty low." "Durante got a big kick out of that, so he sent two of his writers to my house. One was Jack Elinson. . . . [He said] 'Jimmy Durante would like you on his show.' So I sez, how much does he pay? 'Scale.' What is scale? '$175.' Well, he don't want me. My voice is the only thing I've got to sell. He says, 'How much you want?' I sez, $750. He sez, 'You'll never get it,' and they left. Okay? About two days later they're back. 'Mr. Durante sez he'll pay it. Here's the script, read it.'

"I was only booked for one show," says Candy. He recalls part of a sketch he did with Durante. "Durante sez, 'How do ya like that? All these gals with dese long dresses. Ya don't see legs no more unless ya eat a chicken.'" Candy imitates Durante's hoarse voice. "So I walk up to him. I sez, 'I can tell ya about it in a little poem.' He sez, 'Ya ken?' He sez, 'Tell me.' I sez, 'Girls are wearin' their dresses longer (said in little-girl voice), in legs that do not show (said in male adult voice), so now instead of whistling (low male voice), I'm feelin' mighty low (very low male voice).' We did this show, and it got such a howl because they've never heard anything like this, you know. The next two weeks I'm off the show. I understand the Durante show received 50,000 letters wantin' to know who was that little voice. A lot of people thought Durante did it. So they had to bring me back."[26]

Candy's routine was so popular that Elon Packard and Billy Gould, two writers of the Durante show, wrote lyrics and music for a song, "I'm Feeling Mighty Low." MGM recorded the song with Durante and Candido, Candy's name second on the label and in smaller print. It was released in July 1947, the A side, paired with Durante alone on side B doing his classic rendition of "I'll Do the Strut-Away in My Cutaway," credited on the label to Harry Donnelly (Durante's old piano player), Durante, and Irving Caesar. This was the first of ten 78rpm records Durante would make for MGM through 1950, all 20 songs excellent, snappy.

The 1946-47 season saw the show's ratings up slightly from the previous season. The show had a loyal audience but not nearly as large as for Eddie Cantor in the 1930s or for some current weekly comedy hits: Bob Hope; Fibber McGee and Molly; Edgar Bergen and Charlie McCarthy; Jack Benny; Fred Allen; Red Skelton. The Durante Show had ratings this season similar to those for Abbott & Costello, Duffy's Tavern, Judy Canova, Burns and Allen, and Eddie Cantor, but still slightly lower than all these.

This season saw only Frank Sinatra as a guest on the show. He appeared twice, November 8, 1946, and March 21, 1947, as a way to plug the one movie he and Durante made together, *It Happened in Brooklyn*, released by MGM in 1947. The chemistry was always good between these two paisanos—in the one movie, on each other's radio shows, and on Durante's TV show. On the November 8 show, they discuss who gets the girl in the movie, and the answer is Peter Lawford. Sinatra sings a song, then there is a western sketch in which eight aces come out of a deck of cards. On the March 21 show, Sinatra sings a song and takes part in a sketch about drawing the Mason-Dixon Line. Then Sinatra, Durante, and Moore team up to sing "Anything You Can Do (I Can Do Better)," from Irving Berlin's 1946 musical, *Annie Get Your Gun*.

Durante appeared on Sinatra's radio show, *Songs by Sinatra*, February 27 and November 26, 1946, half-hour shows on CBS Wednesday nights, sponsored by Old Gold cigarettes. In the first show, they do a comedy sketch, then Durante sings "I'm the Guy Who Found the Lost Chord," a comedy song he did many times. They do another sketch in which they include Durante's closer, "Who Will Be with You When I'm Far Away." To end the show, they do a duet on Sinatra's "Put Your Dreams Away." For the November 26 show, on which Andre Previn is also a guest, Sinatra and Durante do a comedy sketch which includes the Durante song "So I Ups to Him." Later Durante does a sketch.

On *Lux Radio Theater*, May 5, 1946, CBS, Durante took part in a one-hour dramatization of the MGM movie he had made in 1944, *Music for Millions*. Here he is teamed with the movie's other stars, Margaret O'Brien and Jose Iturbi.

Frank Sinatra, Jimmy Durante, and Garry Moore debate where the song's gotta come from. *The Jimmy Durante–Garry Moore Show*, CBS, November 8, 1946. "The Song's Gotta Come from the Heart."

At the end of the 1946-47 season, on the program of June 27, 1947, Durante announced that next season he would continue with Rexall, but "Garry's gonna have a brand new show of his own" after five years together. He thanked his producer, Phil Cohan; his writers, Stanley Davis, Elon Packard, Bud Pearson, Lester White, Harry Crane, and Jackie Elinson; contact man, Roy Rowan; sound man, Billy Gould; engineer, Joe Schweiger; script girl, Onnie Whizin.

Garry Moore tells how he regretfully left the man he had come to love.

> Durante and I were together for five years, and by that time I was 33, I guess, something like that, and I began to get the feeling that I was becoming—in spite of the fact that in each show I probably had more jokes than he did, because I was on from page one through the last page because I was 'straighting' for Durante, and throwing in a few jokes in the straight man business.... I began to get the feeling ... my humor was ... more cerebral than Durante's.... I was getting more and more identified as Durante's straight man.... [I] had two kids and didn't want to be caught by surprise when I was 35, with my career behind me.

When I announced that I was going to quit at the end of my fifth season, everybody was quite angry. The agency was angry, the network was angry, because I was quitting a successful show and breaking up a successful team. But Durante, after all, had left Clayton and Jackson when it was Clayton, Jackson, and Durante—when they realized he was stronger as a single than he was with the trio. So he was the only one who truly understood when we had our final meeting on it, and people were berating me for—why are you putting the show in possible jeopardy, because you have a winning combination here. Durante was the one who said, "Look, the kid's gotta do what he's gotta do." He was the one who understood. And years later, I had my own variety show on TV, in the late '50s and early '60s, for which we won an Emmy and so forth. I had Carol Burnett with me. [She was on his TV show from 1959 to 1962.] And at the end of '62, Carol came to me and said, "I feel like I've gone as far as I can here, and I'm being offered shows of my own." So she left me. And I understood it thoroughly. She was doing the same thing that I felt I had to do when I was with Durante.

Some years later I walked into Chasen's to have dinner. At one booth there was Durante and his party, and my booth was me and my party, and the booth next to me on the other side was Carol and her party. So here were three generations really, all of whom had helped each other.

The *Jimmy Durante Show*, minus Garry Moore, went on the air without a co-host October 1, 1947, to begin a new season on a new network, switching from CBS to NBC, and moving from Friday to Wednesday night. Howard Petrie continued as announcer, Roy Bargy as musical director, and Candy Candido as unofficial second banana. The dour-faced comic actor Victor Moore was brought on many of the shows as a semi-regular. (Phil Cohan felt Victor Moore didn't really belong on the show.[27]) Added as a regular was Arthur Treacher, a tall Englishman with an imperious, aristocratic tone of condescension, after he had worked the previous season on *The Jack Carson Show*, which went off the air. His role was similar to the butler on the 1933-34 *Chase and Sanborn Coffee Hour* Durante had done, substituting for Cantor. The newly added vocalist was Peggy Lee. Another innovation was that the last five minutes of the half-hour shows would be given over to Tom Harmon for a Rexall sportscast, usually discussing the football games of the week.[28]

The policy for this season was to compensate for the loss of Garry Moore by having a guest star each week. It was decided to have Greer Garson on the season opener. She had won an Oscar for her performance in *Mrs. Miniver*, 1942, and had given outstanding performances in *Random Harvest*, 1942, and *Madame Curie*, 1943. Desi Arnaz, Phil Cohan, and other Durante friends enjoyed telling the story of Durante's first meeting with Greer Garson. As Cohan tells it, the top star at MGM was Greer Garson. Jimmy got MGM to okay her going on the show. The Hollywood movie people hated radio, as later they hated television. They didn't realize how much radio and TV actually promoted their movies. If one of their stars went on the air, they wanted to protect her. Someone had to check the material to make sure it was right. After this was done, the Durante gang, led by the writers Elon Packard and Stan Davis, descended on Greer Garson's home at Stone Canyon, Bel Air. On their way there, they stopped at the Brown Derby for lunch. The writers loved to drink and had two or three martinis apiece. Jimmy warned them to be careful and not say anything offensive or impolite to Miss Garson. He called her "Miss Greer" because he could never say "Greer Garson." "On the way out, Jimmy's driving, and giving the warning. She, like real stars, was just as natural and no problem. She was lonely at that time, just had a divorce. She came down the stairs, 'Would you like a drink?' We shook our heads. Jimmy went to the piano. She had to do a song with Jimmy. Of course Jimmy's songs are always the same: ding-di-dink and then you stop and Jimmy does a line. Jimmy explained, 'Dis is where we get a laugh.' Miss Garson asked, 'What if we don't get a laugh?' Jimmy answered, 'Then we're all in the toilet.'"[29]

The first show set the pattern for the season. It no longer opened with a phone call since Garry was not there to receive the call. Durante opened the show with "You Gotta Start Off Each Day with a Song." Arthur Treacher called Jimmy "James." Miss Greer was fine.

That season brought as guest stars Eddie Cantor, Margaret O'Brien, Victor Moore, Lucille Ball, Bing Crosby, Dorothy Lamour, Carmen Miranda, Charles Boyer, Boris Karloff, and for their first time on radio, Lou Clayton and Eddie Jackson, joining with Durante to recreate the routines of Clayton, Jackson, and Durante. When Durante had to go into the hospital for minor surgery and missed four shows, December 31, 1947, through January 21, 1948, Garry Moore substituted for him the first week, and Victor Moore the remaining three weeks, each week with a different guest star—Red Skelton the first week, Bob Hope, Frank Morgan, and Al Jolson the subsequent weeks.

Candy Candido recalls his entrance on the first show Durante was away. He came on with the voice of a little girl, saying she had a telegram for Mr. Moore. It's a poem for Jimmy in the hospital. Garry Moore asks her to read it. "I'm sorry I can't be with you on this Happy New Year's show, and because I ain't there with my boy [here Candy's voice changes to a deep bass] I'm feelin' mighty low."[30] Then the unbilled Dave Barry, a regular on the show, appears as the continuing character Mr. Ripple, U.S. Commissioner of Rivers and Waterways. He speaks in a rippling voice and sings a few notes of his signature song, "I'm Forever Blowing Bubbles."

Peggy Lee sings her own composition, "It's a Good Day." After a Rexall ad, Garry introduces Red Skelton, who reads a joke that falls flat;

he comments, "You *know* that was written for Durante." Skelton switches to his own strength, doing the voice of one of his character creations, Junior, the little boy, in a long sketch. Then Peggy Lee sings "Mañana." After another Rexall ad, an opera sketch is presented, a narrative poem with Moore, Lee, and Skelton. The refrain is Durante's line, "Hot-cha-cha!" At the end of the show, Garry and Red together say "Good night, Mrs. Calabash." Then Tom Harmon gives his football predictions for the week.

The following week, when Victor Moore and Bob Hope filled in for Durante, they did a spoof on the Hope-Crosby road pictures made for Paramount, "The Road to Pismo Beach." (Pismo Beach is on the California coast north of Santa Barbara.) In the sketch, an Inca idol speaks his native tongue, "Inka Dinka Doo." Candy Candido was the Princess Inka, hitting high and low notes. At the end, Moore and Hope wish Jimmy well and remember to mention Mrs. Calabash.

When Frank Morgan joins Victor Moore in covering for Durante, Howard Petrie announces that Jimmy was discharged today. Morgan and Moore join with Peggy Lee to sing and thus promote Jimmy's exciting new MGM recording made shortly before going into the hospital, "Chidabee, Chidabee, Chidabee (Yah! Yah! Yah!)." It was written with Harry Harris and Harry Crane, the sheet music published by the tiny Jimmy Durante Music Publishing Company, 6317 Yucca Street in Hollywood, run by Durante's friend and later his manager, Lou Cohen.[31]

On the last substitute show before Durante's return, Al Jolson says hello to Jimmy down in Palm Springs, recuperating and expected to return to the show next week. Victor Moore mistakes Jolson for Larry Parks, who had played Jolson in Columbia Pictures' *The Jolson Story*, 1946. Jolson tries to do Durante songs and use Durante expressions. He opens with "You Gotta Start Off Each Day with a Song," interrupting himself like Durante, "Stop da music, stop da music!" and "I got a million of 'em, a million of 'em!" Durante had appeared on Jolson's NBC show, *The Kraft Music Hall*, just one day after his own show of Wednesday, December 17, 1947, and a few days before going to the hospital. On the Jolson December 18 show, Durante plugged his new "Chidabee" recording. He would be a guest on Jolson's show again in the spring of 1948 and twice in the spring of 1949.

Durante returned for the show of January 28, 1948, thanking everyone who covered for him, plugging "Chidabee" by singing all the verses, and plugging the March of Dimes fund-raising campaign.

High points of the 1947-48 season were the shows with Eddie Cantor, October 8, 1947; Bing Crosby, November 5, 1947; Carmen Miranda, November 19, 1947; and most of all, the reunion of Clayton, Jackson, and Durante on April 21, 1948.

Cantor and Durante reminisce about their Coney Island days. With Jimmy at the piano, the duo performs the 1912 vaudeville number "Row, Row, Row" that Cantor and many others had sung on stage. They do a Clayton, Jackson, and Durante routine, singing "I Can Do Without Broadway," Jimmy interrupting with, "Wait a minute, what happened? I musta passed my station!" Then there is a loud crash as Jimmy rips boards off the piano. Roy Bargy's orchestra strikes up and Jimmy sings "Liza" from Ziegfeld's *Show Girl*. Cantor and orchestra do Eddie's "Whoopee." All do "There's No Business Like Show Business." Durante finishes with "Who Will Be with You When I'm Far Away." An excellent show.

Bing Crosby always had a great love for Jimmy Durante and enjoyed doing vaudeville routines with him. Durante appeared as a guest on Crosby's *Philco Radio Time* five times from 1946 to 1949 on ABC. The funniest of those guest appearances was Crosby's show of December 4, 1946. Durante tried to sing Bing's theme song, "Where the Blue of the Night (Meets the Gold of the Day)," and "I Surrender Dear" as a duet. Bing, for his part, tackles Durante's theme song, "You Gotta Start Off Each Day with a Song," as part of a duet, and bravely sings without help Durante's "I'm Jimmy, the Well Dressed Man," changing it to "Crosby, the Well Dressed Man." The show closes with both singing "Blue Skies."

The Crosby guest spot on Durante's show is very good, but pales by comparison with this Crosby show episode. On his November 5, 1947 show, Durante plugs his new MGM film, *This Time for Keeps*, starring Esther Williams, "opening this week in theaters throughout the country," but he does not sing any of the several songs he did in that film. Instead he plugs "Chidabee," Crosby grabbing hold of the tail end of the song. Bing plugs *his* new film for Paramount, *The Road to Rio*. They join to sing "The Song's Gotta Come from the Heart," segueing into "Ochi Chornya," which Durante loved to interpolate into other songs, and back again to "The Song's Gotta...." Dorothy Lamour is announced as next week's guest.

Carmen Miranda and Jimmy Durante were made for each other. Their show of November 19, 1947, is hilarious. Before Carmen appears, Jimmy practices his Spanish with Howard Petrie. Petrie tells him the names he's practicing are just names of Los Angeles streets. Jimmy replies, "That's what I get for takin' lessons wid a bus driver!" He speculates that Carmen might need the name of a new gardener for her mountainous tutti-frutti hats, full of bananas, grapes, and apples. Carmen mispronounces English as well as Jimmy does. He tells her, "Your English isn't broken. It's badly bent." She sings "Banana Song"; they do a sketch about going to the British Consulate's high society ball and a comic duet, "Boom-de-boom," full of interruptions. They practice a dance for a possible invitation to the royal wedding of Prince Philip and then Princess Elizabeth.

(The royal wedding took place in Westminster Abbey on November 20, 1947.)

Clayton, Jackson, and Durante, reuniting for the April 21, 1948 show, go back 25 years to recreate the atmosphere at the Dover Club. They do "Bill Bailey," "I Can Do Without Broadway," "Jimmy, the Well Dressed Man," and "So I Ups to Him." As "straight relief," Peggy Lee sings a number. Victor Moore contributes. (A year later Clayton, Jackson, and Durante will perform for the Friars Club of California, April 16, 1949, sharing the stage with many other stars.)

Toward the end of the 1947-48 season Jackie Barnett joins the staff of writers, contributing new songs for Jimmy to mix in with his heavily worked oldies. Barnett would remain with Durante, increasingly important to his musical material, eventually becoming the associate producer of the television show after the departure of Phil Cohan, and producer of Durante's long-playing records made for Warner Bros. in the 1960s.

It was clear that many of the radio shows started to drag without Garry Moore. Toward the end of the 1947-48 season the writers came up with a new gimmick. A "Magic Carpet" sequence served as an umbrella for related sketches. Each program Jimmy would be whisked away someplace interesting, always begun by his singing a fragment from a new song, "Any State in the Forty-Eight is Great," written by Barnett and Durante. The Magic Carpet idea was continued into the next season, but wasn't very funny. Also added was the character of Hotbreath, at first called Hotbreath Houlihan, a sexy woman played by Florence Halop. She had been on the show occasionally before Garry Moore left, but is now listed as part of the regular cast. Garry recalls that there was an executive at Rexall named Houlihan, so the writers had to drop that name from the Hotbreath character.

The last show of the season contained a surprise. On the June 23, 1948, show, the Magic Carpet trip is to the old Palace Theatre and to the Copacabana. Jimmy speaks to Pierre, the French doorman at the Copa, using a phony French accent. Inside the Copa are Clayton and Jackson. The three sing "There'll Be Some Changes Made." Lou Clayton dances, Eddie Jackson sings. Durante thanks them and adds thanks to drummer Jack Roth. He announces this is his last show for Rexall, but he'll be back in the fall, at a new time. He thanks Rexall for three good years. He thanks his writers Lester White, Stanley Davis, Bud Pearson, Elon Packard, Harry Crane, "and my special song material writer, Jackie Barnett."

In the fall Durante was back working for Camel cigarettes, on Friday nights, with a new co-host, Alan Young, whose own radio show had gone off the air. The new show was called *The Jimmy Durante Show, with Alan Young*. The announcer was Verne Smith, replacing Howard Petrie. Candy Candido and Florence Halop were credited as part of the cast.

Using Alan Young as co-host was the Durante writers' effort to recapture the chemistry of Durante-Moore, but it didn't work. Alan Young said Durante would poke him and push him, trying to get him to be more aggressive. "Hit me, Youngie, hit me!" Durante wanted some of the aggressive interplay he had with Garry Moore. "When I couldn't be what Durante wanted, he reluctantly fired me. 'I gotta let ya go,' Jimmy said, genuinely saddened. He bawled me out just before he fired me. It clearly hurt him to let me go, but he knew and I knew that I was wrong for the role." Despite his being fired, Alan Young calls Durante "the dearest man in the world, gentle and genteel." When asked about the Magic Carpet sketches each week when he was co-host, Alan said they "didn't work." Alan Young went on to have his own shows again and maintained a long-term friendship with Durante associate Candy Candido.[32] When asked about Alan Young, Garry Moore commented, "You know, they made a mistake, and this is nothing against Alan Young. But what they were trying to do was recreate the old Durante-Moore show because Alan Young was young and fresh-looking. It was an unconscious feeling of let's get a younger guy. When Durante used to call me Junior—which wasn't a planned thing, it just happened—that was genuine. So what they were trying to do was recreate that atmosphere and you can't go home again."[33]

The 1948-49 season saw few guest stars and lots of Magic Carpet episodes. The show traveled to Dallas, Texas, for the second and third shows of the season, originating from the Dallas State Fair. Most shows now began not only with "You Gotta Start..." but also piggyback to that, "Inka Dinka Doo." In January 1949, the show, with ratings down, began to add guest stars: Ed Gardner of *Duffy's Tavern*, with Durante visiting *Duffy's Tavern* in reciprocation, Judy Canova, Crosby a second time, Jolson a second time, Hope a second time. After the week with Hope, April 1, 1949, Alan Young was dropped. The April 8, 1949 show was announced by Verne Smith as *The Jimmy Durante Show, with Don Ameche*. A highly skilled and polished Hollywood actor of the '30s and '40s, Don Ameche had had his own show on the air, developed from sketches he and singer Frances Langford had started on *The Charlie McCarthy Show*. Called "The Bickersons," sketches of a squabbling (bickering) married couple, it became an independent show in various forms on NBC, then CBS. Ameche now was called upon to fill out the remainder of the season for the Durante show, ending with the July 1, 1949 program.

Don Ameche returned as co-host for the final, 1949-50 season, which had no guest stars. Howard Petrie was back as the announcer. The cast of regulars was largely the same: Candy Candido with his voices and Florence Halop as Hotbreath, with the addition of Vera Vague for a comedic role. Ameche may have been a better foil for Durante than Alan Young, but not as appropriate a partner as Garry Moore. A few years later,

he would do a very funny Cyrano de Bergerac sketch with Durante on
Durante's television show (February 21, 1951), doing classic drama with
a slight twist. On the series' closing show, June 30, 1950, Durante thanked
"our writers, Norman Paul, Jack Elinson, Morris Freedman, and Bob
Schiller. And the young man who writes my songs, Jack Barnett. Then
there's our producer, Phil Cohan . . . and script assistant, Onnie Whizin."

After Garry Moore's departure, the audience that loved Durante in
the earliest days might have wondered why his production people did not
try Clayton and Jackson as regulars on the show, instead of looking for
other co-hosts. Or one might ask why weren't Clayton and Jackson used
from the start, in the 1930s? Why did Broadway, Hollywood, and radio all
push aside two-thirds of the very good vaudeville team? Why just a rare
guest shot on radio for Clayton and Jackson? Phil Cohan explains his view.

> Eddie Jackson was a sweet guy but not a great talent. He was what they
> call a coon shouter in those days. The one thing he did. Clayton was a
> dancer. They couldn't speak lines. I used them once. Eddie would come
> on sometimes, just for a bit, but he never spoke. And Clayton couldn't
> speak either. One time I think I had the two of them on one shot [April
> 21, 1948], but I fought doing it because to me this was old Broadway stuff.
> I kept Jimmy from doing those old, old things all the time. "I Can Do
> Without Broadway." By the time I was in radio, that's old stuff, old
> Broadway, and Garry Moore, this fresh young guy with a whole different
> wit, whole different contribution, so I deliberately didn't—so we gave
> Durante a whole fresh start. I guess I wasn't conscious of it at the time.
> We got great reviews.[34]

In the fall of 1950, Jimmy Durante would begin the biggest star performance of his career, first in black and white, then color, bringing his
Club Durant old-time material and new Jackie Barnett songs into the living rooms of all America, where he would warm the hearts of Americans
as few vaudeville performers surviving into the 1950s could. He was moving to NBC Television.

First, however, he had to endure the deep, deep heartache of the death
of his partner, manager, protector and friend, Lou Clayton. Cancer took
Clayton's life September 12, 1950, six weeks before Jimmy Durante went
on television for his first live show.[35] Jimmy felt that losing Lou was like
losing his own arms and legs. Loyal to his oldest friends both alive and
dead, Jimmy would use Eddie Jackson regularly on television as he could
not on radio, and always he would say, "Introducing Eddie Jackson, of
Clayton, Jackson, and Durante!"

Chapter 7

TELEVISION AND NIGHTCLUBS— RECREATING THE 1920S

Jimmy Durante went on television for the first time on NBC's *Four Star Revue*, a 60-minute variety comedy show originating from the International Theatre in New York, WNBT-TV, Wednesday night, 8:00 New York time, November 1, 1950. For the 1950-51 season, he was to be one of the program's four rotating hosts, the others being Ed Wynn, Danny Thomas, and Jack Carson. Since Durante was on only once a month, each of his shows could be much better written and planned than if he had a weekly show. Viewing kinescopes of the Durante television shows confirms how good they were: the viewer still laughs and is entertained after a lapse of over forty years. Seeing and hearing Durante are far more rewarding than just listening to Durante.

Commercial television began in 1941 with the granting of licenses to NBC and CBS for their New York stations. NBC got the call letters WNBT on channel one (later WRCA, changing again to WNBC, channel four) and CBS got WCBW on channel two (later WCBS).[1] The New York CBS station, in marking its 50th anniversary in 1991, noted that when it first began, "only 400 New Yorkers had television sets to receive the station's 15 hours of programming each week."[2] World War II stopped progress from this beginning. In 1944, Dumont received a license for a New York station, WABD (later WNEW, then WNYW, channel five).[3] NBC quickly took the lead. Hardly any network programming of significance to the development of comedy variety took place until 1948. That year NBC presented *Texaco Star Theater* starring Milton Berle; CBS presented *Toast of the Town*, starring Ed Sullivan (later *The Ed Sullivan Show*) and *Arthur Godfrey's Talent Scouts*; Dumont presented the *Original Amateur Hour*, with host Ted Mack,[4] which switched to NBC in the fall of 1949. In 1949, no new comedy variety shows of any importance appeared except the *Ed Wynn Show* on CBS; Wynn switched to the *Four Star Revue* on NBC the following fall. Then early in 1950 NBC began a comedy show as important as its Milton Berle program, *Your Show of Shows*, starring Sid Caesar and Imogene Coca, an ambitious 90-minute program every Saturday night. Later that year, NBC began the aforementioned *Four Star Revue*, with Jimmy Durante as one of its hosts; *The Colgate Comedy Hour*, with principal hosts for the first year of a long run, Eddie Cantor, Dean Martin and Jerry Lewis, and Fred Allen; and *You Bet Your Life*, a game show with permanent host Groucho Marx.

In 1949, Chicago became a television center linking the midwest with the east, and in September 1951, the link was completed to the west coast: the result was that the country for the first time had national television. Until the mid-1950s, NBC was dominant; CBS caught up and surpassed NBC at that time; ABC and Dumont struggled for survival far behind the leaders. It became clear that either ABC or Dumont would fail. Since some strength was still derived from the radio networks and all but Dumont had a radio network, it was Dumont that failed, going out of business in 1956. ABC was helped most by its success in attracting Walt Disney to its network in 1954. NBC helped itself enormously by bringing color to its network, and in the process selling RCA color television sets. And in the 1960s, videotape made pre-recorded television shows possible, replacing the excitement and the mistakes of live television.[5]

For the studio audience that attended NBC's *Four Star Revue*, a printed program was distributed, dividing the show into scenes with titles. The idea was to give the audience the feeling of having a real theatrical experience, like reading a *Playbill* for one of the many legitimate Broadway theaters nearby.[6]

For this first appearance of Jimmy Durante on television, the technical crew used an opening film montage, like a newsreel in a movie theater. We see people on telephones telling NBC they want Durante. There is a shot of Durante, unaware of the demand for his talents, soaking in his Beverly Hills swimmming pool. He is floating on an inner tube, cigar in mouth, reading a book. He answers a poolside phone. It's NBC telling him he's wanted in New York to do a TV show. He's not interested. He gets a second call. "Come in, Jimmy, we'll surround you with beautiful women." Jimmy cannot resist this offer. This time he says yes, he's coming to New York. We see Jimmy entering a car, the car speeding, then in a speeding train, then a speeding airplane. He descends from the plane. He's here! He's given a ticker tape parade up Broadway in a convertible, taking in the cheers of the crowds, right up to the NBC studios. "And here he is—Jimmy Durante!"

Jimmy sings "You Gotta Start Off Each Day with a Song," his longtime theme song from radio continuing as theme song on television. As he sings, Jack Roth gets up from his drums to interject, "Sing it, ha-ha, you're hot tonight!" Eddie Jackson comes on, "Sing it, Jimmy boy!" The band is in marching band uniforms. We see the camera of WNBT. People carry welcoming signs and pennants. A photographer takes Durante's picture. Durante stops his opening song to kick out an organ grinder and his monkey, telling them to get their own act. He tells a favorite story about bees seeing Durante's nose poking into the hive, with the punchline, "Run for the hills, boys, it's an anteater!"

Durante goes into the audience, sees a guy in the front row with a TV set. He grabs the set. "Nobody watches *The Goldbergs* while Durante's on!" Back on stage, he throws the TV. An overhead mike descends, startling him. "This is a fine time to get a tooth drilled. Get it away!" He finally finishes his opening song.

In the next scene Jimmy reads his contract, which an exasperated executive rolls out on the floor like a roll of toilet paper. "Now that I've signed it, I want to read it." The beautiful women promised come into the executive's office and make a fuss over Jimmy. He yells the opening line of a song he had used on stage in *Jumbo* in 1935, "Women," and jumps into his "Strut-Away" song from the 1940s, finishing off the scene with a modern new song, "I Beep When I Oughta Bop."

The scene shifts to Milwaukee, backstage at the Riverside Theater, where guest star Donald O'Connor greets Durante. They are there for the Milwaukee opening of their new film, *The Milkman*, November 3. Donald does some dancing in different styles, including a jump against a wall, a milder version of the very acrobatic jump he would do in *Singin' in the Rain*, for MGM, 1952. Durante tells his 1920s story "So I Ups to Him" to a stagehand, but without the music. Durante and O'Connor do a duet, "That's My Boy," used in *The Milkman*. Both strut off as the song ends. In a later scene, set back in New York at NBC, they do "It's Bigger Than Both of Us," another song from their film.

There are other scenes, then the segment that would be kept on all future shows as the next-to-last scene, the Club Durant. Here Durante and, as regular featured performer, his old partner Eddie Jackson, would each month run through some of the Clayton, Jackson, and Durante vaudeville and nightclub routines with the help of the beautiful chorus girls. Sometimes the evening's guest star would be invited into the Club Durant segment, but usually only guests like Sophie Tucker and Eddie Cantor, with genuine roots in vaudeville. Other stars, however talented, are usually kept in the middle of the show, not admitted to the Club.

On this premiere night, the Club Durant segment has eight beautiful dancing girls entering with ballet movements. Durante sings, "I'm Jimmy, That Well Dressed Man." He tries on different hats. He phones "En-zo"

Pinza, singing one note and only one note to him, "just to aggravate 'em."
He plays the piano, throwing a cushion at Jack Roth, then launches into
his famous specialty routine, "The Lost Chord." He destroys the piano,
and the band tosses sheet music, looking for the lost chord. Then Eddie
Jackson comes on. "Introducing my partner, Eddie Jackson, of Clayton,
Jackson, and Durante." Eddie goes into frenetic movements. Jimmy stops
him with, "This is a reunion, not an audition." Eddie sings tonight, and
each night he appears on the Club Durant segment, "Bill Bailey, Won't
You Please Come Home." Both Eddie and Jimmy strut off the stage.

This show, as all future Durante shows, ends with Durante alone on
stage, seated at the piano to sing in a touchingly sad voice the very simple
song written recently with Jackie Barnett, "Goodnight, Goodnight,"
working in a brief mention of "Inka Dinka Doo." Durante turns more fully
to the audience and says good night to everyone and adds, still in a sad
voice, "And good night, Mrs. Calabash, wherever you are." He puts on
his trenchcoat and retreats into the distance, from one spotlight to another
and another. This has much more impact than his effective radio closing.
It is without a doubt the best finish of any television show ever.

The newspaper reviews the day after Durante's television debut were
unanimously enthusiastic. *The New York Times* found, "The Schnozzle is
a TV smash! . . . For sixty minutes on Channel 4 there was bedlam and
hilarity. It was Durante at his very best. Durante, an old hand at working
in the confining quarters of nightclubs, found the intimacy of TV was right
down his alley. Always he was just himself—alternately clowning, singing,
dancing, rough-housing and rewriting the English language. For sheer ex-
uberance of the comic spirit it was something not to be missed."[7] The *New
York Journal-American* found, "About the only thing bigger than Jimmy
Durante's nose is his talent, and it's just as big on television as it ever was
in the saloons, on stage, screen and certainly much bigger than it ever
could be on the radio. His TV debut . . . was happy, wonderful, just about
comic perfection. If you can't see Jimmy where you can reach out and
touch him—and you want always to reach out and literally hug him, he's
that endearing a clown—then television is the answer we've all been
waiting for."[8] The *New York World-Telegram and Sun* was as impressed.
"Television today lies at the proud foot of a conquering hero, one James
Durante. His debut . . . proved that there's nothing wrong with this new
medium that old-time showmanship can't cure. Jimmy was magnificent.
The Durante vitality is staggering. Whether he is tearing the top off a
piano, rubbing noses with a pert little blonde or simply strutting away in
his cutaway, Jimmy is a great show. . . . Radio never gave us the Complete
Durante. The movies gave us even less. In television, you get the Durante
old-timers knew and loved. You get what Edmund Wilson described in
last week's *New Yorker* as the 'wild poetry' of a great personality."[9]

Durante was happy to have Eddie Jackson back working with him on a regular basis. Radio executives had considered Eddie too old-fashioned in style, and Jimmy couldn't convince them otherwise. When Durante went on television, according to Jackson, he didn't ask anyone's permission, just included his old vaudeville partner in the cast.[10]

Among the high points of that 1950-51 television season was the surprise hit combination of Helen Traubel, the great Wagnerian soprano at the Metropolitan Opera, and Jimmy Durante. She appeared the first of several times as guest on the Durante TV show November 29, 1950. Years before, when Durante's people were working on the radio show, they could hear the rehearsal at NBC of *Duffy's Tavern*. Phil Cohan says he heard a woman laughing and laughing. He looked. It was Helen Traubel. (She appeared on that show October 22, 1947.) Years later, the Durante staff was in New York to prepare for Jimmy's first TV show, with guest star Donald O'Connor. For the follow-up show, the writers wanted to do something with opera and knew that Traubel had a great sense of humor. Cohan got the William Morris office to book her.[11]

Helen Traubel wrote her own version of her first encounter with Jimmy Durante in her autobiography, *St. Louis Woman*.

> Durante, I understand, was as frightened and baffled by the proposition as I was. 'Sure, I know she can sing,' he said. 'What I wanna know, can she strut? Everybody around me hasta strut!'
> When I heard of this, it piqued my curiosity. I watched the program to find out what a strut was. I practiced it in private in my bedroom. I guess Durante was practicing his role of Siegfried while I was growling the blues. We were finally brought together and eyed each other with mutual suspicion. Finally Durante went over to the piano and commenced to play and sing. I followed him. We worked out a hilarious act which resulted in that first historic telecast late in 1950.[12]

On her first show with Durante, she sang "Brunnhilde's Battle Cry." When Durante saw her appear in full armor, he gasped, "Holy smoke, she's been drafted!" In a later scene, she and Jimmy did a duet on his turf. Did the audience expect him to sing Wagner? They did "The Song's Gotta Come from the Heart," and buried in the middle was the Russian folk song, "Ochi Chornya" ("Dark Eyes"). Durante then performed "Toscanini, Iturbi and Me," his old song alternately titled "Toscanini, Stokowski and Me," that brags none of these great musicians can really play great piano, while he, Durante, can.

Traubel's appearance with Durante drew thousands of approving letters from Durante and Traubel fans, though a few opera buffs sniffed at her lack of dignity. For her part, Traubel felt good that people liked her, not only for her voice, but for her personality.[13]

Helen Traubel handles comedy as well as opera with Durante and Eddie Jackson on NBC, April 11, 1953.

After the show moved from the International Theatre to the Center Theatre, still in New York, Helen Traubel played her return engagement with Durante, January 24, 1951. When Helen tells Jimmy she hasn't warmed up her voice yet, he tells her to go ahead and "vulcanize" [vocalize]. She sings "Voi lo sapete" from Mascagni's *Cavallera Rusticana*. A later scene has Jimmy conducting Traubel in concert, a maestro waving a baton in front of a symphony orchestra. He is wearing a Stokowski look-alike white wig, long wild hair flowing in all directions. Traubel asks him, "Why the wig?" He replies, "Hair's gotta toss." She says she will sing an aria from *Lohengrin*. They fuss and joke about who's going to do what. She appropriates Durante's line and routine, "This is a catastastroke," appearing annoyed, and grabs the sheet music, throwing it at the orchestra. Jimmy stops her. "Please, Madame Traubel, please. You're supposed to *follow* the music, not throw it all over the joint!" Finally they perform "A Real Piano Player," with "Bill Bailey" interpolated, ending back with the original song.

Traubel's appearances with Durante were so successful that RCA Victor recorded their two duets, "The Song's Gotta Come from the Heart" and "A Real Piano Player," releasing them March 1951 on their *classical* series of Red Seal 12-inch 78s and Red Seal 45s. Traubel was to appear as a guest with Durante again the 1951-52 season, October 6 and December 29, 1951. This was to be followed by one more appearance with him, April 11, 1953.

The Durante-Traubel chemistry was so great that in 1954 they organized an act to play Las Vegas. That city of casinos and nightclubs, jaded by so much great talent, saw something really special.

For the February 21, 1951 show, Durante reunited with Don Ameche, who had been his capable co-host on radio, after Garry Moore and Alan Young. This was like moving from the Metropolitan Opera to the Comédie Française for classical drama. Jimmy plays Cyrano de Bergerac, poet and soldier, to Don Ameche's Christian de Neuvillette, a clumsy young soldier. Both are in love with Roxane, but only Cyrano has a big nose. Elsewhere in the show Don Ameche joins Eddie Jackson and Durante in singing, perhaps in three musketeers' style, Durante's "Who Will Be with You When I'm Far Away."

Durante gets an excellent opportunity to match his mangling of the English language with Carmen Miranda's when she appears as a guest on his March 21, 1951 show, returning March 7, 1953, and to rehearse for a third appearance, August 1955. A very popular singer and comedienne in 1940s musicals for 20th Century Fox, she had appeared with Don Ameche and Betty Grable in her film debut, *Down Argentine Way* (1940); *That Night in Rio* (1941), with Don Ameche again, and Alice Faye; *Weekend in Havana* (1941), with Alice Faye and John Payne; her best role of all, *The Gang's All Here* (1943), with Alice Faye, Phil Baker, and Benny Goodman and his Orchestra; among several others. Doing her first Durante show, she sings in Portuguese "Chica Chica Boom Chic" and "Tico Tico." Jimmy tells her he will sing a romantic song in *her* language. She spouts Portuguese at him and tells him in Eeengleesh, "Hey, Schnozzola, you're hot stuff!" Then she sings an English song by this title, as a duet with Jimmy. She says they'll be a hit, the new dancing team from Brazil, Miranda and Duranda. On her second Durante show, another guest is Cesar Romero. With Durante they sing the Latin-flavored "Miranda, Romero and Gomez." Carmen sings several Portuguese songs, including "Cuanto le Gusta," into which Durante interjects his version of the language, "Inka inka inka."

Carmen Miranda's work on her third Durante show, for NBC's Saturday night *Texaco Star Theatre*, showed her chemistry with Durante better than ever. From an unauthorized recording made from the August 1955 filming,[14] the listener can get some idea of the kind of material and fun Carmen Miranda and Jimmy Durante were able to work out. Carmen worked hard in the rehearsal and taping, including a slight revision of a song she did before with Durante, "Jackson, Miranda, and Gomez." She did a sketch in which Durante met her at the boat after he had booked her as a performer for his Club Durant. She arrives in plain clothes, uncharacteristic of her flamboyant reputation. She and Jimmy embrace. She asks him, "How's my little *cucaracha?*" He answers, "How's my *bonas noches?*" Durante's people wanted her to speak Spanish so Spanish-speaking people in the United States could understand, but for the most part she refused to give up her Portuguese. She did do some rapid-fire sentences in Carioca slang.[15] In the sketch, Jimmy lets her use his apartment, which the landlord forbad him to sublet. She says not to worry, she will be "as quiet as a moose." She sings a few notes, practicing what she calls her "vulcanizing." Jimmy compliments her that her English is getting to be as good as his. Her rendition of the first lines of "To Be or Not to Be" proves the kind of lock on the English language she has. Durante asks her who wrote that. She answers "Xavier Cugat." She sings a few notes of "Delicado" and "Cuanto le Gusta" better than Shakespeare could have. She seemed out of breath, but no one thought anything of it. Back in her Beverly Hills home that night, the lady with the tutti-frutti hat and other wild costuming collapsed and died, the victim of a coronary occlusion.[16]

Although the last guest appearance of Carmen Miranda was filmed in August 1955, that show was not televised until two months after her death, October 15, 1955, repeated July 27, 1957.

One effective regular segment of the Durante television show in later seasons involved interplay between Durante and the Bil Baird puppet shaped in Durante's image, called Conscience. With Bil Baird pulling the strings and Jackie Barnett imitating Durante's voice, many charming scenes were developed. The first appearance of Bil (and Cora) Baird and puppets (not the Durante puppet) occurred on the Christmas-New Year's show of December 27, 1950. The guest that night was Luba Malina. She joked and sang with Durante, but the show was stolen by the interaction between Durante and the puppets. Jimmy sings "(Isn't It a Shame That) Christmas Comes but Once a Year," a song he had sung in his film *The Great Rupert*, plays with children, singing "Falderoll" as they dance about him, the fireplace, the Christmas tree, and opened presents. The puppets perform, imitating Bing Crosby, the Andrews Sisters, and Eddie Cantor. A puppet kisses Jimmy's nose and does somersaults. Jimmy sings to the puppet "Put Yourself in My Hands."

The inaugural 1950-51 season ended with two programs featuring guest stars from the old days of vaudeville. On the April 18, 1951, show, the guest was Sophie Tucker, the last of the red-hot mommas, singer of torch songs and unrequited love. On the May 16, 1951, show, the guests were Fred Allen, the vaudeville and radio wit, and Eddie Cantor. Sophie, who made famous her theme song "Some of These Days" and used it as the title of her autobiography, and Cantor, who was unable to continue the great successes of 1920s vaudeville and 1930s radio, or the relatively minor success of 1930s movies, were both welcomed into the rarified nostalgic confines of the Club Durant.

Sophie Tucker's act was singing her advice to potential lovers and despairing aging women. On Jimmy's show, accompanied by her own piano player, Ted Shapiro, she sings "It's Never Too Late." Jimmy does a few Charleston steps with her and asks her age. She replies only that she's over 40. He goes into an auctioneer's spiel, "I hear 40, do I hear 45, who'll say 50?" When he reaches 65, he says, "Sold to an antique dealer." Later, at the Club Durant, the orchestra plays her theme song, and she and Jimmy do a few lines of "Darktown Strutters' Ball," an old "coon" song. Sophie sings the old minstrel-vaudeville chestnut "Alabamy Bound," then "There's So Much to Do in So Little Time," and ends with "Some of These Days" before exiting. She shows Durante and Jackson that she can strut with the best.

Fred Allen plays two sketches with Durante, one in which Jimmy packs for a trip to Fred's lodge in Maine, and the other at the lodge. Fred, a master of incisive insult humor, tells Jimmy he thought Jimmy's nose was a pickle on the lunch special, "the first pickle I ever saw breathing." They do a song, "(If You've Got) Personality." Fred plays a clarinet, and Jimmy tells him to smile. Fred can't do both at the same time. Says Jimmy, "To have personality, you've gotta do both." Radio listeners, and those few who saw his six movies, will remember that Fred Allen's public image was never ever to smile, like Buster Keaton's trademark deadpan expression. At the cabin in Maine, Durante tells Fred he can't go hunting for rabbits because he doesn't have the heart to shoot them. Says Jimmy, "Any animal with little beady eyes must be on my side."

On the show with Fred Allen, Eddie Cantor is left for the Club Durant segment, as usual just before Durante's good night. After the Durante Girls do a production number, Durante sings "She's a Little Bit This and a Little Bit That." Eddie Cantor enters when Eddie Jackson is announced, "Introducing my partner, Eddie Jackson, of Clayton, Jackson, and Durante!" The orchestra hits "Waiting for the Robert E. Lee" and Cantor, not Jackson, comes out to sing it. Jimmy is surprised. Cantor tells Jimmy he's always wanted to work in the Club Durant. Cantor then sings Jimmy's theme song, "You Gotta Start..." and leaves. Then Eddie Jackson does enter, singing "Is It True What They Say About Dixie?"

For the 1951-52 season, the show was renamed the *All Star Revue*, moved by NBC to Saturday nights, still at the Center Theatre in New York. (After the November 3, 1951 show, the Durante show would originate from the El Capitan Theatre in Hollywood.) The number of hosts for the weekly comedy variety hour expanded beyond the original four. Durante, Ed Wynn, Danny Thomas, and Jack Carson would continue as hosts, but as the audience program read, added would be Olsen & Johnson "and five other great stars." The first season's sponsors had been Motorola TV, Norge (electrical appliances), and Pet milk. This season's sponsors would be Kellogg's (cereals), Snow Crop (frozen foods), and Pet milk.

The core of the Durante staff changed somewhat this season. Phil Cohan left as associate producer, wanting more work than just one show a month. He was replaced by Jackie Barnett, who until now had been credited only for writing special lyrics and music. Roy Bargy continued as musical director, Charles Isaacs and Jack Elinson as chief writers, and Joseph Santley as producer and director. Added to the credits effective the December 1 show was Aida Broadbent for her choreography. Continuing as the core of the Club Durant entertainers were Jimmy Durante, Eddie Jackson, Jack Roth, Jules Buffano, and sometimes Candy Candido.

Another appearance by Helen Traubel began the 1951-52 season October 6, 1951. Their duets were "Our Voices Were Meant for Each Other" and "Waiting for the Robert E. Lee." Earlier in the show the Bil Baird puppet, Conscience, in the image of Durante, made its first, unbilled, appearance.

Just as the previous season's surprise hit had been the Durante-Traubel magic, this season's surprise hit was Durante with the President's daughter, Margaret Truman. A headline in the New York *Daily Mirror* read "To Schnoz She's Mag-nificent: Miss Truman Scores as TV Comic."[17] Harry S Truman was tough, able to take criticism on any political subject. He was fond of saying, "If you can't stand the heat, stay out of the kitchen." But when it came to his daughter's singing, he was thin-skinned, blasting any music critic who found his daughter's talents of less than professional quality. But he had no need to worry when Margaret appeared with Jimmy Durante. True to his reputation, he was kind, and she was, contrary to what some critics said, very good, given her lack of stage experience. Like Traubel, she enjoyed coming off the pedestals on which others had placed her, one from the Metropolitan Opera and one from the White House. And like Traubel, she and Durante would later make nightclub appearances together. Miss Truman enjoyed her first Durante appearance so much she wrote a thank-you note to writer Charles Isaacs[18] and accepted a return engagement later that season.

Jimmy had a way of charming all the women and making them look good on his show; he scored a coup other show hosts could not have in attracting the President's daughter. On her first appearance with Durante, November 3, 1951, Jimmy began by calling her Miss Truman, but within seconds, he began calling her Maggie. Before she's loose enough to do any crazy business with Jimmy, she sings the folk song she must have rehearsed many times for the show, "I Know Where I'm Going." Jimmy and Maggie do a sketch set on a college campus. Margaret is to present an honorary degree at Barnum College (in Washington, DC) to James Francis Durante. He gives an acceptance speech, short but loaded with big words, any one of which could be a land mine for his untrustworthy tongue. Then the two sing, "Why Didn't You Tell Me Before." On her return appearance, March 22, 1952, Margaret Truman again sings one straight number, "One Kiss," before doing a sketch with Durante. On a mock panel show called "Thirst for Knowledge," moderated by Jimmy, she does some funny business with the "I Like Ike" Republican slogan that was ubiquitous in the 1952 presidential campaign year. In a moment of imagination gone wild, she becomes part of the act, Truman, Jackson, and Durante. She twirls a cane and sings "Chidabee, Chidabee, Chidabee (Yah! Yah! Yah!)."

Both appearances of Margaret Truman got much newspaper publicity. *Variety* reported on her second appearance, "What the Schnoz put over, no other comic would have even tried, that of having Margaret Truman fill out the lettering on a blackboard so it will read, 'I Like Ike.' Not bad, eh?"[19]

Variety went on to question whether Margaret's dad knew what she was going to do and whether he gave his approval. The sponsors did not know in advance the "I Like Ike" business that writers Charles Isaacs and Jack Elinson had dreamed up, a daring gag in the face of sponsors wanting to maintain political neutrality. Someone snapped the "I Like Ike" written on a blackboard, with Truman's daughter next to it, sneaked it out, and distributed it to newspapers across the country by Associated Press wirephoto.[20]

Following his coup with Margaret Truman, Durante, really on a hot streak, with great writers, production values, and top guests, coaxed a reluctant Bette Davis to make her first television appearance. Durante's assistant to the producer, Bill Harmon, was a friend of Bette's husband, Gary Merrill, and that connection helped. Like Margaret Truman, Bette enjoyed her experience with Jimmy.

On the night of April 19, 1952, the very popular Academy Award–winning actress spoke her first words on network television. She enters in the second half of the show, in what the studio audience program says is scene 4: "Jimmy Buys Pet Milk to Take on Trip." She's not listed for that scene but appears in a supermarket where Jimmy is shopping. Her first words are, "I'll take two cans of Pet milk!"[21] Hardly Oscar material.

The sketch with Bette Davis imagines what life would be like if they were married to each other and purports to show their budding romance in the fourth grade of public school, then in college. Once married, they quarrel. She's resentful that he made her give up her career and she hasn't won an Oscar in months. Jimmy shoots a row of Bette's Oscars like so many ducks in a shooting gallery. She throws champagne at his portrait.

They decide to separate, splitting their holdings, including the piano, which they rip into two pieces.

Durante could work well with so many different types of women, as long as he avoided seriously sexy sirens. He did well with such types as fractured English comic singers Lupe Velez and Carmen Miranda, big-tonsilled Broadway and opera stars Ethel Merman and Helen Traubel, aristocratic ladies of stage and screen Bette Davis and Tallulah Bankhead—Tallulah called him "my knight in armor"[22]—and a President's daughter with pure amateur charm. On his show of December 1, 1951, his first show from Hollywood at the El Capitan Theatre, Durante works well with the great star of stage and screen, Ethel Barrymore. In addition to a sketch, they do a duet, "There's a Place in the Theatre for You," written by Jackie Barnett and Durante, with the interpolation of "Who Will Be with You When I'm Far Away."

The show Durante did with Bette Davis was the last show of the season. Durante and his troupe, plus fiancee Margie Little, would sail April 23 on the *Queen Elizabeth* for a European tour, primarily a four-week engagement at London's Palladium,[23] opening May 5. The sketch early in the April 19, 1952 show, perhaps the best sketch of the season, deals with preparations for that trip. Jack Roth is yelling at Candy Candido, "Push, push, we've been trying to close the suitcase for an hour." Jules Buffano watches. Another trunk has a sticker marked "England." Durante asks, "Who put that sticker there?" Buffano answers, "I did." Durante yells, "Take it off. We're not going to *England*. We're going to *London*! Dese guys don't know nuttin' about geology!"

Continuing the sketch, the man from the Department of Immigration arrives to give Durante his passport and has Durante push his finger on an ink pad and transfer the print to the passport. "That's the best identification you can have," the official says. "That's the best identification you can have?" echoes Durante. To show the man that he's wrong, Durante puts ink on his nose and presses the nose on the passport. The startled official asks, "What are you doing?" Durante responds, "We're travelin' together, but I don't want my nose stopped at the border."

Durante's puppet, Conscience, wants to go on the trip but can't. They sing a duet, "I Like People." Durante's gang continue their packing. A doctor arrives to give immunization shots to Durante. Jimmy tells Candy Candido, "Candy, you go first to warm up the needle." The doctor chases Candy. With amazing acrobatics and a bit of trickery, Candy climbs the wall behind a recessed bookcase, in a space just wide enough to place his hands and feet, climbing horizontally. Candy describes this scene.[24] "I was a tumbler and a pretty strong-looking guy in those days, you know. I used to do some pretty good stunts. [As the doctor is chasing me] I run up the wall, like a doorway—16 feet high—they built it for me—I'm up there

Lassie noses Durante out by an undisclosed margin in an off-the-set publicity photo from *Two Sisters from Boston* **(MGM, 1946).**

hands and feet. Durante screams, 'Come on down! Take it like a man!' That's when the doctor says, 'Don't worry, Mr. Durante, I've got just the thing for that.' He opens his bag and takes out a telescope needle. So, the guy's about to shoot me, and I pushed. Let me tell you, when a comic sees he can get a laugh he'll do anything. Well, I pushed the set because I feel it's giving away. And I did a pratfall from 16 feet to the floor. Now the doctor's laughing, the cameraman's laughing." When Candy is back on the ground, the doctor jabs him on the knee or leg. Candy says, "He jabbed me mighty low," in his famous bass voice.

Candy recalls that when he got back to his dressing room, Jimmy came up to him and said, "Hey, kid, come in here. That was the funniest thing I seen in my life. The longest laugh I've ever heard. But you know sumtin'? You'll never do it again." Candy, while loving Jimmy, felt Durante was holding him back, not giving him enough to do on most of the shows, and not allowing him to work for anyone else. Jack Benny had wanted Candy to do some work for him, he says, but after Durante spoke to Benny, the offer disappeared. Candy and others who worked with Durante speculated that he wanted to keep his "family" together, with Jimmy offering work and money in exchange for loyalty from them in never crossing him up. Eventually Candy got tired of working with Durante and left him, going on to work as a voice animator for Walt Disney and Roy Disney in a new career spanning 33 years.

This same year there was a report that Paramount Pictures wanted to make the life of Jimmy Durante, buying the movie rights to Fowler's book. Durante's agent, Abe Lastfogel of the William Morris Agency, and Don Hartman, production supervisor at Paramount, had several talks about this. Other studios were said to be interested too. Jimmy would play himself in the film.[25] It is clear how marketable Durante had been made by his success in television, following his success in radio. His nationwide popularity at this stage of his career clearly came not from the movies he continued to make but from his excellent television shows, capturing the immediacy and charm of his nightclub performances which only a relatively few well-to-do patrons had seen from the early days and would continue to see through the '50s and '60s.

The 1952-53 television season, the last for the *All Star Revue*, began for Durante with the show of September 20, 1952. Kellogg and Pet milk continued as sponsors, joined by Del Monte Foods. Bill Harmon was now associate producer, Jackie Barnett back to billing for his songs. Sam Fuller was executive producer, working with Joseph Santley, who continued as producer and director. Receiving billing for the first time were Wanda Smith's Cover Girls. The guest star for the third time was Margaret Truman, plus Phil Harris. On this program Margaret shows an "I Like Durante" button, a take-off on the "I Like Ike" political buttons. Durante plugs the book *The Candidate: A Photographic Interview with the Honorable James Durante*. Compiled by French photographer Philippe Halsman and others, the just-published book poses political questions to Durante and answers are photographic reactions without any words.[26] Phil Harris, a veteran of radio with wife Alice Faye, sings "The Preacher and the Bear." Durante and Truman sing "The Candidate," a song in which they agree

Durante will run for President and Truman (Margaret) for Vice President. Jimmy stops the music to take a phone call from Washington. Mr. Truman says it is okay to carry out their plans as long as Jimmy brings Margaret home early.

Later guests with Durante that season were Frank Sinatra, Fifi D'Orsay, Lily Pons, Sophie Tucker, Linda Darnell, Vic Damone, Ezio Pinza, Carmen Miranda, Cesar Romero, Helen Traubel, Rose Marie, and Gene Fowler.

Durante and Sinatra had worked well on radio and in their one movie together. They continued to work well on television. Sinatra visited shows hosted by Durante on October 18, 1952, and November 8, 1953, and Durante was guest on Frank's ABC-TV variety special, *The Frank Sinatra Timex Show*, October 19, 1959. Durante walked onto Sinatra's show in a surprise appearance near the end of a tribute to Clayton, Jackson, and Durante. Sinatra was playing Lou Clayton; Bing Crosby, Eddie Jackson; Dean Martin, Jimmy Durante. They had sung "You Gotta Start Off Each Day with a Song," "Who Will Be with You When I'm Far Away," "Inka Dinka Doo," and "Bill Bailey, Won't You Please Come Home." On the last number, Mitzi Gaynor joined in, then Durante himself, for the climax of the whole show.[27]

The Durante show with Sinatra's first appearance was also the first Durante show to be televised from the new NBC-TV studios in Burbank. Also guesting on the program was the French-Canandian star Fifi D'Orsay. Sinatra takes part in four of eight scenes, including the show's nostalgia segment, the Club Durant. Fifi D'Orsay is in two scenes, one set in Paris, the other at the Club Durant. Candy Candido recalls that in Sinatra's first scene, "Jimmy Has a Haircut?," "Jack Elinson told me we need something to add to the Durante-Sinatra sketch. Both come into my barbershop at the same time. Both say 'I'm first.' I sez, 'Don't worry, I'll take care of both of you.' So I set them both in the chairs, turn the chairs around and put both heads together. Now I've got the comb in one hand, the scissors in the other. Jimmy looks at me and says, 'Whatcha doin'?' I sez, 'Don't worry, Mr. Durante. I'll never touch your eyebrows. It's the only dependable hair you got!' This was the funny line I gave the guys [the writers Charles Isaacs and Jack Elinson]. They liked it so much they gave me a box of $20 cigars. The next day we have a review—a dress rehearsal, scripts in hand. [Taking the line for himself] Durante messes it up [and the joke is ruined]."[28]

In this same barbershop scene Jimmy tries to interest Sinatra in doing a movie about "The Durante Story," telling Frank he'd be right for the part of Durante as a young man. In a later scene, the real Sheilah Graham does a mock Hollywood gossip telecast about Frank Sinatra playing Jimmy Durante in a forthcoming movie. Sinatra enters as the young Jimmy, saying he's been playing piano at Coney Island and made three bucks. Jimmy, playing his own "dad" tells his "son" to give up piano and work together in the barbershop, "Bartolomeo and Son." Sinatra at the piano starts to play Jimmy's "She's a Little Bit This and a Little Bit That." Jimmy stops him, calling it junk. Then Frank starts "Who Will Be with You When I'm Far Away." Jimmy throws the piano board. Frank says that's a great idea, he can throw boards at the band. As he sings and throws boards, Jimmy remarks, "I've created a frankenfurter!" Durante and Sinatra do a duet on Durante's "Sing Soft," interpolating lines from other Durante songs, "First you tip your hatta" and "You start to turna." This is an excellent, joyfully nostalgic entertainment, and the show not yet to the climactic Club Durant segment. The chemistry of Sinatra and Durante together in vaudeville routines is a wonder to behold.

For the show of January 31, 1953, with guest stars Ezio Pinza and Fifi D'Orsay, the Durante show contributed an innovation to television. Script writer Charles Isaacs described the first use of a two-story set.[29] In the sketch, Pinza is a singing waiter, singing in his bathtub on an upper floor, while the noise drives his downstairs neighbor, Durante, in the company of his girlfriend, Fifi D'Orsay, to bang on the pipes. In desperation, Durante unscrews the pipes, and the tub drops through the ceiling, winding up in Durante's apartment below. Fifi winds up kissing Pinza. Aside from the technology, Charles Isaacs says, "Lots of TV shows picked up on vaudeville sketches and burlesque and silent films, but with a fresh slant." In a later scene, "Pinza's Lament," Durante, Jackson, and Pinza sing "I Want to Be Eddie Jackson." Jackson sings one of the oldies in his repertoire, "After You've Gone," until the song is taken over by Pinza trying to be Eddie Jackson.

On February 5, 1953, Jimmy Durante was presented an Emmy award as best television comedian of 1952. Other nominees were Sid Caesar, Wally Cox, Jackie Gleason, and Herb Shriner. A separate award was given for best comedienne, to Lucille Ball. At the same ceremony Durante was nominated in the category of "Outstanding Personality," but lost to Bishop Fulton J. Sheen. Other nominees for that honor were Lucille Ball, Arthur Godfrey, Edward R. Murrow, Donald O'Connor, and Adlai Stevenson.

The last show of the season and the last for the *All Star Revue*, April 11, 1953, has Helen Traubel again, as wonderful as ever, plus Gene Fowler, author of *Schnozzola*, to introduce the change of scenes, and Rose Marie, who imitates Durante, sitting at the piano and singing "The Lost Chord."

The Colgate Comedy Hour was NBC's big-budget attempt to challenge the dominance of CBS' Sunday night *The Ed Sullivan Show*, running from 8 to 9. The Sullivan show was television's most successful long-term recreation of typical vaudeville bills that, if good enough, played the Palace: it was better than ABC's 1960s *Hollywood Palace* (1964–70, mostly on Saturday nights), partly because of the low-key commentary and experience of Ed Sullivan, and the familiarity of his predictable personality in living rooms every Sunday night.

The Colgate show was, like the *All Star Revue*, composed largely of comedy sketches, with different comedy stars as hosts. *The Ed Sullivan Show*, if you include its earliest programs as *Toast of the Town*, ran on Sunday nights from June 1948 through June 1971, from March 1949 onward always 8 to 9 o'clock. This was a remarkable run with no changes. Durante appeared often on the Sullivan show in the 1960s and hosted *The Hollywood Palace* a few times as well as appearing as a guest on it. *The Colgate Comedy Hour* ran on NBC from September 10, 1950 through December 25, 1955, always opposite Sullivan, to its detriment. Jimmy Durante was the most frequent host the 1953-54 season, appearing with the same monthly regularity as on the *All Star Revue*.

The guests Durante worked with on the Colgate show that season included John Wayne, Frank Sinatra, Ethel Merman, Paul Douglas, Eartha Kitt, Tallulah Bankhead, Carol Channing, Eddie Cantor, Robert Montgomery, Patrice Munsel, Liberace, Marilyn Maxwell, and for the last show of the season, Shelley Winters. Again writing sketches for the Durante entourage and guests were Charles Isaacs and Jack Elinson, with some new Durante songs written by Jackie Barnett alone or in collaboration with Jimmy. Bill Harmon continued as associate producer and Joseph Santley produced and staged the show.

There was not one bad show in the lot. The pattern was set in the *All Star Revue*: the Durante routines and songs, interaction with one or two guests, a Club Durant segment, and Durante's good night. The shows continued much the same, with excellent family entertainment values: funny, touching, wholesome, and uplifting to young and old.

Jimmy Durante's next major television adventure after one season on *The Colgate Comedy Hour* came in the fall of 1954 with the *Texaco Star Theater* on NBC. Milton Berle had been the host from 1948 through 1953, a great comedian finally worn down by the weekly exposure. On radio a comedian could last forever it seemed, but not on television. As Durante put the TV problem, "How many tricks has a guy got, after all? And ya' can't keep doin' the same thing week after week." The most Durante felt he could handle was twice a month.[30] During the 1954-55 season, *The Jimmy Durante Show* would alternate with *The Donald O'Connor Show*. Both programs were 30 minutes—Durante would have preferred a full hour to develop continuity—while Berle had done 60-minute shows. The Durante show was presented live while the O'Connor show was on film. The 1955-56 season saw Donald O'Connor dropped and *The Jimmy Durante*

Show presented weekly. The earlier Durante format was condensed into just the Club Durant. Candy Candido was gone, except for an occasional reappearance, and writer Charles Isaacs left, leaving his chief co-writer, Jack Elinson, to work with Arthur Stander on scripts. The cast of old regulars was Durante, Eddie Jackson, Jules Buffano, and Jack Roth. The show, which first aired October 2, 1954, was produced by Bill Harmon; original words and music by Jackie Barnett; musical director, Roy Bargy; choreography by Aida Broadbent (for the group called the Durante Girls).

Among the guest stars who appeared with Durante on the *Texaco Star Theatre* was Donald O'Connor, on Durante's premiere show. Durante reciprocated the following week by appearing on Donald's show, sharing the guest turn with Mitzi Gaynor. Other Durante guests on his show that season were Jean Hagen and Rusty Hamer (who on *The Danny Thomas Show* played Danny's wife and son, respectively), Vivian Blaine (who recreated her role of Adelaide from the Broadway show and movie, *Guys and Dolls*), Margaret Truman, Lauritz Melchior, George Raft (who did some of his old song-and-dance routines from vaudeville and played a gangster trying to take over the Club Durant), Marilyn Maxwell, Lisa Kirk, comedienne Pat Carroll, Peter Lawford, Patty Andrews (of the Andrews Sisters), George Jessel (who recalled vaudeville and old New York), Dorothy Lamour, Janet Blair, Barbara Whiting (sister of Margaret Whiting), and Cass Daley.

The second season, 1955-56, saw singer Toni Arden, ex-boxing champ Max Baer, Jose and Amparo Iturbi, Carmen Miranda (post-humously), opera star Marguerite Piazza, Jeannie Carson (English singer), Peter Lawford, Peggy Lee, Betty Hutton, Polly Bergen, Vivian Blaine, Jane Froman, George Raft, Tab Hunter, Liberace (twice, very funny in a piano duel with Durante), Milton Berle (who does a duet with Durante, "There's No Business Like the Pizza Business"), Robert Mitchum (tough-guy actor who makes his singing debut), Esther Williams, Charles Laughton, Charles Boyer, Ernest Borgnine (Oscar winner for *Marty*, who makes a singing debut in duets with Durante), George Jessel, opera star Patrice Munsel, Johnny Ray, Connie Russell, Marilyn Maxwell, and Lisa Kirk.

When Durante completed his two-season run for Texaco he bought some or all of those programs, and the live shows preserved as kinescopes ran again June 29 through September 21, 1957, sponsored by Old Gold cigarettes on CBS, summer replacement for Jackie Gleason.

Earlier that year, on March 17, 1957, many stars gathered for an Entertainment Industry Tribute to Jimmy Durante, sponsored by the Jewish Theatrical Guild of America. Held at New York's Waldorf-Astoria, it was a $50-a-plate benefit for needy show business people. George Jessel was toastmaster and narrator for a staged dramatization, "The Jimmy Durante Story," featuring 25 celebrities. Durante and Eddie Jackson performed, as did Garry Moore, and Jackie Barnett wrote a song for the occasion, "The Ballad of Jimmy Durante."[31]

After his regularly scheduled shows for Texaco, Durante made guest appearances on other shows, and for the network's 1959-60 season NBC gave him two specials of his own: *An Evening with Durante*, on September 25, 1959, and *Give My Regards to Broadway*, December 6, 1959. Durante complained that the sponsors and their advertising agencies were getting too powerful and doing the wrong thing: they insisted on putting too many guest stars on the show, with each star expected to get a solo turn and a turn with Durante, and they wanted to keep Eddie Jackson off. Also, the momentum of the show was interrupted too often with commercials. "Nobody's got time ta do nothin'." In the old days when he had just one guest per show, like Traubel, the show was much better.[32]

All through the years of radio and television, reaching out to a national audience more successfully than with motion pictures, Jimmy Durante continued to enjoy most of all the sense of really touching a live audience as he had in nightclubs. The Club Durant on television was fine, but performances in real nightclubs were even better. Durante played the best: the Chez Paree in Chicago, the Copacabana in New York, the Desert Inn in Las Vegas, the Riverside in Reno, Copa City in Miami, and many others.

The listings of Jimmy Durante's nightclub appearances from the 1940s through the 1960s are spotty in the absence of thorough scrapbooks or logs of bookings through the William Morris Agency or other sources that would have kept such records. What information there is comes primarily from newspaper clippings in the Billy Rose Collection of the New York Public Library at Lincoln Center and from the scrapbook maintained by Jack Roth, Durante's drummer through most of their joint careers.

In 1943, after having played theatrical engagements with Eddie Jackson the previous year—eight weeks in Brooklyn, Boston, Hartford, Providence, and Pittsburgh (while Lou Clayton recuperated from a car accident), Durante fulfilled several nightclub engagements. At the time of Jeanne's death, he was in the midst of a 14-week run at the Copacabana, with Roy Bargy having joined his group.

Columnist Earl Wilson reviewed Durante's 1943 Copacabana revue, incredibly his first nightclub appearance since 1931. Durante throws sheet music at the musicians, hurls a piano top at Ted Straeter; the orchestra leader, throws his cigar at the musicians, plays a piano duet with Straeter, and in mock anger for Straeter's playing too well, throws parts of the piano at him, just like the old days with Clayton and Jackson. Jackson, as usual, is included on some of their old vaudeville songs. At one point, Durante helps a ringside table find a woman's glove and gets everyone in on the search; for a "big shot" having champagne with his girl, Jimmy tried to get a two-cent refund on the deposit for the empty bottle.[33]

New York newspapers ran advertisements for Durante's New Year's Eve show at the Copacabana. "Don't get nosed out for New Year's Eve." There was a photo of Durante with Carmen Miranda–style headdress and golf-ball-size earrings and a demure, eyes-downcast smile, with the words "T'anks, Fellers! Your woids trill me, but I maintains me attichude!" Durante was to perform three shows—at 8, 12, and 2 a.m.[34]

It was at the Copa that Jimmy met Margie Little, an attractive young redhead from Plainfield, New Jersey. In an interview, she tells a reporter for *TV Radio Mirror*, "We met in 1944. I was a combination hat-check girl and switchboard operator." Jimmy gave her an engagement ring in December 1950 and married her December 14, 1960. "He was worth waiting for. Jimmy's one of the kindest, most lovable men in or out of show business. He never puts on the dog. He's the same to an errand boy as he is to the sponsor of a show. He's Jimmy to everybody, and he introduces me as 'Margie.' I once asked him if it wasn't a bit undignified. Again, he gave me that hurt look. 'Our names is Jimmy and Margie, ain't they?' he asked. 'I crinch if anyone calls me Mister Durante.'"[35]

In another interview, the new Mrs. Durante says, "There was the time when I had the fleeting and somewhat ridiculous notion I might succeed in getting Jimmy to act more dignified in public." Margie mentions how embarrassed she was, when driving, pedestrians would call out, and Jimmy would shout back, or when elevator boys showed familiarity instead of respect with "Hi, Margie! Hi, Jimmy!" She says she learned to accept this behavior.[36] But some of Jimmy's best friends, his "little family," say Margie never wanted them around the house once she married Jimmy, and they developed a dislike for each other similar to the resentment between Jeanne, Jimmy's first wife, and Lou Clayton, Jimmy's closest buddy. Once Jimmy died, the "little family" and his widow went their separate ways.

As Jimmy entertained in nightclubs, a widower, he had many opportunities to meet and socialize with countless beautiful show girls. He was an enthusiastic womanizer.[37] Women found him always kind, treating them like ladies, with great courtesy, and extremely generous with his money. For one long-time girlfriend, Betty Jane Howarth—a featured singer on a few of his television shows billed as Betty Tyler and on some of his nightclub tours, first as Jane Howard, then as Betty Summers—he bought expensive jewelry, fur coats, property, and a life insurance policy.

Bride Margie kisses groom, December 14, 1960.

Durante told friends he spent a million dollars on her, a report Betty Jane herself was quick to confirm.[38] Another girlfriend, of not as long standing as Betty, was Wanda Smith. She played a prominent role in the Durante television shows as leader of the chorus girls, Wanda Smith and her Cover Girls.[39] No Cyrano de Bergerac pining for unrequited love of Roxane, this Durante got the women he wanted through the charm he exuded, the gentlemanliness and generosity he practiced.

Wanda Smith (at center) and the Cover Girls. 1950s. They were a regular feature on the television shows.

In 1946, the small desert city of Las Vegas was taking a giant step toward becoming the huge gambling and nightclub attraction that we know today. The Flamingo Hotel and Casino, under the guidance of gangster Benjamin "Bugsy" Siegel, was under construction as the first of many lavish Las Vegas spots to feature long-stemmed show girls and major show business stars. On December 26, 1946, the Flamingo's casino opened with Jimmy Durante headlining its show, joined by Xavier Cugat and Rose Marie.[40] Six months later Bugsy was murdered by disgruntled organized crime associates, but Durante remained a favorite Las Vegas performer the rest of his career.

While the Copacabana was Durante's chief venue in New York, the Chez Paree was his favored nightclub in Chicago. Durante's act played the Chez Paree early 1950 after a 12-year absence from Chicago's cafe circuit. Here Durante played the same old favorites like "Inka Dinka Doo" and new stuff like "The Beep in the Bop." Jimmy once again threw piano pieces at Jack Roth. He also kidded Jack Dempsey about taking on and knocking out Gorgeous George, who was widely known then for his perfumed hairdo and burlesque of wrestling.[41]

In 1951, a few months after his plunge into network television, Durante appeared at Copa City, Miami Beach's leading nightclub, with "sixteen Copa lovelies" and Billy Daniels.[42]

Durante recalled how he helped black nightclub acts: Billy Daniels, Sammy Davis, Jr., with the Will Mastin Trio, Buck & Bubbles, in particular. "I've never tried to hurt anybody on the bill with us." He recalled, for instance, an opening night at the Palace. The featured star attraction was always next to last. The last act had to endure people starting to walk out and could not commmand the audience's full attention.

> Buck and Bubbles, a colored team . . . went into a very entertainin'—a great act, great dancin' 'n' singin'. After the show they sez, "We're not gonna follow you." I sez, "Whatsa matter, Buck?" He sez, "No chance, can't we go on aheada you?" So I sez, "Why not?" So Clayton—he managed the act—I sez to Clayton, "Go up to the bookin' office upstairs over the Palace." And the next night or the next matinee they went on ahead of us. And *we* closed the bill.
>   We tried the same thing—I was . . . woikin' down in Florida—at the Copa City. There was an act, not an act, a singer, Billy Daniels. He was in the Lounge. So the boss sez, "Would you care, Jimmy, if"—he was the rage down in the Lounge, great—so he sez, "Would you mind if we put him on the bill wid ya, on the stage in the big room?" I sez, "No." So he went on the bill wid us and that was his start in the big rooms, Billy Daniels. The same thing wid . . . Sammy Davis, Jr. He went on down there also, aheada me. So, I think in this life, I never tried to harm anybody. I think the only good ya get outa dis life, whether it's my business, whether it's your business—I think da only good ya get outa life is da helpin', if ya can help somebody along the way. If ya can help a person along the way I think that's all the satisfaction ya get outa life . . . to help people if you're able to help 'em.[43]

Sammy Davis, Jr., thanked Durante. "I don't know if you remember this or not—in Miami at the Copa City and you being the big star you were, and of course my dad, uncle and I trying to start out and make a little

Opening of Sammy Davis, Jr., at Ciro's in Hollywood, December 1954.
First appearance of Sammy after his auto accident, with Will Mastin and
Sammy Davis, Sr. (Author's collection.)

noise being very hungry performers, it was important to us to get a good
show and be able to do our full act. You could have walked in that night
and said, 'Cut them down to 10 minutes, I'm the star.' You never did, and,
as a matter of fact, I don't think you remember this but . . . you said . . .
'Let the kid [do his stuff] . . . besides I'd like to do a little number with
him myself.' That graciousness . . . was part of your makeup because you
were not only a great performer, but all young people in this business can
learn from you. But you are also one of the nicest human beings that God
ever created."[44]

   After playing the Copa City in Miami, Durante finished the month
of March 1951 back in New York at the Copacabana. Durante's act opened
with "You Gotta Start Off Each Day with a Song," and digressed every
bar or two, including throwing part of the piano or a sheaf of music at his
drummer (Roth). Jimmy does "Umbriago" with Eddie Jackson and comic
bits with chorus girls.[45]

   Durante returned to New York from England aboard the *Queen Mary*
with the core of his television and nightclub group of performers: Eddie
Jackson, Candy Candido, and Jack Roth. Later that month, June 1952, he

opened at the Chez Paree, Chicago. *Variety* reported that he broke that nightclub's first week record, bringing in $68,000; $5,000 more business than the previous high set by Dean Martin and Jerry Lewis.[46] Durante did three shows nightly. Most nightclubs complained of poor business with a furniture convention in town, but the furniture people must have loved Jimmy. After all, he did get his big vaudeville and Broadway number "Wood" from an earlier furniture association brochure, and clearly had a genius for breaking furniture if not building it. Because of Durante's success at the Chez Paree, efforts were made to extend the engagement from three weeks to five and to push back the Durante act's scheduled opening at the Desert Inn in Las Vegas that was set to follow Chicago. The *Chicago Sun-Times* reported, "The lovable Jimmy Durante gives the Chez Paree its third box-office smash in succession," following Jane Froman, then Frank Sinatra. The paper liked Candy Candido, in his first Chicago appearance with Durante, mistakenly calling him a Chicagoan, and mentioned Jack Roth, Eddie Jackson, and Jules Buffano.[47]

The following June (1953), after many more nightclub engagements, Durante returned to the Chez Paree, with his old routines and six shapely cover girls. This time his entourage included Sonny King, replacing Eddie Jackson, who was ill. Possessing a big voice, Sonny King not only did Jackson's kind of routine with Durante but also excerpts from the operetta *The Firefly* and the opera *I Pagliacci*.[48]

From Chicago, Durante went to the Riverside in Reno, theater restaurant, July 1953. The *Chicago American* reviewed the opening night. Durante tore the piano apart, threw sheet music, and hurled a telephone over his shoulder, all objects caught by Jack Roth, who was asked if he ever missed catching these objects. He said he missed the telephone once. Customers would bet on whether he would miss the catch and shatter an expensive mirror in the club. Roth said he was offered $200 to miss, but that bribe offer was not the one time he did miss the phone. Lou Cohen, who served as Durante's manager at this time, said the only time Roth missed a catch was when a light blinded him, and he ended with five stitches over his left eye.[49] Durante and his act returned to the Riverside for what was called his third appearance there, in June 1954.

The hectic pace of nightclub engagements continued. You can get a brief sample of the travel by looking at Jack Roth's scribbled notes for the Durante group's tour for the first five months of 1959. "Started N Y 1959. Copa Jan. 8th—to Feb. 4th. 4 Weeks. Phil. Latin Casino Feb. 6 to 12th. 1 Week. Latin Quarters, Maimi [sic]—Feb. 25th to Mar 17th. 3 Weeks. Palm Beach Towers Hotel, Florida. 2 days, Mar 18 & 19th. Paid $200. New Orleans, La. Mar 21 to Apr. 3. 2 Weeks. Twin Coaches Club, Pittsburgh Pa. April 5 to 12. 1 Week. Play Chicago, Ill. for Old Gold Sunday, Ap. 4. 1 Night—Paid $100. Layed [sic] off—From April 13 to 20 XXXX.

Opened at the Desert Inn Las Vegas April 21 to June 1st/59. For 6 Weeks."
Jack Roth's wife Margie, daughters Eileen and Margie, and son Marty as
usual got only rare moments with the traveling showman.[50] It was a common case of families at home competing with show business for time and
attention.

In the late 1950s and early 1960s, under the guidance of Jackie Barnett
as producer and songwriter, Durante began to do a number of long-
playing albums for Decca and Warner Bros., including one album related
directly to the Club Durant segment of his television shows, called *Club
Durant*.

Durante had made some excellent 78rpm records in the 1940s—for
MGM, Decca, and one for Majestic. The two sides for Majestic, recorded
August 1946, with Eddie Jackson and orchestra directed by Ted Dale,
were "G'wan Home, Your Mudder's Callin'" and "There Are Two Sides
to Ev'ry Girl." Both were related to MGM's 1946 film, *Two Sisters from
Boston*. The sides for Decca, all with Roy Bargy, began with "Inka Dinka
Doo" and "Umbriago," recorded July 26, 1944, with the accompaniment
of Six Hits and a Miss, a vocal group. Decca in 1946 released "Start Off
Each Day with a Song" with Eddie Jackson, back to back with
"Durante—The Patron of the Arts." The same year Decca released "Who
Will Be with You When I'm Far Away?" (with interpolation: "Did You
Ever Have the Feeling"), back to back with "So I Ups to Him" with Eddie
Jackson; also "Jimmy, the Well Dressed Man" with Eddie Jackson, and on
the flip side, "Joe Goes Up—I Come Down." Decca re-released some of
these numbers on a 10-inch long-playing album late in 1949. In the early
1950s (1951–55), Decca recorded nine new Durante performances, re-
leased simultaneously on 78rpm and 45rpm, none of them his old songs:
"How D' Ye Do and Shake Hands" (film *Alice in Wonderland*) and "Black
Strap Molasses," both as a joint effort with Danny Kaye, Jane Wyman,
and Groucho Marx, the first also with Six Hits and a Miss, both with orchestra directed by Sonny Burke; "You Say the Nicest Things" and "If
You Catch a Little Cold," both with Ethel Merman and orchestra accom-
paniment; "Pupalina (My Little Doll)" and "Little People," both with the
Jud Conlon Singers, orchestra directed by Roy Bargy; "It's Bigger Than
Both of Us" and "When the Circus Leaves Town," the first a duet with
Patty Andrews, the second a Durante solo, both with orchestra directed
by Roy Bargy; "Swingin' with Rhythm and Blues" and "I Love You, I
Do," both duets, the first with Peter Lawford, the second with Eddie
Jackson.

Between 1947 and 1950, MGM recorded 20 Durante songs on 78s,
most of the numbers comedy songs with Durante solos, accompanied by
Roy Bargy and orchestra. Some of the numbers were related to MGM

Presenting Eddie Jackson. Duet, 1950s.

films in which Durante performed them. One number recorded in 1947 had Candy Candido with Durante, "I'm Feeling Mighty Low," on the flip side of "I'll Do the Strut-Away in My Cutaway." Others from 1947 include "I'm the Guy Who Found the Lost Chord," "Little Bit This, Little Bit That," "Chidabee-Ch-Ch (Yah-Yah-Yah)," "The Day I Read a Book," "The State of Arkansas," "Dollar a Year Man," "Fugitive from Esquire," and "It's My Nose's Birthday." In 1949, MGM recorded "Any State in the Forty-Eight Is Great," "The Pussy Cat Song (Nyow! Nyot Nyow!)" (with Betty Garrett), "Take an L," and "Bibbidi-Bobbidi-Boo (The Magic Song)" from the 1950 film *Cinderella*. In 1950 MGM recorded two of Durante's earliest vaudeville numbers, "What You Goin' to Do When the Rent Comes 'Round? (Rufus Rastus Johnson Brown)" and "Bill Bailey, Won't You Please Come Home?," both with Eddie Jackson, as well as the children's songs "Frosty the Snowman" and "(Isn't It a Shame That) Christmas Comes but Once a Year."

Durante, as shown from some of his Decca and MGM recordings, was very good at doing songs that would appeal to children as well as to adults. About this time, he made four 78rpm recordings strictly for children, issued on the recognizable yellow vinyl of Golden Records:

"Yankee Doodle Bunny (The Holiday Song)," "Rudolph, the Red-Nosed Reindeer," "Santa Claus Is Comin' to Town," and "I Like People (The Friendly Song)." On the first three titles, Jimmy is assisted by the Sand-pipers; the last title is a solo. All are accompanied by Mitchell Miller and orchestra.

In 1957, Decca released the *Club Durant* album, both as an LP and as an extended-play 45rpm album set, using excerpts of duets Durante did with guests on his radio and TV shows. An outstanding collection, it included "A Real Piano Player" (with Al Jolson); "I'm as Ready as I'll Ever Be" (with Sophie Tucker); "There's a Place in the Theatre for You" (interpolation: "Who Will Be with You When I'm Far Away") (with Ethel Barrymore); "Sing Soft, Sing Sweet, Sing Gentle" (with Bing Crosby); "Our Voices Were Meant for Each Other" (interpolation: "Put on Your Old Grey Bonnet," "Waiting for the Robert E. Lee") (with Helen Traubel); "The Boys with the Proboskis" (with Bob Hope); "The World Needs New Faces" (interpolation: "Start Off Each Day with a Song," "If You Knew Susie") (with Eddie Cantor); "Wingin' with Rhythm and Blues" (with Peter Lawford); Clayton, Jackson, and Durante in a medley of "Start Off Each Day with a Song," "Bill Bailey," "I Can Do Without Broadway," "Jimmy, the Well Dressed Man," "So I Ups to Him," "Because They All Love You." The Clayton, Jackson, and Durante medley was recorded June 1949, a reprise of the Durante radio show of April 21, 1948. The album's liner notes give credit to drummer Jack Roth, "with me since 1920," to his long-time piano player, Jules Buffano, and to songwriter Jackie Barnett, who had first met Durante in 1936, first worked for him in 1941, and by the end of the 1940s was collaborating with Durante on many songs for radio, television, nightclubs, and recordings. Eight songs on the *Club Durant* album are credited to Durante-Barnett.

Profits from songs written by Durante, by members of his group, or in collaboration with Durante went to the Jimmy Durante Music Publishing Company set up for this purpose. The money was to be split with Jackie Barnett and other partners. As in the early days with Lou Clayton, there were no written contracts, and Jackie counted on Jimmy's handshake.[51] When he complained to Jimmy that his name was left off some of the songs they wrote together, Jimmy assured him that when the money mounted up they would all share in the pie. But after Jimmy died, the agreements based on a handshake and trust were no longer valid.[52]

Decca followed the *Club Durant* LP with another, *Jimmy Durante (In Person) at the Piano*, released in 1959. This showed more of Durante's piano technique than any other record he had made or would make. There is no orchestra, just vocals and piano, with Jack Roth quietly on drums. The songs here show the beginning of a change in Durante's recorded material. Ten of the 12 songs are old chestnuts, a mixture of Durante's

Practicing the strut, 1950s. Durante checks with Eddie Jackson, pianist Jules Buffano, and drummer Jack Roth.

songs and other oldies, on the whole very sentimental and sung in a subdued voice with a gentle piano touch. There was nothing approaching mad rushes and no interruptions for stories.

The old-time, energetic, and frantic side of Durante was not gone from the nightclubs. Roulette was the only record company to preserve a live nightclub performance by Durante, and it's a pity more were not taped. *Jimmy Durante at the Copacabana* was released in 1961 and went out of print within one year. This is also the only recording that Sonny King made with Durante and Jackson.

Jimmy referred to Eddie as "my partner," and Sonny as "my junior partner." Sonny had taken over for Eddie Jackson on short notice in 1953, when Eddie was sick, and surprised everybody by how good he was. He was singing at the Copacabana when Durante first heard him. When Eddie Jackson took sick suddenly, Durante and Barnett asked him to join the act at the Desert Inn in Las Vegas. Jimmy liked Sonny King's style, rooted, like his own, in the vaudeville tradition Sonny learned from his father and uncle, George and Joe King, a vaudeville and nightclub team.[53] Jackie Barnett, who was soon to produce a series of Durante albums for Warner Bros., said that after three nights of work with Durante, Sonny King was better than Eddie Jackson.[54] If you were to listen to the live recording at the Copacabana, supplemented by a tape of an appearance of Durante, Jackson, and Sonny King on *The Ed Sullivan Show*, January 7, 1962, you would feel that Sonny King had greater energy and a greater vocal range than Eddie Jackson. For sheer sentimentalism and old-time songs, no one was better than Eddie Jackson, but he was limited.

Jimmy continued to use Eddie both on television and in nightclubs, at the same time giving Sonny an occasional TV appearance and much more to do in nightclubs. Eddie resented the greater attention paid to Sonny.[55]

The Roulette LP shows Durante joking with the audience in a way he could not do on radio and tried, with some success, to do on television with the studio audience. He works both Eddie Jackson and Sonny King into duets and subjects each to extensive ribbing and gruff but good-natured orders.

The Durante show from the Copacabana on this night begins with the announcer introducing "the one and only Jimmy Durante," as the band strikes up his theme song, "You Gotta Start Off Each Day with a Song." Durante enters not with this song on his lips but, in a quick switch, with "I Could Have Danced All Night," from the hugely successful 1956 musical, *My Fair Lady*. Rethinking his decision, he yells, "Stop da music, stop da music! Why should I sing the song and make it a big hit?" Someone yells, "Jimmy, happy birthday." He retorts, "My birthday?" Taking the cue to go into his old song, he sings "It's My Nose's Birthday (Not Mine)." He interrupts with the same comment he always makes at this point in the song, talking about how the nose outweighed the child.

Mentioning the Copa's owner, Jules Podell, Jimmy tells another of his regular gags, about poking his nose in a beehive (on land Podell has shown him) and the bees being frightened by the massive intrusion. He then sings a few notes of "Everywhere You Go," stopping to chat with the chorus girls and audience, as the band continues softly. When he wants the band to stop, he yells "Get off! Get off!" He calls the Copacabana the Copa-ca-basement.

Jimmy turns to an introduction: "Now introducing my partner Eddie Jackson, of Clayton, Jackson, and Durante." The orchestra strikes up Jimmy's oft-used song, "Who Will Be with You When I'm Far Away," with no vocal. Eddie struts in. He and Jimmy sing their old chestnut, "It's Still the Same Old Broadway." Eddie moves into another oldie, "Every Street's a Boulevard." Jimmy encourages him, "Sing it!" and offers other comments as Eddie sings. This segues into Eddie doing "Bill Bailey, Won't You Please Come Home" for what might have been the 5,000th time, Jimmy still interrupting until he tells Eddie "Get off!" meaning end the song. "Take a bow, Eddie, don't waste no time. All right, take another bow, come on, come on! Get off, Eddie!"

Durante now turns to introducing Sonny King. Jimmy gruffly orders Sonny to take the microphone. Sonny, pretending his feelings are hurt by Jimmy's lack of manners, tells him "Say please." Jimmy bawls him out, saying he has *agita* (Italian for heartburn), and Sonny's making it worse. Sonny sings "My Melody Man" with Jimmy at the piano, then "Ragtime Jimmy" as Jimmy tickles the keys. Sonny follows this with what proved to be his big hit working with Durante, Jackie Barnett's collaborative effort "I Love You, I Do." It's a new song in old, sweet ragtime style, starting slowly and building to double-time. Recently, Jackie Barnett demonstrated how he wrote this and all his songs, thousands of them, *all built on three chords*: he says he really wrote the same song 1,500 times. Sitting at the piano, he showed how he used only two thumbs and an index finger.[56]

Durante, in his Copacabana act, talks about the bartender putting $2 in the till and $2 in his pocket. "But I don't say nuttin' . . . Later I get my cut." Some of the people around Durante say this was more than just a joke. In at least a few nightclubs, part of his salary was on the books and part delivered secretly by a "bag man," so as not to attract the tax revenue agents.[57]

Jimmy jokes with the chorus girls, sings a few notes of his own "She's a Little Bit This and a Little Bit That," and interrupts himself to tell a well-worn joke. He launches into another song, "Take Away the Beret," before returning to the earlier song he had started.

Again introducing Sonny King, Jimmy joins Sonny to sing "We're Goin' Home," segueing into "Who Will Be with You When I'm Far Away." Jimmy talks about Las Vegas, then Sonny sings "You Made Me Love You," as Jimmy and the drummer sabotage the love song, causing Sonny to join in the damage. Eddie Jackson appears, and Sonny tells Eddie, "Sing up a storm, Hymie." Eddie sings it straight. Someone calls out, "C'mon, Jackson!" Eddie takes the song's chorus again, and Sonny says,

"Let's give the kid with the big nose a chance, huh?" Jimmy finished the song. Sonny's singing works well in the Durante style, at least as well as Jackson's, but he's more abrasive, more aggressive than Jackson, not always as funny or adorable as Durante's gruff comments and see-through insults.

Jimmy pauses to give everyone a proverb that no one understands. Then he defines a proverb. "You put a pronoun objective in between, and it becomes a proverb." Now the audience knows as much grammatical construction as it did before the explanation, maybe less.

Finally Jimmy gets into a very effective number he often used in nightclubs, "Say It with Flowers," which once had been the lead-in for "Inka Dinka Doo." This leads directly into the closing, "Goodnight, Goodnight." Durante takes a bow and leaves the stage as the orchestra fades with "You Gotta Start Off Each Day with a Song." There is no good night to Mrs. Calabash.

Often a regular part of Durante's nightclub act, also occasionally on the Texaco TV show, were the Borden twins and Sally Davis, three heavyweight girls doing a "fat" act, dancing with Jimmy and bouncing him off their hips. After them came Vega Maddux, a three-hundred pounder. Between the slim chorus girls and the extra-large dumplings, Durante added new, effective comedy routines to his old. The show, with Eddie Jackson and Sonny King, was reported to be fast and hilarious, updated by Jackie Barnett's clever staging and writing. For a change of pace, Durante also sang tender, sentimental ballads like "Young at Heart."

On September 12, 1960, Durante's long-time piano player, Jules Buffano, died in Hollywood of a stroke he suffered two weeks earlier.[58] He was replaced for an October 1960 engagement at the Elmwood Casino, Windsor, Ontario, by George Finley. Finley had briefly been the pianist for Betty Jane Howarth, and she had recommended him.[59] Finley said he loved Durante, loved playing piano for him, never got anything thrown at him like Jack Roth, and retired when Durante had his debilitating stroke in the 1970s.[60]

Later that October 1960, the Durante show once again opened at the Desert Inn, Las Vegas. In Jimmy's clever opening number, "The Man That Makes the Clothes," he changes into several outfits on stage, assisted by the girls. In the Durante group were Jack Roth, Eddie Jackson, Sonny King, and George Finley. Finley was ribbed all night by Durante, like piano players before him—Jules Buffano and Harry Donnelly. Big Sally Davis danced with Jimmy, Eddie, and Sonny. Sonny King nearly stopped the show with "I Love You, I Do." King and Durante together on "Inka Dinka Doo" brought a standing ovation. The show remained there through November 14, 1960.[61]

Jimmy Durante briefly interrupted his nightclub appearances and preparations for his debut on Warner Bros. records to marry Margie Little after a long friendship and engagement. Betty Jane Howarth, who wanted to be Mrs. Durante, was heartbroken, and other women in Jimmy's life were disappointed. Jimmy was 67 and Margie 39; his second marriage, her first. The wedding took place in New York on December 14, 1960, in St. Malachy's Roman Catholic Church, West 49th Street.⁶² When asked by a reporter why he waited so long to marry Margie, Jimmy replied, "I ain't the type who likes to rush into things. I figgered I'd get to know her first. Then if the dame measured up, okay. Anyway, we discussed a lotta things in 15 years, includin' kids."⁶³

Betty Jane said that Jimmy had also given her a diamond ring, signed her to a personal management contract (which she showed, dated January 1, 1960, containing Jimmy's signature), employed her for his television show and nightclub engagements under pseudonyms to hide her from Margie Little, and told her that while Mrs. Calabash once referred to his first wife, Jeanne, it now referred to her.⁶⁴ Wanda Smith also indicated that while she did not receive an engagement ring, Jimmy let her believe he was serious about her.⁶⁵ In 1980, Betty Jane wrote with her sister Mary G. Howarth an unpublished 90-page memoir, "Jimmy Durante and Me," in which she details this love that gave her great happiness, but drove her to a nervous breakdown and hospitalization after she lost Jimmy and his support. She had been a starlet in MGM and Universal pictures, her first role being an extra in *The Pirate*, starring Gene Kelly, and later work with such stars as Clint Eastwood, with studio photographs to prove it. She says Jimmy did not want her to continue in show business—the same desire he had expressed to his first wife years before—and promised to take care of her financially, going so far as to buy her real estate and promising to include her in his will. Her disappointment was crushing.⁶⁶

In February 1961, Jimmy was back at the Copacabana entertaining with his group, including Eddie Jackson, Sonny King, Jack Roth, George Finley, Sally Davis, and Johnny Mack (a tap dancer). They did two shows nightly, at 8 and 12, Fridays also at 2 a.m. From here the Durante show moved to Miami Beach to play the Casanova Room of the Deauville Hotel.

Durante took his show to Harrah's on the South Shore of Lake Tahoe, Nevada, in September 1962, there nightly through September 26. For this engagement he had not only Eddie Jackson, Sonny King, George Finley, and Jack Roth, but as a special added attraction, Helen Traubel, her name in letters as big as Durante's. This great opera star turned pop performer, who had scored so well on the Durante television show, used her own conductor, Richmond Gale. A newspaper article pointed out that the room had a big seating capacity, more than many famous European opera houses. Traubel told the reporter, "I was raised on vaudeville and love it." On stage she sang "Bill Bailey" with Durante and his group.[67]

Before Durante's opening in Lake Tahoe, Jimmy and Margie, now ages 69 and 41, received permission from a California court (June 1962) to adopt the little girl they had brought home as a baby in December 1961. They had named her Cecilia Alicia, nicknamed CeCe. The court proceedings were held to determine if Jimmy were too old to adopt a child, and the judge was obviously moved by Jimmy's sincerity. Chicago Federal Judge Abe Marovitz helped Margie to adopt the child. Margie was the one who wanted to do this. Jimmy felt he was too old to begin raising a baby but went along with Margie's wishes.[68] Before long, Jimmy was crazy about the little girl. Jimmy's great-niece, Rosemary Romano Halderman, who maintains regular contact with CeCe, told about the time Jimmy bought his little girl ten pairs of shoes, and Margie, not wanting CeCe to become too spoiled, made Jimmy take back nine pairs.[69]

In early January 1963, Durante opened at Palumbo's nightclub on Catharine Street in Philadelphia, for a ten-day stay. Here he used his oft-repeated line, "I know there's a million good-looking guys, but I'm a novelty." Sonny King and Durante did their opening duet medley highlighted by "I Love You, I Do." Jimmy sang a special arrangement of "Mack the Knife" and the quiet ballad "Young at Heart." Hefty newcomer Jennie Jackson did the twist, part of the "fat act" that audiences found so hilarious. (Later Vega Maddux would play this role, another large woman bouncing Jimmy off her hips.) Jackson did "Bill Bailey" with assistance from King and Durante, and all three linked up for the "Strut-Away." Jimmy performed "Inka Dinka Doo."[70]

Warner Bros. released a series of five Durante LPs spaced one year apart, each reading "Jackie Barnett Presents. . . ." The first of these, in 1963, was *September Song*. Publicity is given to the claim that this is a "new" Jimmy Durante, the cover reading, "Jackie Barnett Presents the New Jimmy Durante." There are no razz-a-ma-tazz numbers from vaudeville, just very emotionally effective ballads done with careful attention to the lyrics and no humorous interruptions. The cover is a sketch by the artist Fred Williams of Durante seated alone at the piano, just as at the conclusion of his television shows—time to be serious and a bit sad as he said his goodnight to the audience.

Jimmy had resisted doing straight ballads, doubting people would accept this from him. Barnett and other writers and producers convinced Jimmy to try. From the way Durante turned the "Good night, Mrs. Calabash" gag into a statement of touching sincerity, it was clear to some that he could handle straight sentimentality with as great effectiveness as raucous humor. He was already using "Young at Heart" regularly on his nightclub tour. That song was on this album. The title number, "September

Jimmy admires adopted CeCe held by Margie, in an MGM publicity photo off the set of *Billy Rose's Jumbo*, **1962.**

Song," was a big hit for Durante on his television show and on this album, more touching than even Walter Huston's much-admired rendition in *Knickerbocker Holiday* (Broadway, 1938). A 45rpm single of "September Song" sold well, coupled with "Young at Heart." Other songs on the album were "Look Ahead Little Girl," "Count Your Blessings Instead of Sheep," "When the Circus Leaves Town," "I Believe," "Don't Lose Your Sense of Humor," "You'll Never Walk Alone," "One Room Home," and the number Metropolitan Opera tenor Jan Peerce had made famous in the 1940s, "Blue Bird of Happiness." Four of these ten songs are credited on the label to composers Durante and Barnett, including "One Room Home."

Jimmy at first had thought this last song *was* a serious song. But when he performed "One Room Home" on television, it turned out to be unintentionally hilarious, even though it's a song about a serious sentiment: Jimmy not envying anyone who has more material possessions than he has, satisfied with his own small home. It starts out as a sad, charming song, but with breathless lines about the number of rooms someone else might have, counting from one to ten. It's a very unusual song that only Durante could sing and make you laugh or cry, or both.

Durante's second Warner Bros. album was *Hello Young Lovers*, 1964. Like the first album, the songs were arranged and conducted by Roy Bargy, with the John Rarig Singers. This was the last recording Bargy would make with Durante. He retired in 1963, Durante's musical director since 1943. This album was recorded at the Desert Inn in Las Vegas, with photos for the cover taken at the home of Wilbur Clark, the club's owner. Only one number was written by Jackie Barnett and Durante, "In the Other Fellow's Yard." This and all the others are serious, tender ballads: "Hello, Young Lovers," "Try a Little Tenderness," "Smile," "Hi-Lili, Hi-Lo," "Love in a Home," "This Is All I Ask," "The Glory of Love," "You Can't Have Ev'rything," and "The Time Is Now."

On July 18, 1964, CBS-TV tried to bring *The Jimmy Durante Show* back as a situation comedy instead of a variety show. The half-hour show for Texaco, later Old Gold for reissue, had moved in that direction, setting up situations within the confines of the Club Durant. The pilot failed to attract a satisfactory audience rating or sponsors and was not inserted into that fall's lineup. Produced and directed by Hy Averback, written by Billy Friedberg, Mel Diamond, and Mel Tolkin, the proposed series was to have presented Jimmy Banister (Durante), a well-known entertainer, with a grandson, Eddie (Eddie Hodges), who Jimmy wants to enter show business, beginning with a performance on a TV special.[71] Soon, however, Jimmy realizes that it would be better if Eddie went to prep school for a good education.

Eddie Hodges had in fact appeared with Durante in a TV special, "Give My Regards to Broadway," December 6, 1959, on NBC's new series that combined variety and live drama, *Sunday Showcase*. The show was 60 minutes and although viewable today only on black and white kinescope,[72] it was televised in color. Durante, the star, had as guests Jane Powell, Jimmy Rodgers, and Ray Bolger, as well as little Eddie Hodges, who had made a pleasing appearance in a Sinatra film earlier that year, *A Hole in the Head*. On the NBC special, one of the production numbers has Eddie Hodges asking Ray Bolger, "Who was George M. Cohan?" This is the springboard for a tribute to that great showman. Durante and chorus do "Yankee Doodle Dandy." Jane Powell sings "Mary," joined by Durante in a serious mood and Jimmy Rodgers. A duet by Bolger and Hodges becomes a trio with Durante before all five stars sing "Harrigan," "Give My Regards to Broadway," and "That's Entertainment." After the last commercial for Shaeffer pens, Durante on still one more show gets to have the finale to himself, putting on his trenchcoat and saying good night to the audience and Mrs. Calabash.

Warner Bros.' third Durante album, released in 1965, was called *Jimmy Durante's Way of Life*. The William George painting on the cover shows the aging Jimmy looking with appreciation at a daisy he's holding in his hand (instead of a cigar). The title song, "My Way of Life," was written by Jackie Barnett with Sammy Fain. None of the songs were by Durante, and all ten of them are promoted in the liner notes as "moving and emotional songs lovingly performed with the Gordon Jenkins Orchestra and Chorus." Was Jackie Barnett taking Jimmy too far away from his nightclub roots? The mixture of the old and the new, the comic and the serious, was working on television and in nightclubs. Durante had reached his peak as a truly classic show business personality the audience loved, laughing and crying at everything he did. Like Jack Benny, one look, one word, and the audience was in the palm of the performer's hand.

The very title of the album, *Jimmy Durante's Way of Life*, suggests that Jimmy has discovered some secret of happiness. For a man who cannot pronounce English like most professional actors, a man accustomed to bruising if not fracturing the language, Jimmy's attention to the songs' lyrics is admirable and indeed more moving than many singers with bigger voices and better diction. He sings, in addition to the title song, "My Wish," "As Time Goes By," "Make Someone Happy," "I'll Be Seeing You," "When Day Is Done," "When I Lost You," "If I Had You," "Once to Every Heart," and "I'll See You in My Dreams."

Durante was always a gentle, quiet, shy man behind a gruff exterior. Now that exterior was only intermittently seen. His fourth album, *One of Those Songs*, is dedicated to CeCe, his adopted daughter, and to his wife Margie. The original cover shows Jimmy, in his 70s, holding the little girl in his arms. Jackie Barnett, who produced the record, says Margie objected to using CeCe on the cover, so a later printing used a photo of Jimmy standing alone.[73]

The album contains one of the most effective of his serious songs, "Old Man Time" (written by Cliff Friend). We get the same feeling of regret that we got from "September Song," here in particular Jimmy's wish to enjoy his daughter for more years than he knows he has. He does two rousing old songs, "One of Those Songs" and "You're Nobody Till Somebody Loves You," and, for still one more time, with Eddie Jackson as guest star, "Bill Bailey, Won't You Please Come Home." In a tribute to his wife, he sings "Margie."

Other songs here include the very old "Daddy, Your Mama Is Lonesome for You," music Jimmy had written in 1921 with words by Chris Smith and Bob Schafer, but unrecorded by Durante until now; new songs are "Mame," "This Train," and showing he can do rock like the kids of the '60s, "We're Going U.F.O.-ing." Not on the LP but recorded in the fall of 1964 and released as a 45rpm with "Old Man Time" was another rock number, "I Came Here to Swim." "Who wants to swim?", Jimmy first asked, but agreed to record the number when he was shown the Swim was a dance.

With his fifth and last album for Warner, *Songs for Sunday* (1967), Durante showed himself, if one had ever missed seeing it before, a very religious man. All these songs are truly from the heart, especially effective the beautiful "His Eye Is on the Sparrow," which Ethel Waters had done so well, and the simple but touching song Jackie Barnett had recently written with Durante, "Amen." The album was arranged and conducted by Ralph Carmichael, who also contributed the song "One of These Days." Other songs were "Precious Lord" and "Peace in the Valley" by that fine early black writer of spirituals, Thomas A. Dorsey; "Beyond the Sunset," "He Touched Me," "In the Garden," and two additional songs by Jackie Barnett, "Somebody's Keeping Score" (Barnett and Sammy Fain) and "Down by the River-Side" (not the traditional song, but one by Barnett and Durante).

This religious album was reissued by Light Records in Waco, Texas, with the same blue cover showing Jimmy in close-up from the shoulders, old and serious, searchingly looking into the camera. Light Records also used the Durante performance of "One of These Days" in a three-record 45rpm religious album, *Festival: Music from the Oral Roberts Summer TV Special.* The collection of 13 color photographs taken from the Oral Roberts program includes three shots of Durante, one with the full cast of the TV special, one alone, and one shaking hands with Oral Roberts, the evangelist, a rather rare public shot of Jimmy with his hat off for something other than strutting.

Jimmy's appearance in June 1971 at the Oral Roberts Summer Festival, Tulsa, Oklahoma, was taped for television in front of a young audience. With Jimmy were singer Bobby Goldsboro, Ralph Carmichael and his Orchestra, and other guests. The show was telecast in New York on WOR-TV, channel nine, as a Sunday night 60-minute special. It followed the established Oral Roberts formula, inspirational songs leading up to the preacher's ten-minute message. Durante sang "Peace in the Valley" and "One of These Days," songs with a peace-after-death message, delivered with touching impact. The bible of the show business world, *Variety*, not known for its piety, reviewed the telecast.[74]

Durante continued to appear with his nightclub act, including both Eddie Jackson and Sonny King, and on television in specials and as a guest star. In the 1957-58 television season he hosted two installments of NBC's variety series *Club Oasis*, October 26, 1957, and March 1, 1958. He appeared as a guest star with Dinah Shore, Frank Sinatra, Steve Allen, Danny Thomas, Lucille Ball, Ed Sullivan, Merv Griffin, Perry Como, Bob Hope, and Jerry Lewis, among others in the late 1950s and through the 1960s.

As on radio, many hosts who welcomed Durante to their shows wanted to participate in doing Durante's oldest routines. They always had great fun imitating him and his vaudeville partners. Perry Como, for example, one of the most "laid back" entertainers, was very funny trying to strut like Eddie Jackson, participating in the destruction of a piano and the tossing of sheet music. On this NBC show of February 22, 1961, *Perry Como's Kraft Music Hall*, Como, guest star Anna Maria Alberghetti, and Durante do "Bill Bailey" and strut *up* some stairs to the front door of the set, Durante stumbling in the process. Incidentally, on this same show, Durante did an old song he seemed to have abandoned many years ago, in the 1930s, while subbing for Eddie Cantor: "As the Nose Blows (So the Nose Goes)." And as a tribute to the greatness of Durante's own closing, Como allows his own show to end with Jimmy's closing. As Como sings, Jimmy yells "Stop da music! That's no way to say good night!" Jimmy shows Perry how to sing good night, and Perry and Anna Maria join in his song, with Jimmy throwing in at the very end his "Good night, Mrs. Calabash." As credits roll, Jimmy also gets to do his trenchcoat retreat from one spotlight to another.

Durante was a frequent host and guest on *The Hollywood Palace*, a high-budget variety extravaganza that ABC ran in color from 1964 to 1970. Bing Crosby hosted more often than any other star, and every installment of the hour-long show had many singers, comedians, jugglers, and acrobats, just like the old days of vaudeville at the Palace. Among memorable Durante moments that should be counted in any retrospective of *The Hollywood Palace* was Jimmy's duet with Louis Armstrong on "Old Man Time," May 1, 1965, a show devised as a tribute to Armstrong and hosted by him. Another sterling moment on *The Hollywood Palace*, with Durante hosting December 10, 1966, had Jimmy on the piano accompaniment for the fat, cheerful Mrs. Miller, who sang and whistled off-key "Every Little Moment (Has a Meaning of Its Own)" and "Inka Dinka Doo," a show that also had Durante teaming with Peter Lawford as he would do in a few 1960s nightclub performances. Perhaps the best moment was Jimmy's destruction of yet another piano for his old show-stopper, "The Lost Chord," this time in color and in great detail on a show he hosted, March 30, 1968.

Two of Durante's best appearances on television were on children's specials. One was a very brief but noticeably bright appearance in NBC's *Alice Through the Looking Glass*, a musical adaptation of the Lewis Carroll classic, in bright color, November 6, 1966. Durante plays Humpty Dumpty sitting on a wall. He's a fat egg dressed in yellow coat and spats, with gold watch chain. When Alice tells him she read about him in a book, he's impressed, saying, "It must have been a very important book." When Alice corrects his pronunciation of the word "preposterous," he makes her repeat after him the famous nonsense jingle, "Jabberwocky." When she gets it right they sing a song based upon that poem. Then he falls off the wall. On CBS, December 7, 1969, Durante's voice was heard in the wonderful animated color cartoon *Frosty the Snowman*. Durante narrates the story and sings the song. *Frosty* still makes an almost annual reappearance at Christmastime.

Then ABC had an idea that sounded great but in practice did not work so well. They decided to team Jimmy Durante with the four Lennon Sisters for the 1969-70 season, looking for a kindly grandfather-granddaughters chemistry. The Lennon Sisters—Dianne, Peggy, Kathy, and Janet—had been very successful on *The Lawrence Welk Show*, which ABC was still running. The girls projected the kind of wholesomeness that typified Welk's band of clean-cut young Americans. Durante always had a clean act, and despite the unsavoriness of the nightclubs he played, seemed somehow saintly and untouched by any kind of smut incompatible with a family show. Each show would open with Jimmy at the piano and lead into a segment of the Lennons talking to Jimmy, then on to guest stars and the Lennons doing their own thing.

The weekly 60-minute variety show, in color, had the curiously strange title *Jimmy Durante Presents the Lennon Sisters*. According to the Lennon Sisters, who loved Durante, this title caused some confusion: it was unclear whose show it was.[75] The season's premiere was September 26, 1969. This evening brought Durante together with Jack Benny for the first time in their long careers. They did a routine about playing in Carnegie Hall, piano and violin virtuosi. They had too little time, however, since the show also featured as guests Noel Harrison and Jimmy Dean. Durante did his newly recorded sentimental song "Young at Heart" and joined the Lennon Sisters in an oldie from vaudeville days, "Yes Sir, That's My Baby."

Other highlights of the season with the Lennons as far as Durante's role was concerned were Jimmy performing "Be Nice to Your Nose" with Bob Hope, October 24, 1969; George Burns and Jimmy saluting vaudeville and New York City, November 14, 1969; Milton Berle and Jimmy searching for the Fountain of Youth, December 5, 1969; Jimmy's own little girl CeCe, now eight years old, appearing on the show for the Christmas musicale, and singing with her adoring father "Look Ahead, Little Girl" (a song in Jimmy's *September Song* album), December 19, 1969; Eddie Jackson and Sonny King joining Jimmy, Eddie to do "Bill Bailey," Sonny to sing with Jimmy, "Hey, Look Me Over" and "I Love Ya, Love Ya, I Do," December 26, 1969. After the show of April 4, 1970, the program went into reruns through the first week in July 1970, and did not return for the new fall season.

Mixed in with some film work, television appearances, and many nightclub engagements, were many not-always-publicized Durante appearances without charge. He did benefits for charitable organizations that raised money for children in need, like the March of Dimes and the Fraternal

Order of Eagles of America. The Eagles' effort was named the Jimmy Durante Children's Fund.[76] When asked to discuss politics, such as his sentiments on the country's war policies, whether he was a hawk or a dove, Durante liked to say, "I'm an Eagle." He also played free of charge for parties given by Bing Crosby as preludes to his golf tournaments. In addition, whatever weddings or other affairs that the various nightclub syndicates wanted him to play he also would do. He was kind-hearted, couldn't say no, but also, as in the old days, he was still afraid of offending any gangster (though invariably every one of them had genuine affection for him).

On September 29, 1969, three days after the season premiere of his television show with the Lennon Sisters, Durante was given the 1969 Humanitarian Award of the National Conference of Christians and Jews. The dinner at the Beverly Hilton was attended by four hundred. Jack Benny was master of ceremonies, and good friend Danny Thomas presented the award.

The year 1972 started like any other recent year for Jimmy Durante, with television work and lots of nightclub appearances. His energy seemed boundless, and his legs still strong, though his eyesight was not as good as it once had been. Early in the year, the 79-year-old star was given a plaque by the governor of Nevada, Mike O'Callaghan, who proclaimed March 29, 1972, Jimmy Durante Day throughout the state. At the Sands Hotel, Las Vegas, a 90-minute show celebrating Durante's 55th anniversary in show business had Sonny King introducing celebrities for bows. Eddie Jackson was not performing but a guest at a table. Durante showed no signs of fatigue.[77]

That summer Jimmy was named "Father of the Year" by the Los Angeles Press Club.[78] In the fall, late September, he was hospitalized, in St. John's Hospital, Santa Monica. His doctor said he was suffering from fatigue after a heavy television and nightclub schedule. He had been appearing in Las Vegas.[79] Then in November, he startled his family and friends by suffering a massive stroke, leaving him paralyzed and speechless. He was never to make a full recovery.

At a dinner in his honor in November 1973, with Milton Berle as emcee, and Los Angeles Mayor and Mrs. Tom Bradley in attendance, Jimmy feebly tried to sing "Inka Dinka Doo." The result was heartbreaking.[80] Again in April 1974, in a wheelchair after three strokes, Jimmy accepted an award at a luncheon given by the Banshees, an organization of newspaper executives, the first award given by the group to a non-newspaper person. Seated at the Waldorf-Astoria banquet hall table after the award, with microphone held by his old friend from Chicago, Judge Marovitz, and in the company of Margie and CeCe, Jimmy sang a chorus of "Inka Dinka Doo" in a frail voice. One journalist-professor observed, "It was beautifully nostalgic and sad, too, because all of us there knew it was probably the last time we would ever see and hear Jimmy. He was given a huge ovation. And when it stopped, the orchestra played again. And Jimmy sang another chorus of 'Inka Dinka Doo.' And then he sang another. And I think he sang even another. To the point of embarrassment from the viewpoint of the crowd. It was an obvious case of a last hurrah, from a once-great star who knew it was his final appearance and who just wouldn't let it go."[81]

In June 1974, lawyers for Jimmy Durante brought suit in federal court to stop publication of a Durante biography. A writer had a contract with Macmillan for a biography to be released on Jimmy's 80th birthday (February 10, 1973). Durante claimed in the suit that he had been suffering from lapses of memory and did not recall signing a contract to provide material for the book.[82]

On November 19, 1976, a belated tribute to Durante for his 83rd birthday was held at the Beverly Hilton Hotel with 800 guests in attendance. Masters of ceremonies were Danny Thomas and Robert Alda. The event raised more than $100,000 for a Jimmy Durante Pavilion at the Villa Scabrini Home for the Aged in California. Jimmy appeared in his wheelchair.[83]

Two years later, on February 9, 1978, an 85th birthday party was thrown for Jimmy Durante "in absentia" at Jilly's, Sinatra's favorite bar in New York, hosted by ex-boxing champ Floyd Patterson and songwriter John Ottaviano. Mayor Edward I. Koch issued a proclamation making it Jimmy Durante Day.[84]

Throughout his seven-year illness, right up to his death, Margie, aided by nurses, a physical therapist, and some of his best friends, took care of Jimmy. He was not put in a nursing home. Among the most helpful of Jimmy's friends was Desi Arnaz. He and Jimmy had enjoyed each other's company for many summers vacationing near Del Mar, north of San Diego, and betting on horses at the racetrack there. After Jimmy's strokes, with his right side more affected than his left, he watched Desi trying to teach him to play the piano again, using his left hand. Margie told Jimmy's friend, Judge Marovitz, how much help Desi was.[85] George Finley also regularly dropped by to play the piano for his boss and pass the time.

After all Jimmy had done for others, his friends did not forget him, and fans by the hundreds of thousands wrote letters to him from all over the country.

The town of Del Mar, known for its beautiful racetrack built in the mid–1930s with Bing Crosby's money,[86] had already immortalized Durante the way Frenchmen immortalize their famous writers. Durante, with a vacation home there and a box for the thoroughbred racing season, was made honorary mayor (1969). The street leading to the track was named Jimmy Durante Boulevard, and one gate was called the Jimmy Durante Gate (another the Pat O'Brien Gate).

Jimmy placed many small bets on the horses over the years. Few of them came in, even with bets on multiple numbers in the same race. Once he picked six horses out of a field of nine and shouted as they came down the stretch, "Come on, anybody!"[87] But Jimmy, the well dressed man, was a winner, and by more than just a nose.

Chapter 8

CONCLUSION

Jimmy Durante died January 29, 1980, after being admitted to St. John's Hospital, Santa Monica, on January 7 for treatment of pneumonia. At his death, he was 86, just short of his 87th birthday. Rosary and mass were held in Good Shepherd Roman Catholic Church, Beverly Hills, January 31, with tributes led by Bob Hope and Danny Thomas before five hundred mourners. Burial was in Holy Cross Cemetery, February 1, with Desi Arnaz leading the list of pallbearers. Eddie Jackson was there in a wheelchair.

Two weeks to the day of Jimmy's death, February 12, 1980, Jack Roth died of a heart attack at his home in Yonkers, New York. Five months later, July 15, 1980, Eddie Jackson died at the Sherman Oaks Community Hospital after suffering a massive stroke at his Van Nuys, California, home.

Jimmy left CeCe behind, a child who would develop into a beautiful young lady, an accomplished rider and trainer of horses near Del Mar, and more recently, a wife and mother.

In the interview he gave Professor Herman Harvey on television in 1962, Jimmy had said something meaningful about cemeteries. He recalled a line from "Broadway, My Street," written many years ago with columnist Sidney Skolsky.[1] The song, featured by Clayton, Jackson, and Durante in Ziegfeld's *Show Girl*, talks about the phony elements of Broadway, how all the ritzy people who think they're so important all wind up with tombstones pretty much the same. "That line [about tombstones] stuck to me for years back. And I think [of] my first wife, Lord have mercy on her soul, she's buried out here in California, and there's not a Sunday that I'm in town that I don't go out to the cemetery. . . . God has taken us, and that's the end. We worry about triteful little things, and we worry about the things that are nothing, and I think it's a wonderful education goin' to a cemetery."[2]

Given a byline as a guest editorial writer for a magazine in 1934, Durante in a serious mood wrote, "All of us have schnozzles, if not on our faces, then in our characters, minds, or habits. We are, in short, ridiculous in one way or another. When we admit our schnozzles, instead of defending them, we begin to laugh, and the world laughs with us. Life isn't serious any more, and death is pretty much of a grin. What a great world it would be if we all learned to laugh at our schnozzles. We wouldn't have wars, suicides, race hatreds, or economic distress, and sickness of soul and body would be rare indeed."[3]

Durante held no grudges against anyone. He tried not to hurt anyone. He never became too self-important to be friendly to the poor as well as the rich, to the unknown as well as the famous. With all the deaths in his family, and with financial pressures, he still had an open hand and an open heart to anyone in need, even to those who took him for a sucker. Judge Marovitz told the story of the time he, Sonny King, and Jimmy, after a good steak dinner at the Cart restaurant in Chicago, walked a few blocks down State Street to the Chez Paree, where Jimmy and Sonny were performing later that evening. The area they walked through had lots of panhandlers, pubs, and peep shows. A man approached them, asking for money. The judge said, "Ah, you're drunk." Jimmy, always the soft touch, said, "Ah, give him a buck." Sonny gave the guy a dollar, and the judge gave him another, with Jimmy handing over still another bill. The panhandler looked at Jimmy with vision clear enough to see who it was. "You're Jimmy Durante. I'm a wino. I'm a mooch. I'd take money from anybody, but not from you, Jimmy. You made too many people happy." And with that, the man gave Jimmy back his dollar.[4]

Fans of Durante can still see him in their mind's eye. He is sitting at an upright piano, 5'7", 155 pounds or thereabouts, famous big nose, twinkling blue eyes, baggy pants, and battered old hat on balding head, a chewed cigar stump nearby, launching into the song that had begun so many of his shows—a song that offered good advice on how to live every single day of one's life:

> You gotta start off each day with a song,
> Even when things go wrong.
> You'll feel better, you'll even look better.
> I'm here to tell you you'll be a go getter.
> For the way that you shake my hand
> Will tell me where I stand.
> Ain't it better to go thru life, with a smile and a song,
> Than walkin' around with a face that's a hundred miles long.
> You'll find that you can't go wrong
> If you start off each day with a song.[5]

As the second chorus begins, Eddie Jackson jumps in, spurring him on like a faithful parishioner at a revival meeting, "Sing it, Jimmy boy! Sing it for the hoi polloi." Durante interrupts himself a couple of times to tell jokes and stories. The number's not finished. Durante goes into still another chorus, Eddie Jackson encouraging him with "Oh boy, you're singin' now!" and Durante with still another one of his "I got a million of 'em" stories to tell.[6]

The Lower East Side neighborhood where Jimmy Durante grew up still has old-timers, many Italian, who remember him as a native son, one of their own who brought them glory. Tommy and Nick Leonessa, florist sons of Tommy, Senior, who knew the Durante family when they were neighbors, commented, "It's about time someone wrote a book about this great man, an Italian who made us proud and was a sweet, good man who never forgot his friends."[7] Two women working in St. Joseph's rectory, Arlene and Patty, recalled their fathers' friend who had a rooftop pigeon coop with a picture of Durante in it, a place of honor.[8]

Almost everyone who spoke about Durante felt he knew Durante well, embellishing the importance of his own role in working or being with Durante, and like *Rashomon*, giving a different spin to the ball, a different aspect or interpretation. There was a protectiveness about discussing Durante's personal life, not just on the part of his relatives but by his extended family of closest associates. Some would have unkind words to say about so and so, but no one ever wanted anything damaging to be said or revealed about the man who was for everyone the "purest" man they had ever known. What is a rich man? A man who can count such fierce loyalty among so many friends and love even from strangers.

NOTES

Chapter 1: Overview of a Career

1. Robert Kimball, ed., *The Complete Lyrics of Cole Porter* (New York: Alfred A. Knopf, 1983), pp. 119–20.
2. "Parlez Moi D'Amour" or "Speak to Me of Love" was a popular French song in 1930s nightclubs, stage, and radio. Copyright 1930, music and lyrics by Jean Lenoir, it also appeared in an American version by Bruce Siever. Durante never went beyond singing the French title and a few additional, mangled French words.
3. *Sum and Substance*, Professor Herman Harvey, host, KNXT Public Affairs (CBS-TV affiliate in Los Angeles), 30 minutes, 1962.
4. Bob Hope, as told to Pete Martin, *Have Tux, Will Travel* (New York: Simon & Schuster, 1954), p. 264.
5. Phil Cohan, interview (Jan. 19, 1991, Pacific Palisades, California).
6. Garry Moore, interview (April 25, 1991, by telephone, Hilton Head, South Carolina).
7. Moore interview.

Chapter 2: Beginnings and Family Roots

1. *New York City Guide*, prepared by the Federal Writers' Project of the Works Progress Administration in New York City (New York: Random House, 1939), pp. 404, 186. See also, Stan Fischler, *Uptown, Downtown: A Trip Through Time on New York's Subways* (New York: Hawthorn/Dutton, 1976), p. 251.
2. Gene Fowler, *Schnozzola: The Story of Jimmy Durante* (New York: Viking Press, 1951), p. 10. Throughout his career Durante told reporters much the same story about his family, his early life, and how he got his start in show business. Short and long versions are scattered through decades of magazines and newspapers. The fullest written report is Fowler's biography, used by many other authors, often without credit given. As valuable as *Schnozzola* is, there are too few specifics about sources of information and no index for the many names and places scattered throughout. We know only that Fowler befriended Durante and taped many hours of interviews with him, Lou Clayton, and others, tapes that would later be the subject of painful wrangling "with people who were guiding the affairs of Jimmy Durante," especially on the matter of movie rights to *Schnozzola*.

H. Allen Smith, *The Life and Legend of Gene Fowler* (New York: William Morrow, 1977), pp. 299–301.

3. Fowler, pp. 10–11.

4. Fowler, p. 11.

5. *Sum and Substance.*

6. Accounts of Durante's childhood say Jimmy was born in 1893 and was baptized at St. James Catholic Church on Oliver Street. The Baptism Register at St. James immaculately preserves, in ornate handwriting, all records from 1849 on, but, surprisingly, no record of James Francis Durante. Some neighborhood old-timers said they had heard that the famous Jimmy Durante had been baptized at St. Joachim, a neighborhood church that no longer exists. Jimmy Durante, they said, had been on the committee to save St. Joachim in the 1950s, petitioning Cardinal Spellman, but the church was torn down for a housing project. An inspection of the St. Joachim registry, housed at St. Joseph's Church on Catherine Street, showed nothing close to the reputed birthdate of February 10, 1893. It was suggested that Jimmy Durante may have been baptized at home (it was then the custom to perform the baptism on the day of birth because of high infant mortality) or that the priest may have neglected to enter the baptism in the registry. In any case, on the day before Jimmy got married in 1921, he was "conditionally baptized" in Holy Innocents Church on West 37th Street, where the wedding ceremony took place. He, too, apparently was unable to find records of his original baptism, and the 1921 baptism register gave his birth as a year earlier, February 10, 1892.

7. *Monitor*, NBC Radio, Feb. 9, 1963.

8. Fowler, p. 14.

9. Julie Romano, interview (Jan. 13, 1991, Oceanside, California).

10. Fowler, p. 15.

11. Albert J. Durante, Jr., interview (Nov. 13, 1990, New York City).

12. *Variety*, April 24, 1934.

13. Marion Romano, interview (July 6, 1990, Los Angeles); Julie Romano, interview.

14. *Variety*, March 12, 1941; *NY Times*, Feb. 28, 1941.

Chapter 3: Ragtime and Nightclubs

1. Oliver Pilat and Jo Ranson, *Sodom by the Sea: An Affectionate History of Coney Island* (Garden City, NY: Doubleday, Doran, 1941), p. 93.

2. Pilat and Ranson, p. 108.

3. The youthful Joe Weber and Lew Fields, soon-to-be vaudeville comedy stars, performed there about 1878 as 11-year-olds, having debuted in show business at the age of nine. They were both born the same year, 1867, in New York City. Weber and Fields earned $2 a day and five beer checks from Duffy for working 10 a.m. to midnight. They got an extra fifteen cents daily by selling the beer checks to the waiters instead of drinking the beer. Felix Isman, *Weber and Fields: Their Tribulations, Triumphs and Their Associates* (New York: Boni and Liveright, 1924), p. 45.

4. The boardwalk that would make the place still more popular was, when Durante came on the scene, still a decade away from being built.

5. The youngest child of orthodox cantor Moses Baline, he emigrated in

1893 with his family to New York's Lower East Side. They arrived September 14, seven months after Jimmy Durante was born, and lived on Cherry Street, the same street where Durante's father had his barbershop. Laurence Bergreen, *As Thousands Cheer: The Life of Irving Berlin* (New York: Viking, 1990), pp. 5, 8.

6. Bergreen, pp. 21–27.

7. One of the most popular songs ever written, a song not in ragtime but about ragtime, "Alexander's Ragtime Band" is a "coon" song. "Coon" was then a common term for "race" music, and Alexander was thought to be a comically unlikely name for a black man. Bergreen, p. 19. Clayton, Jackson, and Durante would soon be performing a coon song favorite, "Rufus Rastus Johnson Brown."

8. Fowler, pp. 16–24.

9. Eddie Cantor with Jane Kesner Ardmore, *Take My Life* (Garden City, NY: Doubleday, 1957), pp. 53–54.

10. Pilat and Ranson, p. 109.

11. Pilat and Ranson, p. 110.

12. Pilat and Ranson, p. 111.

13. Fowler, p. 25.

14. *Jazz Odyssey, Vol 3—The Sound of Harlem*, Columbia recorded album C3L-33, released 1964, booklet notes by George Hoefer.

15. *Variety*, Feb. 20, 1914, p. 22.

16. Fowler, p. 26.

17. The same owner controlled two establishments called the College Inn, one near the Alamo on 125th Street and the other in Coney Island, as well as the College Arms, closed when the College Inn opened in Coney Island, and the Steeplechase Ballroom in Rockaway Beach. *Variety*, June 9, 1916.

18. Samuel B. Charters and Leonard Kunstadt, *Jazz: A History of the New York Scene* (Garden City, NY: Doubleday, 1962), p. 58.

19. Al Rose and Edmond Souchon, *New Orleans Jazz: A Family Album*, rev. ed. (Baton Rouge: Louisiana State University Press, 1978; orig. 1967), pp. 144, 156; also, H.O. Brunn, *The Story of the Original Dixieland Jazz Band* (Baton Rouge: Louisiana State University Press, 1960), p. 60.

20. Charters and Kunstadt, p. 80.

21. Brian Rust, *Jazz Records 1897–1942*, 2 vols. 4th rev. enl. ed. (New Rochelle, NY: Arlington House, 1978). Most recording dates and personnel in the Ragtime chapter are derived from Rust's reference work, invaluable despite mistakes (corrections here partly by Mark Berresford).

22. Rust, *Jazz Records 1897–1942*, with corrections.

23. It's possible that Durante and the Alamo house band made other recordings. Len Kunstadt, publisher of *Record Research Magazine*, Brooklyn, NY, and coauthor with Samuel B. Charters of *Jazz: A History of the New York Scene* (1962), says that Durante's Club Alamo orchestra signed an exclusive contract with Olympic Records, reported in a late 1921 Olympic press release, "Alamo Band to Make Records," *The New York Clipper*, September 14, 1921, p. 30. Durante would have been the piano player and Doc Behrendson on saxophone. Kunstadt says it's uncertain whether any of these Olympic sides were made or released. Whatever records were released by Olympic, a very small company, are very rare today. Kunstadt, interviews, 1988 and 1993, New York.

24. David A. Jasen, *Tin Pan Alley: The Composers, the Songs, the Performers and Their Times* (New York: Donald I. Fine, 1988), p. 129; See also, Bruce Bastin, *Never Sell a Copyright: Joe Davis and His Role in the New York Music Scene 1916–1978* (Chigwell, England: Storyville, 1990).

25. Jasen, p. 84.

26. Perry Bradford, *Born with the Blues* (New York: Oak Publications, 1965), p. 131.

27. "Final Bar," *Down Beat*, April 1980, p. 12.

28. Rudi Blesh and Harriet Janis, *They All Played Ragtime*, 4th ed. (New York: Alfred A. Knopf, 1950; rpt. New York: Oak, 1971), pp. 224–225.

29. Gunther Schuller, *Early Jazz: Its Roots and Musical Development* (New York: Oxford University Press, 1968), p. 183.

30. Gunther Schuller, *The Swing Era: The Development of Jazz, 1930–1945* (New York: Oxford University Press, 1989), pp. 15–16.

31. "Coon" songs, imitating Negro mannerisms, were, like "mammy" songs, popular entertainment in minstrel shows and elsewhere, often supplemented by blackface makeup.

32. Paul Whiteman, given a by-line, "Paul Whiteman Denies 'Jazz'; Plays 'Syncopated Rhythm'," *Variety*, Jan. 3, 1924, p. 4. See also, "First American Jazz Concert Will Be Paul Whiteman's—at Aeolian Hall, New York, Feb. 12," *Variety*, Dec. 13, 1923, p. 1.

33. Paul Whiteman and Mary Margaret McBride, *Jazz* (New York: J.H. Sears, 1926).

34. Fowler, pp. 54–55.

35. Fowler, pp. 31–33.

36. Dave Stryker, a trombonist, recalled Jeanne first coming into the Alamo, where he said he worked with Durante's band for three years (c. 1918–c. 1921). Stryker interview (Aug. 18, 1984, by telephone; Jan. 6, 1985, Lake Worth, Florida).

37. Not in St. Malachy's as Fowler writes.

38. Maud Jeanne Olson, age 32, was born, according to the Church's marriage register, August 31, 1889. She was the daughter of divorced parents, John Olson and Marie Doncoes, a mixture of Swedish, Scottish, and French-Canadian immigrant stock. She had been baptized in that same church October 13, 1918. The wedding ceremony was performed by Father John J. Laughlin. The Church of the Holy Innocents, located at 128 West 37th Street in New York, was at that time known as the actors' chapel, popular with Catholic show business people. (When Jimmy married a second time, St. Malachy's on West 49th Street was the actors' chapel.) Jimmy listed his address as 2556 Palmetto Street, Brooklyn, and Jeanne as 610 West 150th Street, New York.

39. Interview with daughters of Jack Roth, Eileen Euler and Margie Sexton (Sept. 23, 1990, Pearl River, New York); also Fowler, p. 38.

40. Flushing, Queens, folklore places the Durante house at 161st or 163rd Street, but the Queens Historical Society found a James F. Durante listed in a 1926 telephone directory at 29-05 162nd Street. This author confirmed through an interview with the owners of that house, March 27, 1993, that this was the Durante house. Enrico M. Conetta, a medical doctor, and his wife, immigrants from Italy, bought the house in April 1947 for $17,500. Jimmy gave it to his cousins, the Romano family. While digging in the garden, Dr. Conetta discovered a religious medallion from the funeral of Bartolomeo Durante, placed there by the Romanos. He mailed it to the Durante relatives who had decided to join Jimmy in Los Angeles.

41. *Variety*, March 22, 1923.

42. *Variety*, April 12, 1923.

43. *Variety*, April 19, 1923.

44. "Coney Island's Early Start Boomed by Big Boardwalk," *Variety*, May 10, 1923.

45. "Police Beg Women Not to Go Leg Bare on Coney Strands," *Variety*, June 8, 1923.

46. *Variety*, several issues, including Jan. 13, 1923.

47. William Cahn, *Good Night, Mrs. Calabash: The Secret of Jimmy Durante* (New York: Duell, Sloan and Pearce, 1963), p. 43.

48. Maurice Zolotow, *No People Like Show People* (New York: Random House, 1951), p. 111.

49. Zolotow, p. 107.

50. Fowler, p. 49.

51. George S. Chappell, *The Restaurants of New York* (New York: Greenberg, 1925), p. 117.

52. Albert J. Durante, Jr., interview (Nov. 13, 1990, New York); Fowler, p. 57.

53. Fowler, p. 70.

54. Fowler, p. 77.

55. Fowler, pp. 65–66.

56. Fowler, p. 82.

57. *Variety*, Oct. 6, 1926.

58. April 21, 1948.

59. "Speaking of Pictures: Jimmy Durante Shows How to Wreck a Baby Grand," *Life*, Sept. 20, 1948, pp. 14–15.

60. Craig Thompson and Allen Raymond, *Gang Rule in New York: The Story of a Lawless Era* (New York: Dial Press, 1940), pp. 104–105.

61. Fowler, p. 135.

62. Ethel Merman, with George Eells, *Merman: An Autobiography* (New York: Simon & Schuster, 1978), p. 33; See also, Ethel Merman, as told to Pete Martin, *Who Could Ask for Anything More* (Garden City, NY: Doubleday, 1955), p. 71. The 1955 biography was published in England under a different title, with different pagination for the same material, different arrangement of the same photographs, and gives no credit to Pete Martin: Ethel Merman, *Don't Call Me Madam* (London: W.H. Allen, 1955).

63. Bob Thomas, *I Got Rhythm!: The Ethel Merman Story* (New York: G.P. Putnam's Sons, 1985), p. 27.

64. Jimmy Durante and Jack Kofoed, *Night Clubs* (New York: Alfred A. Knopf, 1931), p. 205.

65. Gilbert Seldes, "Jimmie Is Exhubiliant," *The New Republic*, Jan. 16, 1929, pp. 247–48; advertisement for the Parody Restaurant from a New York theater program, week of May 30, 1927.

66. "Whiteman's Own Club Has Grand Opening," *Billboard*, Feb. 26, 1927; Thomas A. DeLong, *Pops: Paul Whiteman, King of Jazz* (Piscataway, NJ: New Century Publishers, 1983), p. 106.

67. Polly Rose Gottlieb, *The Nine Lives of Billy Rose* (New York: Crown, 1968), pp. 79–80.

68. Gottlieb, p. 80.

69. Durante and Kofoed, pp. 62–65.

70. Durante and Kofoed, p. 247.

Chapter 4: Vaudeville and Broadway

1. Bernard Sobel, *A Pictorial History of Vaudeville* (New York: Citadel Press, 1961), pp. 17–18.

2. See Morton Minsky and Milt Machlin, *Minsky's Burlesque* (New York: Arbor House, 1986).

3. Irving Zeidman, *The American Burlesque Show* (New York: Hawthorn Books, 1967), "Censorship" chapter, pp. 219–35.

4. "Twenty Years of Vaudeville," *The New York Dramatic Mirror*, Dec. 24, 1898, pp. 90–93.

5. "Twenty Years...," *Dramatic Mirror*, p. 91.

6. "Twenty Years...," *Dramatic Mirror*, p. 92.

7. F.F. Proctor, "A Pre-Historic 'Continuous Performance'," *The New York Dramatic Mirror*, Dec. 24, 1898, p. 94. See also, Parker Zellers, *Tony Pastor: Dean of the Vaudeville Stage* (Ypsilanti, MI.: Eastern Michigan UP, 1971), pp. 71–72.

8. Langston Hughes and Milton Meltzer, *Black Magic: A Pictorial History of Black Entertainers in America* (Englewood Cliffs, NJ: Prentice-Hall, 1967; rpt. New York: Bonanza Books, 1967), p. 69.

9. A. Herbst, *New York Star*, Nov. 6, 1918.

10. *New York Star*, July 9, 1919.

11. Brian Rust with Allen G. Debus, *The Complete Entertainment Discography: from the Mid-1890s to 1942* (New Rochelle, NY: Arlington House, 1973), p. 514.

12. *Variety*, March 16, 1927.

13. *Variety*, April 18, 1928.

14. Fowler, pp. 125–26.

15. Gerald Bordman, *American Musical Theatre: A Chronicle* (New York: Oxford University Press, 1978), p. 452. Much of the basic information on all seven of the Durante shows comes from Bordman, supplemented by the original theater programs and other sources.

16. *New York Times*, July 3, 1929; rpt. *On Stage: Selected Theater Reviews from The New York Times 1920–1970*, ed. Bernard Beckerman and Howard Siegman. New York: Arno Press/Quadrangle, 1973), p. 98.

17. Herbert G. Goldman, *Jolson: The Legend Comes to Life* (New York: Oxford University Press, 1988), pp. 190–92.

18. Goldman, p. 193.

19. Bordman, p. 453.

20. *New York Times*, rpt. *On Stage*, p. 98.

21. The theater program fails to give composer credit for "Money!," while giving credit for three other Durante compositions. *The Complete Lyrics of Cole Porter* (1983) attributes proper credit, p. 105. Fowler mentions "the Money to Burn creation," p. 149.

22. Stanley Green, *The Great Clowns of Broadway* (New York: Oxford University Press, 1984), p. 56.

23. Bordman, pp. 465–66.

24. *Variety*, April 12, 1932.

25. Bordman, pp. 482–83.

26. Regina Crewe, "Spencer Tracy as 'The Show-Off' Wins Laughs on Capitol Screen; Durante and Holtz and Polly Moran in Merry Stage Show," *New York American*, March 17, 1934. Also, "Lou Holtz and Jimmie Durante Reunited in Antic Stageshow on Capitol Boards," *New York World-Telegram*, March 19, 1934.

27. *The Biographical Encyclopedia & Who's Who of the American Theatre*, ed. Walter Rigdon (New York: James H. Heineman, 1965), p. 787.

28. Gottlieb, p. 103.

29. *Broadway Highlights of 1936* (1936), part of Adolph Zukor's annual

newsreel series, starring Ted Husing reporting major doings on Broadway and show business.

30. *Richard Rodgers Fact Book* (New York: The Lynn Farnol Group, 1965), p. 158.

31. *Variety*, Oct. 7, 1936.

32. *Richard Rodgers Fact Book*, p. 160.

33. "Red, Hot and Blue," *Stage, 14* (Nov. 1936), 44–45. The article includes seven performance photographs including Durante in a polo outfit.

34. *Stage*, Nov. 1936, p. 44.

35. Bordman, p. 499.

36. Merman with Eells, p. 82.

37. Merman with Eells, p. 81; also George Eells, *The Life That Late He Led: A Biography of Cole Porter* (New York: G.P. Putnam's Sons, 1967), p. 159.

38. *The Complete Lyrics of Cole Porter* (1983), p. 147.

39. For example, "'Red, Hot, Blue!' Opens and All Is De-lovely," *Chicago Herald-Examiner*, April 14, 1937, the review finding Durante in top form, Hope breezy, and Merman heaven's gift to the lyric writers. Also, Ashton Stevens, "Two Great Comics Shine in Second Night Opening of 'Red, Hot 'n' Blue,'" *Chicago American*, April 15, 1937. [The critic had missed opening night.]

40. *The Chicago Tribune*, April 28, 1937.

41. Hope, *Have Tux, Will Travel*, pp. 127–28.

42. *The Chicago Tribune*, April 28, 1937.

43. Bordman, p. 514.

44. Merman with Eells, p. 101.

Chapter 5: Movies

1. William MacAdams, *Ben Hecht: The Man Behind the Legend* (New York: Charles Scribner's Sons, 1990), p. 117.

2. The author has an audiotape of the racial dialogue in the context of the soundtrack, as well as a videotape of the film with the abrupt deletion. It appears that the deletion was made after the film's release, perhaps for its television showing.

3. Norman Krasna, "Yuh Take This Here Now Durante Guy: Just $3,000 a Week of Bone!," *Exhibitors Herald-World*, Jan. 18, 1930, p. 28.

4. Even as late as 1960s television, as outstanding a comedy writer as Goodman Ace could not write the kind of material Durante needed for his peculiar kind of act. For a Durante TV special, airing August 9, 1961, with Bob Hope, Garry Moore, and Janice Rule his guests, Durante complained, "'Somebody hired Goodman Ace and his team of four writers to write da thing, but they didn't know how to write Durante. Ace is fine for Perry Como and da light comedy stuff, but it ain't for Durante.'" Hal Humphrey, "Durante to Debut as Cereal Seller," *L.A. Times*, Sept. 27, 1965, in reporting Durante's next special, Oct. 30, 1965.

5. The Billy Rose Collection of the New York Public Library at Lincoln Center has an extensive clippings scrapbook of this film's reviews from across the country.

6. The Get Rich Quick Wallingford stories had been used for silent movie plots since 1915.

7. Durante performs a much shorter excerpt of this song in Warner Brothers' 1941 film *The Man Who Came to Dinner*.

8. The second edition of the *Oxford English Dictionary* (1989) lists these terms, saying they apply particularly to Jimmy Durante, and gives examples of their use by or about Durante. Vol. 14, p. 628.

9. Neal Gabler, *An Empire of Their Own: How the Jews Invented Hollywood* (New York: Crown, 1988), pp. 3–4.

10. Gabler, p. 82.

11. Gabler, p. 79.

12. Rudi Blesh, *Keaton* (New York: Macmillan, 1966), p. 302.

13. Buster Keaton, with Charles Samuels, *My Wonderful World of Slapstick* (Garden City, NY: Doubleday, 1960), p. 237.

14. Blesh, p. 311.

15. Tom Dardis, *Keaton: The Man Who Wouldn't Lie Down* (New York: Charles Scribner's Sons, 1979), p. 202.

16. Keaton with Samuels, p. 201.

17. Keaton with Samuels, p. 237.

18. Thalberg's life was the basis for F. Scott Fitzgerald's final, uncompleted novel, *The Last Tycoon*, published posthumously in 1941. The character Monroe Stahr becomes at age 23 the *wunderkind* of Hollywood. In 1937, the Academy of Motion Picture Arts and Sciences established the Irving G. Thalberg Memorial Award, given each year as a special Oscar for production achievement by an individual producer.

19. Keaton with Samuels, p. 237.

20. Dardis, p. 230; see also, Bob Thomas, *Thalberg: Life and Legend* (Garden City, NY: Doubleday, 1969), p. 204.

21. Keaton with Samuels, pp. 242–43.

22. As a guest on the Rudy Vallee radio show, March 13, 1941, Durante would show how well he could work with John Barrymore, doing a very good half-hour boxing sketch.

23. "Stardom for Durante," *Variety*, Oct. 18, 1932; also, *Hollywood Reporter*, Oct. 14, 1932.

24. John Douglas Eames, *The MGM Story: The Complete History of Fifty Roaring Years* (New York: Crown, 1975), p. 95.

25. Harrison B. Summers, comp., *A Thirty-Year History of Programs Carried on National Radio Networks in the United States, 1926–1956* (Columbus, OH: Ohio State University, 1958; rpt. New York: Arno Press, 1971), p. 31.

26. Eames, p. 94.

27. The evolution of the film's script and the film's ultimate fragmentation is detailed at length by Henry Jenkins, *What Made Pistachio Nuts?: Early Sound Comedy and the Vaudeville Aesthetic* (New York: Columbia University Press, 1992), pp. 107–26.

28. Copyrighted by MGM September 9, 1933, this song had words by Lorenz Hart, with music by Richard Rodgers and Jimmy Durante.

29. Jeanne also made a brief appearance with Jimmy in one of Paramount's behind-the-scenes shorts for the "Hollywood on Parade" series. This particular short starred the songwriting team of Harry Revel and Mack Gordon, with Rudy Vallee, John Boles, Durante, Ben Turpin, Ted Healy and the Stooges, and Florence Desmond (imitator of celebrities).

30. John McCabe, *George M. Cohan: The Man Who Owned Broadway* (Garden City, NY: Doubleday, 1973), pp. 219–20.

31. Ward Morehouse, *George M. Cohan: Prince of the American Theater* (Philadelphia and New York: J.B. Lippincott, 1943), p. 186.

32. McCabe, p. 265.

33. Rigdon, p. 912.

34. Fowler, p. 200.

35. In 1951, Durante sued Paramount Pictures and Hal Wallis Productions in New York Supreme Court for using the title *That's My Boy* for a Dean Martin and Jerry Lewis film. He claimed the expression was his catchphrase that had become identified with him, and that, moreover, his Jimmy Durante Music Publishing Company had turned out a tune of the same title, written by Jackie Barnett and Sammy Fain. *Variety* reported that Durante lost the first round in the $350,000 damage suit with the court's denial of a temporary injunction against Paramount's use of the title. The Martin and Lewis movie was released with that title.

36. Fowler, pp. 202–3. Fowler reports that despite his brother-in-law's apparent lack of concern for his family in America, Jimmy paid for Genaro's return to America during World War II, where he would live with Jimmy's help in California until his death.

37. Associated Press wirephoto, Oct. 14, 1936.

38. *Variety*, Sept. 20, 1978. In September 1978, a syndicated TV series *That's Hollywood*, made by 20th Century Fox, showed the Temple-Durante song-and-dance outtake on its season opener of a regular Saturday night series, shown in New York City on WABC-TV. That one installment presented scenes that were cut from movies and funny fluffs in filming of movies and TV shows.

39. *Variety*, Oct. 18, 1939.

40. Gene Autry, with Mickey Herskowitz, *Back in the Saddle Again* (Garden City, NY: Doubleday, 1978), p. 75.

41. Fowler, p. 216.

42. Autry with Herskowitz, p. 76.

43. Autry with Herskowitz, p. 76.

44. Information taken from Warner Brothers Archives at the University of Southern California.

45. Warner Brothers Archives.

46. Warner Brothers Archives.

47. Warner Brothers Archives. Letter to Warner Bros. Pictures, Inc., from the law offices of Wright and Millikan, Los Angeles, dated Dec. 31, 1941, counsel for Charles Chaplin and Charles Chaplin Film Corporation, charging infringement of copyright.

48. Warner Brothers Archives.

49. Warner Brothers Archives.

50. *The New York Times*, April 29, 1943.

51. Largely completed by mid–August 1944, the film ran too long, as seemed evident even before a first sneak preview that November and was cut. After a second preview in the spring of 1945, it was cut again. After opening the film in Boston that August, MGM thought of cutting it further but let it go at 110 minutes for its Broadway first run in April 1946. Stephen Harvey, *Directed by Vincente Minnelli* (New York: The Museum of Modern Art/Harper & Row, 1989), p. 58.

52. This included Durante's "You Gotta Start Off Each Day with a Song" and his sketches "Death and Taxes," with Edward Arnold and Kay Williams, and "The Pied Piper," as well as a routine he did with Lucille Ball and Marilyn Maxwell. James Robert Parish and William T. Leonard, *The Funsters* (New Rochelle, NY: Arlington House, 1979), pp. 237–38.

53. NBC Monitor radio interview, Feb. 9, 1963.

54. Aside from the films involving Durante, Pasternak produced such musical comedies as *One Hundred Men and a Girl* (1937), a Deanna Durbin feature for Universal, that also highlighted Leopold Stokowski; *Destry Rides Again* (1939), Universal, starring Marlene Dietrich; *Presenting Lily Mars* (1942), MGM, starring Judy Garland; *Anchors Aweigh* (1945), MGM, starring Frank Sinatra, Gene Kelly, and Kathryn Grayson, with Jose Iturbi.

55. The Italianate word "umbriago" had the connotation of a friendly inebriate. It had been used by Durante in his act long before it became a song copyrighted by Caesar and Durante.

56. Both Roth and Jackson are listed in the opening credits.

57. See note in Chapter 7: TV & Nightclubs—Recreating the 1920s.

58. Leslie Halliwell, *Halliwell's Filmgoer's Companion*, 9th ed. (New York: Charles Scribner's Sons, 1988), p. 539.

59. "No-Good Squirrel," *Life* magazine, April 3, 1950, p. 34.

60. Music by Charles B. Lawlor, lyrics by James W. Blake, "Sidewalks of New York" was turned into a 1927 Broadway musical by the same title. For another good sample of what vaudeville was like, watch Bob Hope playing vaudeville great Eddie Foy in the 1955 Paramount film, *The Seven Little Foys*.

61. Letter to the author, Feb. 9, 1993, from the British Film Institute.

62. Robert F. Hawkins, "Active Italians," *New York Times*, Aug. 27, 1961, reprinted in *The New York Times Encyclopedia of Film*, 1958–1963 volume (New York: Times Books, 1984).

63. *Epoca*, April 2, 1961, p. 460, as mentioned in John Darretta, *Vittorio De Sica: A Guide to References and Resources* (Boston: G.K. Hall, 1983), p. 99.

64. "Il Giudizio Universale," in Darretta's De Sica Guide, "The Films: Synopses, Credits, and Notes," pp. 95–99; also, "Il Giudizio Universale," *Variety Film Reviews 1907*–1980, 16 vols., (New York: Garland, 1983), originally *Variety*, Sept. 13, 1961, dateline Venice, Sept. 2, 1961. The screenplay for the film, with a diary of production notes and 80 film stills, was published in a book: Vittorio De Sica and Cesare Zavattini, *Il Giudizio Universale*. Ed. Alberto Bevilacqua. Rome: Salvatore Sciascia Editore, 1961.

65. Kathleen Post, "Durante: The New Groom Takes On a New Sidekick," *TV Radio Mirror*, Sept. 1961, p. 77. Primarily a report on Durante's long premarriage relationship with Margie Little, the article touches upon his brief role in the De Sica film.

Chapter 6: Radio

1. Irving Settel, *A Pictorial History of Radio* (New York: Citadel Press, 1960), p. 41; see also, Erik Barnouw, *A History of Broadcasting in the United States*, vol. 1: "A Tower in Babel" (New York: Oxford University Press, 1966), p. 145.

2. Settel, pp. 42–43.

3. Settel, pp. 48–49.

4. Settel, pp. 49–50, 52, 55.

5. Settel, pp. 57, 59.

6. Most information about what radio shows were on the air each season and their audience ratings comes from the book by Harrison B. Summers, cited in an earlier endnote.

7. "As the Nose Blows" resurfaced, on rare occasion, as on a guest appearance with Perry Como, a TV show February 22, 1961.

8. Tapes made from original discs and scripts of Durante radio programs were studied at the USC Cinema-Television Library and Archives of Performing Arts, Los Angeles. Tapes of the Cantor show with Durante substituting omit all Ruth Etting songs.

9. Fowler, p. 38.

10. Jimmy Durante, *Jimmy (Schnozzle) Durante's Jumbo Song Book* (New York: Harry Engel, 1936). The song book's cover was printed two ways: beneath the crossed noses, one version read "FUNNY Songs, Jokes, Pictures"; the other version read "Starring in Billy Rose's JUMBO."

11. Tapes of Rudy Vallee radio shows were provided for study upon request from the Rudy Vallee Collection, Thousand Oaks Library, Thousand Oaks, California.

12. Paul Robeson, the politically controversial singer-actor, was listed as a guest on this show, but the tape received from Thousand Oaks omitted Robeson.

13. Abraham Lincoln Marovitz, interview (July 25, 1991, by telephone, Chicago).

14. Garry Moore, interview (April 25, 1991, by telephone, Hilton Head, South Carolina).

15. Phil Cohan, interview (Jan. 19, 1991, Pacific Palisades, California).

16. Moore interview.

17. Cohan interview.

18. When this bit of mayhem wasn't done on the show itself, it was used before the show to warm up the studio audience.

19. Maggie Arnold was housekeeper to Jimmy Durante for many years until he married his second wife, Margie Little. Maggie's sister Ethel, who worked for the Durantes briefly before Maggie, married Tom Bradley, a police officer later to be mayor of Los Angeles.

20. Cohan interview.

21. Moore interview.

22. Scripts from USC Archives.

23. Cohan interview; see also, Glenhall Taylor, *Before Television: The Radio Years* (South Brunswick and New York: A.S. Barnes, 1979), pp. 152, 154–55; George Burns, with David Fisher, *All My Best Friends* (New York: G.P. Putnam's Sons, 1989), pp. 119–20; Jhan Robbins, *Inka Dinka Doo: The Life of Jimmy Durante* (New York: Paragon House, 1991), p. 149.

24. Moore interview.

25. Roger D. Kinkle, *The Complete Encyclopedia of Popular Music and Jazz 1900–1950*, vol. 2 (New Rochelle, N.Y.: Arlington House, 1974), p. 669; see also, Jimmie Hollifield II, "A Voice Sweet as Candy," *Comics Scene*, #17 (Feb. 1991), 61–64ff.

26. Candy Candido, interviews (July 15, 1991, by telephone; Aug. 31, 1991, in Burbank, California).

27. Cohan interview.

28. Scripts in USC Archives.

29. Cohan interview; see also Desi Arnaz, *A Book* (New York: Morrow, 1976), pp. 258–59; George Burns with David Fisher, pp. 122–23.

30. Candido interview; supported by script in USC Archives.

31. The Jimmy Durante Music Publishing Company had Lou Cohen as President; Eddie Jackson, Secretary; Jack Roth, General Manager.

32. Alan Young, interview (Dec. 12, 1990, by telephone, San Fernando Valley, California).

33. Moore interview.
34. Cohan interview.
35. "Lou Clayton's Death Recalls Close Kinship with Durante-Jackson," *Variety*, Sept. 13, 1950; "Lou Clayton, Former Durante Partner, Dies," *Los Angeles Times*, Sept. 13, 1950.

Chapter 7: Television and Nightclubs—Recreating the 1920s

1. Tim Brooks and Earle Marsh, *The Complete Directory to Prime Time Network TV Shows, 1946–Present* (New York: Ballantine Books, 1979), p. ix.
2. "50 Years Together: Channel 2 and You," CBS-TV, Channel 2, New York, *60 Minutes*, July 10, 1991; see also, *New York Times*, July 10, 1991.
3. Brooks and Marsh, p. ix.
4. Harry Castleman and Walter J. Podrazik, *The TV Schedule Book: Four Decades of Network Programming from Sign-on to Sign-off* (New York: McGraw-Hill, 1984), p. 3.
5. Brooks and Marsh, pp. xi–xii.
6. Charles Isaacs, head writer of Durante's TV shows, with Jack Elinson, donated his extensive collection of programs and scripts to the Theater Arts Library, UCLA, Los Angeles, where they were examined. The scripts are in five bound volumes, covering 1950–54, the *Four Star Revue*, the *All Star Revue*, and the *Colgate Comedy Hour*. UCLA also has a few scattered Durante shows, early and later, on videotapes for research viewing. A few additional Durante shows and guest appearances were in the collection of the Museum of Television & Radio, New York.
7. Jack Gould, "Durante a 'Smash' in His Video Debut," *New York Times*, Nov. 2, 1950.
8. Jack O'Brian, "Jimmy Durante Still the Funniest Man in the World," *New York Journal American*, Nov. 2, 1950.
9. Harriet Van Horne, "TV Debut Shows Off Durante at His Best," *New York World-Telegram and Sun*, Nov. 2, 1950.
10. Eddie Jackson interview by Hal Humphrey, "He Really Steams Me," *The Mirror* [Los Angeles], Dec. 15, 1952.
11. Cohan interview.
12. Helen Traubel, with Richard G. Hubler, *St. Louis Woman* (New York: Duell, Sloan and Pearce, 1959), p. 246.
13. Traubel with Hubler, pp. 246–47.
14. Maracaibo 809, *Jimmy Durante & Carmen Miranda*. The same show is described in great detail by a Miranda biographer, Martha Gil-Montero, *Brazilian Bombshell: The Biography of Carmen Miranda* (New York: Donald I. Fine, 1989), pp. 253–57.
15. Gil-Montero, p. 253.
16. Gil-Montero, p. 258.
17. Nick Kenny, in *New York Daily Mirror*, Nov. 5, 1951.
18. Dated November 20, 1951, from Wakulla Springs, Florida, on personal stationery with the monogram MMT. From the Charles Isaacs Collection at UCLA.
19. *Variety*, March 24, 1952.

20. Charles Isaacs, interview (Jan. 24, 1991, by telephone, Los Angeles); Jack Elinson, interview (July 16, 1991, by telephone, Los Angeles).

21. UCLA Archive script; see also, Whitney Stine, with a running commentary by Bette Davis, *Mother Goddam: The Story of the Career of Bette Davis* (New York: Hawthorn Books, 1974), p. 243.

22. Tallulah Bankhead, *Tallulah: My Autobiography* (New York: Harper & Brothers, 1952), p. 293.

23. *Variety*, May 14, 1952.

24. Candy Candido, interview (Jan. 17, 1991, Burbank, California).

25. Thomas M. Pryor, *New York Times*, Feb. 21, 1952. This project did not get far. In 1959–60, plans for another film project failed to materialize.

26. Philippe Halsman and others, *The Candidate: A Photographic Interview with the Honorable James Durante* (New York: Simon & Schuster, 1952). A similar photo book was done on French comedian Fernandel.

27. Dean Martin, Bing Crosby, and Frank Sinatra were interested in making a movie about Clayton, Jackson, and Durante. Director Frank Capra turned in a script he had written to Columbia Pictures for planned 1959–60 release. A biographer of director Frank Capra says the three stars lost interest and that the script was a "formless and bathetic treatment" of Fowler's *Schnozzola*. Joseph McBride, *Frank Capra: The Catastrophe of Success* (New York: Simon & Schuster, 1992), p. 639; see also, Frank Capra, *The Name Above the Title: An Autobiography* (New York: Macmillan, 1971), pp. 465–68. A Crosby biographer wrote, "The actors' strike meant the project had to be dropped." Charles Thompson, *Bing: The Authorized Biography* (New York: David McKay, 1975), p. 211.

28. Candy Candido interview.

29. Charles Isaacs interview.

30. Hal Humphrey, "'It's Eatin' Us All Up!," *The Mirror* [Los Angeles], May 10, 1954.

31. The souvenir program is part of the Billy Rose Collection at the New York Public Library at Lincoln Center.

32. Hal Humphrey, "TV Getting Too Crowded for J. Durante," *Mirror News* [Los Angeles], Dec. 1, 1959. Incidentally, the NBC radio network's last expensive effort to keep radio entertainment shows alive failed at least partly for the same reason: overloading a show with too many guests doing too many things. Premiering November 5, 1950, four days after Durante's television debut, *The Big Show*, 90 minutes weekly, was spearheaded by Tallulah Bankhead, as hostess, and Fred Allen, who was talked out of retirement. Durante appeared several times.

33. Earl Wilson, "It Happened Last Night" column, with lead story and headline, "Durante Does Moider 'Em in New Copacabana Revue," *New York Post*, March 5, 1943; "Jimmy Durante: The Great Schnozzle Has Hit the Jackpot with a Comeback Act That Is 20 Years Old," *Look*, June 1, 1943, pp. 70–71.

34. For example, *New York Sunday Mirror*, Dec. 26, 1943, p. 31.

35. Kathleen Post, *TV Radio Mirror*, Sept. 1961, pp. 25ff.

36. Margie Little, as told to John M. Ross, "My Husband—Jimmy Durante," *The American Weekly*, Jan. 22, 1961.

37. While careful not to give details or names, Durante's nephew Julie Romano says his uncle was a "womanizer." Julie Romano interview. Marty Roth, son of Jack Roth, says his father was often the "beard," the ostensible date, for Durante girlfriends. Marty Roth, interview (Jan. 17, 1991, Burbank, California).

38. Betty Jane Howarth, interviews (May 29, 1991, by telephone, Pittsburgh, and in person, July 19, 1991, Pittsburgh). Parish and Leonard, p. 239, also took

note of this relationship: "For years Durante had also been dating actress Betty Jane Howarth."

39. Wanda Smith, interview (Aug. 8, 1991, by telephone, Venice, California).

40. Otto Friedrich, *City of Nets: A Portrait of Hollywood in the 1940's* (New York: Harper & Row, 1986), p. 262; also, Jefferson Graham, *Vegas: Live and in Person* (New York: Abbeville Press, 1989), p. 20.

41. Jack Roth's scrapbook, clipping from an unnamed newspaper, Sunday, Feb. 12, 1950.

42. Jack Roth scrapbook, clipping dated March 1951.

43. *Sum and Substance*, Herman Harvey, host, 1962; also interview with Herman Harvey (July 30, 1991, by telephone, Rancho Palos Verdes, California).

44. *Monitor*, Feb. 9, 1963.

45. Jack Roth's scrapbook, clipping dated March 29, 1951.

46. "Schnoz's $68,000 Cracks Chi Chez Paree Mark," *Variety*, June 25, 1952.

47. Jack Roth scrapbook.

48. William Leonard, "Durante Back at Chez with Old Routines," *Chicago Sunday Tribune*, June 14, 1953.

49. Stan Delaplane, "Stan Delaplane's Postcard from Reno," *Chicago American*, July 22, 1953.

50. Eileen Euler and Margie Sexton, interview; also, Marty Roth, interview (Jan. 17, 1991, Burbank, California).

51. Jackie Barnett, interview (July 12, 1990, Marina del Rey, California).

52. Barnett says he wrote "One Room Home," a revised version of Jimmy's old "One Room House," but the newer copyright was assigned to Durante alone. Controversy surrounds this composition. According to Fowler, Durante got the idea for "One Room Home" from a drunk police captain in a nightclub, and the song Durante wrote was used in the Boston tryout of the musical *Show Girl*. Some years later Durante used it again on radio and was sued, with NBC, by the poet Alfred Kreymborg who claimed it ridiculed his own serious, free verse. The court ruled there was no infringement of copyright. Details of the lawsuit are given by Fowler (pp. 136–37) and the media, including *The New York Times*, "Poet Asks $100,000 for His Free Verse," March 22, 1934; *Newsweek* ("Poet Sues Durante," March 31, 1934, p. 34); and *Radio Stars* (Dora Albert, "I'll Be Suing You," Oct. 1934, p. 82). A 1952 amendment of the copyright law gave owners of non-dramatic material control of performance rights (Barnouw, vol. 2, p. 100).

The Barnett version, "One Room Home," was used by Durante on NBC-TV in the 1950s and recorded for Warner Bros. in 1963. Many years later Barnett contended that he collaborated on a revised version of this very funny and emotionally moving song but was not given proper credit. ASCAP lists "One Room House" and credits only Durante. On the *September Song* album, credits list "One Room Home" composers as Durante-Barnett. When in 1989 the musical *Durante* was touring the country in a failed effort to reach Broadway, Barnett wanted to sue the producers for failing to list his name in the program as coauthor of the song "One Room Home" and for failing to pay him royalties.

53. Sonny King, interview (July 14, 1991, by telephone, Chicago).

54. Jackie Barnett interview.

55. Robert Golden, interview (April 23, 1991, by telephone, Rancho Mirage, California). He is Eddie Jackson's stepson and the surviving family member with whom Eddie felt closest (more so than with Eddie's own children).

56. Jackie Barnett interview.

57. The sources wished to remain anonymous.

58. *Variety,* Sept. 21, 1960.

59. Betty Jane Howarth interview.

60. George Finley, interview (Jan. 10, 1991, by telephone, Los Angeles).

61. Unmarked clipping from Jack Roth's scrapbook.

62. Witnesses were Clement Hirsch and Edith Hirsch. The priest was Thomas De Luca. Jimmy's parents were listed in the registry as Bartolomeo Durante and Katherine Novilino (not Rosa). Margaret's parents were listed as Samuel Little and Cecilia Knothe. She had last been baptized recently, December 2, 1960, at St. Victor's Church, 8634 Hollywood Drive, West Hollywood, California, and she was listed as living in West Hollywood. Jimmy was listed as living at 511 N. Beverly Drive, Hollywood.

63. Lloyd Shearer, "When Is a Man Too Old to Adopt a Baby?," *Parade* magazine, [Syracuse, NY] *Herald American*, September 9, 1962, pp. 4–5. From Jack Roth's scrapbook.

64. Betty Jane Howarth interview.

65. Wanda Smith interview.

66. Betty Jane Howarth interview.

67. *Nevada State Journal and Reno Evening Gazette*, Sept. 22, 1962. From Jack Roth's scrapbook.

68. Abraham Lincoln Marovitz, interview (July 25, 1991, by telephone, Chicago).

69. Rosemary Romano Halderman, interview (Jan. 13, 1991, Oceanside, California; also previously, Nov. 11, 1990, by telephone).

70. Jerry Gaghan, "The Schnoz Returns," *Philadelphia Daily News*, Jan. 11, 1963.

71. The rest of the cast included Audrey Christie (as Rosie), John McIntyre (as Duveen), Ralph Bell (as Chet Hudson), Daryl Richard (as Frank Peterson), Kevin O'Neal, Barry Gordon, and Dorothy Konrad.

72. UCLA Archives.

73. Jackie Barnett interview. This writer saw only the cover with CeCe.

74. *Variety,* June 9, 1971.

75. Dianne, Peggy, Kathy and Janet Lennon, *Same Song—Separate Voices: The Collective Memoirs of the Lennon Sisters* (Santa Monica, CA: Roundtable Publishing, 1985), p. 227.

76. An informational sheet issued by the Fraternal Order of Eagles in late 1966 or early 1967 said its Fund had presented grants to the Milwaukee Children's Hospital and St. John's Hospital of Pediatrics in Santa Monica, California. Durante, it was noted, was the "gentlest and kindliest of men," and had entertained without charge at eight consecutive Eagles conventions and other Eagles gatherings over the years. He was an active life member.

77. "Durante at 79: 55 of 'Em in the 'Biz,'" *Variety,* April 5, 1972, p. 100.

78. *L.A. Herald Examiner,* May 26, 1972. From Jack Roth's scrapbook.

79. *Van Nuys (Calif.) News,* Sept. 26, 1972. From Jack Roth's scrapbook.

80. *Newsweek,* Nov. 26, 1973.

81. Robert E. Rhodes, Atwood Professor of Journalism, University of Alaska, Anchorage, letter to author, Oct. 30, 1990. Also, newspaper reports of the event: Earl Wilson, "It Happened Last Night," *New York Post,* April 24, 1974, p. 52; "Inka Dinka Doo in His Veins," New York *Daily News,* April 24, 1974, p. 24; Jack O'Brian, "The Voice of Broadway," syndicated column, various newspapers including one in Wilkes-Barre, PA, May 8, 1974. The first two clippings come from

the New York Public Library, the third from Charles Stumpf clippings collection, Conyngham, PA.

82. "Durante Wants Out," *Variety*, clipping, dateline Hollywood, June 11, 1974. The author named was Charles Mangel, *Look* Senior Editor, who had interviewed Durante for an article, "Pinocchio Lives!," *Look*, March 4, 1969, pp. 93–98.

83. Parish and Leonard, p. 239.

84. *Variety*, February 15, 1978.

85. Abraham Lincoln Marovitz interview.

86. Thompson, pp. 77–78.

87. Mangel, p. 94.

Chapter 8: Conclusion

1. He didn't recall whether the words were by Skolsky or Walter Winchell, with whom he had also collaborated on one song in the 1920s. The song written with Walter Winchell was "She Doesn't," words by Winchell, music by Durante and Chick Endor.

2. *Sum and Substance.* The lines from the song were reprinted in the book by Dayton Stoddart, *Lord Broadway, Variety's Sime* (New York: Wilfred Funk, 1941), pp. 306–07.

3. "Laughter," *American Magazine*, May 1934, p. 61.

4. Abraham Lincoln Marovitz interview.

5. Copyright © 1936 (Renewed 1964) EMI Robbins Catalog, Inc. Used by permission of CPP/Belwin, Inc., P.O. Box 4340, Miami, FL 33014. International copyright secured. Made in U.S.A. All rights reserved.

6. The song, with Durante's narrative interruptions included, was recorded on a 1946 Decca 78, reissued on LP, and much later on cassette.

7. Tommy and Nick Leonessa, of Nick the Florist, interview (June 1990, New York).

8. Interview (June 1990, New York).

Appendix A

CHRONOLOGY

1893: February 10, James Francis Durante is born on New York's Lower East Side, the fourth and youngest child of a barber father and a mail-order bride, Bartolomeo and Rosa Durante, both immigrants from Salerno, Italy.

1908: Jimmy is playing ragtime piano at neighborhood parties, in Bowery clubs, and between bouts at a prizefighting arena.

1910: Losing the last of several menial jobs, he begins in earnest a career as a piano player, in Coney Island, at Diamond Tony's. That fall he plays in Chinatown, at the Chatham Club.

1911: Back in Coney Island, playing at Carey Walsh's, he is nicknamed "Ragtime Jimmy." Here he meets Izzy Iskowitch, soon to be famous as Eddie Cantor.

1914: Playing piano at many clubs around New York, Jimmy gets an important break when he begins to work at the Alamo Club in Harlem.

1917: Jimmy, leading the white jazz band at the Club Alamo on 125th Street in Harlem, books Eddie Jackson, a shimmy dancer, and his vaudeville partner, blues singer Dot Taylor.

1918: Winter, Jimmy meets Maude Jeanne Olson, a young lady from Toledo, Ohio, who comes into the Club Alamo looking for a singing job. November, in a New York recording studio, the Original New Orleans Jazz Band, with Durante on piano, records for the Okeh label, "Ole Miss" and "Ja Da (Intro. 'You'll Find Old Dixieland in France')." The same numbers are rerecorded for the Gennett label January 1919.

1920: January 16. Prohibition Amendment (18th to the Constitution) is ratified by the necessary two-thirds of the states and goes into effect. In May, Durante records with his own group, Jimmy Durante's Jazz Band, "Why Cry Blues," for Gennett.

1921: January 1, Jimmy's mother dies of a blood clot in the brain. He has the first of his many song compositions published, including "Let's Agree to Disagree," written with the famous black jazz singer Mamie Smith and black composer Chris Smith. The most popular of the songs he has published this year is "I've Got My Habits On," which earns him almost $1,500 in royalties, with lyrics by Chris Smith and Bob Schafer. On June 19, Jimmy, age 28, marries Maude Jeanne Olson, age 32, in Holy Innocents Church, New York. In August, Ladd's Black Aces, a white jazz group

193

organized by Sam Lanin, makes its first recordings for Gennett, Durante on piano. In October, Bailey's Lucky Seven, another Sam Lanin jazz group, makes its first records.

1923: Club Durant opens with Durante's partner Eddie Jackson, and soon after, with new partner Lou Clayton.

1924: Club Durant is padlocked for Prohibition violations. Clayton, Jackson, and Durante open the Dover Club.

1927: C, J&D perform on regular basis at the Parody Club. In March, they make their vaudeville debut at Loew's State.

1928: In April, C, J&D headline a vaudeville bill at the Palace, breaking box office records. In May C, J&D leave the Parody Club to begin a vaudeville tour of Keith-Albee theaters in Cincinnati, Chicago, and Milwaukee, adding Minneapolis. In the fall, they open at the Silver Slipper cafe in New York, but ten days later the place is closed by Prohibition agents.

1929: In May, C, J&D make their first and only recording, "Can Broadway Do Without Me?" and "So I Ups to Him," for Columbia. July 2, C, J&D open on Broadway in Ziegfeld's *Show Girl*. Before the end of the year, the trio works at Paramount's Astoria studio on the film *Roadhouse Nights*.

1930: December 8, C, J&D open on Broadway in Cole Porter's *The New Yorkers*. Here they do their famous "Wood" routine, piling the stage with anything they can find made of wood.

1931: Early in the year Durante's book coauthored with journalist Jack Kofoed is published, *Night Clubs*. In May, C, J&D play the Palace. When *The New Yorkers* closes, Jimmy and wife Jeanne move to Hollywood where Jimmy has a five-year contract from MGM. Films for MGM in 1931—*The New Adventures of Get Rich Quick Wallingford* and *The Cuban Love Song*.

1932: MGM films this year—*The Passionate Plumber*, *The Wet Parade*, *Speak Easily*, and *Blondie of the Follies*. For Paramount—*The Phantom President*. In April, he works alone on stage for the first time without Clayton and Jackson, playing a week in Pittsburgh.

1933: Durante's most successful composition, "Inka Dinka Doo," is published, with lyrics by Ben Ryan. Immediately several dance and jazz bands record their own arrangements of it. March 4, Durante opens on Broadway in *Strike Me Pink*. In the fall, Durante substitutes for Eddie Cantor on his NBC radio show. MGM films this year—*What! No Beer?*, *Hell Below*, *Broadway to Hollywood*, and *Meet the Baron*.

1934: On February 13, Los Angeles, Durante records "Inka Dinka Doo" and "Hot Patatta" for Columbia. In March, he headlines a stage show at Broadway's Capitol Theatre, with Lou Holtz and Polly Moran. On April 18, Jimmy's brother Albert J. Durante dies in New York. In the summer, Durante again substitutes for Eddie Cantor on radio. Films this year—*Palooka* (United Artists), *George White's Scandals* (Fox), *Hollywood Party* (MGM), *Strictly Dynamite* (RKO), and *Student Tour* (MGM).

1935: Film—*Carnival* (Columbia). In the fall, Durante takes over Ed Wynn's radio program for Texaco. On November 16, Jimmy opens in Billy Rose's *Jumbo*, Broadway spectacle.

1936: Publication of *Jimmy (Schnozzle) Durante's Jumbo Song Book*, all songs with words and music by Durante: "I'm Jimmy, That Well Dressed Man"; "I

Know Darn Well I Can Do Without Broadway (Can Broadway Do Without Me?); "You Gotta Start Off Each Day with a Song"; "I Got a Million of 'Em"; "It's Mutiny!"; "Hot-Cha-Cha!"; "I'm Mortified"; "It's the Gypsy in Me!". On June 1, JD opens at the London Palladium after touring Paris, Rome, Dublin, Glasgow, and Liverpool. While in England, he makes the film *Land Without Music,* later released in the United States as *Forbidden Music.* On October 29, JD opens on Broadway in Cole Porter's *Red, Hot and Blue!*

1938: JD guest stars on the radio shows of Jack Oakie and Rudy Vallee. Films— *Start Cheering* (Columbia), *Sally, Irene and Mary* (20th Century Fox), *Little Miss Broadway* (20th Century Fox).

1939: On February 9, JD opens on Broadway in *Stars in Your Eyes.* He guest stars on the Rudy Vallee radio show. In October, he appears at the Paramount Theatre in New York.

1940: Film—*Melody Ranch* (Republic).

1941: February 27, Jimmy's father dies at age 92, in New York, while Jimmy was appearing at Earl Carroll's theater restaurant in Hollywood. Films— *You're in the Army Now* (Warner Bros.), *The Man Who Came to Dinner* (Warner Bros.).

1942: Early in the year, JD is offered eight weeks of vaudeville engagements. He asks Eddie Jackson to join him, while Lou Clayton recuperates from a car accident. J&D play Brooklyn, Boston, Hartford, Providence, and Pittsburgh. On June 24, Jimmy's sister, Lilian Romano, dies in Brooklyn, and Jimmy flies from Hollywood for the funeral.

1943: On February 14, wife Jeanne, age 52, dies in California. On February 26, JD appears on *The Camel Comedy Caravan,* NBC radio, New York, with a young comedian unknown to him, Garry Moore, on another segment of the show. In late spring, Durante and Moore sign to do a new radio show for Camel cigarettes, on CBS. They also substitute for Abbott & Costello on NBC during Costello's illness. JD appears at the Copacabana much of the year, his first nightclub appearance since 1931. He also appears at the Capitol Theatre, New York. Roy Bargy becomes JD's musical director, to remain with him until retirement in 1963.

1944: January 24, *Time* magazine features JD on its cover. JD meets Margie Little, a hat-check girl and switchboard operator at the Copacabana. They date. He gives her a ring December 1950, and they marry December 1960. Films this year, made under new MGM contract—*Two Girls and a Sailor, Music for Millions.* He shoots scenes for MGM musical *Ziegfeld Follies,* but film runs long, and all his scenes are cut before release in January 1946.

1945: April 6, Rexall Drugs replaces Camel as sponsor of the Durante-Moore radio show. October 31, JD leaves imprint of nose and hand on sidewalk of Grauman's Chinese Theatre.

1946: Billy Rose, in his syndicated column "Pitching Horseshoes," addresses a letter to Louis B. Mayer, head of MGM, critical of the way the studio has handled Durante. June 5, *Variety* publishes a tribute to JD's 30th anniversary in show business. June 17, *Newsweek* features JD on its cover. MGM film this year—*Two Sisters from Boston.* August, release of two songs from the MGM film, JD assisted by Eddie Jackson, on the Majestic label. Decca releases a Durante album in its Personality Series. December 4, JD is guest on Bing Crosby's radio show the first of five times. December 26, Durante is the headliner at the grand opening of the Flamingo casino in Las Vegas, built by Benjamin "Bugsy" Siegel.

1947: June 27, Garry Moore's last appearance as co-host of the Durante-Moore radio show. December 18, JD is guest on the Kraft Music Hall, starring Al Jolson, NBC radio, the first of four times. MGM films—*It Happened in Brooklyn, This Time for Keeps.*

1948: April 21, on JD's radio show Clayton, Jackson, and Durante recreate the Dover Club in a 25th-year reunion, the vaudeville team's first appearance on radio. June 23, last Durante radio show for Rexall. October 8, start of new season on radio, the show has switched to NBC, sponsored by Camel, and Alan Young becomes co-host. A-1 Comics issues two Jimmy Durante Comics. MGM film—*On an Island with You.*

1948–51: MGM releases 20 Durante songs.

1949: April 8, Don Ameche replaces Alan Young as co-host of the radio show. April 16, Clayton, Jackson, and Durante perform for the Friars Club of California. December, JD appears for six weeks at the Copacabana, three shows nightly.

1950: February, JD takes his act to the Chez Paree, Chicago, after a 12-year absence from Chicago's cafe circuit. June 30, last appearance of the Durante radio show. September 12, partner and personal manager Lou Clayton dies in Santa Monica, California, at age 63. November 1, debut of JD on NBC television, *Four Star Revue.* December, Jimmy gives Margie Little an engagement ring. Films—*The Great Rupert* (Eagle-Lion), *The Milkman* (Universal).

1951: March, RCA Red Seal (classical division) releases a recording of Helen Traubel and JD duets from two JD television shows. April, JD wins the prestigious George Peabody Award for his television comedy. June, *Collier's* magazine begins a six-part serialization of Gene Fowler's new book on Durante, *Schnozzola.* NBC signs Durante to a new 15-year contract. October 6, JD begins second season on television in revamped format of *Four Star Revue,* now titled *All Star Revue.*

1952: Paramount shows interest in filming the life of JD, buying the rights to Fowler's book. JD's agent, Abe Lastfogel, head of the William Morris Agency, and Don Hartman, production supervisor at the studio, have talks about this. JD is to play himself in the film. May 5, JD and his troupe open their show at the London Palladium. While there he promotes the launching of the British publication of the Fowler book. He also promotes *The Candidate: A Photographic Interview with the Honorable James Durante,* photo book compiled by Philippe Halsman and others. June, JD breaks the house record at the Chez Paree, Chicago.

1953: February 5, JD is presented an Emmy Award as best television comedian of 1952. June, JD appears with his "junior partner," Sonny King. July, the show goes to the Riverside, theater restaurant in Reno. Fall, JD becomes principal host for the 1953-54 season of *The Colgate Comedy Hour,* on NBC, appearing himself about once a month.

1954: October 2, premiere of *The Jimmy Durante Show* on the *Texaco Star Theatre,* NBC, biweekly, alternately with *The Donald O'Connor Show.*

1955: September 24, second season for Texaco, now weekly.

1957: March 17, Entertainment Industry Tribute to JD at New York's Waldorf-Astoria, with a staged dramatization of his life. June 29, first of Durante show reruns, NBC Texaco shows, kinescopes purchased by Durante and run on CBS through September 21, as summer replacement for Jackie Gleason. Film—*Beau James* (Paramount, unbilled appearance with Bob Hope). Decca releases album *Club Durant*, with excerpts from JD's radio and TV shows, featuring duets with show business greats, and presenting Clayton, Jackson, and Durante.

1958: March 3, U.S. Representative from Illinois, Hon. Melvin Price, enters remarks about JD's "Fifty Years in Show Business for a Great American Comedian" into the *Congressional Record*, 85th Congress, Second Session, praise deserved but premature by several years.

1959: Decca issues album *Jimmy Durante (in Person) at the Piano*. October 19, JD is a surprise guest on *The Frank Sinatra Timex Show*, ABC-TV variety special, after a tribute to Clayton, Jackson, and Durante with Sinatra as Lou Clayton, Bing Crosby as Eddie Jackson, and Dean Martin as Durante.

1960: Film—*Pepe* (Columbia). September 12, Jules Buffano, Durante's long-time piano player, dies in Hollywood, age 62. December 14, JD, age 67, marries Margie Little, age 39, in New York.

1961: JD's act at the Copacabana is recorded and released by Roulette, *Jimmy Durante at the Copacabana*. The only commercial recording of Durante in a nightclub, it includes Eddie Jackson and Sonny King. Film—*Il Giudizio Universale* (Italian; English title, *The Last Judgment*). August 9, JD NBC-TV special. December 24, JD and Margie bring home a baby girl, Cecilia Alicia, seeking to adopt her.

1962: June 8, JD, age 69, and Margie, 41, are given permission to adopt CeCe, after California court proceedings to determine if JD were too old to adopt a child. September, Helen Traubel appears with JD in the South Shore Room of Harrah's, Lake Tahoe, through September 26. Film—*Billy Rose's Jumbo* (MGM). JD gives an interview for telecast on a Los Angeles station, KNXT, *Sum and Substance*, hosted by Professor Herman Harvey.

1963: January 10, JD opens at Palumbo's nightclub, Philadelphia, with Sonny King in the troupe. February 9, *Monitor*, NBC radio, presents a 70th birthday tribute to JD. JD's first album for Warner Bros. is released, *September Song*.

1964: JD's second album for Warner Bros. is released, *Hello Young Lovers*. July 18, CBS-TV pilot for a situation comedy, *The Jimmy Durante Show*, is aired but fails to attract sponsors and is not inserted into the fall lineup. September, the Hollywood Press Club honors JD on his 50th anniversary in show business.

1965: JD's third album for Warner Bros. is released, *Jimmy Durante's Way of Life*. May 1, JD is guest on *The Hollywood Palace*, ABC-TV, a show on which he will serve as host several times in the next few years, through 1968. October 30, first JD TV special in four years, *Jimmy Durante Meets the Lively Arts*, ABC.

1966: March 7, JD speaks at a National Press Club luncheon, Washington, DC, ostensibly revealing the source of Mrs. Calabash. March 9, U.S. Representative from Florida, Hon. Claude Pepper, introduces into the *Congressional Record* remarks about JD, "Jimmy Durante—The Eighth Wonder of the World," 89th Congress, Second Session. Earlier, March 3, the *Congressional Record* carried a tribute to JD, "Fifty Years in Show Business for a Great American Comedian." Also in March, Washington, DC, in a ceremony at the White House for Easter Seals, JD is declared national chairman of the Society for Crippled Children and Adults. Warner Bros. releases fourth JD album, *One of Those Songs*. Little CeCe is photographed with JD on the jacket. November 6, JD appears on the NBC-TV musical special, *Alice Through the Looking Glass*, playing Humpty Dumpty.

1967: JD launches a ten-week nightclub tour. Warner Bros. releases the fifth and last JD album, *Songs for Sunday*. JD makes guest appearances on several TV shows, including Danny Thomas and Bob Hope shows.

1968: For JD's 75th birthday, friends give a big surprise party at Chasen's in Hollywood, with seven-year-old CeCe popping out of the cake. December 26, JD hosts *The Hollywood Palace*, ABC-TV, ringmaster of special circus show.

1969: May 8–28, JD opens at the Music Hall of the Frontier Hotel, Las Vegas, equal billing with the Lennon Sisters. July 30, JD show opens 71st Annual International Convention Grand Aerie Fraternal Order of Eagles, Radisson Hotel, Minneapolis, JD's ninth consecutive appearance at an Eagles convention. JD is named honorary mayor of Del Mar, California. September 26, *Jimmy Durante Presents the Lennon Sisters* premieres as a weekly musical variety show on ABC. The show lasts one season. September 29, JD is given the 1969 Humanitarian Award of the National Conference of Christians and Jews, at a Beverly Hilton dinner. October 13, JD is guest on the Bob Hope variety special, NBC-TV. December 7, JD's voice narrates the story of the animated *Frosty the Snowman*, CBS-TV.

1970: JD continues his usual busy schedule of nightclub engagements. Late June, JD at the Frontier Music Hall, Las Vegas. July 9, JD is stricken with dizzy spells after leaving the stage at the Frontier, just before the midnight show. Vic Damone is rushed in to replace him. JD is flown to Los Angeles, admitted to a hospital. Diagnosis is an infection of the inner ear.

1971–72: JD continues a hectic pace of nightclub engagements and playing benefits. November 1972, JD suffers a massive stroke, leaving him partially paralyzed.

1973: November, Milton Berle is emcee at a dinner in Los Angeles honoring JD. JD tries to sing "Inka Dinka Doo" from a wheelchair.

1974: January 15, Roy Bargy, JD's musical director, dies in Vista, California. April 24, JD in wheelchair after three strokes, tries to sing in public after receiving the 22nd annual Silver Lady Award of the Banshees, organization of newspaper executives, at the Waldorf-Astoria, New York.

1976: November 19, tribute to JD, Beverly Hilton Hotel, with Danny Thomas, emcee.

1978: February 9, an 85th birthday party is thrown for JD "in absentia" at Jilly's, Sinatra's favorite bar in New York, hosted by ex-boxing champ Floyd Patterson and songwriter John Ottaviano. Mayor Koch issues a proclamation making it Jimmy Durante Day.

1980: January 29, JD dies at St. John's Hospital in Santa Monica, California, age 86, just short of his 87th birthday, from pneumonia. February 12, Jack Roth, JD's drummer and friend, dies at age 81 in Yonkers, New York. July 15, Eddie Jackson dies in Sherman Oaks, California.

Appendix B

FEATURE FILMS
AND BROADWAY PLAYS

Feature Films

Roadhouse Nights. Paramount, 1930. Stars Helen Morgan, Charles Ruggles, and Fred Kohler, with Clayton, Jackson, and Durante and the Durante orchestra. Directed by Hobart Henley. 69 minutes.

This is a detective story about a murder in a nightclub run by a mobster and bootlegger, played by Fred Kohler. Charles Ruggles is an investigator who gets killed. Helen Morgan and Clayton, Jackson, and Durante perform in the club but all too briefly. Durante is Daffy. Clayton and Jackson are Moe and Joe.

New Adventures of Get Rich Quick Wallingford. MGM, 1931. Stars William Haines, with JD, Leila Hyams, Clara Blandick, Walter Walker, Ernest Torrence, Guy Kibbee, Hale Hamilton, Robert McWade, Henry Armetta. Directed by Sam Wood. 96 minutes.

William Haines plays a hustler who bilks people of their money. Durante is his helper, Schnozzle.

The Cuban Love Song. MGM, 1931. Stars Lawrence Tibbett, with Lupe Velez, Ernest Torrence, JD, Karen Morley, Hale Hamilton, Louise Fazenda, Mathilda Comont, Phillip Cooper, Ernesto Lecuona and the Palau Brothers' Cuban Orchestra. Directed by W.S. Van Dyke. 80 minutes.

It is a musical romance. Durante is O.O. Jones, Marine buddy of Lawrence Tibbett as Tibbett woos Lupe Velez.

The Passionate Plumber. MGM, 1932. Stars Buster Keaton, with JD, Irene Purcell, Polly Moran, Gilbert Roland, Mona Maris. Directed by Edward Sedgwick. 73 minutes.

The film is set in Paris with Keaton a plumber and set-up lover to make another man jealous. Durante is a chauffeur, Elmer Tuttle from Yonkers, New York, pleased to discover in Keaton a fellow American.

The Wet Parade. MGM, 1932. Stars Walter Huston, with Myrna Loy, Neil Hamilton, Lewis Stone, Dorothy Jordan, Robert Young, JD, Wallace Ford. Directed by Victor Fleming. 120 minutes.

This serious, crusading film studies the damage brought by alcoholism and bad liquor. Durante plays Abe Shilling, a Prohibition agent.

Speak Easily. MGM, 1932. Stars Buster Keaton, with JD, Ruth Selwyn, Thelma Todd, Hedda Hopper, Sidney Toler. Directed by Edward Sedgwick. 82 minutes.

Keaton is a naive, unworldly college professor who joins traveling actors, including James "Jimmy" Dodge, played by Durante. The film focuses on the group's effort to open a show on Broadway.

The Phantom President. Paramount, 1932. Stars George M. Cohan, with Claudette Colbert, JD, Sidney Toler. Directed by Norman Taurog. 80 minutes.

In a singing-talking style of rhyming dialogue, Rodgers and Hart music underlies a story about a medicine man (Cohan) who is a dead ringer for the President of the United States and is hired as a double. Durante is the medicine man's assistant, Curly.

Blondie of the Follies. MGM, 1932. Stars Marion Davies and Robert Montgomery, with Billie Dove, JD, ZaSu Pitts, Sidney Toler, Louise Carter, James Gleason. Directed by Edmund Goulding. 93 minutes.

New York show girls compete for love and success in the Follies. Durante's bit part in the film's second half lasts not over three minutes, but is the high point. Davies and Durante spoof Garbo and Barrymore in *Grand Hotel*.

What! No Beer? MGM, 1933. Co-stars Buster Keaton and JD (both names above the title), with Roscoe Ates, Phyllis Barry, John Miljan, Edward Brophy, Henry Armetta. Directed by Edward Sedgwick. 66 minutes.

Keaton as a taxidermist and Durante as barber Jimmy Potts are friends who try to make money on beer as the nation votes on Prohibition.

Hell Below. MGM, 1933. Stars Robert Montgomery, Walter Huston, Madge Evans, JD, Robert Young, Sterling Holloway, Eugene Pallette. Directed by Jack Conway. 105 minutes.

The drama about a submarine crew is given comic relief by sailor Durante.

Broadway to Hollywood. MGM, 1933. Stars Alice Brady, Frank Morgan, Jackie Cooper, Russell Hardie, Madge Evans, Mickey Rooney, Eddie Quillan, Fay Templeton, JD, Nelson Eddy, May Robson, Una Merkel. Directed by Willard Mack. 85 minutes.

Three generations of show business, The Three Hacketts, played by Morgan, Brady, and Cooper, struggle to reach the top. Durante has a very brief scene in the last quarter of the film.

Meet the Baron. MGM, 1933. Stars Jack Pearl and JD, with ZaSu Pitts, Edna May Oliver, Ted Healy and his Stooges, Ben Bard, Henry Kolker, Wiiliam B. Davidson, the Metro-Goldwyn Girls. Directed by Walter Lang. 65 minutes.

Pearl plays a pants presser who impersonates the Baron von Munchausen, with tales of adventure. Durante, his manager, Joseph McGoo, is not given much to do.

Palooka. UA/Reliance, 1934. Stars JD, Lupe Velez, and Stu Erwin, with Marjorie Rambeau, Robert Armstrong, Mary Carlisle, William Cagney,

Thelma Todd, Gus Arnheim and his orchestra. Directed by Benjamin Stoloff. 86 minutes (Reliance Pictures, distributed by United Artists; prints that read "Astor Pictures" run 74 minutes).

Ham Fisher's comic strip character comes to life, played by Stu Erwin, with Durante as the boxer's manager, Knobby Walsh. Lupe Velez plays the opportunist who goes with any fighter wearing the champion's belt. A high point is Durante's introduction of his song "Inka Dinka Doo."

George White's Scandals. Fox, 1934. Stars Rudy Vallee, JD, Alice Faye, Adrienne Ames, Gregory Ratoff, Cliff Edwards, Dixie Dunbar, Gertrude Michael, George White. Directed by George White. 80 minutes.

A backstage romance takes the back seat to the very fine musical numbers of a George White revue. Durante as Happy McGillicuddy works well in musical numbers with Cliff Edwards and Rudy Vallee.

Hollywood Party. MGM, 1934. Stars JD, Lupe Velez, Laurel & Hardy, Charles Butterworth, Jack Pearl, Ted Healy and the Three Stooges, Mickey Mouse, Polly Moran, Eddie Quillan, June Clyde, George Givot, Robert Young. No director credited. 68 minutes (some prints run 63 minutes with color Disney cartoon deleted, "Hot Chocolate Soldiers").

In this disjointed but often funny screwball comedy Durante dreams that he's Schnarzan, a muscular jungle star, at a party, with his girlfriend Lupe Velez mad at him.

Strictly Dynamite. RKO, 1934. Stars JD and Lupe Velez, with Norman Foster, William Gargan, Marian Nixon, The Mills Brothers, Eugene Pallette, Sterling Holloway. Directed by Elliott Nugent. 71 minutes.

Durante is Moxie, star of a radio show looking for fresh material. Lupe Velez is his girlfriend. Both sing, Durante introducing "Hot Pattata."

Student Tour. MGM, 1934. Stars JD, Charles Butterworth, Phil Regan, Douglas Fowley, Florine McKinney, Betty Grable, Herman Brix (Bruce Bennett), Nelson Eddy. Directed by Charles F. Riesner. 87 minutes.

A college sculling (rowing) crew tours Europe tutored by a professor whose philosophy course they failed. Durante is Hank Merman, trainer of the crew.

Carnival. Columbia, 1935. Stars Lee Tracy and Sally Eilers, with JD, Florence Rice, Thomas Jackson, John Richard [Dickie] Walters. Directed by Walter Lang. 75 minutes.

A carnival puppeteer fights for custody of his baby boy after his wife dies. Durante is the man's loyal friend, called Fingers for his pickpocket skills.

Land Without Music. British, Capitol Films, 1936; U.S. title, *Forbidden Music*; reissued in U.S. as *That's My Boy*. Stars Richard Tauber, JD, Diana Napier, June Clyde, Derrick de Marney. Directed by Walter Forde. 80 minutes (cut to 63 minutes in U.S.).

Tauber in this operetta by Oscar Straus is a singer in a land that bans music. Durante is his friend, Jonah J. Whistler.

Start Cheering. Columbia, 1938. Stars JD, Gertrude Niesen, Charles Starrett, Joan Perry, Walter Connolly, Hal LeRoy, The Three Stooges, Raymond Walburn, Broderick Crawford, Ernest Truax, Louis Prima Orchestra, Johnny Green Orchestra. Directed by Albert S. Rogell. 78 minutes.

A movie star joins a college football team, falls in love, and plays in the big game. The Three Stooges try out for the team. Durante as the coach's assistant, Willie Cumbatz, gets to sing his "I'll Do the Strut-away in My Cutaway."

Sally, Irene and Mary. 20th Century–Fox, 1938. Stars Alice Faye, Tony Martin, Fred Allen, Joan Davis, Marjorie Weaver, Gregory Ratoff, JD, Louise Hovick (Gypsy Rose Lee). Directed by William A. Seiter. 72 minutes.

Three manicurists dreaming of Broadway careers turn a ferry into a showboat. Fred Allen plays their agent and Durante his assistant, Jefferson Twitchell.

Little Miss Broadway. 20th Century–Fox, 1938. Stars Shirley Temple, with George Murphy, JD, Phyllis Brooks, Edna May Oliver, George Barbier. Directed by Irving Cummings. 70 minutes.

A theatrical boarding house musical, Shirley Temple has musical numbers with Murphy. Durante is Jimmy Clayton, leader of a jazz band.

Melody Ranch. Republic, 1940. Stars Gene Autry, with JD, Ann Miller, George "Gabby" Hayes, Barton MacLane, Barbara Allen, Jerome Cowan, Mary Lee, Joseph Sawyer. Directed by Joseph Santley. 84 minutes.

The singing cowboy catches a horse thief. Durante is Cornelius J. Courtney, acting· as both prosecutor and defense counsel at the trial.

You're in the Army Now. WB, 1941. Stars JD, Phil Silvers, and Jane Wyman, with Regis Toomey, Joe Sawyer, Donald Mcbridge, the Navy Blues Sextette, Matty Malneck and his orchestra. Directed by Lewis Seiler. 79 minutes.

Durante and Phil Silvers play Jeeper Smith and Breezy Jones, two vacuum cleaner salesmen who wind up in the army in a boot camp comedy.

The Man Who Came to Dinner. WB, 1941. Stars Monty Woolley, Bette Davis, and Ann Sheridan, with Billie Burke, JD, Richard Travis, Grant Mitchell, Mary Wickes, Elizabeth Fraser, Reginald Gardiner. Directed by William Keighley. 112 minutes.

This screen adaptation of the George S. Kaufman and Moss Hart play about a celebrity guest who drives his host family crazy during a protracted visit features Monty Woolley in the same role he played on Broadway. Durante plays Banjo, a rambunctious friend of the Woolley character.

Two Girls and a Sailor. MGM, 1944. Stars Van Johnson, June Allyson, and Gloria DeHaven, with Jose and Amparo Iturbi, JD, Lena Horne, Donald Meek, Virginia O'Brien, Harry James and his orchestra, Xavier Cugat and his orchestra, Gracie Allen, Helen Forrest, Linda Romay, Tom Drake, Frank Sully. Directed by Richard Thorpe. 124 minutes.

A love triangle merely serves as the frame for the real interest, many good musical numbers for all. Durante plays Billy Kipp, an old vaudevillian who befriends and advises the two grown sisters whose family was in vaudeville.

Music for Millions. MGM, 1944. Stars Margaret O'Brien, Jose Iturbi, June Allyson, JD, and Marsha Hunt, with Hugh Herbert, Connie Gilchrist, Harry Davenport, Larry Adler, Marie Wilson. Directed by Henry Koster. 120 minutes.

A young girl helps her big sister overcome fear about her husband in the war. JD plays Andrews, pianist and manager for Iturbi's Manhattan Philharmonic. The overwrought melodrama is helped by Durante's songs, especially "Umbriago," written for this film, and by the many snippets of classical music.

Two Sisters from Boston. MGM, 1946. Stars Kathryn Grayson, June Allyson, Lauritz Melchior, JD, and Peter Lawford, with Ben Blue. Directed by Henry Koster. 112 minutes.

The film has Grayson and Allyson working in Spike's (Durante's) turn-of-the-century saloon. Its music ranges from nostalgic-sounding popular songs to opera.

It Happened in Brooklyn. MGM, 1947. Stars Frank Sinatra, Kathryn Grayson, JD, Peter Lawford, and Gloria Grahame. Directed by Richard Whorf. 105 minutes.

Sinatra returns to Brooklyn as a G.I. after the war to stay with his old friend, Nick Lombardi, a high school janitor played by Durante. Both Sinatra and Lawford fall for Grayson. The chemistry between Sinatra and Durante is terrific: a high point is their duet on "The Song's Gotta Come from the Heart."

This Time for Keeps. MGM, 1947. Stars Esther Williams, Lauritz Melchior, JD, Johnnie Johnston and Xavier Cugat and his orchestra, with Dame May Whitty, Sharon McManus, Dick Simmons, Mary Stuart, Ludwig Stossel, Dorothy Porter, Tommy Wonder. Directed by Richard Thorpe. 105 minutes. Color.

A love story and water ballet sequences are supplemented by excellent Durante musical numbers, especially "I'm the Guy Who Found the Lost Chord" and another less famous number played at a piano sinking into a pool. Durante is Ferdi Farro, family friend and accompanist for Esther Williams.

On an Island with You. MGM, 1948. Stars Esther Williams, Peter Lawford, Ricardo Montalban, JD, Cyd Charisse, Xavier Cugat, and Leon Ames. Directed by Richard Thorpe. 107 minutes. Color.

Esther Williams must choose between Peter Lawford and Ricardo Montalban as they make a film in Hawaii. Durante is Buckley, business agent with the film company. A musical high point is Durante's singing of "I Know Darn Well I Can Do Without Broadway, but Can Broadway Do Without Me?" and "I'll Do the Strut-away in My Cut-away."

The Great Rupert. Eagle-Lion, 1950. Stars JD, Terry Moore, and Tom Drake, with Queenie Smith, Chick Chandler, Sara Haden, Frank Orth. Directed by Irving Pichel. 86 minutes.

Durante is the Great Amendola, an old vaudevillian who has trouble paying the rent for his family while also taking care of another old trouper's trained squirrel named Rupert. This modest, sentimental movie works well and includes interesting George Pal Puppetoon sequences.

The Milkman. Universal, 1950. Stars Donald O'Connor and JD, with Joyce Holden, Piper Laurie, Henry O'Neill. Directed by Charles Barton. 87 minutes.

Durante is Breezy, a milkman nearing retirement, and O'Connor a likeable but bumbling newcomer. The two work well together with the comedy and songs.

Beau James*. Paramount, 1957. Stars Bob Hope, with Vera Miles, Paul Douglas, Alexis Smith, Darren McGavin, narrated by Walter Winchell. Unbilled guest appearances by Jack Benny, George Jessel, and JD. Directed by Melville Shavelson. 105 minutes. Color.

Hope is excellent as New York Mayor Jimmy Walker in a film biography based on the book by Gene Fowler. Durante's brief appearance is also excellent, working with Hope in song and dance.

Pepe*. Columbia, 1960. Stars Cantinflas, Dan Dailey, and Shirley Jones, with Ricardo Montalban, Vicki Trickett, Matt Mattox, Hank Henry, Suzanne Lloyd, Carolos Rivas, and the following guest stars (in alphabetical order)—Maurice Chevalier, Bing Crosby, Michael Callan, Richard Conte, Bobby Darin, Sammy Davis, Jr., JD, Zsa Zsa Gabor, Hedda Hopper, Joey Bishop [credits error listing star under "J"], Ernie Kovacs, Peter Lawford, Janet Leigh, Jack Lemmon, Jay "Dennis the Menace" North, Kim Novak, Andre Previn, Donna Reed, Debbie Reynolds, Edward G. Robinson, Cesar Romero, Frank Sinatra, and ?? [included in the credits]. Together with Billie Burke, Ann B. "Schultzy" Davis, William Demarest, Col. E.E. Fogelson, "Big" Jack Entratter, Jane Robinson, Bunny Waters, and Charles Coburn. Directed by George Sidney. 195 minutes (later cut to 157 minutes). Color.

Cantinflas leaves his Mexican village to try to retrieve his beloved horse from Hollywood buyers and in the process runs across many stars. Durante's small role is that of a gambler at a Las Vegas casino.

The Last Judgment*. Italian, 1961, *Il Giudizio Universale*. All-star cast with European actors plus a few American actors: Vittorio Gassman, Silvana Mangano, Alberto Sordi, Vittorio De Sica, Fernandel, Ernest Borgnine, Akim Tamiroff, Anouk Aimee, Melina Mercouri, Jack Palance, JD, and others. Directed by Vittorio De Sica. 98 minutes. B&W/Color. Not released in the U.S.

A series of vignettes that reveal life in Naples before the Last Judgment that the people are awaiting. Fearful people vow to repent but forget their vows when the threat recedes. Durante plays a man with a big nose who wanted to ask God why he was given such a face.

Billy Rose's Jumbo*. MGM, 1962. Stars Doris Day, Stephen Boyd, JD, and Martha Raye, with Dean Jagger. Directed by Charles Walters. 125 minutes. Color.

Durante is Pop Wonder, co-owner of a financially troubled circus with his daughter, Doris Day. He works well with Day and with Martha Raye in musical numbers and dramatic action.

It's a Mad, Mad, Mad, Mad World*. UA, 1963. Stars Spencer Tracy and an all-star cast, including, in alphabetical order, Milton Berle, Sid Caesar, Buddy Hackett, Ethel Merman, Mickey Rooney, Dick Shawn, Phil Silvers, Terry-Thomas, Jonathan Winters, also Edie Adams, Dorothy Provine, Eddie "Rochester" Anderson, Jim Backus, Ben Blue, Joe E. Brown, Alan Carney, Barrie Chase, William Demarest, Andy Devine, Peter Falk, Norman Fell, Paul Ford, Sterling Holloway, Edward

Everett Horton, Marvin Kaplan, Buster Keaton, Don Knotts, Charles McGraw, ZaSu Pitts, Carl Reiner, Madlyn Rhue, Arnold Stang, The Three Stooges, Jesse White, "a few surprises, and in alphabetical order, Jimmy Durante." Directed by Stanley Kramer. 192 minutes (later cut to 155 minutes, recently restored on home video version to 175 minutes). Color.

Durante's death early in the film sets off a mad chase for his buried money by hordes of people.

(*Note:* Durante was filmed in scenes for the 1946 MGM musical *Ziegfeld Follies.* Completed in 1944, it ran too long, and was cut before its release at 110 minutes in January 1946. In the film's released form Durante does not appear at all.)

Broadway Plays

Show Girl. Ziegfeld Theatre, July 2, 1929. Produced by Florenz Ziegfeld. Written and dialogue stage by Wm. Anthony McGuire. Based on the novel by J.P. McEvoy. Music by George Gershwin, special numbers by Vincent Youmans; lyrics by Gus Kahn and Ira Gershwin. Stars Ruby Keeler, with Clayton, Jackson, and Durante, Eddie Foy, Jr., Harriet Hoctor, Duke Ellington and his Cotton Club Orchestra.

The New Yorkers. Broadway Theatre, December 8, 1930. Produced by E. Ray Goetz. Billed as "A Sociological Musical Satire." Book by Herbert Fields, based on a story by E. Ray Goetz and Peter Arno. Music and lyrics by Cole Porter. Cast included Hope Williams, Clayton, Jackson, and Durante, Waring's Pennsylvanians.

Strike Me Pink. Majestic Theatre, March 4, 1933. Produced by Lew Brown and Ray Henderson as their new musical revue. Songs by Brown and Henderson. Stars Lupe Velez, JD, and Hope Williams, with Hal Le Roy, Roy Atwell, Eddie Garr, George Dewey Washington.

Jumbo. Hippodrome, November 16, 1935. Produced by Billy Rose. Libretto by Ben Hecht and Charles MacArthur. Music and lyrics by Richard Rodgers and Lorenz Hart. Stars JD and Paul Whiteman and his Orchestra, with Rosie the elephant.

Red, Hot and Blue! Alvin Theatre, October 29, 1936. Produced by Vinton Freedley. Words and music by Cole Porter. Book by Howard Lindsay and Russel Crouse. Stars JD, Ethel Merman, and Bob Hope, with Polly Walters, The Hartmans.

Stars in Your Eyes. Majestic Theatre, February 9, 1939. Produced by Dwight Deere Wiman. Book by J.P. McEvoy. Lyrics by Dorothy Fields. Music by Arthur Schwartz. Stars Ethel Merman and JD, with Tamara Toumanova, Richard Carlson, Mildred Natwick.

Keep Off the Grass. Broadhurst Theatre, May 23, 1940. Produced by the Messrs. Shubert. Music by James McHugh; lyrics by Al Dubin. Sketches in revue by Mort Lewis; Parke Levy and Lan Lipscott; S. Jay Kaufman; Panama and Frank. Stars JD, Ray Bolger, Jane Froman, and Ilka Chase, with Betty Bruce, Nan Rae, Maude Davis, Larry Adler, Virginia O'Brien, John McCauley, Sunnie O'Dea, Jack[ie] Gleason, The DeTuscans, Jose Limon, Emmet Kelly, Dodson's Monkeys.

Appendix C

RADIO APPEARANCES

Shows Hosted by Durante

1933-34 Season

THE EDDIE CANTOR SHOW (THE CHASE & SANBORN HOUR). First aired Sept. 13, 1931, lasting until 1934. NBC, Sun. 8:00 (time given is always New York, Eastern, time), 60 min.

Durante, still unknown to radio audiences, substituted for Eddie Cantor September 10 through November 12, 1933, while Cantor was busy filming *Roman Scandals* for Samuel Goldwyn (released December 1933). With Rubinoff and his orchestra. Vocalist, Ruth Etting. Next summer, JD was Cantor's replacement, July 22 through September 30, 1934. There were no guest stars with Durante.

1935-36 Season

JIMMY DURANTE: JUMBO FIRE CHIEF. NBC, Tues. 9:30, 30 min. (Previous three years had been ED WYNN: TEXACO FIRE CHIEF.) Premiered Oct. 29, 1935, running through March 3, 1936. Intended to promote Billy Rose's *Jumbo*, playing at the Hippodrome. Vocalists were Donald Novis and Gloria Grafton from the cast of *Jumbo*.

1942-43 and 1943-44 Seasons

THE ABBOTT AND COSTELLO SHOW. NBC, Thurs. 10:00, 30 min., sponsored by Camel cigarettes. First aired Oct. 8, 1942, running for five years. When Costello became ill with rheumatic fever, JD and Garry Moore substituted, from March 25, 1943, through the end of the season, September 30, 1943. The March 25 script was marked "New Camel Program," program no. 1. When Abbott & Costello were still not prepared to resume their program in the new fall season, JD and Moore continued to fill in, from October 7 through October 28, 1943 (with scripts now marked "Substitute Program No. 1). There were almost no guest stars. Marlene Dietrich appeared on the September 9, 1943, show.

208

1943-44 Season through 1949-50 Season

CAMEL COMEDY CARAVAN. CBS, Fri. 10:00, 30 min., beginning October 8, 1943. JD and Garry Moore, co-hosts.

Durante had made guest appearances on this show as early as February 26, 1943, appearing after unknown comedian Garry Moore. Later guest spots included the March 19, 1943, show.

Durante and Moore became the regular hosts when the show premiered the 1943-44 season on Friday, October 8, 1943. The show originated in New York, but was broadcast from Los Angeles with increasing frequency.

On April 6, 1945, Rexall became the sponsor, same time and length. Name changed to THE JIMMY DURANTE-GARRY MOORE SHOW. Few guest stars during the 1944-45 season (May 4, 1945, Marilyn Maxwell; June 29, 1945, Ray Bolger). No guest stars on the 1945-46 season, but several in the 1946-47 season: Nov. 8, 1946, Frank Sinatra; Nov. 15, 1946, surprise guest Phil Baker; March 21, 1947, Frank Sinatra.

Most shows were from Los Angeles, but shows were also broadcast from Minneapolis, San Francisco, and New York. Last show for Garry Moore as co-host, June 27, 1947.

October 1, 1947: THE JIMMY DURANTE SHOW, still sponsored by Rexall, changed networks, moving to NBC, Wed., 10:30, 30 min. And Rexall gave way for Camel to again become the sponsor. There was now a weekly guest star: Oct 1, 1947, Greer Garson; Oct. 8, 1947, Eddie Cantor; Oct. 15, 1947, Margaret O'Brien; Oct. 22, 1947, Victor Moore; Oct. 29, 1947, Lucille Ball; Nov. 5, 1947, Bing Crosby; Nov. 12, 1947, Dorothy Lamour; Nov. 19, 1947, Carmen Miranda; Nov. 26, 1947, Victor Moore; De. 3, 1947, Charles Boyer; Dec. 10, 1947, Boris Karloff; Dec. 17, 1947, Victor Moore; Dec. 24, 1947, Margaret O'Brien; Dec. 31, 1947 (Garry Moore and Red Skelton sub for ailing JD); Jan. 7, 1948 (Bob Hope and Victor Moore sub for ailing JD); Jan. 14, 1948 (Frank Morgan and Victor Moore sub for ailing JD); Jan. 21, 1948 (Al Jolson and Victor Moore sub for ailing JD); Jan. 28, 1948, Victor Moore; Feb. 4, 1948, Victor Moore; Feb. 11, 1948 (with Victor Moore, by this time almost a co-host, a semi-regular); Feb. 18, 1948 (with Victor Moore); Feb. 25, 1948 (with Victor Moore); March 3, 1948 (with Victor Moore); March 10, 1948, Van Johnson; March 24, 1948 (with Victor Moore); March 31, 1948 (with Victor Moore); April 7, 1948, Dorothy Lamour; April 14, 1948 (first five min. preempted by Pres. Truman speech for opening of security loan drive, with Victor Moore now a regular part of the cast, listed second, after JD); April 21, 1948, CLAYTON AND JACKSON in a reunion, 25 years after the Dover Club, plus Victor Moore, reprising an old nightclub act; April 28, 1948, Lucille Ball; May 5, 1948 (with Victor Moore); May 12, 1948 (with Victor Moore); May 19, 1948 (with Victor Moore); May 26, 1948 (with Victor Moore); June 2, 1948, no guest; June 16, 1948 (with Victor Moore); June 23, 1948 (no guest. Last program for Rexall. Last show of season).

October 8, 1948: THE JIMMY DURANTE SHOW, WITH ALAN YOUNG, returned to Fridays, NBC, 10:30, 30 min., back under Camel sponsorship. Alan Young stayed through April 1, 1949. He was replaced by Don Ameche, with the program from April 8, 1949, onward called THE JIMMY DURANTE SHOW, WITH DON AMECHE. Ameche stayed through the end of the season, June 30, 1950, when Durante left radio to prepare for his entry into television. Season's guests on Jan. 7, 1949, Ed "Archie" Gardner (of DUFFY'S TAVERN); Jan. 21, 1949, Judy Canova; Feb. 4, 1949, Bing Crosby; March 4, 1949, Al Jolson;

April 1, 1949, Bob Hope; June 17, 1949, Hal March; June 24, 1949, Marion Hutton; July 1, 1949, last show of season.

Oct. 7, 1949. Final season began with all shows originating from Hollywood except Nov. 25, Dec. 2, Dec. 9, Dec. 16, Dec. 23, and Dec. 30 (taped Dec. 19), which were from New York, and Feb. 24, March 3, and March 10 from Chicago. No guest stars. June 30, 1950, last show.

Other Durante Commercial Network Radio Appearances

THE RUDY VALLEE SHOW (also popularly known as THE FLEISCHMANN HOUR and THE ROYAL GELATIN HOUR). The first major network variety hour, the show debuted on NBC, Oct. 24, 1929 and ran ten years, until Sept. 28, 1939.
    NBC. Thurs. 8:00, 60 min. Durante guest appearances with Vallee: May 11, 1933, July 14, 1938, Feb. 23, June 1, Aug. 24, Sept. 28, 1939.

THE RUDY VALLEE SHOW (for Sealtest). Musical variety show debuted March 7, 1940 and ran until July 8, 1943; John Barrymore was a regular part of the show from a few months after its inception until shortly before his death on May 29, 1942.
    NBC, Thurs. 10:00, 30 min. Durante guest appearance with Vallee: March 13, 1941.

BROADCAST CELEBRATING OPENING NBC'S HOLLYWOOD RADIO STUDIOS. Special, Dec. 7, 1935, NBC (WJZ in New York), Sat. 10:30, 120 min.
    Radio, screen, and opera stars were featured, including Al Jolson as host and performer, Bing Crosby, Bill Robinson, James Melton, Rudy Vallee, Ruth Etting, John Charles Thomas, Phil Regan, Paul Whiteman, JD, and others.

JACK OAKIE SHOW, for Camel, CBS, Tues. 9:30, 30 min. Oakie's first season, 1936-37, the show was called JACK OAKIE'S COLLEGE and ran 60 min., same network and starting time. First aired Dec. 29, 1936. Second season, 1937-38, called the JACK OAKIE SHOW. Ran until March 22, 1938.
    Jan. 18, 1938: JD was a guest star.

THE BENNY RUBIN SHOW [ONLY YESTERDAY]. CBS (WABC, New York), Sun. 8:00, 30 min.
    March 14, 1943: JD was a guest star.

THE FRED ALLEN SHOW [TEXACO STAR THEATRE]. CBS (WABC, New York), Sun. 9:30, 30 min.
    April 4, 1943 and Jan. 23, 1944: JD was a guest star.

PAUL WHITEMAN PRESENTS. NBC, Sun. 8:00, 30 min. Summer replacement for Edgar Bergen, 1943. Premiered June 6, ran through August 29. Paul Whiteman and his orchestra and hostess Dinah Shore. Sponsored by Chase and Sanborn. 13-week run. High point: July 4, 1943 reunion of Bing Crosby with Harry Barris and Al Rinker, the Rhythm Boys' first professional reunion since they appeared with Whiteman in 1930.
    Aug. 15, 1943: JD was a guest star.

THE DANNY KAYE SHOW [BLUE RIBBON TOWN]. CBS (WABC, New York), Sat. 8:00, 30 min. Sponsored by Pabst Blue Ribbon Beer, premiered Jan. 6, 1945, with guest Eddie Cantor. Switched to Fri., 10:30, April 27 through June 1, 1945, returning Fridays at 10:30 for a second season Nov. 16, 1945, immediately following the Durante-Moore show, running through May 31, 1946.

April 27, 1945: Guests are JD and Garry Moore.

(An Armed Forces Radio Service transcription was made of this program, labeled DANNY KAYE #14.)

PHILCO RADIO HALL OF FAME (Paul Whiteman, ABC). Dec. 5, 1943. *Winged Victory*. ABC network (WJZ in New York), Sun. 6:00, 60 min. Debut of show reviewing the top hits from all fields of entertainment, as judged by *Variety*. First program: presentation of B'wy's *Winged Victory* (a patriotic play by Moss Hart about the training of a bomber's crew, featuring the Army Air Forces, original music composed and conducted by Sgt. David Rose, opened Sat., Nov. 21, 1943, profits going to the Army Emergency Relief Fund).

In the radio cast: Bob Hope, JD, Hildegarde, Quentin Reynolds, Rocco, Paul Whiteman, Deems Taylor, emcee.

Jan. 21, 1945. ABC, Sun. 6:00, 60 min. Paul Whiteman, host. This show included JD, Arthur Treacher, Carmen Miranda.

Feb. 17, 1946. ABC, Sun. 6:00, show reduced to 30 min. Paul Whiteman, host. Guest: Jack Haley, but also JD as unannounced visitor at show's end, to plug his appearance next week.

Feb. 24, 1946. ABC, Sun. 6:00, 30 min. Paul Whiteman, host. Guest: JD.

PHILCO RADIO TIME (Bing Crosby, ABC; the first major transcribed [canned] network show, debuted October 16, 1946 with guest Bob Hope, and ran through June 1, 1949; from 1949 through 1952 Crosby's show was sponsored by Chesterfield on CBS, Wed. 9:30, 30 min.)

Dec. 4, 1946. ABC, Wed. 10:00, 30 min. JD is guest on Bing Crosby's show, first of five times. (Crosby had just switched from ten years with the KRAFT MUSIC HALL).

Other four times: April 16, 1947; Oct. 8, 1947; Feb. 4, 1948; Feb. 2, 1949.

SONGS BY SINATRA. CBS, Wed. 9:00, 30 min. Sponsored by Old Gold cigarettes.

Feb. 27 and Nov. 26, 1946: JD was a guest star, the second appearance with additional guest star Andre Previn.

LUX RADIO THEATER. CBS, Mon. 9:00, 60 min.

May 5, 1946. Dramatization of MGM movie *Music for Millions*. Program stars Margaret O'Brien, Jose Iturbi, JD, and Frances Gifford.

REXALL CHRISTMAS GREETINGS, 1946, special pressing "The Rexall Song."

THE VICTOR BORGE SHOW STARRING BENNY GOODMAN. NBC, Mon. 9:30, 30 min. Sponsored by Mobil Oil.

Feb. 3, 1947: Guests are JD and Phil Silvers.

(An AFRS transcription was made of this program, minus Victor Borge portions, labeled THE BENNY GOODMAN SHOW, program #31.)

LOUELLA PARSONS. WKECA, Los Angeles, ABC network, 15 min., 6:15–6:30 Pacific Time. Sponsor: Woodbury (facial soap). Program #96. Oct. 19, 1947. Guest: JD.

THE KRAFT MUSIC HALL (Jolson; *The Kraft Music Hall*, a major NBC variety show, began June 26, 1933, starring Paul Whiteman and his orchestra, including Roy Bargy, who would work many years for Durante; Al Jolson took over from Whiteman late in 1933, leaving the following year, returning the fall of 1947; Bing Crosby hosted the show beginning 1935 and remained until 1946. The show, with Jolson as host, lasted until 1949.)

Dec. 18, 1947: First of four JD guest appearances with Jolson. Also April 1, 1948, March 10 and April 21, 1949.

SCREEN GUILD PLAYERS. CBS radio, 1948. "Snow White and the Seven Dwarfs." Stars Margaret O'Brien, and JD, with Mary Jane Smith for the Motion Picture Relief Fund.

SEALTEST VARIETY THEATRE. NBC, Thurs. 9:30, 30 min., November 4, 1948. Dorothy Lamour, host. JD and Edward G. Robinson are the guests.

DUFFY'S TAVERN. NBC, Wed. 9:00, 30 min.
March 30, 1949: Guests JD and Ann Sothern.

THE DEAN MARTIN & JERRY LEWIS SHOW. NBC, premiered Sun., April 3, 1949, 6:30, 30 min. Their third show, April 17, 1949 had JD as guest star.

THE BOB HOPE SHOW. NBC, Tues. 9:00, 30 min.
April 19, 1949: JD was guest star, with regulars Doris Day, Irene Ryan, and the Les Brown Orchestra.

THE BIG SHOW. NBC, premiere show, Nov. 5, 1950, Sun., 90 min. Hosted each week by Tallulah Bankhead, accompanied regularly by Fred Allen, who came out of retirement. (Expensive show lasted only one season.) With JD on the first show were other guests: Ethel Merman, Paul Lukas, Jose Ferrer, Frankie Laine, and Danny Thomas.

Dec. 10, 1950. Guests: Eddy Arnold, Charles Boyer, JD, Imogene Coca, Mindy Carson.

Dec. 24, 1950. Guests: JD, Bert Lahr, Robert Merrill, Margaret O'Brien, Edith Piaf, Ed Wynn, Fran Warren.

Jan. 14, 1951. Guests: Louis Calhern, JD, Fran Warren, Martha Raye, Jack Carter, Florence Desmond.

April 8, 1951. Guests: Vivian Blaine, JD, Portland Hoffa, Jane Morgan, Rudy Vallee.

April 29, 1951. Guests: Milton Berle, Rosemary Clooney, JD, Frank Lovejoy, Gordon MacRae, Ethel Merman.

Feb. 4, 1952. Guests: Jane Pickens, Laraine Day, JD, Judy Holiday, Leo Durocher, Robert Cummings, Portland Hoffa, Frankie Laine. Meredith Willson's orch.

FIBBER McGEE AND MOLLY. NBC, Tues. 9:30, 30 min., March 11, 1952. 20th Anniversary on NBC. JD is guest star.

At end of the show, after the President of the Hollywood Chamber of Commerce reads a statement, JD reads a statement of congratulations from many radio comedians, lauding the show's wholesome family humor.

CLYDE GILMOUR'S MUSIC PROFILES. CBC broadcast, August 1, 1953, c. 30 min. Profile of JD.

KFI's 50th ANNIVERSARY (of broadcasting), Los Angeles. c. 12 hours. No date given. Ralph Edwards begins, "KFI, This Is Your Life!" Many guest stars, including JD, tell anecdotes about the golden days of radio. The show had to be no later than 1959 since Lou Costello, a participant, died that year. With Don Ameche, Harry von Zell, Jim Jordan, Bud Abbott, Bing Crosby, Rudy Vallee, Harold Peary, Walter O'Keefe, Jack Haley, JD, Roy Rogers, John Conte, Bob Hope, Jack Benny, Carleton E. Morse, Edgar Bergen and many others.

JOURNEYS #5, "Jimmy Durante: The Merchant of Mirth." No date or station. A series of audio portraits of America in the 20th century. Each 60 min.

DIMENSION. A program service of the CBS owned radio stations. "Dorothy Kilgallen Introduces You to People You'd Like to Know." 1961. Very brief excerpts of stars, giving their short statements, about 2 min. each. Jimmy Durante segment runs 2:12.

MONITOR. NBC, Feb. 9, 1963. 70th Birthday Tribute to JD. 45 min. Durante talks about his early career. Plus excerpts from JD shows, and tributes from Jack Benny, Sammy Davis, Jr., Joey Bishop, Garry Moore, Ethel Merman, and Bob Hope.

SAME TIME, SAME STATION. Radio series? After 5 parts on Bing Crosby, 3 parts on JD: Nov. 5, 12, 19, 1972. No other information.

AFRS (Armed Forces Radio Service) Programs

AFRS had regular weekly shows from March 1942 to 1949, 30 min. each except for specials.

Some of the CAMEL CARAVAN programs featuring JD and Garry Moore were recorded by the AFRS for rebroadcast to the troops overseas, 16-inch transcription discs no. 14, 58, 59, 78, 86, 89, 93, 95, 103, and 104, among others. Avoiding a brand name, the show was called COMEDY CARAVAN.

Another AFRS series, COMMAND PERFORMANCES, involved JD on several programs, not rebroadcasts.

Durante also appeared several times on the MAIL CALL series and the G.I. JIVE series, and at least once on the JUBILEE series aimed at black troops, using a black emcee and mostly black entertainers. The AFRS also distributed to American troops a large number of V-discs with many musical celebrities involved, but JD was not included.

Exact or approximate dating and number in series come from a combination of Jerry Valburn tapes, SPERDVAC tapes, Larry Kiner catalog, Lonstein and Marino's THE REVISED COMPLEAT SINATRA (1979), Coleman's THE COMPLETE JUDY GARLAND (1990), and from internal evidence like plugs for new films released. There are some confusing discrepancies.

Command Performances

#81. c. 1943. Judy Garland, Bing Crosby, JD, Kay Kyser. As on many of these shows the announcer was Ken Carpenter, broacasting from Los Angeles.

#92. c. 1943. Bob Hope, emcee, The Charioteers, Betty Hutton, Lana Turner, JD, Judy Garland.

#120. c. June 1944. Paulette Goddard, emcee, Anita Ellis, Louis Armstrong, JD, Johnny Mercer, Georgia Gibbs.

#124. July 1944. JD, Bette Davis, Marilyn Maxwell, Jose Iturbi.

#128. c. Aug. 1944. Claudette Colbert, JD, Ronald Colman, Dale Evans, Alan Hale, Betty Hutton.

#132. Sept. 4, 1944. Ginger Rogers, emcee, Virginia O'Brien, JD, George Murphy, Golden Gate Quartet.

#148. c. July 1945. "Encore." Edgar Bergen and Charlie McCarthy, JD, Bette Davis, Gypsy Rose Lee, Fred Allen.

#149. c. July 1945. JD, Claudette Colbert, Tommy Dorsey, Bob Burns.

#155(?). Much reissued show (Curtain Call LP, also Scarce Rarities LP, Radiola's Sandy Hook LP, and Pro Arte CD). "Dick Tracy in B-Flat," Feb. 15, 1945. Featured JD as The Mole, in support of Bing Crosby as Dick Tracy, Dinah Shore as Tess Truehart. Also featured Harry Von Zell, Jerry Colonna, Bob Hope, Frank Morgan, Judy Garland, the Andrews Sisters, Frank Sinatra, and Cass Daley. SPERDVAC lists Dick Tracy as show #155, Jerry Valburn as #162, Coleman and Lonstein both assign #166 and date it April 29, 1945.

#157. Linda Darnell, JD, Arthur Treacher, and Janet Blair.

#166. 1945. Herbert Marshall, emcee, Janet Blair, JD, Sons of the Pioneers, Lauren Bacall, Humphrey Bogart, Edward Arnold.

#172. 1945. JD, Bing Crosby, Lauritz Melchior.

#183. 1945. Janet Blair, emcee, JD, Rise Stevens, Victor Borge.

#198. JD, Ginny Simms, Ensign Dennis Day.

#202. Andrews Sisters, emcee, Celeste Holm, Durante and Garry Moore, Delta Rhythm Boys.

#250. c. Dec. 1946. Janet Blair, Bob Burns, JD, Tommy Dorsey and Orch.

#251. c. Dec. 1946. Victor Borge, Shirley Ross, Garry Moore & JD.

#254. Dec. 29, 1946. Carole Landis, Frank Sinatra, Clark Dennis, JD.

#268. 1947. Ava Gardner, Marion Morgan, JD.

CHRISTMAS 1943 SPECIAL. 90 min. Stars Bob Hope, emcee, JD, Kay Kyser and His Orchestra, Gen. George C. Marshall, Frances Langford, Ed "Archie" Gardner, Nelson Eddy, Spike Jones and the City Slickers (with Red Ingle), Ginny Simms, Navy Secretary Frank Knox, The Charioteers, War Secretary Henry L. Stimson, Dinah Shore, Jack Benny, and Fred Allen, The Ken Darby Chorus.

CHRISTMAS 1944 SPECIAL. c. 120 min. Stars Bob Hope, emcee, Xavier Cugat, Jerry Colonna, Spike Jones and His City Slickers, Virginia O'Brien, Ginny Simms, JD, Secretary of War Henry Stimson, Dinah Shore, Jack Benny, Fred Allen, Kay Kyser, Frances Langford, Dorothy Lamour, Johnny Mercer, Navy Secretary James Forrestal, Danny Kaye, W.C. Fields, Judy Garland, Spencer Tracy, Ken Darby Chorus.

VICTORY EXTRA, Aug. 15, 1945. c. 103 min. Bing Crosby, emcee, Ronald Colman, Rise Stevens, Dinah Shore, Bette Davis, JD, Jose Iturbi, Lionel Barrymore, Marlene Dietrich, Burgess Meredith, Ginny Simms, Frank Sinatra, Janet Blair, King Sisters, Johnny Mercer, Danny Kaye, Carmen Miranda, Claudette Colbert, Ed Gardner, Lena Romay, others.

CHRISTMAS 1945 SPECIAL. c. 120 min. Bob Hope, emcee, Bing Crosby, Dinah Shore, Harry James, Herbert Marshall, JD, Ginny Simms, Jerry Colonna, Johnny Mercer, Judy Garland, the Pied Pipers, Ed Gardner, Frances Langford, Kay Kyser, Cass Daley, Frank Sinatra, Mel Blanc, Pres. Harry S. Truman, chorus.

CHRISTMAS 1946 SPECIAL. 60 min. Lionel Barrymore and Bob Hope, emcee, Vera Vague, Jerry Colonna, Andrews Sisters, Linda Darnell, Groucho Marx,

Audrey Totter, Dinah Shore, Garry Moore and JD, Gloria DeHaven, Esther Williams, Frances Langford, Edgar Bergen & Charlie McCarthy, Pres. Truman.

5th ANNIVERSARY SHOW, May 29, 1947. 60 min. Lionel Barrymore, emcee, starring Judy Garland, George Murphy, Ginny Simms, Lauritz Melchior, Greer Garson, Jack Benny, Frank Sinatra, Orson Welles, Danny Kaye, Dinah Shore, Fred Allen, JD, Nelson Eddy, Eddie "Rochester" Anderson, Paul Lukas, Ernst Lubitsch, few others.

6th ANNIVERSARY SHOW, May 29, 1948. 60 min. Contains excerpts from earlier shows, including the Durante-Colbert skit from Command Performance #128.

1977: 35th ANNIVERSARY SHOW. 60 min. Bob Hope, emcee, excerpts from earlier shows, including Eddie Cantor, Dinah Shore, Frank Sinatra, Bing Crosby, Fanny Brice, Hanley Stafford, Jack Benny, Abbott & Costello, Burns & Allen, Bergen & McCarthy, Red Skelton, JD, Judy Garland.

Mail Call (1940s)

#91. 1944. Judy Garland, Bing Crosby, JD and Arthur Treacher. This particular episode is dedicated to servicemen from Minnesota. This show was released on side 1 of Tandem LP 1903, MAIL CALL (see Appendix E).
#111. 1944. Ginny Simms, JD, Harry James, The Pied Pipers, Johnny Mercer and Jo Stafford.
#125. Dinah Shore, Virginia O'Brien, Monty Woolley, JD, and Carlos Ramirez.
#134. c. Feb. 1945. Dick Haymes, emcee, King Sisters, Georgia Gibbs, Dick Stabile (saxophone), JD, and later, Eddie Jackson.
#283. c. Dec. 1947. Chili Williams, Frank Sinatra, JD & Garry Moore, Jo Stafford and The Starlighters, The Four Blazes, Candy Candido.

G.I. Journal (1940s)

#9. AFRS. Arthur Q. Bryan, Bing Crosby, JD, Trudy Erwin, Linda Darnell.
#14. AFRS. Bob Hope & JD, among others.
#58. AFRS. Jack Carson, emcee, Johnny Mercer, JD, Elvia Allman, Pied Pipers, Connie Haines, Linda Darnell.
#69. AFRS. Bing Crosby, emcee, Joan Blondell, JD, Pat Friday (female singer), Mel Blanc (as the Sad Sack), and The Charioteers, who accompany Bing but are not credited.

Jubilee (1940s)

#207. c. 1946. c. 34 min. Ernie "Bubbles" Whitman, emcee (with jive talk). King Cole Trio, Barney Bigard, Betty Roche, Benny Carter and his Orchestra, with special guest, JD.

Additional Programs for the U.S. Military and Other Governmental Agencies

THIS IS THE ARMY.* 1" spot, 1943, world transcription #B836384. JD plugs Irving Berlin's film *This Is the Army* (Warner, 1943). All proceeds go to the Army Emergency Relief.

GUEST STAR #9. (U.S. Treasury Dept., promoting U.S. Savings Bonds) 15 min. April 3, 1947. JD, Garry Moore, Elvia Allman, Dennis Agay. Host: Howard Petrie. The Savings Bond Orch. with singers under the direction of Dennis Agay.

GUEST STAR #68. July 11, 1948. 15 min. JD and Peggy Lee.

REGISTRATION. CBS, September 13, 1944. Program aimed at voter registration. Non-partisan, public service 30 min. show. Stars George Coulouris, Gene Kelly, JD, Olivia de Havilland.

MUSIC FOR THE WOUNDED: AFRS Hollywood Bowl Series #33, Aug. 5, 1948. 130 min. Ed "Archie" Gardner, Red Skelton, Danny Kaye, Frankie Laine, Frank Sinatra, Irving Berlin, Jack Haley, JD, Gene Autry, Edgar Bergen, Frances Langford, Virginia O'Brien, and others.

MUSIC ON DECK (Navy), program #19. 15 min. Mid-1950s. Guest: JD.

MUSIC ON DECK (Navy). No program number or date. 15 min. Pat Boone, JD, Sammy Davis, Jr.

STARS FOR DEFENSE. Program #24. March 17, 1957. 15 min. Featuring JD with Ray Bloch and his orchestra.

HERE'S TO VETERANS. Program #1426. 1973 (rebroadcast of excerpts from 1947). 15 min. JD, Arthur Treacher, Peggy Lee.

MUSIC YOU CAN'T FORGET (new series of 15-minute radio shows, presented by Social Security). 1970s. Hosted by Carol Channing.
    Show #2 (LP, part of 7-LP set) features numbers by JD as well as Liza Minnelli and Carol Channing with Webb Pierce.
    Show #64 (LP, part of different 7-LP set) features songs by Ethel Merman, Channing, JD with Eddie Jackson in medley.

Programs Recorded for Private Charitable Organizations, Political and Other Fundraising Events

RED CROSS WAR FUND PROGRAM. NBC, May 26, 1940, 60 min. Eddie Cantor, emcee. Speakers included Eleanor Roosevelt, others. Talent included Vivien Leigh and Laurence Olivier, Gertrude Lawrence, Jerry Colonna, Bob Hope, Walter Huston, JD, Lynn Fontanne and Alfred Lunt, Jack Benny and Don Wilson, Edgar Bergen and Charlie McCarthy, Judy Garland, few others.

AMERICAN RED CROSS 1946 FUND APPEAL. NBC, 5 min. JD and Garry Moore.

CATHOLIC CHARITIES APPEAL. NBC, April 18, 1948, 30 min. 29th Annual Appeal for the New York Catholic Diocese. Bing Crosby, JD, Maureen O'Sullivan, Pat O'Brien, Ann Blyth, Bob Hope, and the Crosby boys, Gary and Lindsay.

CHRISTMAS SEALS CAMPAIGN. Dec. 4, 1948, 15 min. JD and Garry Moore.

UNITED RED FEATHER CAMPAIGN OF AMERICA. NBC, September 30, 1951. 30 min. Jane Wyman, Judy Garland, Dinah Shore, Bing Crosby, JD, Mario Lanza, Ray Milland, Tony Martin, Richard Warfield, with a special address by President Harry S Truman.

MARCH OF DIMES. C. early 1950s, c. 30 min. Bob Hope, emcee. With Phil Harris, Bing Crosby, Paul Nero, Johnny Green, Ferde Grofe, James Roosevelt, JD, others.

"YOUR RHYTHM REVUE," 1953 FUND APPEAL FOR THE SISTER ELIZABETH KENNY FOUNDATION, for polio treatment. 15 min. Recorded at Kenny Foundation national headquarters in Minneapolis. JD recordings introduced individually by unnamed announcer.

"CALLING ALL HEARTS," 1957 HEART FUND. 15 min. JD and Helen Traubel.

ALL-STAR REVIEW, 1958 CANCER CRUSADE VARIETY SHOW. John Daly narrates and plays excerpts of past ten years of shows: Bob Hope, Jackie Gleason, Bing Crosby and Frank Sinatra duets, Joan Crawford, Fibber McGee & Molly, Dinah Shore, JD, and Helen Traubel.

"CLOSE TO YOUR HEART," 1960 HEART FUND. 15 min. JD and Garry Moore, with Eddie Cantor.

EASTER SEAL CAMPAIGN 1968. 7-inch LP, CPM-72605. Side A-Senator Everett M. Dirksen reading "The Crippled Child's Bill of Rights." Side B—JD has a singing spot (56 seconds) and a talking spot (24 seconds). JD sings a song addressed to crippled children, "One Little Step," only a few bars vocal and piano, then addresses contributors. His second spot, straight talking.

Appendix D

TELEVISION APPEARANCES

Shows Hosted by Durante

1950-51 Season

FOUR STAR REVUE. First telecast Oct. 4, 1950, last time, with changed title, April 18, 1953. NBC, Wed. 8:00 (time given is always Eastern), 60 min. JD's debut Nov. 1, 1950. Durante was the host once a month, alternating with Ed Wynn, Danny Thomas, and Jack Carson. This season sponsored by Motorola, joined later by Norge and Pet milk.

Nov. 1, 1950; guest: Donald O'Connor. Nov. 29, 1950; guest: Helen Traubel. Dec. 27, 1950; last show from the International Theatre, New York; guest: Luba Malina. Jan. 24, 1951; first time originating from the Center Theatre, New York; guest: Helen Traubel. Feb. 21, 1951; guest: Don Ameche. March 21, 1951; guest: Carmen Miranda. April 18, 1951; guest: Sophie Tucker, with Ted Shapiro at the piano. May 16, 1951; guests: Fred Allen and Eddie Cantor.

1951-52 Season

Retitled ALL STAR REVUE. Moved to Sat. 8:00, 60 min. Still originated at Center Theatre, New York. This season sponsored by Kellogg's, Snow Crop, and Pet Milk. Additional comedians headlined: Martha Raye (four times), Olsen & Johnson, Spike Jones, Victor Borge, Bob Hope, the Ritz Brothers, and Paul Winchell. Season premiere September 8, 1951, with JD in small segment on film. JD continued once a month.

Oct. 6, 1951; guest: Helen Traubel. Nov. 3, 1951; guest: Margaret Truman. Dec. 1, 1951. (First show from Hollywood, the El Capitan Theatre) Guest: Ethel Barrymore. Dec. 29, 1951; guest: Helen Traubel. Jan. 26, 1952; guest: Mickey Rooney. Feb. 23, 1952; guest: Gloria Swanson. March 22, 1952; guest: Margaret Truman. April 19, 1952; guest: Bette Davis.

1952-53 Season

ALL STAR REVUE. Only JD remained of original hosts, with other performers starring in single programs: the Ritz Brothers, Dennis Day, Walter O'Keefe, Perry Como, Sonja Henie, and Ben Blue. JD continued to do the show once a month.

Show now sponsored by Pet milk, Kellogg's, Del Monte Foods, Band-Aid Plastic Strips, Beacon wax, and Studebaker.

Sept. 20, 1952; last show from the El Capitan Theatre in Hollywood; guests: Margaret Truman and Phil Harris. Oct. 18, 1952; first show from the new NBC-TV studios in Burbank; guests: Frank Sinatra and Fifi D'Orsay. Nov. 15, 1952; guest: Lily Pons. Dec. 13, 1952; guest: Sophie Tucker. Jan. 3, 1953; guests: Linda Darnell and Vic Damone. Jan. 31, 1953; guests: Ezio Pinza and Fifi D'Orsay. March 7, 1953; guests: Carmen Miranda and Cesar Romero. April 11, 1953; guests: Helen Traubel, Rose Marie, Gene Fowler.

1953-54 Season

THE COLGATE COMEDY HOUR. First telecast Sept. 10, 1950, last time Dec. 25, 1955. NBC, Sun. 8:00, 60 min. JD was the principal host 1953–54. He did the show once a month that season.

Oct. 11, 1953; from the El Capitan Theatre, Hollywood; guest: John Wayne. Nov. 8, 1953; guest: Frank Sinatra. Dec. 6, 1953; guest: Ethel Merman. Jan. 3, 1954; guests: Paul Douglas and Eartha Kitt. Feb. 7, 1954; guests: Tallulah Bankhead and Carol Channing. March 14, 1954; guests: Eddie Cantor, Robert Montgomery, Patrice Munsel.

1954-55 Season

TEXACO STAR THEATER. (Had been hosted by Milton Berle, 1948–53, NBC, Tuesdays, 60 min.) Continued 1954-55 season, Sat. 9:30, 30 min., alternating between THE DONALD O'CONNOR SHOW and THE JIMMY DURANTE SHOW. JD's first telecast, Oct. 2, 1954. JD's show was live (as he preferred) and set in the Club Durant; Donald O'Connor's on film.

Oct. 2, 1954; guest for premiere show: Donald O'Connor; from Hollywood; live (early in the season most shows live, though toward the end of the season most shows are on film). Oct. 9, 1954; THE DONALD O'CONNOR SHOW. Premiere. Musical situation comedy. Guests: JD, Mitzi Gaynor, and comedian Sidney Miller (who would become a regular on the O'Connor show). All O'Connor shows are on film. Oct. 16, 1954. THE JIMMY DURANTE SHOW. Guests: Jean Hagen and Rusty Hamer, from THE DANNY THOMAS SHOW, where they play Danny's wife and son. Oct. 23, 1954; Texaco pre-empted by a special. Nov. 6, 1954; THE JIMMY DURANTE SHOW. Guest: Vivian Blaine. Nov. 20, 1954; Texaco pre-empted by a special. Nov. 27, 1954; guest: Margaret Truman. Special guest appearance by Dean Martin and Jerry Lewis. Dec. 11, 1954; guest: Lauritz Melchior. Dec. 18, 1954; Texaco pre-empted by *LOOK* magazine awards. Jan. 1, 1955; guest: George Raft. Jan. 15, 1955; Texaco pre-empted by a special. Jan. 22, 1955; guest: Vivian Blaine. Feb. 5, 1955; guest: Marilyn Maxwell. Feb. 12, 1955; Texaco pre-empted by Academy Awards Nominations. Feb. 26, 1955; guest: Lisa Kirk, singer. March 12, 1955; Texaco pre-empted by a special. March 19, 1955; guest: Pat Carroll. April 2, 1955; guest: Peter Lawford, star of DEAR PHOEBE (on TV). April 16, 1955; Texaco pre-empted by a special. April 23, 1955; guest: Patty Andrews. May 7, 1955; Texaco pre-empted by a special. May 14, 1955; guest: George Jessel. May 28, 1955; guest: Dorothy Lamour. June 4, 1955; Texaco pre-empted by special. June 18, 1955; guest: Janet Blair, singer-dancer-actress. July 2, 1955; Texaco pre-empted by special. July 9, 1955; guest:

Barbara Whiting (seen on CBS-TV in "Those Whiting Girls," with older sister Margaret Whiting). July 23, 1955; guest: Cass Daley, comic singer. July 30, 1955; Texaco pre-empted for a special. August 13, 1955; *TV Guide* says 8:30 to 9:00 this week. No guests. Eddie Jackson's birthday celebrated, a surprise. August 27, 1955; Texaco pre-empted for a special. Sept. 3, 1955; Back to normal time, 9:30 to 10. guest: Dave Barry (who had been on JD's radio show). Sept. 10, 1955; This is the last DONALD O'CONNOR SHOW. Sept. 17, 1955; guest: Comedienne Pat Carroll; on film; last Durante show of the season.

1955-56 Season

TEXACO STAR THEATER. JD's show, but not Donald O'Connor's show, lasted a second season, through June 2, 1956. Durante now appeared weekly, Saturday from 9:30 to 10:00.

Sept. 24, 1955; guests: Toni Arden, singer, and Max Baer, former boxing champ. Oct. 1, 1955; Texaco pre-empted for a special. Oct. 8, 1955; guests: Jose and Amparo Iturbi. Oct. 15, 1955; guest: The late Carmen Miranda (Filmed early August 1955, just before her death; her last professional appearance). Oct. 22, 1955; guest: Marguerite Piazza, "formerly of the Metropolitan Opera, lately of nightclubs." Oct. 29, 1955; guest: Peter Lawford. Nov. 5, 1955; Texaco pre-empted for a special. Nov. 12, 1955; guests: Jeannie Carson, English singer, and Peter Lawford. Nov. 19, 1955; guest: Peggy Lee. Nov. 26, 1955; Texaco pre-empted by a special. Dec. 3, 1955; guest: Betty Hutton. Dec. 10, 1955; guest: Polly Bergen, singer-actress. Dec. 17, 1955; guest: Vivian Blaine. Dec. 24, 1955; Texaco pre-empted by a special. Dec. 31, 1955; guest: Jane Froman, singer. Jan. 7, 1956; guest: George Raft. Jan. 14, 1956; guests: Tab Hunter and Jeannie Carson. Jan. 21, 1956; Texaco pre-empted by a special. Jan. 28, 1956; guest: Liberace (with brother George). Feb. 4, 1956; guest: Milton Berle. Feb. 11, 1956; guest: Robert Mitchum (actor makes his debut as a singer). Feb. 18, 1956; Texaco pre-empted for Academy Awards Nominations. (JD on orange cover of *TV Guide* this week, wearing earmuffs and smaller muffs on nose.) Feb. 25, 1956; guest: Esther Williams. March 3, 1956; guest: Charles Laughton. March 10, 1956; guest: Liberace (in return appearance, again with brother George). March 17, 1956; Texaco pre-empted by TV Emmy Awards. March 24, 1956; guest: Gordon MacRae. March 31, 1956; in color; guest: Charles Boyer. April 7, 1956; black and white again; guest: Ernest Borgnine (Durante persuaded him to make his singing debut). April 14, 1956; Texaco pre-empted by a special. April 21, 1956; guests: George Jessel and Patrice Munsel. April 28, 1956; guests: Johnny Ray, Liberace, Peter Lawford, and George Raft, plus Lloyd Mangrum and Dr. Cary Middlecoff, two top golfers in the annual tournament for the Damon Runyon Memorial Fund; from the Desert Inn in Las Vegas. May 5, 1956; guest: Peter Lawford. May 12, 1956; Texaco pre-empted by a special. May 19, 1956; guest: Connie Russell. May 26, 1956; guest: Marilyn Maxwell. June 2, 1956; guest: Lisa Kirk.

1957 Summer Reruns

THE JIMMY DURANTE SHOW. CBS reruns (orig. NBC's 1955-56 season), Sat. 8:00, 30 min., June through September. Last few shows at 8:30. Sponsored by Old Gold cigarettes, not Texaco. Produced by JD's own company, with NBC having no financial interest. Series ran June 29, 1957 to Sept. 21, 1957, on CBS, summer replacement for Jackie Gleason.

June 29, 1957; guest: Jane Froman, singer; orig. shown Dec. 31, 1955. July 6, 1957; guest: Peter Lawford; orig. shown May 5, 1956. July 13, 1957; guest: Lisa Kirk; orig. shown June 2, 1956. July 20, 1957; no guests; Jimmy stages surprise birthday party for Eddie Jackson; orig. shown Aug. 13, 1955. July 27, 1957; guest: Carmen Miranda; orig. shown Oct. 15, 1955. August 3, 1957; guest: George Sanders; orig. shown ? August 10, 1957; guest: Cass Daley; orig. shown July 23, 1955. August 17, 1957; guest: Connie Russell; orig. shown May 19, 1956. August 24, 1957; guest: Polly Bergen; orig. shown Dec. 10, 1955. August 31, 1957; guests: Peter Lawford and Anna Maria Alberghetti, in "The Necklace"; orig. shown ? Sept. 7, 1957; guest: Barbara Whiting; orig. shown July 9, 1955. Sept. 14, 1957; pre-empted by a CBS special. Sept. 21, 1957; tonight only, began 8:30 (to 9:00); guest: Marilyn Maxwell; orig. shown May 26, 1956.

Durante Television Specials
(see also individual listings by year)

AN EVENING WITH DURANTE. 1959-Sept. 25. JD NBC-TV special. Guests: Lawrence Welk, Sal Mineo, Gisele MacKenzie, Bobby Darin, Ginny Tiu (five-year-old pianist from Hong Kong).

GIVE MY REGARDS TO BROADWAY. 1959-Dec. 6. JD NBC-TV special, Guests: Jane Powell, Jimmy Rodgers, Eddie Hodges, Ray Bolger.

THE JIMMY DURANTE SHOW. 1961-Aug. 9. JD NBC-TV special. Guests: Bob Hope, Garry Moore, Janice Rule.

JIMMY DURANTE MEETS THE LIVELY ARTS. 1965-Oct. 30. First JD TV special in four years, ABC, 60 min., color. JD explores opera, art, drama, dance, and music with guests Roberta Peters, Max Showalter, Robert Vaughn, Rudolf Nureyev, Lynn Seymour, and The Shindogs.

THE JIMMY DURANTE SHOW (SITCOM) 1964. CBS-TV tried to bring THE JIMMY DURANTE SHOW back in a drastically different format, a situation comedy instead of a variety show. The pilot failed to attract an audience rating or sponsors and was not inserted into that fall's lineup. It was aired as part of a series of failed pilot shows, SUMMER PLAYHOUSE, July 18, 1964.

Variety Shows

CLUB OASIS. Variety series, bi-weekly, NBC, Sat. 9:00, 30 min. Ran just one season, first telecast Sept. 28, 1957, last time Sept. 6, 1958. Hosts included JD, Dean Martin, Eddie Fisher, Frank Sinatra, Spike Jones, others. JD hosted just twice.

THE HOLLYWOOD PALACE. ABC's effort to recapture the feeling of vaudeville as it existed at the famous Palace was less successful than CBS' ED SULLIVAN SHOW. First telecast Jan. 4, 1964 (with host Bing Crosby), last time Feb. 7, 1970 (again with Crosby). Throughout its run the show was on ABC, first on Sat. 9:30-10:30, moved to Tues. 10-11:00 from Sept. 5, 1967 to Jan. 2, 1968, back to Sat. 9:30-10:30 from Jan. 13, 1968 to its end Feb. 7, 1970. Had many hosts,

Bing Crosby the most frequent (30-plus appearances), followed by Fred Astaire, Milton Berle, JD, Sid Caesar and Imogene Coca, Sammy Davis, Jr., and Don Adams. Fewer vaudeville acts later as the show became more of a straight musical-comedy variety hour. Never had what could be called a regular host. JD hosted irregularly.

JIMMY DURANTE PRESENTS THE LENNON SISTERS. Sept. 26, 1969–July 4, 1970. Premiere of new weekly musical variety show, ABC, Fri. 10:00, 60 min. Last telecast July 4, 1970. (Special preview of this series, May 6, 1969, called THE LENNON SISTERS SHOW.) This season was the first after the Lennon Sisters had left THE LAWRENCE WELK SHOW. When the Durante–Lennon Sisters show was moved in February to Saturdays at 9:30, it ran immediately after the hour given to Lawrence Welk, aiming to draw the audience that had adored these girls on their long stay with Welk. It was cancelled at the end of its first and only season.

May 6, 1969. THE LENNON SISTERS SHOW. ABC special, Tues. 10:00, 60 min., color. Preview of the Lennon Sisters' forthcoming weekly ABC series with JD. Guests: JD, Bobby Goldsboro, and Hines, Hines & Dad.

Sept. 26, 1969. Premiere. ABC, Fri. 10:00, 60 min., in color each week. JD and the Lennon Sisters (4)—Dianne, Peggy, Kathy, and Janet—are the stars of this new variety series. Show usually opened with JD at piano, leading into segment of chatter and songs with Lennons.
    Guests: Jack Benny, Noel Harrison, Jimmy Dean. (JD and Jack Benny appearing together for the first time in their long careers.)

Oct. 3, 1969. Guests: Glen Campbell, Arte Johnson (Laugh-In), The Lettermen.

Oct. 10, 1969. Guests: Joey Bishop, O.C. Smith, Roy Rogers & Dale Evans.

Oct. 17, 1969. Guests: Martha Raye, Buddy Ebsen, Bobby Goldsboro.

Oct. 24, 1969. Guests: Bob Hope, Andy Williams, Osmond Brothers.

Oct. 31, 1969. Guests: Danny Thomas, Jimmie Rodgers.

Nov. 7, 1969. Guests: Fess Parker, John Byner, and Hines, Hines & Dad.

Nov. 14, 1969. Guests: George Burns, John Gary, Sonny James and his Southern Gentlemen.

Nov. 21, 1969. Guests: Kate Smith, Louis Nye, Rosie Grier.

Nov. 28, 1969. Guests: Don Ho, Merle Haggard, comic Corbett Monica.

Dec. 5, 1969. Guests: Milton Berle, pianist Jo Ann Castle, singer John Stewart.

Dec. 12, 1969. Guests: Mike Douglas, Norm Crosby, and the folk-singing Stoney Mountain Cloggers (from the Grand Ole Opry).

Dec. 19, 1969. Guests: Lorne Greene, JD's eight-year-old daughter CeCe, and 25 members of the Lennon family join in a Christmas musicale. (TV Guide says the program was taped before an audience composed entirely of the girls' family, friends, and neighbors.)

Dec. 26, 1969. Guests: Raymond Burr, Al Martino, Eddie Jackson, and Sonny King.

Jan. 2, 1970. Pre-empted by a movie.

Jan. 9, 1970. Guests: Mel Torme, Kaye Ballard, Monty Hall (whose *Let's Make a Deal* series takes a ribbing).

Jan. 16, 1970. Guests: Ed Ames, impressionist David Frye, duo pianists Ferrante & Teicher.

(Last show until Feb. 14, when it moved to Sat., 9:30.)

Sat., Feb. 14, 1970, 9:30-10:30, still ABC. Return. (Now immediately after the hour of THE LAWRENCE WELK SHOW.) Guests: Jack Benny, Sammy Davis, Jr.

Feb. 21, 1970. Guests: Dinah Shore, Walter Brennan, Watts Community Choir.

Feb. 28, 1970. Guests: Wayne Newton, Tony Randall, ventriloquist Senor Wences.

March 7, 1970. Guests: Leslie Uggams, Vic Damone, Arte Johnson (of *Laugh-In*).

March 14, 1970. Guests: Jerry Lewis, Jack Jones.

March 21, 1970. Guests: Desi Arnaz, Bobby Goldsboro, and Hines, Hines & Dad.

March 28, 1970. Guests: Perry Como, John Hartford, comic Charlie Callas.

April 4, 1970. Guests: Jimmy Dean, honky-tonk pianist Jo Ann Castle, impressionist Rich Little.

April 11, 1970. Reruns began with this show. Guests: Glen Campbell, Arte Johnson, The Lettermen; orig. televised Oct. 3, 1969.

April 18, 1970. Guests: Danny Thomas, Jimmie Rodgers; orig. televised Oct. 31, 1969.

April 25, 1970. Guests: Milton Berle, pianist Jo Ann Castle, singer John Stewart; orig. televised Dec. 5, 1969.

May 2, 1970. Guests: Leslie Uggams, Vic Damone, Arte Johnson; orig. televised March 7, 1970.

May 9, 1970. Guests: Fess Parker, John Byner, and Hines, Hines & Dad; orig. televised Nov. 7, 1969.

May 16, 1970. Guests: Raymond Burr, Al Martino, Eddie Jackson and Sonny King; orig. televised Dec. 26, 1969.

May 23, 1970. Guests: Mel Torme, Kaye Ballard, Monty Hall; orig. televised Jan. 9, 1970.

May 30, 1970. Guests: George Burns, John Gary, Sonny James and his Southern Gentlemen; orig. televised Nov. 14, 1969.

June 6, 1970. Pre-empted by ABC News Special.

June 13, 1970. Guests: Jerry Lewis, Jack Jones; orig. televised March 14, 1970.

June 20, 1970. Guests: Desi Arnaz, Bobby Goldsboro, Hines, Hines & Dad; orig. televised March 21, 1970.

June 27, 1970. Pre-empted by a football game.

July 4, 1970 (final program). Guests: Wayne Newton, Tony Randall, ventriloquist Senor Wences; orig. televised Feb. 28, 1970.

Other Durante Television Appearances

March 26, 1951. THE EDDIE CANTOR SHOW. NBC, Sun. 8:00, 60 min. Guests: JD and Eddie Jackson.

Dec. 23, 1951 (?). THE BOB HOPE SHOW. NBC, Sun. 7:00, 30 min. Guest: JD.

1954-Dec. 5. SPOTLIGHT. NBC, Sun. 7:30, 90 min., color. Revue on ice, originates from Colonial Theatre, New York City. Skating, songs, and sketches. Produced by Max Liebman. Stars Sonja Henie, JD, Jack Buchanan, Jeannie Carson (last two are British musical-comedy stars), Pat Carroll (comedienne).

Feb. 21, 1956. THE MILTON BERLE SHOW. NBC, Tues. 8:00, 60 min., color. Guests: Eddie Cantor, JD, Cyd Charisse, Dan Dailey, Peggy Lee, The Four Aces.

Nov. 30, 1956. THE WALTER WINCHELL SHOW. NBC, Fri. 8:30, 30 min. Short-lived variety show. Guests: JD, Jill Corey.

Oct. 13, 1957. STANDARD OIL 75TH ANNIVERSARY SHOW. NBC, Sun. 9:00, 90 min., color. Special. Tyrone Power, host, starring JD, Marge and Gower Champion, Bert Lahr, Duke Ellington, Brandon de Wilde, Eddie Mayehoff, Jane Powell, Kay Thompson, Donald O'Connor.
    JD and Bert Lahr do a comedy turn together for the first time ever and perform very early Durante songs.

Oct. 26, 1957. CLUB OASIS. NBC, Sat. 9:00, 30 min. JD hosts tonight. His guest: Jeannie Carson, British singer-comedienne.

Dec. 1, 1957. THE DINAH SHORE CHEVY SHOW. NBC, Sun. 9:00, 60 min., color. Guests: Rossano Brazzi, JD, Pat Suzuki, the Steiner Brothers (tap-dancing trio).

Jan. 7, 1958. THE EDDIE FiSHER SHOW. NBC, Tues. 8:00, 60 min., color. Guests: George Gobel (regular guest who had his own show alternating weeks with Eddie Fisher), JD, Lily Pons, Jimmy Rodgers.

March 1, 1958. CLUB OASIS. NBC, Sat. 9:00, 30 min. JD hosts tonight. His guests: Jane Kean, singer-comedienne; Ronnie Fletcher, dancer.

Oct. 12, 1958. THE DINAH SHORE CHEVY SHOW. NBC, Sun. 9:00, 60 min., color. Guests: JD, Peter Lawford, Julius La Rosa, Ella Fitzgerald.

Nov. 12, 1958. MILTON BERLE STARRING IN THE KRAFT MUSIC HALL. NBC, Wed. 9:00, 30 min., color. Guest: JD.

Sept. 25, 1959. AN EVENING WITH DURANTE. JD special, NBC, Fri. 8:30, 60 min., color. (First of two comedy shows JD would do this fall, the second being Dec. 6, 1959.) Guests: Lawrence Welk, Sal Mineo, Gisele MacKenzie, Bobby Darin, Ginny Tiu (five-year-old pianist from Hong Kong).

Oct. 19, 1959. THE FRANK SINATRA TIMEX SHOW. ABC, Mon. 9:30, 60 min. Special. Guests: Bing Crosby, Dean Martin, and Mitzi Gaynor, with JD's appearance unbilled.
    Durante walked on stage near end of a tribute to Clayton, Jackson, and Durante with Sinatra (as Lou Clayton), Crosby (as Eddie Jackson), and Martin (as Jimmy Durante).

Fall, 1959. SUNDAY SHOWCASE. NBC, Sun. 8:00, 60 min., color, combining variety and live drama. Lasted only through that one season.
Oct. 25, 1959. "A Tribute to Eleanor Roosevelt on Her Diamond Jubilee." Starring Marian Anderson, Lauren Bacall, Ralph Bellamy, Gertrude Berg, Milton Berle, Eddie Cantor, Art Carney, Maurice Chevalier, JD, Henry Fonda, Arthur Godfrey, Cedric Hardwicke, Helen Hayes, Bob Hope, Jose Iturbi, Henry Morgan, Sidney Poitier, and Elizabeth Taylor. With former President Harry S Truman, Vice President Richard M. Nixon, other world leaders.
Dec. 6, 1959. One variety presentation in the series was "Give My Regards to Broadway," starring JD, with guests Jane Powell, Jimmy Rodgers, Eddie Hodges, Ray Bolger.

Jan. 18, 1960. STEVE ALLEN PLYMOUTH SHOW. NBC, Mon. 10:00, 60 min., live, color. Guests: JD, Peggy Lee.

April 19, 1960. THE GARRY MOORE SHOW. CBS, Tues. 10:00, 60 min. Guests: JD, singer Anna Maria Alberghetti.
The first appearance of Durante and Moore since their show on radio.

Oct. 7, 1960. DIAMOND JUBILEE—PLUS ONE! [Saluting Eleanor Roosevelt]. NBC, Fri. 9:00, 60 min. Host, Bob Hope. Guest stars: Lucille Ball, Jack Benny, George Burns, Carol Channing, Nat "King" Cole, Irene Dunne, JD, Mahalia Jackson, Mary Martin, Paul Newman, Richard Rodgers, Simone Signoret, and Joanne Woodward. Special appearances by Mrs. Eleanor Roosevelt, Vice President Richard M. Nixon, Senator John F. Kennedy, General Omar N. Bradley, and Dr. Tom Dooley. The tribute was to benefit the Eleanor Roosevelt Cancer Foundation.

Dec. 6, 1960. OPEN END. NBC, Tues. 10:00, 60 min. Special edition with host David Susskind. (Show usually syndicated, Sundays in New York on WNBT, channel 13, 10:00, open-ended. An earlier panel of five comics ran 3 hours and 15 minutes.) Panel of five comics: Joey Bishop, George Burns, JD, Buddy Hackett, and Groucho Marx. Only Hackett had appeared on the earlier show.

Dec. 12, 1960. BOB HOPE BUICK SHOW. NBC, Mon. 9:30, 60 min. Starring Bob Hope and Polly Bergen. Special guest: JD.

Feb. 22, 1961. PERRY COMO'S KRAFT MUSIC HALL. NBC, Wed. 9:00, 60 min. Guests: JD and Anna Maria Alberghetti.

Aug. 9, 1961. THE JIMMY DURANTE SHOW. NBC Special, Wed. 10:00, 60 min., taped. Guests: Bob Hope, Garry Moore, Janis Rule.

Nov. 27, 1961. THE DANNY THOMAS SHOW. CBS, Mon. 9:00, 30 min. Episode entitled "Danny and Durante." Guest: JD.

Jan. 7, 1962. THE ED SULLIVAN SHOW. CBS, Sun. 8:00, 60 min. Guests: JD, with his partner Eddie Jackson and his "junior partner" Sonny King, Rosemary Clooney, others.

1962. THE NEW MARCH OF DIMES. Syndicated show, 60 min. Benefit for polio research. Host, JD. Guests: Ed Wynn and Buster Keaton (the three doing sketch, "The Scene Stealers"). Plus Rosemary Clooney, The Limelighters, Eartha Kitt, Roger Williams, Nanette Fabray, Fabian, Dorothy Provine. Other stars appear briefly: David Janssen, Ralph Edwards, Fritz Feld, Dr. Frank C. Baxter, Lorne Greene, Dan Blocker, James Garner, Jackie Cooper, Abby Dalton. Also,

Mr. Basil O'Connor, Pres., National Foundation, and Debbie, the poster girl for the March of Dimes.

1962. SUM AND SUBSTANCE. Local Los Angeles program, 30 min. Host, Herman Harvey. Guest: Jimmy Durante. Series of interviews by Professor Herman Harvey, who created the series, in association with University of Southern California and KNXT-TV Public Affairs. CBS affiliate, Los Angeles.

Feb. 24, 1963. THE ED SULLIVAN SHOW. CBS, Sun. 8:00, 60 min. From Las Vegas. Guests: JD, Carol Lawrence, Pat Buttram (comic), Eddie Seifert and Co. (contortionists), the Nitwits (slapstick artists from England), Eric Brenn (plate-spinner). JD is joined by Sonny King, Eddie Jackson, and the Desert Inn Dancing Girls.

Sept. 21, 1963. THE JERRY LEWIS SHOW. ABC, Sat. 9:30, 120 min. Premiere of live talk show, which was cancelled after three months. Early surprise appearances by Robert Stack, then JD.

Sept. 29, 1963. THE ED SULLIVAN SHOW. CBS, Sun. 8:00, 60 min. Opens new fall season with JD, Peter Lawford, and Frank Sinatra, Jr., as guests.

Jan. 23, 1964. PERRY COMO SPECIAL. NBC, Thurs. 10:00, 60 min. Guests: JD, Dorothy Provine, Russ Tamblyn, and Texas Boys Choir. Live from the Dallas State Fair Music Hall.

April 18, 1964. THE HOLLYWOOD PALACE. ABC, Sat. 9:30, 60 min. JD host. Guests: Liberace, Jack Carter, Piccola Pupa (singer), Silvio Francesco (dancer-juggler), Sylte Sisters (singers), The Hardy Family (acrobats), Colvin and Wilder (comics), Otto and Maria (balancing act).

July 18, 1964. THE JIMMY DURANTE SHOW. CBS, Sat. 9:30, 30 min. Pilot for situation comedy series. Stars JD and Eddie Hodges. Part of SUMMER PLAYHOUSE series.

Nov. 8, 1964. THE ED SULLIVAN SHOW. CBS, Sun. 8:00, 60 min. Guests: JD, Nipsey Russell, singer Jean Paul Vignon, London's rock 'n' rolling Bachelors, comic Richard "Mr. Pastry" Hearne, pianist Ginny Tiu and her singing-dancing company, the juggling Del Ray Brothers, and Brizio the Clown.

Dec. 10, 1964. THE DANNY THOMAS SHOW. CBS, Mon. 9:00, 30 min. Guests: JD, Eddie Fisher, Joey Bishop.

Feb. 7, 1965. THE ED SULLIVAN SHOW. CBS, Sun. 8:00, 60 min. Guests: JD, Vaughn Monroe, Leslie Uggams, Stiller & Meara, comedienne Jean Carroll, Israeli vocalist Rebecca Raz, the Royal Welsh Male Choir, the folk-singing Womenfolk, the Brascia & Tybee dance team, and the Petroffs' novelty act.

May 1, 1965. THE HOLLYWOOD PALACE. ABC, Sat. 9:30, 60 min. Host, Louis Armstrong. Guests: Rowan & Martin, Diahann Carroll, Edward G. Robinson, JD, Ballet Folklorico of Mexico.

Louis Armstrong and Jimmy: "Between your trumpet and my nose, we could blow 100 years." They do a duet on "Old Man Time."

Oct. 30, 1965. JIMMY DURANTE MEETS THE LIVELY ARTS. ABC, 9:30, 60 min., color. JD's first TV special in four years. Guests: Max Showalter on Sandy Warlock (painting), Robert Vaughn (drama), Rudolf Nureyev and Lynn Seymour (ballet).

Feb. 7, 1966. THE LUCY SHOW. Lucille Ball's CBS series, Mon. 8:30, 30 min., color. Cameo appearances in this episode, "Lucy Goes to a Hollywood Premiere": Kirk Douglas, Edward G. Robinson, Jimmy Durante, and Vincent Edwards.

April 17, 1966. THE ED SULLIVAN SHOW. CBS, Sun. 8:00, 60 min., color. Guests: JD, Petula Clark, the rock 'n' rolling Animals, Franco Corelli and Dorothy Kirsten, Myron Cohen, contortionist Gita Morelly, and on a taped segment, the Swingle Singers.

Oct. 2, 1966. THE ED SULLIVAN SHOW. CBS, Sun. 8:00, 60 min., color. Guests: JD, Dame Margot Fonteyn and Rudolf Nureyev, Alan King, Connie Francis, Gwen Verdon and cast members from *Sweet Charity*, ventriloquist Arthur Worsley, winners of the New York Harvest Moon Ball dance contest.

Oct. 19, 1966. BOB HOPE CHRYSLER THEATER. NBC, Sun. 9:00, 60 min., color. Special. An episode called "Murder at NBC." Hope and 15 other comedians: Don Adams, Milton Berle, Red Buttons, Johnny Carson, Jack Carter, Bill Cosby, Wally Cox, Bill Dana, JD, Don Rickles, Dan Rowan and Dick Martin, Dick Shawn, and Jonathan Winters. (Rerun Sun., March 15, 1967, 9:00.)

Nov. 6, 1966. ALICE THROUGH THE LOOKING GLASS. NBC, Sun. 7:30, 90 min., color. Special. A musical adaptation of the Lewis Carroll classic. JD played Humpty Dumpty. Alice was played by Judi Rolin.
    Others in the cast included Roy Castle as Lester the Jester; Robert Coote as The Red King; Richard Denning as The Father; Nanette Fabray as The White Queen; Ricardo Montalban as The White King; Agnes Moorehead as The Red Queen; Jack Palance as The Jabberwock; Tom Smothers and Dick Smothers as Tweedledum and Tweedledee.
    RCA Victor released an LP of the show the same year.

Dec. 10, 1966. THE HOLLYWOOD PALACE. ABC, Sat. 9:30, 60 min., color. JD host. Guests: The Turtles, George Carlin, Elaine Dunn, Mrs. Miller, Peter Lawford.

Jan. 14, 1967. THE HOLLYWOOD PALACE. ABC, Sat. 9:30, 60 min., color. Bing Crosby host. Guests: Senate Minority Leader Everett Dirksen (R., IL.), JD, Tim Conway, Edie Adams, Danny Sailor (pole-climber).

April 12, 1967. DANNY THOMAS SPECIAL. NBC, Wed. 9:00, 60 min., color. Guests: JD, Vic Damone, Sammy Davis, Jr., Jane Powell, and Dennis Day.

Sept. 5, 1967. THE HOLLYWOOD PALACE. ABC, Tues. 10:00, 60 min., color. Bing Crosby, host. Guests: JD, Milton Berle, Diahann Carroll, Joey Heatherton, Every Mother's Son (vocal group), Ravi Shankar. Season premiere.
    Bing, Berle, and JD recreate Clayton, Jackson, and Durante.

Sept. 20, 1967. THE BOB HOPE SHOW. NBC, Wed. 9:00, 60 min., color. Variety special. Guests: JD, Phyllis Diller, Kaye Stevens, Jack Jones, Rudy Vallee, Dan Rowan and Dick Martin.

Nov. 11, 1967. MISS TEENAGE AMERICA PAGEANT. CBS, 10:00, 90 min., color. From Dallas, Texas. Hosts Dean Jones and Jane Powell. Guest star, JD.

Dec. 5, 1967. THE HOLLYWOOD PALACE. ABC, Tues. 10:00, 60 min., color. JD host. Guests: Ethel Merman, The Lennon Sisters, Grass Roots (rock group), Noel Harrison, Larry Bishop (son of Joey Bishop) and Rob Reiner (as comedy team), Milt Kamen, The Berosinis (acrobats).

Dec. 26, 1967. THE HOLLYWOOD PALACE. ABC, Tues. 10:00, 60 min., color. JD host (ringmaster) of the "Palace" circus show. Guests: performing dogs, ponies, monkeys, elephants, acrobats, clowns, and a trapeze artist.

Jan. 13, 1968. THE HOLLYWOOD PALACE. ABC, Sat. 9:30, 60 min., color. Bing Crosby, host. Guests: Phil Harris, Peggy Lee, JD, Milton Berle, Lawrence Welk, Roosevelt Grier of the L.A. Rams, acrobats of the Moscow Circus, plus clips of past guests. Premiere of fifth season, returning to its original time slot.

Feb. 15, 1968. PERSONALITY. NBC, Mon.-Fri. 11 A.M., 30 min., color. Game show, three celebrity panelists live, changing each week, plus daily guest joining on film. On-film guest: JD, Thursday, joining Joan Fontaine, Van Johnson, and Joan Rivers.

Feb. 17, 1968. THE HOLLYWOOD PALACE. ABC, Sat. 9:30, 60 min., color. JD host. Guests: Vicki Carr, Jimmy Dean, Pat Henry, Van Johnson, Mac Ronee, The Temptations.

March 30, 1968. THE HOLLYWOOD PALACE. ABC, Sat. 9:30, 60 min., color. JD host. Guests: The Beatles (on film), Tim Conway, Fred and Mickey Finn, Grand Ballet Classique from Paris, Liza Minnelli, comedian Jerry Shane.

   Jimmy Durante is introduced as "75 years young." With four chorus girls and four tuxedoed gents, he and they sing "Old Man Time." Studio audience stands to sing "Happy Birthday" to Jimmy. The show was taped February 23, 1968. His birthday was February 10, 1893.

April 21, 1968. ROMP!! ABC special, Sun. 7:00, 60 min., color. Variety show for teenagers headlined by Ryan O'Neal and Michele Lee. Guests: JD, Barbara Eden, James Darren, Sammy Davis, Sr. [not Jr.], the Harpers Bizarre, Cream, Celebration.

Oct. 5, 1968. THE HOLLYWOOD PALACE. ABC, Sat. 9:30, 60 min., color. JD host. Guests: Joey Heatherton, Don Ho, The Lennon Sisters, Lewis and Christy (comedy team), six gymnastics finalists in the U.S. Olympic trials.

Dec. 14, 1968. THE HOLLYWOOD PALACE. ABC, Sat. 9:30, 60 min., color. JD host. Guests: Ethel Merman, Sugar Ray Robinson, Bill "Jose Jimenez" Dana, Vikki Carr, Leland Palmer (singer-dancer), Hendra and Ullett (comedy team), The Iriston Horsemen from the Moscow State Circus.

Jan. 11, 1969. THE HOLLYWOOD PALACE. ABC, Sat. 9:30, 60 min., color. JD host. Guests: Ella Fitzgerald, Sergio Franchi, Marvin Gaye, Pat Cooper, the Tahiti Nue Revue, the Society of Seven (rock group).

March 2, 1969. MOTHERS-IN-LAW. NBC, Sun. 8:30, 30 min., color. Situation comedy series. This week's episode called "Every In-Law Wants to Get Into the Act." Series stars Eve Arden and Kaye Ballard. Regular Jerry Fogel debuts his nightclub act, featuring an imitation of JD (who makes a cameo appearance). Produced by good friend Desi Arnaz.

March 19, 1969. CHRYSLER PRESENTS THE BOB HOPE SPECIAL. NBC, Wed. 9:00, 60 min., color. Guests: JD, Nancy Sinatra, Ray Charles, Cyd Charisse.

Oct. 13, 1969. THE BOB HOPE SHOW. NBC, Mon. 9:00, 60 min., color. Program of vaudeville-style music, songs, and comedy. Guests: JD, Barbara McNair, Donald O'Connor, Tom Jones.

Dec. 7, 1969. FROSTY THE SNOWMAN. CBS, Sun. 7:30, 30 min., color. Animated short film, based on the hit song by Steve Nelson and Jack Rollins. JD's voice narrating the story and singing the title song. Also starring the voices of Billy De Wolfe and Jackie Vernon, with Paul Frees and June Foray.

MGM released the original soundtrack recording. Videocassette released 1989 has copyright date 1969.

Repeated Dec. 5, 1971, CBS, Sun. 7:30, and many Christmas seasons thereafter.

Jan. 3, 1970. THE ANDY WILLIAMS SHOW. NBC, Sat. 7:30, 60 min., color. Musical variety. Guests: JD, Leslie Uggams, James Garner, Judy Carne.

Feb. 7, 1970. THE HOLLYWOOD PALACE. ABC, Sat. 9:30, 60 min., color. Last show of the long series. Host: Bing Crosby. Sponsored by Faberge. Taped clips of many acts and stars who appeared over the years. Includes Mrs. Miller and JD (only a portion of their act from Dec. 10, 1966 show); JD falling off a glass chair; JD flubbing lines while introducing Peter Lawford, and the two dressed as British rockers listening to off-stage directions and confused as to what to say (from Dec. 10, 1966 show). Ends with collage of stars saying goodnight, including JD.

Sept. 20, 1970. THE ED SULLIVAN SHOW. CBS, Sun. 8:00, 60 min., color. Premiere of 23rd season. Presents first AGVA awards ceremony (American Guild of Variety Artists), awards called Georgies in honor of George M. Cohan. At Caesar's Palace in Las Vegas. Among the awards: Entertainer of the Year, Bob Hope; Comedy Stars, Carol Burnett and Flip Wilson; Golden Award, JD.

March 6, 1971. THE PEARL BAILEY SHOW. ABC, Sat. 8:30, 60 min., color. Guests: JD, Tony Bennett, The Supremes.

June 6, 1971. ORAL ROBERTS SUMMER FESTIVAL. Syndicated. WOR-TV, New York, Sun. 10:00, 60 min., color. Taped in Tulsa, Oklahoma, in front of a young audience. With JD, Bobby Goldsboro, Ralph Carmichael Orch., others.

Light Records released a 45rpm three-record set, FESTIVAL: MUSIC FROM THE ORAL ROBERTS SUMMER TV SPECIAL.

Aug. 1, 1971. THE SONNY & CHER COMEDY HOUR. CBS, Sun. 8:30, 60 min., color. Premiere of variety series. Guest: JD.

Sept. 10, 1972. A SALUTE TO TELEVISION'S 25TH ANNIVERSARY. ABC, Sun. 9:30, 90 min., color. Top stars in person and highlights from the past 25 years: Judith Anderson, Russell Arms, James Arness, Lucille Ball, Milton Berle, Sid Caesar, George Chakiris, Maria Cole, JD, Dave Garroway, Lorne Greene, Florence Henderson, Bob Hope, Snooky Lanson, Gisele MacKenzie, Dewey Murrow, Harry Reasoner, George C. Scott, Rod Serling, Dinah Shore, Smothers Brothers, Ed Sullivan, John Wayne, Eileen Wilson, Robert Young, and Efrem Zimbalist, Jr.

Oct. 13, 1972. THE SONNY & CHER COMEDY HOUR. CBS, Fri. 8:00, 60 min., color. Guests: JD, Gilbert O'Sullivan.

Related Durante Television Items

Sept. 25, 1978. THE PEOPLE. CBS series, Sat. 2:00, 30 min., color. Tribute to JD.

Sept. 16, 1978. THAT'S HOLLYWOOD. Syndicated TV documentary series made by 20th Century Fox. Executive producer, Jack Haley, Jr. Narrator, Tom Bosley. WABC-TV, New York, 7:30, 30 min.

The premiere of this show concerned scenes that were cut from movies and funny fluffs in filming of movies and TV shows. "Included was a song-and-dance number with Shirley Temple and Jimmy Durante. Unfortunately, no reason for its deletion from the film was given." (*Variety*, Sept. 20, 1978).

Major Television Awards

April 1951. JD wins the George Peabody Award for his TV comedy, "Entertainment" category, 1950.

Feb. 5, 1953. JD is presented an Emmy Award as best TV comedian of 1952. (Other nominees were Sid Caesar, Wally Cox, Jackie Gleason, and Herb Shriner.) A separate award was given that year for best comedienne, to Lucille Ball.

The same year JD was nominated in the category of "Outstanding Personality" but lost to Bishop Fulton J. Sheen. Others nominated included Lucille Ball, Arthur Godfrey, Edward R. Murrow, Donald O'Connor, and Adlai Stevenson.

Appendix E

Discography

Works helpful in compiling this list are many, but most helpful for the 78s are the reference books by Brian Rust, especially *Jazz Records 1897–1942* (2 vols. New York: Arlington House, 1978). Corrections to Rust from researcher Mark Berresford are incorporated through 1921. For the LPs the monthly Schwann catalogues were most useful.

Durante with Groups—78rpm Records

Original New Orleans Jazz Band

477-B Ole Miss
  Okeh 1156. New York, c. November 1918.
  Personnel*: JD, piano; Alfred "Pantsy" Laine or Frank Christian, cornet; Frank Lhotak, trombone; Achille Baquet, clarinet; Arnold Loyacano, drums.

478-B Ja Da (Intro. You'll Find Old Dixieland in France)
  Okeh 1155. New York, c. November 1918.
  Personnel: same.

6026 He's Had No Lovin' for a Long, Long Time
6027 Ja-Da (Intro. You'll Find Old Dixieland in France)
  Gennett 4508. New York, January 1919.
  Personnel: same.

6091, -A Ja-Da (Intro. You'll Find Old Dixieland in France)
6092-A He's Had No Lovin' for a Long, Long Time
  Gennett 4508, reissued Ristic 2.
  New York, c. March 1919.
  Personnel: same except trombonist changes, possibly Miff Mole (according to Berresford. "The trombone here is more muscular and rhythmic than on the preceding OK and Gennett session, which is typical Lhotak. Mole, furthermore,

*Possibly Dave Stryker, whom I interviewed in West Palm Beach, Florida, on January 6, 1985, was the trombonist on some of this group's and other groups' sessions that involved Durante. Stryker said he played at the Alamo Club with Durante's band for three years, and recalled playing and recording with Achille Baquet, clarinet; Johnny Stein, drums; later, Jack Roth, drums.

231

in a 1950s interview with Record Research, New York City, claimed he worked with Durante at this time.")

"Ja-Da Medley" and "He's Had No Lovin' for a Long, Long Time" were reissued on the LP, NEW ORLEANS BOYS 1918-1927, (Dutch) Riverside RM-8818, part of the "Classic Jazz Masters" series. This LP was pressed in Holland for continental release. The source was Gennett 4508, matrix 6091-A and 6092-A, c. March 1919, although liner notes give Nov. 1918.

Jimmy Durante's Jazz Band

7246 Why Cry Blues
> Gennett 9045, and Sterling (Canada) 9028.
> New York, May 1920.
> Personnel: Frank Christian, cornet; possibly Dave Stryker, trombone; possibly Achille Baquet, clarinet; JD, piano; Johnny Stein, drums.

Lanin's Southern Serenaders

Matrix not given Memphis Blues
> The St. Louis Blues.
> Arto 9097, Bell P-97, and Hy-Tone K-97.
> New York, c. July 1921.
> Personnel: Phil Napoleon, trumpet; possibly Moe Gappell or Dave Stryker, trombone; Doc Behrendson, clarinet; Loring McMurray, alto sax; JD, piano; unknown, drums.

41924-1-3 Shake It and Break It
> Emerson 10439, 10566, Medallion 8239, Regal 9134, and Tempo (U.K.) R-27.
41925-2-3 Aunt Hagar's Children Blues
> Emerson 10439, 10566, Banner 1182, Regal 9134, 9456.
> New York, c. August 1, 1921.
> Personnel: same, with Sam Lanin vocal on first.

69330 Shake It and Break It
> Pathe 20634 (vertical cut recording, USA issue).
> New York, c. August 1921.
> Personnel: same, with Sam Lanin vocal.

837-1-2 Aunt Hagar's Children Blues (Aunt Hagar's Blues*) (Aunt Haggar Blues**)
> Paramount/Bluebird 20068 (rare West Coast early 1920s label, not RCA), Paramount 20222*, Banner 1015, Black Swan 2034, Claxtonola 40068, Famous 3062, 3216*, National 12222*, Puritan/ Triangle 11068*, 11222*, Imperial 1253** (U.K.).
> New York, c. August 30, 1921.
> Personnel: same, without vocal.

838-1-2 Shake It and Break It
> Paramount/Bluebird 20068, Banner 1015, Black Swan 2034, Broadway/Puritan/Triangle 11068, Claxtonola 40068, Famous 3062.
> New York, c. August 30, 1921.
> Personnel: same, with Sam Lanin vocal.

Note: (Both 837-1-2 and 838-1-2, as they appeared on Black Swan 2034, on an all–Negro label, under the name HENDERSON'S DANCE ORCH., sought to mislead the public into thinking the group was black and led by Black Swan's house band leader Fletcher Henderson.

69392 I've Got the Joys
69393 Mandy 'n' Me
        Pathe 20649 (vertical cut recording, USA issue), 10256 (mx 69392 only).
        New York, c. September 1921.
Personnel: same, no vocal by Lanin.

42044-1 Gypsy Blues
        Emerson 10467, Regal 9143.
42045-1-3-4 My Sunny Tennessee
        Emerson 10467, Regal 9139.
        New York, c. November 3, 1921.
        (Regal 9143 and 9139 as KENTUCKY SERENADERS.)
        Personnel on both: Phil Napoleon, trumpet; maybe Moe Gappell or Dave Stryker, trombone; Doc Behrendson, clarinet; Loring McMurray, alto sax; JD, piano; maybe John Cali, banjo; unknown, drums.

42095-2-4 Arkansas Blues
42096-2-3 Lonesome Lovesick Blues
        Emerson 10496, Regal 9164.
        New York, c. December 7, 1921.
Personnel: same except Jack Roth replaces unknown, drums.

42162-1-3 Eddie Leonard Blues
42163-1-2-3 Satanic Blues
        Emerson 10508, Regal 9191.
        New York, c. January 24, 1922.
Personnel: same except Cali omitted.

42196-1-3 Virginia Blues
42197-2-3 Doo Dah Blues
        Emerson _____, Regal 9200.
        New York, c. February 24, 1922.
Personnel: same.
Note: On Lanin's Southern Serenaders' next, and last, recording in July 1922 ("Good Morning" and "I'm Just Wild About Harry," Banner 1100 and Regal 9355), Durante was replaced on piano by Frank Signorelli, and Miff Mole took over on trombone, among other changes. Phil Napoleon and Jack Roth continued.

Ladd's Black Aces

7577-A Aunt Hagar's Children Blues
7578 Shake It and Break It
        Gennett 4762, Connorized 3011, Starr 9150 (Canada), Rich-Tone 7011. New York, August 1921.
        (Some copies show mx 7577-A as "Aunt Hager's Children's Blues." Connorized 3011 as CONNORIZED JAZZ HOUNDS; Rich-Tone 7011 as WHITE BROTHERS ORCH.; Starr 9150 as LANIN'S JAZZ BAND.)

Personnel: Phil Napoleon, trumpet; maybe Moe Gappell or Dave Stryker, trombone; Doc Behrendson, clarinet; JD, piano; unknown, drums; Sam Lanin, vocal. (Rust: "This personnel is based on the recollections of Sam Lanin and Jimmy Durante." Berresford amends this: "Roth was absent from pre–November 1921 sessions. His style is quite distinctive....The drummer on the Lanin Southern Serenaders and Ladd's sides is nowhere as rhythmic, tending to emphasize the beat rather than the afterbeat.")

7666, A-B Gypsy Blues
7667-A-B I'm Just Too Mean to Cry
          Gennett 4794, Connorized 3030, Rich-Tone 7014 (1st number only),
          Starr 9177. New York, October 1921.
          (Connorized as CONNORIZED JAZZERS.) Personnel: Added Loring
McMurray, alto sax; John Cali, banjo.

7685, -B-C Brother Low Down
          Gennett 4806, Connorized 3034.
7686, -A I've Got to Have My Daddy Blues (Lonesome Lovesick Blues*)
          Gennett 4806, Connorized 3035, Starr 9189* (Canada, second num-
          ber only).
7685-C Brother Low Down (Take "C" on Starr 9189)
          New York, October 1921.
          (Connorized as CONNORIZED JAZZERS.)
          Personnel: McMurray and Cali omitted.

7695, -A She's a Mean Job
7696, -A-B I Got It, You'll Get It
          Gennett 4809, Starr 9196, Connorized 3059 (second number only).
New York, November 1921.
          (Connorized as CONNORIZED JAZZERS.) Personnel: Benny Bloom, cor-
net; maybe Moe Gappell or Dave Stryker, trombone; Doc Behrendson, clarinet;
JD, piano; Jack Roth, drums; Billy de Rex, vocals on both numbers.
          Note: On Ladd's Black Aces' next recording ("Virginia Blues," c. February
25, 1922) and subsequent recordings for Gennett, Durante was replaced by Frank
Signorelli on piano. Phil Napoleon and Jack Roth continued with the group
through its last recording for Gennett, August 1924. All the group's 78s were
reissued on three LPs by Fountain (U.K.) Vintage Jazz Series: FJ-102 (Vol. 1:
1921-1922), released 1971; FJ-106 (Vol. 2: 1922-1923), 1973; FJ-111 (Vol. 3:
1923-1924), 1975.

Bailey's Lucky Seven

7668, -A-B How Many Times?
7669, -A Wimmin (I Gotta Have 'Em, That's All)
          Gennett 4795, Connorized 3034, Rich-Tone 7014, Starr 9178 (2nd
          number also on Edison Bell Winner 3697 [U.K.] and Westport 468
          [U.K.]).
          New York, October 1921.
          (Rich-Tone as THE JAZZ HARMONIZERS.) Probable personnel: Benny
Bloom, trumpet; Moe Gappell, trombone; Doc Behrendson, clarinet & tenor sax;
Loring McMurray, alto sax; JD, piano; Jack Roth, drums.

7711-A-B I've Got My Habits On
7712-B-C In My Heart, on My Mind, All Day Long
         Gennett 4815, Connorized 3045, Starr 9193 (second number also on
         Rich-Tone 7022 under group name THE JAZZ HARMONIZERS).
         New York, December 1921.
     Personnel: Phil Napoleon, trumpet; maybe Charlie Panelli, trombone; Doc
Behrendson, clarinet; Loring McMurray & Bennie Krueger, alto sax & tenor sax;
maybe JD, piano; Jack Roth, drums.
     Note: The next recording by BAILEY'S LUCKY SEVEN ("My Mammy
Knows" and "On the 'Gin 'Gin Ginny Shore," c. February 1, 1922) has changes
in personnel, not all of them known, probably without Durante. The group continued to record for Gennett through February 1926, with Miff Mole, trombone,
from Oct. 1923 on, and Red Nichols, trumpet, from August 1924 on. Jack Roth
continued as the drummer until about 1924.

Leona Williams and Her Dixie Band

     Some researchers, including Berresford, suggest that Leona Williams and Her
Dixie Band included Durante on piano on recordings made for Columbia in New
York, January 1922, replaced by Frank Signorelli in March 1922. The prevailing
view, however, seems to be that Durante was not on any of these sessions. A British
LP, Fountain FB-303, reissued the recordings of what Brian Rust in his liner notes
calls "vaudeville-type blues," a white group backing a Creole singer.

Clayton, Jackson, and Durante

148495-2 Can Broadway Do Without Me?
158496-2 So I Ups to Him
         Columbia 1860-D, (U.K.) DB-153 (first number only also on Harmony
         HS-11353). New York, May 9, 1929.
     Personnel: vocal, acc. by studio orchestra.

Durante Solo—Singles and LPs

Brunswick/Columbia 78s

LA-105-A Inka Dinka Doo
LA-106-A Hot Patatta
         Brunswick 6774, 01754, Columbia (U.K.) DB-1806 (first number
         only also on Harmony HS-11353).
         Los Angeles, February 13, 1934.
     Personnel: Jimmy Durante vocal, acc. by studio orchestra. Reissued on Col-
umbia 36732, August 1944.

Majestic 78s

T-785 G'wan Home, Your Mudder's Callin'
T-784 There Are Two Sides to Ev'ry Girl

(both from film *Two Sisters from Boston*) Majestic 1059. New York, August 1946. Reissued on Varsity 168, September 1949, and as part of Royale 10" LP 68, reissued as Royale 1812, and Royale 45rpm EP-269.
Personnel: Durante vocals with Eddie Jackson, orchestra directed by Ted Dale.

Decca 78s and Their Reissues, 1940s

June 1946. Release of Decca 78rpm album JIMMY DURANTE in its Personality Series, Decca A-442. All songs written entirely or in part by JD. With orchestra under direction of Roy Bargy. Same album released 1949 as Decca 10" long-playing record, Decca DL-5116, and as Decca 45rpm album 9-110 on four records.

L-3480 Inka Dinka Doo
L-3481 Umbriago
  Decca 23351. Recorded July 26, 1944.
  Personnel: with Six Hits and a Miss, on both.

L-3613 Start Off Each Day with a Song
L-3612 Durante—The Patron of the Arts
  Decca 23566. Recorded 1946.
  Personnel: first with Eddie Jackson.

L-3624 Who Will Be with You When I'm Far Away?
  (Interpolation: Did You Ever Have the Feeling)
L-3650 So I Ups to Him
  Decca 23567. Recorded 1946.
  Personnel: Second with Eddie Jackson.

L-3652 Jimmy, the Well Dressed Man
L-3651 Joe Goes Up—I Come Down
  Decca 23568. Recorded 1946.
  Personnel: First with Eddie Jackson.

Some of these recordings were reissued as part of the Decca "Curtain Call" Series, "devoted to the great performers of our times and the recorded songs which helped to make them famous." Released on Decca 78rpm DU-1502, and Decca 45rpm 9-11046, were "Start Off Each Day with a Song" and "Inka Dinka Doo." Another reissue was the 45rpm coupling of "Inka Dinka Doo" and "Umbriago" on Decca 23351.

MGM 78s and Their Reissues

Note: Matrix numbers are not visible on the pressings. Matrix and recording dates were provided through the courtesy of Charles Garrod, researcher who compiled with Ed Novitsky a booklet MGM RECORD LISTINGS 3000, 2000, 5000, 55000 AND 6000 for the Joyce Record Club, Zephyrhills, Florida, June 1989.) All but one 78 have Roy Bargy conducting the orchestra.

47-S-3104-2 I'm Feeling Mighty Low
47-S-3105-2 I'll Do the Strut-Away in My Cutaway
  MGM 30015. Los Angeles, Spring 1947? (Released July 1947)
  Personnel: First with Candy Candido.

47-S-3106-2 I'm the Guy Who Found the Lost Chord (film *This Time for Keeps*)
47-S-3107-1 Little Bit This, Little Bit That
    MGM 30035. Los Angeles, Spring 1947? (Released Oct. 1947)

47-S-3277-2 Chidabee-Ch[idabee]-Ch[idabee] (Yah-Yah-Yah)
    MGM 30084. Los Angeles, Nov. 28, 1947.
47-S-3297-3 The Day I Read a Book
    MGM 30084. Los Angeles, Dec. 5, 1947.

47-S-3278-4 The State of Arkansas
47-S-3279-2 Dollar a Year Man
    MGM 30169. Los Angeles, Nov. 28, 1947.

47-S-3280-2 Fugitive from Esquire
47-S-3296-3 It's My Nose's Birthday
    MGM 30207. Los Angeles, Dec. 5, 1947.

49-3014-3 Any State in the Forty-Eight Is Great
49-3015-2 The Pussy Cat Song (Nyow! Nyot Nyow!)
    MGM 30176. Los Angeles, 1949.
    Personnel: both with Betty Garrett.

49-S-445 Take an L
49-S-446 Bibbidi-Bobbidi-Boo (The Magic Song)(film *Cinderella*)
    MGM 30226. Los Angeles, 1949. (Released Jan. 1950)
    Personnel: First with Marion Colby; both with orchestra conducted by
Michael Durso.

50-S-3091-1 A Razz-a-Ma-Tazz
50-S-3094-2 I'm a Vulture for Horticulture
    MGM 30238. Los Angeles, 1950. (Released c. June 1950)

50-S-3092 What You Goin' to Do When the Rent Comes 'Round? (Rufus Rastus
        Johnson Brown)
50-S-3093 Bill Bailey, Won't You Please Come Home?
    MGM 30255. Los Angeles, 1950. (Released Aug. 1950)
    Personnel: both with Eddie Jackson.

50-S-3099-2 Frosty the Snowman
50-S-3100-1 Christmas Comes but Once a Year (Isn't It a Shame That)
    MGM 30257. Los Angeles, 1950. (Released Sept. 1950)
    Personnel: First with unidentified child or woman.

    Reissued on MGM 10" LP, JIMMY DURANTE, MGM E-542: I'll Do the
Strut-Away in My Cutaway; I'm the Guy Who Found the Lost Chord; Chidabee-
Ch-Ch; Dollar a Year Man; Fugitive from Esquire; It's My Nose's Birthday; The
Day I Read a Book; The State of Arkansas.
    Again reissued, 1958, in MGM's Lion series as JIMMY DURANTE IN PER-
SON, Lion 12" LP L70053: the above plus Bill Bailey, Won't You Please Come
Home; What You Goin' to Do When the Rent Come 'Round (Rufus Rastus
Johnson Brown); A Razz-a-Ma-Tazz; I'm a Vulture for Horticulture.
    Also, with the same album title, on 12" LP, MGM E-3256, and under the title
THE SPECIAL MAGIC OF JIMMY DURANTE on 12" LP, (British) MGM
Select 2353.083. This material was reissued again in 1964 on MGM 12" LP, THE
VERY BEST OF JIMMY DURANTE, MGM E-4207.

Four of these MGM numbers were also reissued on MGM 45rpm extended-play album X101B, A-RAZZ-A-MA-TAZZ: A-Razz-a-Ma-Tazz; I'll Do the Strut-Away in My Cutaway; Bill Bailey Won't You Please Come Home?; What You Goin' to Do When the Rent Comes 'Round? (Rufus Rastus Johnson Brown)

RCA Victor 78s and 45s

The Song's Gotta Come from the Heart
A Real Piano Player
    RCA Victor 12" 78rpm, 12-3229; Victor 45rpm, 49-3229. March 1951.
    Equal billing for Durante and Helen Traubel, with orchestra conducted by Roy Bargy. Recorded from Durante's TV shows: first, Nov. 29, 1950; second, Jan. 24, 1951.

Decca 78s and 45s, 1950s

L-6388 How D' Ye Do and Shake Hands (film *Alice in Wonderland*)
L-6389 Black Strap Molasses
        Decca 27748. c. June 1951. (Released Sept. 1951) Also released on
        Decca 45rpm 9-27748.
    Personnel: Danny Kaye, Jimmy Durante, Jane Wyman, Groucho Marx. First with 4 Hits and a Miss, and orchestra directed by Sonny Burke. Second, with chorus and orch. dir. by Burke.

81782 You Say the Nicest Things
81784 If You Catch a Little Cold
        Decca 27865. October 26, 1951. Also released on Decca 45rpm
        9-27865.
    Personnel: Jimmy Durante and Ethel Merman, with orchestra accompaniment.

81783 A Husband—a Wife.
        Decca 29248. October 26, 1951. Also released on Decca 45rpm.
    Personnel: Durante and Merman.
    The above numbers were reissued 1987 on Ethel Merman LP, THE WORLD IS YOUR BALLOON, MCA MCL-1839 (England).

L-7969 Pupalina (My Little Doll)
L-7970 Little People
        Decca 29354. c. Nov. 1954. Also released on Decca 45rpm 9-29354.
    Personnel: JD with Jud Conlon Singers, orch. dir. by Roy Bargy.

L-8351 It's Bigger Than Both of Us (label does not state it is from 1950 film *The Milkman*)
L-8352 When the Circus Leaves Town
        Decca 29537. c. May 1955. Also released on Decca 45rpm 9-29537.
    Personnel: First JD and Patty Andrews, second JD alone, both with orch. dir. by Roy Bargy.

L-8353 Swingin' with Rhythm and Blues
L-8354 I Love You, I Do
        Decca 29581. c. May 1955. Both are also on a Decca 45rpm.

Personnel: First JD with Peter Lawford, second JD with Eddie Jackson, both with orch. dir. by Roy Bargy.

Golden 78s (for Children)

Yankee Doodle Bunny (The Holiday Song)
I Like People (The Friendly Song)
    Golden BR9. Released March 1, 1952. No matrix on label. Also on Little Golden Record SR99 (6" 78 rpm).
Personnel: First JD with the Sandpipers, second alone, both with Mitchell Miller and orchestra.

Rudolph the Red-Nosed Reindeer
Santa Claus Is Comin' to Town
    Golden BR13. 1952. No matrix on label.
Both with the Sandpipers and Mitchell Miller and orchestra.

Decca LPs and Related 45rpm Issues

Decca DL-5116. THE ONE AND ONLY JIMMY DURANTE. 10" LP. 1949. With Eddie Jackson on three numbers, with Six Hits and a Miss on two numbers, all eight songs accom. by orch. Dir. by Roy Bargy. Duplicated from 78rpm album, 1946 (see above).
    Also available on a British 10" LP, Brunswick LA-8582, JIMMY DURANTE SINGS.
    In 1962, six of these eight songs were reissued on one side of a British 12" LP, Ace of Hearts (Decca) 25, JIMMY DURANTE SINGS/EDDIE CANTOR SINGS.

Decca DL-9049. CLUB DURANT. 12" LP. 1957. Mono. Also issued in England on Brunswick LAT-8218. Excerpts from Durante's radio and TV shows. All numbers performed as duets with guest stars. Nine numbers including one medley. SIDE 1—A Real Piano Player (with Al Jolson); I'm as Ready as I'll Ever Be (with Sophie Tucker); There's a Place in the Theatre for You (Interpolation: Who Will Be with You When I'm Far Away) (with Ethel Barrymore); Presenting—Clayton, Jackson, and Durante: medley of Start Off Each Day with a Song, Bill Bailey, I Can Do Without Broadway, Jimmy, the Well Dressed Man, So I Ups to Him, Because They All Love You (recorded June 1949, a reprise of the Durante radio show of April 21, 1948, a reunion of the team, celebrating 1923, 25 years since they performed these songs at the Club Durant and the Dover Club). SIDE 2—Sing Soft, Sing Sweet, Sing Gentle (with Bing Crosby); Our Voices Were Meant for Each Other (Interpolation: Put on Your Old Grey Bonnet, Waiting for the Robert E. Lee) (with Helen Traubel); The Boys with the Proboskis (with Bob Hope); The World Needs New Faces (Interpolation: Start Off Each Day with a Song, If You Knew Susie) (with Eddie Cantor); Wingin' with Rhythm and Blues (with Peter Lawford).
    Liner notes by Durante mention drummer Jack Roth ("with me since 1920"); songwriter Jackie Barnett, who collaborated with JD on most songs on this album and who had been working with JD since 1941, having first met in 1936; his longtime piano player Jules Buffano.
    These selections were also released on three extended-play 45s, Decca ED-2526,

ED-2527, and ED-2528. The first, entitled "Club Durant," is with Jolson, Sophie Tucker, and the team of Clayton, Jackson, and Durante; the second, entitled "The Jimmy Durante Show," is with Traubel and Ethel Barrymore; the third is with Hope, Crosby, and Cantor.)

Decca DL-8884. JIMMY DURANTE (IN PERSON) AT THE PIANO. 12" LP. 1959. Mono and stereo. Vocals and piano, Jack Roth drums, no orchestra. SIDE 1—Start Off Each Day with a Song; Mad Bird Melody (Toodle De Doo); I Want a Girl (Just Like the Girl That Married Dear Old Dad); Inka Dinka Doo; You Made Me Love You (I Didn't Want to Do It); Carolina in the Morning. SIDE 2—By the Light of the Silvery Moon; Take An "L"; Shine on Harvest Moon; The Best Things in Life Are Free; Ida, Sweet as Apple Cider; Good Night.

Royale LP

Royale LP-68. JIMMY DURANTE PRESENTS TV ON RECORDS. 10" LP. With Paul Douglas, Eddie Jackson, Lily Ann Carol, Louis Prima and Orch. Reissued on Royale 10" LP 1812, JIMMIE DURANTE TV SHOW. Only Durante material is the reissue of the Majestic 78rpm sides, G'wan Home, Your Mudder's Callin,' and There're Two Sides to Ev'ry Girl, both with Eddie Jackson. No liner notes.

Durante and Eddie Jackson's rendition of "G'wan Home, Your Mudder's Callin'" was again reissued on a 12" LP, ALL STAR SHOW, released as Ultronic 50238 and Halo 50238. The other Durante-Jackson side was not included.

Roulette LP

Roulette 25123. JIMMY DURANTE AT THE COPACABANA. 12" LP. 1961. Mono and stereo. Also issued in England on Columbia SCX-3395. Recorded live at the famous New York nightclub. Features Eddie Jackson and introduces Durante "find," "my junior partner" Sonny King. Six medleys:

SIDE 1—Medley 1) I Could Have Danced All Night; It's My Nose's Birthday; Everywhere You Go; Medley 2) It's Still the Same Old Broadway; Every Street's a Boulevard; Bill Bailey, Won't You Please Come Home; And They Became Good Friends; Medley 3) My Loving Melody Man; Ragtime Daddy; I Love You, I Do. SIDE 2—Medley 4) She's a Little Bit This, a Little Bit That; Take Away the Beret; Medley 5) We're Goin' Home; Who Will Be with You; Don't Talk About Us When We're Gone; You Made Me Love You; Medley 6) Say It with Flowers; Inka Dinka Doo; Goodnight.

Warner Bros. LPs and Related 45rpm Issues

Warner Bros. 1506. SEPTEMBER SONG. 12" LP. 1963. Mono and stereo. Cover reads "Jackie Barnett Presents The New Jimmy Durante." Sentimental songs. Arranged and conducted by Roy Bargy with the John Rarig Singers, produced by Jackie Barnett.

SIDE 1—September Song; Look Ahead Little Girl; Count Your Blessings Instead of Sheep; When the Circus Leaves Town; I Believe. SIDE 2—Young at Heart; Don't Lose Your Sense of Humor; You'll Never Walk Alone; One Room Home; Blue Bird of Happiness.

Warner Bros. 1531. HELLO YOUNG LOVERS. 12" LP. 1964. Mono and stereo. Presented by Jackie Barnett. Arranged and conducted by Roy Bargy, with the John Rarig Singers. Produced by Jimmy Hilliard. Recorded at United Recording Studios, Las Vegas, in collaboration with Wilbur Clark's Desert Inn.

SIDE 1—Hello, Young Lovers; Try a Little Tenderness; Smile; Hi-Lili, Hi-Lo; Love in a Home. SIDE 2—This Is All I Ask; The Glory of Love; You Can't Have Ev'rything; In the Other Fellow's Yard; The Time Is Now.

Warner Bros. 1577. JIMMY DURANTE'S WAY OF LIFE. 12" LP. 1965. Mono and stereo. Presented by Jackie Barnett. Produced by Jimmy Hilliard. With the Gordon Jenkins Orchestra and Chorus.

SIDE 1—A Way of Life; My Wish; As Time Goes By; Make Someone Happy; I'll Be Seeing You. SIDE 2—When Day Is Done; When I Lost You; If I Had You; Once to Every Heart; I'll See You in My Dreams.

Warner Bros. 1655. ONE OF THOSE SONGS. 12" LP. 1966. Mono and stereo. Presented by Jackie Barnett. Produced by Jimmy Hilliard. With special guest star Eddie Jackson. Arranged and conducted by Ernie Freeman.

SIDE 1—One of Those Songs*; You're Nobody Till Somebody Loves You; Bill Bailey (Won't You Please Come Home) (with Eddie Jackson); What Became of Life*; Margie. SIDE 2—Old Man Time; We're Going U.F.O.-ing; Daddy (Your Mama Is Lonesome for You); This Train; Mame

Warner Bros. 1713. SONGS FOR SUNDAY. 12" LP. 1967. Mono and stereo. Presented by Jackie Barnett. Produced by Jackie Barnett. Arranged and conducted by Ralph Carmichael.

SIDE 1—Down by the River-side; Precious Lord; He Touched Me; In the Garden; Somebody's Keeping Score. SIDE 2—Amen; Beyond the Sunset; Peace in the Valley; His Eye Is on the Sparrow; One of These Days.

LP reissued on Light Records, Waco, Texas, LS-5565, with the same Warner LP title, and liner notes shortened; "One of These Days" also appeared on Light Records 45rpm three-record set FESTIVAL: MUSIC FROM THE ORAL ROBERTS SUMMER TV SPECIAL.

Warner Bros. 45s Released in Conjunction with LPs

Warner Bros. Pro 152.
    F13145. September Song (from SEPTEMBER SONG LP)
    F13307. Reflections on My First Fifty Years in Show Business (Durante speaking)

Warner Bros. S-1506.
    S38831. September Song
        I Believe
        Young at Heart
    S38832. You'll Never Walk Alone
        Count Your Blessings Instead of Sheep
    Promotion, intended for Seeburg jukeboxes.

Warner Bros. 5382.
    F13145. September Song
    F13143. Young at Heart
    Both from SEPTEMBER SONG LP.

Produced by Dick Glasser.

Warner Bros. 5410.
F13458. Hello, Young Lovers
F13460. This Is All I Ask
Both from HELLO YOUNG LOVERS LP.

Warner Bros. 5456.
GX13854. When Love Flies Out the Window
GX13860. This Train
Both arranged and conducted by Perry Botkin, Jr.,* produced by Jimmy Hillard. Second from ONE OF THOSE SONGS LP. (*LP credits Ernie Freeman for arranging and conducting all songs including "This Train." No mention of Botkin, but song arrangement is identical.)

Warner Bros. 5483.
GX14114. Old Man Time
GX14113. I Came Here to Swim
First from ONE OF THOSE SONGS LP. Both produced by Jackie Barnett, arranged and conducted by Ernie Freeman.

Warner Bros. 5686.
HX14881. One of Those Songs
HX14882. What Became of Life (I Wonder)
Both arranged by Ernie Freeman and produced by Dick Glasser, from ONE OF THOSE SONGS LP.

Warner Bros. 5843.
J15117. Margie
J15133. Bill Bailey (Won't You Please Come Home)
Both from ONE OF THOSE SONGS LP, second with Eddie Jackson.

Warner Bros. 7024.
K15667. Hellzapoppin' (from the Alexander Cohen production *Hellzapoppin' '67*)
K15669. M.F. O'Brien
Both songs produced by Jackie Barnett, arranged and conducted by Ralph Carmichael.

Warner Bros.-Seven Arts 7241.
J15134. We're Going U-F-Oing
L16745. Dear World (from Broadway production *Dear World*)
First, from ONE OF THOSE SONGS LP, Durante solo, arranged and conducted by Ernie Freeman, produced by Jimmy Hilliard; second, Durante with Maurice Chevalier, arranged and conducted by Bob Mersey, produced by Jackie Barnett.

Warner Bros.-Seven Arts 7253.
K15869. Amen
K15867. He Touched Me
Both from SONGS FOR SUNDAY LP.

Warner Bros.-Seven Arts 7367.
F13150. Look Ahead Little Girl
M17940. He Ain't Heavy, He's My Brother
First from SEPTEMBER SONG LP, arranged and conducted by Roy Bargy; second by Ernie Freeman.

Other Long-Playing Recordings Involving Durante
(listed alphabetically by label)

Ace of Hearts 69 (British Decca). HOLLYWOOD SINGS, VOL. 3: THE BOYS & GIRLS. 12" LP. 1964. Mono. Includes Durante and Merman singing " You Say the Nicest Things" from the Decca 78rpm (q.v.).

AEI 2118. JUDY HOLLIDAY: A LEGACY OF LAUGHTER. 12" LP. 1984. Mono. Includes two non-singing skits with Durante, "Anne of the Thousand Days" and "Not-So-Private Lives." Archival source not given.

AEI 2121. GREETINGS FROM HOLLYWOOD! 12" LP. 1984. Mono. Christmas and New Year's greetings and songs from celebrities. Includes JD singing "Christmas Comes but Once a Year."

AEI 1176. GREETINGS FROM BROADWAY! 12" LP. 1985. Mono. Includes "I'm Gonna Hang My Hat in Brooklyn," sung by Betty Hutton, Claudette Colbert, Ronald Colman, and JD. Also "The Floradora Sextette," sung by Tallulah Bankhead, Rudy Vallee, JD "et al."

Ajazz 526. THE EARLY BING CROSBY PLUS THE BING CROSBY SHOW. 12" LP. n.d. Mono. Includes c. 1946 appearance of JD, singing "You Gotta Start Off Each Day with a Song" and a few notes of Bing's theme song plus some jokes and a duet, "C'mon Out, The Band Is Playing" (using the tune of "G'wan Home, Your Mudder's Callin'"—song recorded 1946). Bing plugs JD's new Rexall show and new film, *This Time for Keeps*, released 1947.

Ambassador Artists (Pittsburgh, PA) 1003-3. THE LEGENDS OF AL JOLSON, JIMMY DURANTE, EDDIE CANTOR. 3 12" LPs. n.d. Mono. With commentary by Walter Winchell and George Jessel. 1 LP per personality. Winchell narrates the Durante LP. Reissued as individual LPs by Award (Hollywood), 1971.
    SIDE 1 songs by JD—I Could Have Danced All Night; What a Day, What a Day, What a Day; You Gotta Start Off Each Day with a Song; A Razz-a-Ma-Tazz; It's Kinda Hard to Put It in Words; The State of Arkansas; Pike's Peak or Bust. SIDE 2 songs—I Love Ya, Love Ya, Love Ya; The Boys with the Proboscis (with Bob Hope); If You Knew Susie (with Eddie Cantor); I'm as Ready as I'll Ever Be (with Sophie Tucker); Inka Dinka Doo; I'll Do the Strut-Away; September Song; Young at Heart; Goodnight.

American Heritage DL-734712 (MCA Special Markets). MUSIC OF THE 1920'S AND 1930'S. 12" LP. n.d. Stereo. Includes Durante with Six Hits and a Miss, singing "Inka Dinka Doo" from the Decca 78rpm (q.v.).

Black Lion (U.K.) 52013. BING CROSBY WITH SPIKE JONES AND JIMMY DURANTE. 12" LP. 1983. Mono.
SIDE 1—Recorded Oct. 23, 1946. Nothing with JD. SIDE 2—Recorded Dec. 4, 1946. JD opens doings with a few bars of Bing's theme song "When the Blue of the Night (Meets the Gold of the Day)," Bing and JD join on Durante's oft-used song "You Gotta Start Off Each Day with a Song," and they do a duet on Bing's oft-used song "Blue Skies."

Caliban 6006. IT HAPPENED IN BROOKLYN (1947). See Hollywood Soundstage 5006.

Caliban 6013. STRICTLY DYNAMITE (1934). 12" LP. n.d. Mono. Soundtrack of RKO film starring Durante and Lupe Velez. Durante sings "Hot Pattata" and "I'm Putty in Your Hands." Coupled with soundtrack excerpts from *The Singing Kid* (1936), *Playboy of Paris* (1930), *The Way to Love* (1933), *Beloved Vagabond* (1936). No liner notes.

Caliban 6022. TWO GIRLS AND A SAILOR (1944). See Sound/Stage Recordings 2307.

Caliban 6031. SALLY, IRENE AND MARY (1938). 12" LP. n.d. Mono. Soundtrack of 20th Century Fox film starring Alice Faye, with Durante. Coupled with soundtrack excerpts from *Tea for Two* (1950). No liner notes.

Colpix 507. PEPE. 12" LP. Mono and stereo. 1961. Soundtrack of 1960 Columbia film starring Cantinflas, with Dan Dailey, Shirley Jones, and 35 guest stars including Jimmy Durante. LP contains nothing with Durante.

Columbia 5860. BILLY ROSE'S JUMBO. 12" LP. 1963. Mono and stereo. Soundtrack of 1962 MGM musical. Stars Doris Day, Stephen Boyd, JD, and Martha Raye. JD joins with Doris Day and Martha Raye to sing "The Circus on Parade," sings solo the reprise of "The Most Beautiful Girl in the World" (earlier sung by Stephen Boyd), and joins in the finale, "Sawdust, Spangles and Dreams" with Doris Day, Stephen Boyd, Martha Raye, and chorus.

Columbia Musical Treasury P2M 5287. OLD TIME RADIO. 2 12" LPs. 1968. Mono. Includes Durante performing "Inka Dinka Doo" and Clayton, Jackson, and Durante doing "Can Broadway Do Without Me."

Columbia Musical Treasury P5M 5872. THE SULLIVAN YEARS. 5 12" LPs. 1973. Mono. Highlights of THE ED SULLIVAN SHOW, on CBS-TV for 23 years beginning May 21, 1948, Sunday nights 8:00, for 60 minutes. Includes Durante on the show of April 17, 1966, performing "Start Off Each Day with a Song," "One of Those Songs," and "Inka Dinka Doo."

Columbia Musical Treasury DS-515. GREAT MEMORIES FROM OLD TIME RADIO. 12" LP. n.d. Simulated stereo. Includes Durante's "Inka Dinka Doo."

Columbia Special Products CSS-1508. THE GREAT OLD TIME RADIO STARS. 12" LP. n.d. Simulated stereo. Includes Durante's "Inka Dinka Doo."

Columbia Special Products CSS-1509. THE GREAT STARS OF VAUDEVILLE. 12" LP. n.d. Simulated stereo. Includes "Can Broadway Do Without Me" with Clayton, Jackson, and Durante. (Also issued on 45 rpm, Columbia Priceless Editions 4-PE.3, coupled with Al Jolson's "Rock-a-Bye Your Baby with a Dixie Melody," accompanied by Guy Lombardo & his Royal Canadians.)

Columbia Special Products CSPS-1065 (Canada). RICHARD RODGERS: THE SOUND OF HIS MUSIC. 12" LP. n.d. Stereo. Includes "The Most Beautiful Girl in the World" from *Jumbo*, sung by Durante.

Columbia Transcriptions (Presented by Ken-L-Ration Canned Dog Food). GREAT COMEDIANS OF THE CENTURY. 10" LP. n.d. Brief segments, totalling 30 minutes. Narrated by Eddie Cantor. Includes Jimmy Durante, as well as W.C. Fields, Willie and Eugene Howard, Burns and Allen, Will Rogers, Weber and Fields, Harry Hershfield, Moran and Mack, George Jessel.

Curtain Calls 100/1. DICK TRACY IN B-FlAT. 12" LP. n.d. Mono. The Armed Forces Radio Service (AFRS) Command Performance, recorded for broadcast Feb. 15, 1945. Featured JD as The Mole, in support of Bing Crosby as Dick Tracy, Dinah Shore as Tess Trueheart. Also featuring Harry Von Zell, Jerry Colonna, Bob Hope, Frank Morgan, Judy Garland, the Andrews Sisters, Frank Sinatra, and Cass Daley. JD sings "The Music Goes 'Round & 'Round." LP also issued on Scarce Rarities Productions 5504, n.d., and on Sandy Hook (Radiola) 2052 in 1981. Reissued on a Compact Disc, Pro Arte 505, in 1990.

Decca 7018. CURTAIN CALL, VOL. 1. 10" LP. 1952. Mono. Includes Durante performing "Start Off Each Day with a Song" and "Inka Dinka Doo," the first with Eddie Jackson, the second with Six Hits and a Miss. (Also on 78s — Decca DU-1502, and separately on Decca 78s 23566 and 23351.)

Decca DL-4205. OPEN HOUSE. 12" LP. 1963. Mono. Includes Durante performing "Ida, Sweet as Apple Cider" from Decca LP, JIMMY DURANTE IN PERSON. A sampler released to promote several Decca and Coral LPs.

Decca DL-4206. HOUSE PARTY. 12" LP. 1963. Mono. Includes Durante performing "Shine on Harvest Moon" from Decca LP, JIMMY DURANTE IN PERSON. A sampler released to promote several Decca and Coral LPs.

Decca DEA 7-1. THOSE WONDERFUL THIRTIES: THE STARS OF HOLLYWOOD'S GOLDEN ERA. 2 12" LPs. 1969. Simulated stereo. Includes Durante's "Inka Dinka Doo" from the Decca 78rpm (q.v.).

Decca DEA 7-2. THOSE WONDERFUL THIRTIES: THE STARS OF BROADWAY, NIGHT CLUBS AND VAUDEVILLE. 2 12" LPs. 1969. Simulated stereo. Includes "Club Durant Medley" from the Decca LP, CLUB DURANT.

DRG 2-2100. 25 YEARS OF RECORDED SOUND FROM THE VAULTS OF M-G-M RECORDS, VOLUME ONE. 2 12" LPs. 1979. Mono. Includes Durante's duet with Betty Garrett "Any State in the Forty-Eight Is Great," recorded Dec. 29, 1948.

Epic LN-3234. GREAT MOMENTS IN SHOW BUSINESS. 12" LP. 1956. Mono. 11 selections include Clayton, Jackson, and Durante performing "I Know Darn Well I Can Do Without Broadway (But Can Broadway Do Without Me?), reissued from Columbia 78rpm (q.v.), recorded May 9, 1929. Plus Walter Huston; Bill Robinson; Eddie Cantor; Cliff Edwards; Burns and Allen; Gene Raymond; Al Jolson; Dick Powell; Fred Astaire; Eddie "Rochester" Anderson.

Folkways RFS-603. SOPHIE TUCKER & TED LEWIS. 12" LP. 1982. Mono. SIDE 1 — Sophie's television debut, on the Jimmy Durante Show. Liner notes do not mention it was NBC, April 18, 1951. Joking and singing. Second half of side 1 is taken from Sophie's appearance on the radio variety show from the early 1950s, THE BIG SHOW, starring Talullah Bankhead. SIDE 2 — Ted Lewis singing.
    The same material was also released on Soted 1200, with no liner notes.

Folkways RFS-604. A TRIBUTE TO GEORGE M. COHAN. 12" LP. 1983. Mono.
    SIDE 2 — Excerpts from the soundtrack of Cohan's only film, Paramount's 1932 *The Phantom President.* Durante steals the show from Cohan, barking hoarsely in song "Dr. Barney Will Cure You." No outstanding songs despite talents of Rodgers & Hart.

SIDE 1—Cohan singing his own songs, and speaking.
The same material was also released on Old Shep 1000, with no liner notes.

GNP 9048. BING CROSBY: THE RADIO YEARS, VOL. 4. 12" LP. 1986. Mono. Includes Crosby-Durante duet, "You Gotta Start Off Each Day with a Song," recorded Nov. 28, 1946. Reissued on a compact disc.

Golden 38. THE STARS SING (FOR CHILDREN OF ALL AGES). 12" LP. 1959. Mono. 12 performers, 1 number each. Includes Durante singing "I Like People" from the Golden 78rpm (q.v.).

Golden Age 5023. THE BING CROSBY RADIO SHOWS. 12" LP. 1978. Mono. From Crosby's "own private collection of transcriptions," no dates given. Includes Durante singing "You Gotta Start Off Each Day with a Song."

Hall of Fame 1010. THE BEST LOVED SONGS OF JIMMY DURANTE. 12" LP. c. 1978. Mono. Reissue of twelve songs made for MGM plus four made for Decca.

Halo 50238. ALL STAR SHOW. 12" LP. 1957. Mono. Includes Durante's "G'wan Home, Your Mudder's Callin'" (from a Majestic 78). LP reissued as Ultraphonic 50238 in 1958.

Harmony 11287 (budget subsidiary of Columbia Records). AS TIME GOES BY. 12" LP. c. 1968. Mono and stereo. Jimmy Durante in selections previously released on Warner Bros. Records.
SIDE 1—As Time Goes By; When Day Is Done; I'll See You in My Dreams; Try a Little Tenderness; If I Had You. SIDE 2—Smile; Make Someone Happy; Hi-Lili, Hi-Lo; The Glory of Love

Hollywood Soundstage 5006. IT HAPPENED IN BROOKLYN. 12" LP. 1981. Mono. Soundtrack of 1947 MGM release, starring Frank Sinatra, Kathryn Grayson, Peter Lawford, Jimmy Durante. JD joins Sinatra and Bobby Long in singing "I Believe" and Sinatra in duet on "The Song's Gotta Come from the Heart." Both songs, music and lyrics by Sammy Cahn and Jules Styne.
Also on Caliban 6006. Coupled with soundtrack excerpts from ON MOONLIGHT BAY (1951) and THREE SMART GIRLS (1936). No liner notes.

JJA 19765 (Music Masters, NYC). BERT LAHR ON STAGE, SCREEN AND RADIO. 12" LP. 1976. Mono. Includes excerpts of comic turn Lahr did with JD on the STANDARD OIL 75TH ANNIVERSARY SHOW, NBC-TV, Oct. 13, 1957 [liner notes give wrong date, Oct. 27, 1957].

JJA 19766 (Music Masters, NYC). RODGERS AND HART IN HOLLYWOOD, VOL. 1, 1929-1935. 2 12" LPs. 1976. Mono. Remastered excerpts from original soundtracks. Includes what little music there was in *The Phantom President* (1932), with George M. Cohan and Durante, and *Hollywood Party* (1934), with Durante and Jack Pearl.

Kasha King 1935. BIG BROADCAST OF 1935. 12" LP. n.d. Mono. Radio performances by Bing Crosby, Bill "Bojangles" Robinson, Al Jolson, James Melton, Rudy Vallee, Ben Bernie and his orchestra, Ruth Etting, John Charles Thomas, Phil Regan, Paul Whiteman and his orchestra, Harry Owens, and last on the record, Jimmy Durante with the Whiteman orchestra.

King of Comedy 1226. BOB HOPE AND HIS FRIENDS. 3 12" LPs. 1979. Mono. Includes duet with Durante, performing "Start Off Each Day with a Song" and "The Boys with the Proboskis" (with banter not included on Durante's CLUB DURANT Decca LP), and trio with Durante and Doris Day in "Mad About That Man," taken from Hope's NBC-TV Specials.

Living Era AJA-5011 (British). HOLLYWOOD SINGS. 12" LP. 1982. Mono. Includes "Can Broadway Do Without Me?" with Clayton, Jackson, and Durante, from the Columbia 78rpm (q.v.).
Also released as a CD, no. 5011.

London HA-P 2056. BEAU JAMES (THE LIFE AND TIMES OF JIMMY WALKER). 12" LP. Mono. Soundtrack of 1957 Paramount film starring Bob Hope. Durante has excellent but unbilled appearance, singing and hoofing with Hope (Jimmy Walker) and chorus "Sidewalks of New York" (included in the LP).

Longines Symphonette Recording Society LWS-117 (MGM Custom Records Division). BROADWAY! BROADWAY! BROADWAY! 12" LP. n.d. Stereo. Includes Durante's "I'll Do the Strut-Away in My Cutaway" and "It's My Nose's Birthday."

Longines Symphonette Society LWS-465 (MCA Special Markets). THOSE MEMORY YEARS. 12" LP. n.d. Stereo. Includes Durante with Six Hits and a Miss, singing "Inka Dinka Doo" from the Decca 78rpm.

Magic (U.K.) 10. BING CROSBY AND FRIENDS, VOL. 2. 12" LP. 1984. Mono. 15 songs, each a duet with a friend, including "The Song's Gotta Come from the Heart" with Durante. All numbers backed by the John Scott Trotter Orchestra.

Maracaibo 809. JIMMY DURANTE & CARMEN MIRANDA. 12" LP. n.d. Mono. Also, as Records Macumbeiros Churrasco M-809. CARMEN MIRANDA. SIDE 1: Contains Carmen Miranda's very effective guest appearance on JD's TV show, taped just before her death August 5, 1955. SIDE 2: Songs from Carmen Miranda's 1940s films, including "The Lady in the Tutti-Frutti Hat," and "Paducah" with Benny Goodman and his orchestra, from *The Gang's All Here*.

MCA (England) MCL-1839. ETHEL MERMAN: THE WORLD IS YOUR BALLOON. 12" LP. 1987. Mono. Reissue of 78s, 3 vocal duets with Durante (q.v.) and 8 with Ray Bolger, plus 9 other rare recordings Merman made 1950-51.

MCA 2-11002. THAT'S ENTERTAINMENT. 2 12" LPs. 1974. Mono. Music from the original MGM movie soundtrack. Includes Durante performing "Singin' in the Rain" from *Speak Easily* (1932) and "The Song's Gotta Come from the Heart" as a duet with Frank Sinatra in *It Happened in Brooklyn* (1947).

Memorabilia 721. JIMMY DURANTE AND GARRY MOORE SHOW. 12" LP. n.d. Mono. Part of series WHEN RADIO WAS KING! No liner notes. Radio show from May 23, 1947.

M.F. Distribution Co. 207/5. BING CROSBY: THE GREATEST RADIO BROADCASTS. 5 12" LPs. 1978. Mono. Ten complete half-hour programs, 1946-47, including Durante as a guest on the Dec. 4, 1946 Crosby show.

MGM E-4733. FROSTY THE SNOWMAN. 12" LP. 1969-70. Mono and stereo. Soundtrack of CBS-TV half-hour animated film, presented December 7, 1969. Voice of Jimmy Durante used as the narrator.

MGM 5301. THAT'S ENTERTAINMENT, PART 2. 12" LP. 1976. Mono. Music from the original MGM movie soundtrack. Includes Durante performing "Inka Dinka Doo" in *Two Girls and a Sailor* (1944).

Murray Hill 894637. BING CROSBY AND HIS FRIENDS. 4 12" LPs. n.d. Mono. Commemorating Crosby's 50th year as an entertainer, excerpts from original radio broadcasts, with guest stars, including Durante.

Murray Hill 931699. THE GREAT RADIO COMEDIANS. 5 12" LPs. n.d. Mono. Original radio broadcasts. The JD Show, Nov. 22, 1946; also The Abbott & Costello Show; The Lucky Strike Program Starring Jack Benny; Amos 'n' Andy; The Fred Allen Show; The Charlie McCarthy Show (also known as "The Edgar Bergen–Charlie McCarthy Show"); The Eddie Cantor Pabst Blue Ribbon Show; Duffy's Tavern; The George Burns and Gracie Allen Show; The Great Gildersleeve. All shows 30 minutes each.

Old Shep 1000. THE ORIGINAL YANKEE DOODLE DANDY, GEORGE M. COHAN. See Folkways RFS-604.

Paramount PAS-5006. THOSE DARING YOUNG MEN IN THEIR JAUNTY JALOPIES. 12" LP. 1969. Music from the 1969 British-American Paramount film soundtrack, including the title song (with interpolation of "The Man Who Broke the Bank at Monte Carlo") sung by Jimmy Durante.
Title song also released on a 45rpm single, Paramount 3, in 1969.

PJ International 001. THE FRANK SINATRA DUETS. 12" LP. 1984. Mono. Radio (1945-47) and television (1952-77). Includes duet with Durante, "Who Will Be with You When I'm Far Away?", Feb. 27, 1946.

PJ International 003. SONGS BY SINATRA. 12" LP. 1988. Mono. Radio broadcasts.
SIDE 1—Feb. 27, 1946 (Armed Forces Radio). Guest JD with the Pied Pipers. JD joins Sinatra for a comedy sketch, sings without Sinatra "The Lost Chord," the two do another comedy sketch which includes the song JD often used, "Who Will Be with You When I'm Far Away?," and to end the show a duet on "Put Your Dreams Away." SIDE 2—Nov. 26, 1946 radio show. Guests JD and Andre Previn, with the Pied Pipers. Sinatra and JD do a comedy sketch which includes the Durante song "So I Ups to Him." Later JD does a sketch.

Radiola MR-1002. SON OF JEST LIKE OLD TIMES. 12" LP. 1971. Mono. An LP of radio comedy excerpts. Includes Eddie Cantor appearing as a guest with Jimmy Durante (on television, not radio—Cantor mentions Warner Bros. preparing his life story, which was released in late 1953, and being in show business 40 years.) The two comedians recall old times and sing bits of their old songs. And Durante sings a few bars of "Liza" from Ziegfeld's *Show Girl*, 1929.

Radiola MR-1080. JIMMY DURANTE ON RADIO. 12" LP. 1977. Mono.
SIDE 1—The JD Show, NBC, Dec. 3, 1947. Guest star Charles Boyer. Jimmy as Cyrano de Bergerac. SIDE 2—JD recalls his first days in radio, recorded 1972.
More recollections from JD, on early days in show business on the Bowery, with Benny Rubin, recorded March 14, 1943 (including JD singing "Broadway, My Street").
Clayton, Jackson, and Durante, their first radio appearance, the JD show April 21, 1948, recreating the 1923 Club Durant and Dover Club, singing and dancing "Bill Bailey" and other numbers in medley (see CLUB DURANT LP).

Guest spot with Tallulah Bankhead on her NBC radio THE BIG SHOW, Nov. 5, 1950, singing "It's Kinda Hard to Put It in Words."
Undated JD show with guest Victor Borge, JD alone singing "Toscanini, Iturbi and Me" and "Chidabee-Ch-Ch."
JD's closing, "Good Night."

Radiola MR-1100. COMMAND PERFORMANCE: VICTORY EXTRA. 12" LP. 1979. Mono. One-hour special, August 15, 1945, with many stars including Durante (bantering with Bette Davis and matching a few keyboard notes with Jose Iturbi).
Also released as a CD, no. 1100.

Radiola 3MR-2. AL JOLSON RADIO RARITIES. 3 12" LPs. 1985. Mono. Six broadcasts, including program of April 21, 1949, with guest Jimmy Durante. They do duet, "A Real Piano Player." Tapes are Armed Forces Radio Service re-broadcasts, with original Kraft Music Hall commercials and any mention of Kraft cut.

RCA Victor LOC-1130. ALICE THROUGH THE LOOKING GLASS. 12" LP. 1966. Mono and stereo. Soundtrack of NBC-TV special, Nov. 6, 1966. Jimmy Durante as Humpty Dumpty. On LP Durante and Judi Rolin (as Alice) recite famous nonsense poem "Jabberwocky."

RCA VICTOR LOC-1011. SHOW BIZ: FROM VAUDE TO VIDEO. 12" LP. 1953. Mono. (Also as a 45rpm extended-play album, RCA Victor EOD-1011. 8 sides). Narrated by George Jessel. Intended as companion to the book by Abel Green and Joe Laurie, Jr., published by the same title, 1951. Includes brief excerpts of the actual voices of performers or their music. Includes JD singing "Jimmy, the Well Dressed Man" and "I Can Do Without Broadway."
Also released by C.S.G. Records (Camden, NJ), CG-1, as THOSE HAPPY DAYS, 20's TO 40's [on label] and THOSE GOOD OLD DAYS, 1918 to 40's [on cover]. 12" LP. n.d. Mono. Narrated by George Jessel.

Reader's Digest. HEAR THEM AGAIN! 10 12" LPs. 1968 (custom pressed by RCA Records). Mono. Includes JD performing with Helen Traubel "The Song's Gotta Come from the Heart."

Reader's Digest. THE GOLDEN AGE OF ENTERTAINMENT. 10 12" LPs. 1980 (custom pressed by RCA Records, 1979). Mono. Includes JD with Eddie Jackson performing "You Gotta Start Off Each Day with a Song" and "Inka Dinka Doo" with Six Hits and a Miss.

Rhino 820. DR. DEMENTO PRESENTS THE GREATEST NOVELTY RECORDS OF ALL TIME: VOL. 1, THE 1940s AND BEFORE. 12" LP. 1985. Mono. Includes Durante's earliest recorded version of "Inka Dinka Doo" (Feb. 13, 1934).

Sandy Hook (Radiola) 2052. DICK TRACY IN B-FLAT. See Curtain Calls 100/1.

Sayville (England) SVL-209. "SINGIN' IN THE RAIN": FAMOUS STAGE & SCREEN PERSONALITIES. 12" LP. 1990. Mono. Includes Durante singing "Hot Patatta," from Feb. 13, 1934 recording.
Also released as a CD, no. 209.

Scarce Rarities Productions 5504. DICK TRACY IN B-FLAT. See Curtain Calls 100/1.

Soted 1200. SOPHIE TUCKER & TED LEWIS. See Folkways RFS-603.

Sound/Stage Recordings 2307. TWO GIRLS AND A SAILOR. 12" LP. 1974. Mono. Soundtrack of 1944 MGM musical starring Gloria DeHaven, Van Johnson, and June Allyson, with JD, Lena Horne, Harry James and his Orch., Xavier Cugat and his Orch., Gracie Allen, Jose and Amparo Iturbi, Lina Romay, Tom Drake. JD sings "Inka Dinka Doo" with chorus. Gracie Allen performs hilarious "Concerto for Index Finger."
　　　Also on Caliban 6022, with no liner notes.

Tandem 1903. MAIL CALL. 12" LP. n.d. Mono. SIDE 1, though not so marked, was taken from Mail Call #91, c.1944 because it mentions Judy Garland's "The Trolley Song" as coming from her latest picture (MGM's *Meet Me in St. Louis*, 1944). Program stars Judy Garland, who is the m.c., Bing Crosby, JD, and Arthur Treacher. JD has some funny chatter with Treacher and is included on one number, with Crosby and Garland singing "The Groaner, the Canary and the Nose."
　　　SIDE 2 is from another undated MAIL CALL program, starring Judy Garland, Bing Crosby, Frank Sinatra, Bob Hope, and Jerry Colonna.
　　　Recording made for the Armed Forces Radio Service.
　　　Also released as a CD, on LaserLight 15.413, in 1992.

United Artists (U.K.) 30115. THE GOLDEN AGE OF AMERICAN RADIO— STARRING BING CROSBY. 12" LP. 1978. Mono. Excerpts from Crosby's radio broadcasts 1946-54, including Durante as a guest on the Dec. 4, 1946 show.

Wonderland 148. RUDOLPH THE RED-NOSED REINDEER AND OTHER CHRISTMAS FAVORITES. 12" LP. 1978. Mono. Title song by Durante. The album also includes Bing Crosby and Roy Rogers, among others.

Yeddo 83. BING CROSBY & JIMMY DURANTE. 12" LP. n.d. Mono. Tape of Durante as guest on Crosby's radio show. The closing plugs JD's radio show for Rexall and new film THIS TIME FOR KEEPS (1947). Coupled with THE RADIO CAVALCADE OF 1936, featuring Harry Richman presenting Gertrude Niesen and Kay Thompson. Also coupled with brief segment of Dick Powell and wife Joan Blondell entertaining the U.S. Armed Forces in 1943.

　　　Note: There are numerous other miscellaneous recordings of Jimmy Durante, or reissues of his recordings, made at 78rpm and 33⅓, released by the Armed Forces Radio Service, the U.S. Treasury Department, and various other governmental agencies that use stars to entertain and pro- mote governmental objectives, plus recordings made by charity organiza- tions. All were meant to be played on radio. Only those that have been subsequently released on LP for the general public are listed above. See a separate listing of radio programs involving Durante.

Compact Discs Involving Durante
(listed alphabetically by label)

Box Office/Encore. 2 CDs. 1991. THE MUSIC OF BROADWAY 1939. A cross- section of songs "available on 78's during the shows' original runs," some by original cast, including Ethel Merman and Durante's duet in STARS IN YOUR EYES, "It's All Yours." This number was taken from a radio transcription, February or March 1939.

Decca MCAD-10611. 1992. BOB HOPE & FRIENDS: THANKS FOR THE MEMORIES. Hope's complete Decca recordings, including duet with Durante, "The Boys with the Proboscis," originally on Durante's Decca LP, CLUB DURANT, 1957. Ten of the thirteen numbers were collected on a previous Hope LP, BOB HOPE IN HOLLYWOOD, MCA-906, 1984, but not the Durante duet.

Epic EK-53764. 1993. SLEEPLESS IN SEATTLE. Original motion picture soundtrack. Includes JD's Warner Brothers recordings of "As Time Goes By" and "Make Someone Happy."

Epic EK-57682. 1993. MORE SONGS FOR SLEEPLESS NIGHTS. Additional songs not used in the SLEEPLESS IN SEATTLE movie. Including JD's Warner Brothers recording of "I'll See You in My Dreams."

Intersound CD-1013. 2 CDs. 1991. THE FABULOUS THIRTIES. Performers include Durante, doing "Inka Dinka Doo."

JSP Records (England) CD-701. 1990 (England). BING CROSBY AND JIMMY DURANTE: START OFF EACH DAY WITH A SONG. Songs and dialogue from Crosby radio shows 1946-49.

Living Era CD-5011. Reissue of 1982 LP, HOLLYWOOD SINGS, including Clayton, Jackson, and Durante's "Can Broadway Do Without Me?" from 1929.

Natasha Imports 4026 [subsidiary of Stash Records]. 1993. SEPTEMBER SONG. Songs and banter taken mostly from 1940s Armed Forces Radio Service transcriptions, other 1940s radio shows, and 1950s TV shows. Includes some rare material.

Pro-Arte CDD-483. 1989. LEGENDARY ENTERTAINERS. Performers from the 1920s, including Clayton, Jackson, and Durante's "Can Broadway Do Without Me?"

Tall Poppy/Conifer TQ-157. 1987. HOORAY FOR HOLLYWOOD. Includes Durante's "Hot Patatta" from 1934.

Varese Sarabande VSD-5321. 1991. CITY SLICKERS. Original motion picture soundtrack. Includes JD's Warner Brothers recording of "Young at Heart."

Vintage Jazz Classics 1031-2. 1991. BOB HOPE'S CHRISTMAS PARTY: COMMAND PERFORMANCE—CHRISTMAS 1945. 77 min. (of original show that ran close to two hours). CD cuts some of the dialogue, but includes all the music. JD sings "So I Ups to Him." (See Durante radio listings.)

Vintage Jazz Classics 1048. 1993. HOLLYWOOD STARS GO TO WAR: G.I. JIVE. Armed Forces Radio Service broadcasts from 1943-45, including JD joking with Harry James about Betty Grable.

Warner Archives 9.45456-2. 1993. AS TIME GOES BY: THE BEST OF JIMMY DURANTE. Includes 12 selections chosen from the first three of five LPs JD made for Warner Brothers: "As Time Goes By," "If I Had You," "Smile," "Hi-Lili, Hi-Lo," "Make Someone Happy," "Young at Heart," "Hello, Young Lovers," "Try a Little Tenderness," "The Glory of Love," "I'll Be Seeing You," "September Song," and "I'll See You in My Dreams." (The CD runs only 34 minutes.)

Related 78rpm Recordings

Note: An early imitator of Jimmy Durante (and many other celebrities) was the British singer-comedienne Florence Desmond. She made 78rpm records in the 1930s. Among them:

"A Hollywood Party," part 1 OB-2380-2
                part 2 OB-2381-1
HMV B-4264, Victor 24210. London. July 25, 1932. Orch. acc. cond. by Ray Noble.

"A Hollywood Bridge Game," part 1 OB-6084-1-2
                    part 2 OB-6085-1-2
HMV rejected. London, March 8, 1934.

"A Hollywood Bridge Game," part 1 OB-6084-3
                    part 2 OB-6085-3
HMV B-8159 and HMV B.D. 275. London, March 23, 1934.

On the earlier recording, Miss Desmond impersonates Janet Gaynor and all the guests who arrive at her party: ZaSu Pitts arrives first, then Durante (saying "Ach-cha-cha, I'm mortified! I got a million of 'em, a million of 'em!), then Greta Garbo (looking for a corner in which to be alone), Tallulah Bankhead, Marlene Dietrich, Gracie Fields, and Marie Dressler. "Gracie Fields" sings "Lancashire Blues."

On the later recording, Miss Desmond impersonates the voices of Durante and ZaSu Pitts, his novice bridge partner, and their opponents Lupe Velez and Mae West. Jimmy teaches ZaSu how to cheat. The sketch ends with "Durante" saying, "I know the hand I dealt 'ya. I got a million of 'em, a million of 'em!"

Related LP Recordings (Durante associates listed first,
then performers of his songs, including imitators)

Audio Fidelity 1909. EDDIE JACKSON! 12" LP. 1959. Mono. Songs by JD's long-time partner, with his Dixielanders. All 12 songs are well-known. The only song he used with Durante and Lou Clayton is "Bill Bailey."

Colpix 402. FOR LOSERS ONLY. 12" LP. 1959. Mono. Songs by JD's "junior partner," Sonny King. Twelve songs, with no Durante-related material.

Folkways 35. ROY BARGY: PIANO SYNCOPATIONS. 12" LP. 1978. Mono. 17 rags composed by JD's long-time orchestra director, composed and published in the early 1920s. Performed by Bargy on discs and piano rolls. Compiled and annotated by David A. Jasen.

Coral 57083. AND THEN I WROTE... 12" LP. 1956. Mono. Irving Caesar vocals with piano accompaniment, including song he wrote with JD, "Umbriago" (1944). Excellent imitation of JD's voice too! Preceded by anecdote about meeting JD at train station, traveling to California for the first time, from New York, with his old father, and how Mr. Durante wanted to give him a haircut.

Columbia CL-1377. HAPPY DAYS! 12" LP. 1960. Mono. The Buffalo Bills (barbershop group and banjo). They harmonize well on Durante's "Inka Dinka Doo."

Dot 3143. JACK KANE SALUTES THE COMICS. 12" LP. n.d. Mono. With his orchestra in big band arrangements of songs associated with 12 comedy acts, including JD's "Inka Dinka Doo."

Fona (Chicago) (no number). A SALUTE TO JIMMY DURANTE. 12" LP. n.d. Stereo. Danny Rio, who looks like JD, does a Chicago nightclub act singing JD's songs in a style imitative of JD. LP has 10 songs associated with Durante.

Label credits for songs used gives "public domain" for "Start Off Each Day with a Song," "Everywhere You Go" and "Bill Bailey."

"Love You, I Do" is credited to B. Abram and Hank Levine ("I Love You, I Do" was written by Durante-Buffano-Barnett).

"Good Night" is credited to Guy Bagar (it was written by Durante & Barnett).

Other songs on the LP appear to be correctly attributed: "Young at Heart," "My Nose's Birthday," "Old Man Time," and "Inka Dinka Doo."

Major Minor Records (England) SMCP-5029. MINSTREL SHOW. 12" LP. 1969. Stereo. The Mississippi Minstrels. Geoff Love sings JD's "Inka Dinka Doo."

Painted Smiles 1366. BEN BAGLEY'S RODGERS AND HART REVISITED, VOL. 3. 12" LP. c. 1978. Stereo. Arthur Siegel sings "Women," the solo Durante had in *Jumbo* (1935), with voice imitating Durante.

Also released as CD-106 in 1989.

Pickwick/33 PC/SPC-3002. THE MANY FACES OF SAMMY DAVIS, JR. 12" LP. c. 1965. Mono and stereo. Includes JD's "Inka Dinka Doo."

Reissue of Capitol material originally recorded July 29, 1949, released April 3, 1950 on Capitol 943, the flip side of "Laura." Song is occasion for Sammy to imitate not only Durante but other celebrities—James Cagney, James Stewart, Mel Blanc, and the Ink Spots' Bill Kenney.

Also released as Capitol CD D-124808 in 1990, SAMMY DAVIS, JR.: THE CAPITOL COLLECTOR'S SERIES.

RCA Camden CAL-2100. THE MICKEY FiNN THEME AND OTHER FAVORITES. 12" LP. 1966. Mono and stereo. The Ragtimers include a medley of "One of Those Songs" (often sung by Durante) and Durante's "Inka Dinka Doo."

20th Century–Fox 3124. DICK SHAWN SINGS WITH HIS LITTLE PEOPLE. 12" LP. 1963. Mono and stereo. Includes JD's "Inka Dinka Doo" and 11 other songs Shawn sings "with some of the most talented youngsters in show business." Arranged and conducted by Milton DeLugg.

Related Compact Discs (Performers of Durante songs)

ProArte CDD-592. 1991. GUY LOMBARDO: AULD LANG SYNE. Guy Lombardo's Royal Canadians, dance band. Recordings from 1928-37, including Durante's "Inka Dinka Doo," with a vocal trio, Nov. 27, 1933.

Concord Jazz CCD-6003. n.d. SOFT SHOE. Herb Ellis and Ray Brown lead a jazz quintet in instrumental numbers that include Durante's "Inka Dinka Doo." Recorded 1974.

Appendix F

DURANTE AS COMPOSER

Information on many of these songs comes from the Library of Congress Copyright Office's *Catalogue of Copyright Entries* (Washington: Government Printing Office, issued annually), plus the *ASCAP Index of Performed Compositions (New York: ASCAP, 1979), and The Blue Book of Hollywood Musicals*, by Jack Burton (Watkins Glen, NY: Century House, 1953). Much additional information, but no dates, was provided by Durante songwriter from the 1950s and '60s, Jackie Barnett.

In some cases, actual sheet music or lead sheets were examined. Copyright dates and numbers are given where known, but songs are listed by approximate dates of first known performance where possible if presented much earlier than copyright date. Some early songs seem to have been used many years before being registered, and others not registered at all. There are certain to be many omissions and some errors since, as far as can be determined, no comprehensive listing of Durante compositions has ever been published.

Asterisks (*) precede the songs Durante continued to perform with some frequency throughout his career.

Dec. 8, 1919. THE SYMPHONY JASS FOX-TROT, by JD and Jefferson D. Loyacano. L.C. copyright number E463502. Instrumental.

Dec. 8, 1919. WHY CRY BLUES, by JD and Achille Baquet. L.C. copyright number E463503. Instrumental.

Recorded May 1920, by Jimmy Durante's Jazz Band, on Gennett 9045. It was the only early recording issued under Durante's own name. [*Note:* While the recording gave Baquet credit as collaborator, the copyright registration lists Jefferson D. Loyacano, not Baquet, as Durante's collaborator.)

June 7, 1920. THE FRETTIN' BLUES, by JD and Achille Baquet. E481055. Instrumental.

June 6, 1921. I DIDN'T START IN TO LOVE YOU (UNTIL YOU STOPPED LOVING ME), words by Bob Schafer and Sam Coslow; music by JD, arranged by George F. Briegel. E512335; Triangle Music Co., New York.

254

It was recorded by Daisy Martin ("Colored Blues Singer"), accompanied by the Five Jazz Bell-Hops, on Okeh 8009, c. Aug. 2, 1921.

June 13, 1921. DADDY, YOUR MAMA IS LONESOME FOR YOU, words by Chris Smith & Bob Schafer; music by JD. E512503; Triangle Music Pub. Co., New York. Copyrighted a second time, May 27, 1925, blues fox trot performance accompanied by ukelele, arranged by May Singhi Breen, E616213; Triangle, New York.

It was recorded by Bennie Krueger and his orchestra, vocal by Al Bernard (white vaudeville singer), on Olympic 15117, c. June 1921; also by Mamie Smith and Her Jazz Hounds on Okeh 4416, c. Aug. 5, 1921. Much later recorded by JD himself on Warner Bros. LP, ONE OF THOSE SONGS, 1966.

July 18, 1921. SWEETNESS, words by Bob Schafer & Dave Ringle; music by JD, arranged by George F. Briegel. E514944; Triangle Music Co., New York.

Aug. 23, 1921. YOU'RE TALKING TO THE WRONG MAN NOW, lyrics by Chris Smith; music by JD. E518655; Triangle Music Pub. Co., New York.

Sept. 24, 1921. LET'S AGREE TO DISAGREE, words and music by Mamie Smith, Chris Smith, and JD. E519494; Triangle Music Pub. Co., New York. Copyrighted a second time Oct. 1, 1921; E522722; Triangle, New York.

Mamie Smith recorded this for Okeh 4511, c. Oct. 12, 1921, with Her Jazz Hounds.

Sept. 26, 1921. I'M ON MY WAY TO NEW ORLEANS, words by Sugarfoot Gaffney and Bartley Costello; music by JD, arranged by Robert W. Ricketts. E519491; Triangle, New York. Second copyright Oct. 1, 1921, E522723, dropping arranger's name.

Sept. 26, 1921. MEAN DADDY BLUES, words by Fred Hamburger; melody by Irving Bloom and JD, arranged by Robert W. Ricketts. E519493; Triangle Music Pub. Co., New York. Second copyright with changes noted, Dec. 3, 1921, E523428, Triangle.

Mamie Smith and Her Jazz Hounds recorded this for Okeh 4631, May 1922.

Oct. 10, 1921. I'VE GOT MY HABITS ON, words by Chris Smith & Bob Schafer; music by JD. E519920; Goodman & Rose, Inc., New York. (First copyright says words by Chris Smith, melody by Bob Schafer and JD, arranged by Robert W. Rickets. Second copyright, Nov. 25, 1921, says words by Chris Smith and Bob Schafer, music by JD. The published sheet music gives the second copyright credits.) Copyright a third time, March 20, 1922, E546771, American Piano Co., New York, for Ampico piano roll no. 202351-F, played by Edgar Fairchild; in B flat, with copyright claimed on the interpretation.

Bailey's Lucky Seven recorded this, with Durante the probable piano player, on Gennett 4815, Dec. 1921; by Joseph Samuels' Jazz Band on Okeh 4477, c. Oct. 29, 1921; Miss Patricola on Victor 18838, Nov. 22, 1921; also by [Ben] Selvin's Dance Orch. on Vocalion 14277, c. Nov. 16, 1921; Bennie Krueger and his orchestra on Brunswick 2181, c. Dec. 1921; James P. Johnson piano roll solo, QRS 1814, New York, Jan. 1922 (reissued on 10" LP, JAMES P. JOHNSON: EARLY HARLEM PIANO, Riverside RLP-1011, and in England, London AL-3511, c. 1954).

The cover of the commercially released sheet music has blackface sketch plus insert photo of white singer Patricola.

256   APPENDIX F

1921. ONE OF YOUR SMILES, words by Bartley Costello and John J. Kenny; music by JD. Published by Triangle Music Pub. Co.

April 3, 1922. AT THE HONKY-TONK STEPPERS' BALL, words by Chris Smith; melody by JD; arr. by Claude Lapham. E533046; Goodman & Rose, Inc., New York. Second copyright, words and music by the above, May 30, 1922, E535982; Goodman & Rose.

Photographed sheet music cover, in Thomas L. Morgan and William Barlow's FROM CAKEWALK TO CONCERT HALLS: AN ILLUSTRATED HISTORY OF AFRICAN AMERICAN POPULAR MUSIC FROM 1895 TO 1930 (Washington, DC: Elliott & Clark, 1992), p. 82.

May 3, 1922. I AIN'T NEVER HAD NOBODY CRAZY OVER ME, words and music by JD, Johnny Stein, and Dave Ringle; arr. by Teddy Eastwood. E538098; Broadway Music Corp., New York. Second copyright, Feb. 21, 1923, says words and melody by JD, Johnny Stein, and Jack Roth, arr. by George Holman, E560268; Fred Fisher, Inc., New York. Third copyright, May 8, 1923, keeps information of second copyright except dropping of arranger's name, E562136.

The Broadway Syncopators recorded this for Vocalion 14598, May–June 1923. Also recorded by Ladd's Black Aces, after Durante had left the group, Gennett 5164, May 19, 1923.

Nov. 22, 1922. MY MOLLY, melody by Billy McGill and JD, arr. by McGill. E552152; Billy McGill and JD, New York.

Nov. 22, 1922. BARNEY DEAR, melody by Billy McGill and JD, arr. by McGill. E552153; Billy McGill and JD, New York.

March 12, 1923. LULLABY LADY, melody by Johnny Stein and JD. E560840; Johnny Stein, New York.

March 27, 1923. YOU'LL FIND ME WHERE YOU LEFT ME (BUT I WON'T BE ALONE), words by Alex Sullivan; melody by JD. E558922; Leo Feist, Inc., New York. Second copyright, May 15, 1923, E562469, adds orch. version arr. by Sam Danks. Third copyright, June 19, 1923, E563208, copyrights an arrangement.

Aug. 30, 1923. PAPA STRING BEAN: NEW ORLEANS BLUES, words by Al Bernard; music by JD. E570765; Edward B. Marks Music Co., New York. Second copyright, Sept. 15, 1923, adds arranger William J.C. Lewis, E569378; Marks.

Oct. 24, 1923. WHAT'LL I DO, words by Sam Coslow and Jack Roth; music by JD. E576367; All Star Music Corp., New York.

March 20, 1924. WE ALL HAD ENOUGH OF IT NOW, words by Henry Creamer; music by JD and Bob Schafer. E586802; Jack Mills, Inc., New York.

1924. EVERYBODY WANTS TO GET INTO THE ACT, by JD.
Mentioned by Lou Clayton as a number sung at the Dover Club, Fowler, p. 82. The Durante exclamation of faked exasperation is often used, not the song.

1924. *AGAIN YOU TURNA, words and music by JD. Copyright May 18, 1948. EU131003. Renewed June 3, 1975 by JD. R606579.
Clayton said it was sung at the Dover Club, Fowler, p. 82.

1924. SKEET, SKAT, by JD.
Used in 1920s nightclub routine, when important customers entered, telling the waiter where to seat them.

See Dayton Stoddart's book on Sime Silverman, *Lord Broadway*, *Variety's Sime*, 1941, p. 299, for five lines of the song; also John Fisher's *Call Them Irreplaceable*, 1976, p. 49.

1924. EAST WIND (BLOWS FROM THE WEST), by JD.
From a poem by a New York neighbor, a Mr. Bloomish (see Fowler's book, p. 38). Used by JD on radio 1933–34.

May 4, 1925. DON'T SAY YOU WILL (WHEN YOU KNOW THAT YOU WON'T), words and music by Sam Coslow, JD, and Jack Roth; pf. acc., with ukulele arr. David Berend. E613767; Robbins-Engel, Inc., New York.

Nov. 25, 1925. SHE DOESN'T, words by Walter Winchell; music by JD and Chick Endor, pf. acc., with ukelele arr. Jeanne Gravelle. E628789; Henry Waterston, Inc., New York.
Photographed sheet music, in Cahn's *Good Night Mrs. Calabash*, p. 37.

April 27, 1928. *I KNOW DARN WELL I CAN DO WITHOUT BROADWAY (BUT CAN BROADWAY DO WITHOUT ME?), words & music by JD. E691040; Jimmy Durante, Flushing, L.I., N.Y.
Title later shortened to just CAN BROADWAY DO WITHOUT ME? Published by Robbins Music Corp.
Introduced by C,J&D in SHOW GIRL, 1929, and recorded by them on Columbia 1860-D, May 9, 1929. Sung by JD in *On an Island with You*, 1948 film. Collected in the 1936 song book (with no mention of 1928 copyright). Also included in *Show Biz Song Folio*, Robbins Music Corp., 1953, the folio a tie-in with the 1951 book by Abel Green and Joe Laurie, Jr., and the RCA Victor LP, c. 1954.
Clayton said this song was performed at the Dover Club (c. 1924–26), Fowler, p. 82.

April 27, 1928. *(I'M) JIMMY, THE WELL DRESSED MAN, words & music by JD. E691041; Jimmy Durante, Flushing, L.I., N.Y. Second copyright, May 18, 1948; EU130999. Renewed June 3, 1975; R606575.
Song was introduced by C,J&D on Broadway in *Show Girl*, 1929. Collected in *Jimmy (Schnozzle) Durante's Jumbo Song Book* (New York: Harry Engel, Inc., 1936).

April 27, 1928. *SHE'S A LITTLE BIT THIS AND A LITTLE BIT THAT, words & music by JD. E691042; Jimmy Durante, Flushing, L.I., N.Y. Second copyright, May 18, 1948; EU131007 [using a comma instead of word "and"]. Renewed June 3, 1975; R606583.
Used on radio 1934. Featured in the 1947 MGM film *This Time for Keeps*.

1929. *ONE ROOM HOME, by JD.
EU260460, Jan. 7, 1952.
Used in Boston tryout of *Show Girl*, 1929. Much later, on SEPTEMBER SONG LP, credit is given to JD and Jackie Barnett. See a long note for Chapter 7 on the controversy surrounding credit for this song and its variations.
See Maurice Zolotow's book *No People Like Show People*, 1951, p. 115, for eleven lines of the song as it was recited by Durante in *Show Girl*.

June 6, 1929. *SO I UPS TO HIM (AND HE UPS TO ME), words & melody by JD. E unp. 7658; Jimmy Durante, Flushing, L.I., N.Y. Second copyright, May 18, 1948; EU131000. Renewed June 3, 1975; R606576.
Introduced by JD (without C&J) in *Show Girl*, 1929, and recorded, with minimal interjections by C&J, on Columbia 1860-D, May 9, 1929.

1929. BROADWAY, MY STREET, words by Sidney Skolsky; music by JD. Copyright May 18, 1948; EU131001. Renewed by JD, June 3, 1975; R606577.

Sung by Clayton, Jackson, and Durante on Broadway in *Show Girl*, 1929. ASCAP credits only JD, not Skolsky.

Referred to by Clayton as BROADWAY'S A PHONY, performed at the Dover Club (c. 1924-c. 1926), Fowler, p. 82; Dayton Stoddart's book on Sime Silverman quotes several lines from the same song, which he entitles BROADWAY IS A FAKE, A PHONY, BUT IT'S MY STREET, pp. 306–07.

c. 1929. *WHO WILL BE WITH YOU WHEN I'M FAR AWAY, words and music by William H. Farrell and JD, derived from Farrell's WHO WILL BE WITH YOU WHEN I GO AWAY. Copyright Feb. 2, 1955; EP86928; Leo Feist, Inc., New York. "Appl. states prev. reg. 15 Dec. '13, E321957. NM: 'new lyric and change in melody.'"

JD used this song with great frequency, from at least the early 1930s onward, especially on radio.

The source of the song was acknowledged by JD on a 1946 Decca recording, but usually Durante claimed the song as his own, without mentioning its source. (The 1913 sheet music released by the F.B. Haviland Pub. Co., New York, carries as its full title, WHO WILL BE WITH YOU WHEN I GO AWAY (OR WHEN I'M FAR AWAY FROM YOU). Durante's title is very close but he uses only a portion of the song's chorus.]

1929. EVERYTHING IS ON THE UP AND UP; EVERYBODY WANTS MY GIRL; HELLO, EVERYBODY, FOLKS. Words and music by JD. Copyright Jan. 7, 1952; EU260506. Also as a variant, HELLO, HELLO, HELLO.

Feb. 1930 release of Paramount film *Roadhouse Nights* contained, according to *Photoplay*, these three of JD's songs: (This viewer caught only the first and third. Either the print was edited, or the middle song was cut by Paramount.)

The variant, HELLO, HELLO, HELLO, was featured in HOLLYWOOD PARTY, 1934 film, again with some variation in 1946 film *Two Sisters from Boston*.

1930. HOT PATATTA, words & music by JD.

Performed by Clayton, Jackson, and Durante on Broadway in *The New Yorkers*, Dec. 1930. Later featured in the 1934 film *Strictly Dynamite*. Recorded on Brunswick with INKA DINKA DOO.

1930. *WOOD, words & music by JD. Copyright Jan. 7, 1952; EU260469.

Performed by Clayton, Jackson, and Durante in *The New Yorkers*, Dec. 1930, inserted into the Cole Porter musical. They had performed it at the Palace two years earlier.

1930. A DISSA AND A DATTA, words & music by JD. Copyright Jan. 7, 1952 as DATA. EU260482.

Performed by Clayton, Jackson, and Durante in *The New Yorkers*, Dec. 1930, entitled DATA in the playbill.

1930. MONEY!, words & music by JD.

Performed by Clayton, Jackson, and Durante in *The New Yorkers*, Dec. 1930.

1931. *DID YOU EVER HAVE THE FEELING, by JD. Copyright Jan. 7, 1952 as DID YOU EVER HAVE THAT FEELING, EU260481.

Used in Durante's first MGM film, *New Adventures of Get Rich Quick Wallingford*, 1931. Included on 1946 Decca 78RPM album JIMMY DURANTE, as an interpolation within the song "WHO WILL BE WITH YOU WHEN I'M FAR AWAY?" Used by JD on radio 1943.

Sept. 9, 1933. REINCARNATION, words by Lorenz Hart; music by Richard Rodgers and JD. E unp. 76160; Metro-Goldwyn-Mayer Corp. Renewed Sept. 21, 1960; R263039.
Sung by JD in 1934 film *Hollywood Party*.

Sept. 9, 1933. YES ME, words and music by Lorenz Hart, Richard Rodgers and JD. E unp. 76164; Metro-Goldwyn-Mayer Corp. Renewed Sept. 21, 1960; R262724.

Nov. 7, 1933. *INKA DINKA DOO, words by Ben Ryan; melody by JD. E unp. 78547; Irving Berlin, Inc. Renewed Nov. 15, 1960; R266593. Second copyright, Dec. 7, 1933, adds that the song is from *Joe Palooka*, words by Ben Ryan, music by Jimmy "Schnozzle" Durante, with arr. for ukulele, etc., E pub. 39319; Irving Berlin, Inc. Second copyright renewed, Dec. 7, 1960; R267341 and R267342.
The song was also published under the 1933 copyright by Bourne, Inc., New York, with no tie-in to the Palooka film. On the 1946 Decca 78rpm album the composers are listed as Durante-Ryan-Donnelly, adding the name of JD's pianist Harry Donnelly. After JD sang the song in UA/Reliance Pictures' *Palooka*, 1934, he performed it again in two MGM films, *Two Girls and a Sailor*, 1944, and *This Time for Keeps*, 1947. It was used by JD on radio for the first time in 1933.
In addition to JD recordings, Ferde Grofe and his Orchestra, with vocal by The Rhythm Boys (not Crosby, Barris, and Rinker), recorded "Inka Dinka Doo" for Columbia 2858-D, Nov. 21, 1933; Sam Robbins recorded a vocal of it with his own dance band, S.R.'s Hotel McAlpin Orch., for Bluebird 5276, Nov. 22, 1933 (also on Montgomery Ward M-4408-A); Guy Lombardo and His Royal Canadians, vocal trio, Brunswick 6714, Nov. 27, 1933; Will Osborne and his orchestra, with vocal trio, for Banner 32927, Mellotone 12880, and other labels, Dec. 4, 1933; Jimmie Noone and his jazz band, with an Ed Pollack vocal, for Vocalion 2619, Dec. 15, 1933 (reissued on 10" LP, Jazz Society 15, "Jimmie Noone And His Orchestra"); Don Bestor and his dance orch., vocal by The Chanters, for Victor 24503, Jan. 24, 1934.

1933. AS THE NOSE BLOWS (SO THE NOSE GROWS), probably by JD.
Used on radio, 1933, as JD's opening theme. JD had sung a few notes in the 1932 film *The Phantom President*.

1934. THE BEE AND THE ROSE, possibly by JD.
Used on radio, 1934.

1934. I'M PUTTY IN YOUR HANDS, words and music by JD.
Featured in the 1934 film *Strictly Dynamite*.

1934. I SAY IT WITH MUSIC, words and music by JD.
Featured in the 1934 film *Student Tour*.

1934. TAKE A W, words and music by JD. Also as variant same year, *TAKE AN L, which was copyrighted July 29, 1949 by JD. EU174699; Jimmy Durante Music Publishing Co. Renewed by JD, Sept. 27, 1976; R642120.
Used on radio 1934. TAKE A W was dropped before 1940s. TAKE AN L was used again by JD in radio 1947. Featured in 1950 film *The Great Rupert*.

Jan. 2, 1936. JIMMY (SCHNOZZLE) DURANTE'S JUMBO SONG BOOK, words and music by JD, compiled and ed. Jean Herbert; with arr. for guitar, etc.

E pub 52923; Harry Engel, Inc., New York. Renewed by Jean Herbert, Jan. 7, 1963; R308361.

Includes eight songs, in this order: *I'M JIMMY THAT WELL-DRESSED MAN (previously copyrighted in 1928, with "THE," not "THAT" in the title; earlier copyright is not mentioned in the SONG BOOK); *I KNOW DARN WELL I CAN DO WITHOUT BROADWAY (CAN BROADWAY DO WITHOUT ME?) (previously copyrighted in 1928; earlier copyright is not mentioned in the SONG BOOK); *YOU GOTTA START OFF EACH DAY WITH A SONG, words and music by JD (also published alone by Robbins Music Corp., 1936) I GOT A MILLION OF 'EM; IT'S MUTINY!; HOT-CHA-CHA!; I'M MORTIFIED; IT'S THE GYPSY IN ME!

These last five songs were almost never performed but very commonly used as expressions.

1940. I'M A FUGITIVE FROM ESQUIRE, by JD & Howard Dietz. Copyright May 18, 1948; EU131002. Renewed by JD, June 3, 1975; R606578.

Sung by JD on Broadway in *Keep Off the Grass*, 1940. Used on radio in 1943.

1940. TOSCANINI, STOKOWSKI, AND ME, by Harold Spina, JD, and Walter Bullock. Also as variant, 1943, TOSCANINI, TCHAIKOVSKY AND ME, and most popular, 1944 variant, *TOSCANINI, ITURBI AND ME.

First version sung by JD in out-of-town (Boston) previews for *Keep Off the Grass*, 1940. Dropped before Broadway opening. Variant, TOSCANINI, TCHAIKOVSKY AND ME, sung on Paul Whiteman's ABC show PHILCO RADIO HALL OF FAME, Dec. 5, 1943. Variant, TOSCANINI, ITURBI AND ME, sung in 1944 film *Music for Millions*, and in 1940s and '50s radio and TV.

1941. VACUUM CLEANER OF THE DAY, words and music by JD.

Composed for the 1941 film *You're in the Army Now*, but reworked and retitled IF YOU OWNED A WHIRLAWAY.

1941. I AM AN ARMY MAN, words and music by JD.

Composed for the 1941 film *You're in the Army Now*, but dropped.

1944, April 12. *UMBRIAGO, words and music by Irving Caesar and JD. E unp. 371175; Irving Caesar, New York. Second copyright, May 8, 1944; E pub. 124878; Robbins Music Corp., New York.

Introduced by JD in 1944 film *Music for Millions*. Although the song was copyrighted 1944, the word itself was part of C,J&D's 1920s act long before it became a song.

May 18, 1944. I'D LIKE TO WRITE A SONG TO WIN THE WAR, words and music by Irving Caesar, Alfred Bryan, and JD. EU389013. Renewed by JD, May 18, 1971; R506195, and by Alfred Leo Bryan (child of the deceased), R506196.

June 28, 1944. *I'LL DO THE STRUT-AWAY IN MY CUTAWAY, words and music by Harry Donnelly, JD, and Irving Caesar. E pub. 129976; Leo Feist, Inc., New York. Renewed by JD, June 29, 1971; R508240.

Featured in the 1948 MGM film *On an Island with You*.

1946. JOE GOES UP—I COME DOWN, by JD. Copyright Jan. 7, 1952; EU260467.

On 1946 Decca album.

1946. *DURANTE—THE PATRON OF THE ARTS, by JD. Copyright under the title I'M DURANTE, THE PATRON OF THE ARTS, lists words and music

by JD, Les White, and Buddy Pierson. May 18, 1948; EU130997. Renewed by JD, June 3, 1975; R606573.
On 1946 Decca album, DURANTE—THE PATRON OF THE ARTS credits JD alone.

1946, Dec. 23. *THE LOST CHORD, words and music by Earl K. Brent and JD. EU57033; Loew's Inc. Renewed by JD, Jan. 24, 1974; R568597, again giving title THE LOST CHORD, repeating both names, Brent and JD. Also copyright Jan. 7, 1952, as *I'M THE GUY WHO FOUND THE LOST CHORD, listing only JD as composer. EU260476.
Recorded, with the longer title, for MGM, 1947. Used in MGM's *This Time for Keeps*, 1947.

1947, Nov. 20. *CHIDABEE, CHIDABEE, CHIDABEE (YAH! YAH! YAH!), words and music by JD, Harry Crane, and Harry Harris. E pub. 19052. Jimmy Durante Music Pub. Co./Harry Harris Music Pub. Co. Renewed by Harry Harris, Dec. 19, 1974; R593506.
Radio, 1947. Often used by JD on radio. Recorded for MGM, 1947.

Nov. 20, 1947. YOU'RE ONE IN A MILLION. Lyrics by Harry Harris; music by JD. E pub. 19053. Jimmy Durante Pub. Co. Renewed by Harry Harris, Dec. 19, 1974; R593507.

1947. I'M FEELIN' MIGHTY LOW, words by Bill Gould and Elon Packard, music by JD. Jimmy Durante Music Pub. Co. copyright Jan. 7, 1952. EU260500.
Recorded by JD and Candy Candido for MGM in 1947.

1947. THE DAY I READ A BOOK, by JD & Jackie Barnett. Copyright Jan. 7, 1952 as (I'LL NEVER FORGET) THE DAY I READ A BOOK. JD/JB. EU260497.
Recorded by MGM, 1947.

May 18, 1948. I CAN'T READ A MENU, words by Harry Harris and Harry Crane; music by JD. EU130998. Renewed by JD, June 3, 1975; R606574.

May 18, 1948. I CAN'T READ AMENS, words and music by JD, Harry Harris, and Harry Crane. EU130998 [Library of Congress catalogue error, same number as given for I CAN'T READ A MENU. Possibly the same song, "Amens" a misprint for "A Menu."] Renewed by Harry Harris, Dec. 5, 1975; R619542.

May 18, 1948. THE STATE OF ARKANSAS, by JD and Jackie Barnett. EU131004. Renewed by JD, June 3, 1975; R606580.
Radio, 1947. Recorded by MGM, 1947.

May 18, 1948. *IT'S MY NOSE'S BIRTHDAY (NOT MINE), by JD, Harry Crane, and Harry Harris. EU130996; Jimmy Durante Music Pub. Co. Renewed by JD, June 3, 1975; R606572.
Recorded for MGM, 1947.

May 18, 1948. I'M DEFINATELY THE LATIN TYPE, words and music by JD and Jackie Barnett (hereafter referred to as JB). EU131005. Renewed by JD, June 3, 1975; R606582.
Library of Congress catalogue spells "definitely" as "definately."

May 18, 1948. I'D MAKE A WONDERFUL SKY-WRITER IF I ONLY KNEW HOW TO SPELL, words by JB; music by JD. EU131006. Renewed by JD, June 3, 1975; R606582.

May 18, 1948. IF WASHINGTON NEEDS ME I'LL ANSWER THE CALL (BUT THEY BETTER NOT CALL ME COLLECT), words by Irving Caesar; music by JD. EU131008. Renewed by JD, June 3, 1975; R606584.
Used on radio, 1944.

May 18, 1948. I'LL WORK FOR WASHINGTON FOR A DOLLAR A YEAR, words and music by JD, Harry Harris, and Harry Crane. EU131009. Renewed by JD, June 3, 1975; R606585. Renewed by Harry Harris, Dec. 5, 1975; R619543.
Recorded by MGM, 1947, with title DOLLAR A YEAR MAN.

June 28, 1948. ANY STATE IN THE FORTY-EIGHT IS GREAT, by JB/JD. EU136851; Jimmy Durante Music Pub. Co. Renewed by JD, June 30, 1975; R608294.
Recorded for MGM, 1949. Used regularly on radio.

March 4, 1949. SUMMER LOVE. JD/JB. EU159185. Renewed by JD, April 19, 1976; R631263.

March 4, 1949. THE WAY SHE LOOKS. JD/JB. EU159186. Renewed by JD, April 19, 1976; R631264.

March 4, 1949. THINGS ARE GONNA BE FINE IN FORTY-NINE. JD/JB. EU159187. Renewed by JD, April 19, 1976; R631265. Also copyright Jan. 7, 1952 under the title EVERYTHING WILL BE FINE IN FORTY-NINE. JD/JB. EU260508.

March 4, 1949. *SING SOFT. JD/JB. EU159188. Renewed by JD, April 19, 1976; R631266.
A variant title, SING SOFT, SING SWEET, SING GENTLE, was recorded on the CLUB DURANT LP.

March 4, 1949. IN THE HILLS OF BROOKLYN. JD/JB. EU159189. Renewed by JD, April 19, 1976; R631267. Also copyright Jan. 7, 1952, crediting both JD & JB. EU260493.

March 4, 1949. MODESTY PREVENTS ME FROM TALKING. JD/JB. EU159190. Renewed by JD, April 19, 1976; R631268.

March 4, 1949. I'M A LONG FLANNEL GUY. JD/JB. EU159191. Renewed by JD, April 19, 1976; R631269.

March 4, 1949. THE THINKER. JD/JB. EU159192. Renewed by JD, April 19, 1976; R631270.

March 4, 1949. RIDIN' THE RANGE ON MY PINTO. JD/JB. EU159193. Renewed by JD, April 19, 1976; R631271.

July 29, 1949. *A REAL PIANO PLAYER. JD/JB. EU174689; Jimmy Durante Pub. Co. Renewed by JD, Sept. 27, 1976; R642110.
RCA Victor Red Seal 78 and 45 recordings, 1951, credit Barnett alone. CLUB DURANT LP credits both.

July 29, 1949. (ISN'T IT A SHAME THAT) CHRISTMAS COMES BUT ONCE A YEAR, by JD and Harry Crane. EU174690. Renewed by JD, Sept. 27, 1976; R642111.
MGM recording, 1950, adds to the credits, "assisted by Jules Buffano" (JD's pianist). Featured in Universal's 1950 film *The Great Rupert*.

1949. Film score for *The Great Rupert*, Universal, 1950.

July 29, 1949. I'M STUCK WITH ELIZABETH. JD/JB. EU174691. Renewed by JD, Sept. 27, 1976; R642112.

July 29, 1949. A SUIT WITH TWO PAIRS OF PANTS. JD/JB. EU174692. Renewed by JD, Sept. 27, 1976; R642113. Also copyright Jan. 7, 1952, giving both JD and Barnett credit. EU260489.

July 29, 1949. I BEEP WHEN I OUGHTA BOP. JD/JB. EU174693. Renewed by JD, Sept. 27, 1976; R642114.

July 29, 1949. IT'S HIS MUSIC. JD/JB. EU174694. Renewed by JD, Sept. 27, 1976; R642115.

July 29, 1949. MY OLD MAN. JD/JB. EU174695. Renewed by JD, Sept. 27, 1976; R642116.

July 29, 1949. THE BOYS WITH THE PROBOSKIS. JD/JB. EU174696; Jimmy Durante Music Pub. Co. Renewed by JD, Sept. 27, 1976; R642117.
On CLUB DURANT LP.

July 29, 1949. WHY DIDN'T YOU TELL ME BEFORE? JD/JB. EU174697. Renewed by JD, Sept. 27, 1976; R642118.

1950. NOBODY WANTS MY MONEY. JD/JB. Copyright Jan. 7, 1952. EU260462.
Used in Universal's 1950 film *The Milkman*.

1952. *Note:* All the following songs listed in this year were copyrighted **Jan. 7, 1952**, unless otherwise noted. Most are collaborations between Durante and Jackie Barnett for Durante's television series. All are assigned to the Jimmy Durante Music Publishing Co., Hollywood, unless otherwise noted. Songs are listed alphabetically.
    ACADEMY AWARDS; JD/JB; EU260478. ANYONE FOR TENNIS; JD/JB; EU260479. BORN ON THE EAST SIDE; JD alone; EU260473. BORN TO BE PUSHED AROUND; JD/JB; EU260480. April 21, 1952: COCKTAIL MUSIC; JD/JB; EU274297. THE CONTINENT; JD alone; EU260477. DON'T COMPLAIN, MAKE THE BEST OF IT; JD/JB; EU260487. DON'T TALK; JD alone; EU260486. March 28, 1952: THE DURANTE FLIP; JD/JB; EU269554. THE DURANTE STORY; JD/JB; EU260452. DURANTE THE PEOPLE'S CHOICE; JD and Victor Moore; EU260485. DURANTE THE SCIENTIST; JD/JB; EU260484. DURANTE'S ENGLISH LESSON; JD/JB; EU260483. HATS; JD, Jules Buffano, JB, Benny Davis, and Harry Akst; EU260507. March 28, 1952. I LIKE MY WOMEN HARD TO GET; JD/JB; EU269552. March 28, 1952. I REFUSE TO WEAR A BERET; JD/JB; EU269551. IF YOU'VE GOT PERSONALITY; JD, Jules Buffano, and JB; EU260503. I'M A HARD MAN FOR A MASSAGE; JD/JB; EU260504. I'M A LONG FLANNEL GUY; JD/JB; EU260502. I'M A ONE GIRL MAN; JD/JB; EU260501. I'M A ROMANTIC GONDOLIER; JD/JB; EU260499. I'M FROM MILWAUKEE; JD/JB; EU260494. I'M GOING HOME; JD alone; EU260495. I'M THE TOAST OF PARIS; JD/JB; EU260496. IT'S KINDA HARD TO PUT IT IN WORDS; JD/JB; EU260492. IT'S NOT HIS MIND, IT'S HIS MUSIC; JD/JB; EU260505. IT'S THE DANCE OF UMBRIAGO; JD/JB; EU260498. JAMES THE FIFTH; JD/JB; EU260491. JIMMY DURANTA CLAUS; JD/JB; EU260468. KNICKERS; JD alone; EU260466. LANA TURNER'S SWEATER;

JD alone; EU260465. LOVE IS A TWO LANE HIGHWAY; JD/JB; EU260463.
April 21, 1952. A LOVE SCENE TO END ALL LOVE SCENES; JD/JB;
EU274299. A MAN'S HOME IS HIS CASTLE; JD/JB; EU260490. MONEY
SONG; JD/JB; EU260464. MY PSYCHIATRIST; JD/JB; EU260461. THE
NEW DANCING TEAM FROM BRAZIL; JD/JB; EU260450. April 21, 1952.
ONE FOR ALL AND ALL FOR ONE; JD/JB; EU274298. P.S. THIRTY-
THREE; JD/JB; EU260457. PEEDLE DE DEE; JD/JB; EU260455. PIKES
PEAK OR BUST; JD/JB; EU260459. POLITICAL JIMMY; JD/JB; EU260458.
PUT YOURSELF IN MY HANDS; JD, Jules Buffano, and Jack Roth;
EU260454. SOMEBODY'S OVERLOOKING A GOLD MINE BY NOT
LOOKING OVER ME; JD/JB; EU260456. March 28, 1952. THERE'S A
PLACE IN THE THEATRE FOR YOU; JD/JB; EU269553 (included on CLUB
DURANT LP). THE WAY SHE LOOKS; JD/JB; EU260451. March 28, 1952.
WHAT THEY NEED IN THE OPERA IS RHYTHM; JD/JB; EU269550.
WHATEVER YOU WANT IS YOURS; JD, Jules Buffano and JB; EU260449.
WILL HE PASS; JD/JB; EU260474. WORCESTERSHIRE ON THE SAUCE;
JD/JB; EU260470. YOU GOTTA KEEP ON TRYIN'; JD/JB; EU260471. YOU
WANTED TO BET; JD alone; EU260472. YOU, YOUR HUSBAND AND
ME; JD/JB; EU260475. YOU'RE MUCH TOO PRETTY FOR ME; JD/JB;
EU260488.

1953. *Note:* All Library of Congress listings for this year are unpublished music
registered Jan. 5, 1953, and Nov. 10, 1953, all attributed to the Jimmy Durante
Music Publishing Co., Hollywood. Almost all are collaborations with Jackie
Barnett. Songs are listed alphabetically under Jan. 5, then under Nov. 10.

1953: Jan. 5 AIN'T THIS BETTER THAN AN ASHTRAY; JD/JB; EU298967.
THE CANDIDATE; JD/JB; EU298963. GEE, I'M A LUCKY GUY; JD and
Clarence Stout; EU298959. GO TO THE POLLS AND VOTE, BOYS; JD/JB;
EU298964. I LOVE A MAN WHO PLAYS THE PIANO; JD/JB; EU298965.
I WILL WRITE YOU LOVE SONGS; JD, JB, and Jules Buffano; EU298957.
*IT'S TIME TO SAY GOODNIGHT; JD/JB; EU298968 (also called GOOD-
NIGHT, GOODNIGHT by JD/JB; listed as GOOD NIGHT on AT THE
PIANO LP, 1959; used on JD's first TV show, Nov. 1, 1950, and often thereafter);
I'VE BEEN TO PICCADILLY; JD/JB; EU298961. LET YOUR CONS-
CIENCE BE YOUR GUIDE; JD/JB; EU298966. *LOVE YOU, LOVE YOU,
LOVE YOU, BABY MINE; EU298972; JD, Jules Buffano, and JB; Jackie
Barnett's ASCAP list shows (1) BABY MINE, (2) I LOVE YA, LOVE YA, LOVE
YA, I DO and (3) I LOVE YOU, I DO as three separate items, all with same three
collaborators (I LOVE YOU, I DO was recorded by JD with Eddie Jackson, Decca
29581, c. June 1955, also on 45rpm; additionally I LOVE YOU, I DO was re-
corded by Guy Lombardo and his Royal Canadians, vocal by Carmen Lombardo,
on Capitol 45rpm 5926). SEE YOU AROUND; JD/JB; EU298962. TAKE
YOUR PICK; JD, JB, and Jules Buffano; EU298971. THOUGH I'M A BUM
TODAY; JD/JB; EU298960. TRUMAN, JACKSON, AND DURANTE; JD/JB;
EU298958 (used for Margaret Truman's second appearance on JD's TV show,
March 22, 1952). WITH DURANTE YOU'LL NEVER KNOW; JD/JB;
EU298969. YOU CAN TELL BY THE TALK; JD alone; EU298970. **Nov. 10,
1953.** DON'T MENTION IT; JD/JB; EU337497. FIRE AND ICE; JD/JB;
EU337496. I'M AS READY AS I'LL EVER BE; JD/JB; EU337503 (on CLUB
DURANT LP). I'M THE DADDY WHO CAN COOL HER DOWN; JD/JB;
EU337501. JIMMY CHANGED HIS CLOTHES; JD/JB; EU337502. LIGHT

HER CIGARETTE; JD/JB; EU337500. MAN WE DATE; JD/JB; EU337495. MR. AND MRS. JIVE; JD/JB; EU337504. SING A SONG I WROTE; JD/JB; EU337498. WE'LL TAKE YOU ALONG; JD/JB; EU337499.

Oct. 6, 1955. DON'T LOSE YOUR SENSE OF HUMOR. Words by JB; music by JD. EU412893. Jimmy Durante Music Publishing Co., Hollywood. On SEPTEMBER SONG LP.

1955. WHEN THE CIRCUS LEAVES TOWN, by JD and JB. Jimmy Durante Music Pub. Co. Released on Decca 78rpm, 1955. Also on SEPTEMBER SONG LP, 1963.

1950s. I'VE GOT A GIRL CRAZY ABOUT ME, by JB, Jules Buffano, and JD. JD Music Pub. Co. I'M JIMMY'S GIRL, by JB and JD. Published by the Jimmy Durante Music Pub. Co. SWINGIN' WITH RHYTHM AND BLUES, by JD and JB. Jimmy Durante Music Pub. Co. (on CLUB DURANT LP). THE WORLD NEEDS NEW FACES, by JD and JB. Jimmy Durante Music Pub. Co. (on CLUB DURANT LP). OUR VOICES WERE MEANT FOR EACH OTHER, by JD and JB. Jimmy Durante Music Pub. Co. (on CLUB DURANT LP). I'M AS READY AS I'LL EVER BE, by JB and JD. Jimmy Durante Music Pub. Co. (on CLUB DURANT LP). MAD BIRD MELODY (TOODLE DO DOO), by JD. Jimmy Durante Music Pub. Co. (on AT THE PIANO LP, 1959).

1960s. IN THE OTHER FELLOW'S YARD, by JB and JD. Jimmy Durante Music Pub. Co. (on HELLO YOUNG LOVERS LP, 1964). WE'RE GOING U-F-OING, by JB and JD. Jimmy Durante Music Pub. Co./Jaybar Music Co. (on ONE OF THOSE SONGS LP, 1966). DOWN BY THE RIVER-SIDE, by JB and JD. Jimmy Durante Music Pub. Co./Jaybar Music Co. (on SONGS FOR SUNDAY LP, 1967). AMEN, by JB and JD. Jimmy Durante Music Pub. Co./Jaybar Music Co. (on SONGS FOR SUNDAY). HAS ANYBODY HERE SEEN MY GIRL?, by JB and JD. JD Music Pub. Co. WHAT A DAY, by JD. JD Music Pub. Co.

Note: There are many other songs credited to Jackie Barnett and Jimmy Durante on Jackie Barnett's ASCAP list, which he was kind enough to show this writer. Dates are not provided. Like a good number of those in the above listing, many of these are special material for specific TV shows, all from 1950s–60s. They are omitted here unless also found listed in the Library of Congress Catalogue.

Related Musical Compositions

1929. I WAS MADE TO LOVE YOU, words by Charles Tobias; music by Harold Veo and Doris Tauber. Mills Music, Inc., New York.
Song featured by Clayton, Jackson, and Durante, with a photo of the trio on the sheet music cover.

1931. DON'T TAKE LIFE SERIOUSLY, words by Geo. Solotaire; music by Sol Cohan and Clarence Kay. Modern Music Co., New York.
Song featured by Clayton, Jackson, and Durante, with a photo of the three on the cover.

1934. SCHNOZZOLA, words by Dave Oppenheim; music by Teddy Powell and Ira Schuster. Kornheiser Schuster Inc., New York.

MGM photo of Durante on cover with inscription, "Best Always, Schnozzle Durante. Hot-Cha."

1945. I LOVE TO READ THE FUNNIES, by Perry Alexander and "Woody" Frisino. Dubonnet Music Publishing, New York.
Song featured by Durante, with a photo of him on the cover.

1951. IF THE WORLD WERE FULL OF DURANTES, by Eddie Cantor and Charlie Tobias. Tobias and Lewis, New York.
Tribute to Durante. Seventeen photos of Durante on the cover.

1952. YANKEE DOODLE BUNNY, by Cliff Friend. Ben Bloom Music Corp., New York.
Durante on cover, having recorded this children's song.

1961. OLD MAN TIME, by Cliff Friend and Jack Reynolds. Miller Music, New York.
Warner Bros. Records photo of Durante on cover.

1972. GOODNIGHT, MRS. CALABASH, lyrics by Yip Harburg; music by Sammy Fain. Never published.

BIBLIOGRAPHY

Adler, Irene. *I Remember Jimmy: The Life and Times of Jimmy Durante*. Westport, CT: Arlington House, 1980.

Allen, Steve. *Funny People*. New York: Stein and Day, 1981.

Autry, Gene, with Mickey Herskowitz. *Back in the Saddle Again*. Garden City, NY: Doubleday, 1978.

Bankhead, Tallulah. *Tallulah: My Autobiography*. New York: Harper & Brothers, 1952.

Barnouw, Erik. *A History of Broadcasting in the United States*. vols. 1 and 2 (of 3): to 1933 — "A Tower in Babel"; 1933 to 1953 — "The Golden Web." New York: Oxford University Press, 1966, 1968.

Bastin, Bruce. *Never Sell a Copyright: Joe Davis and His Role in the New York Music Scene 1916–1978*. Chigwell, England: Storyville, 1990.

Bergreen, Laurence. *As Thousands Cheer: The Life of Irving Berlin*. New York: Viking, 1990.

The Biographical Encyclopedia & Who's Who of the American Theatre. Ed. Walter Rigdon. New York: James H. Heineman, 1965.

Blesh, Rudi. *Keaton*. New York: Macmillan, 1966.

————, and Harriet Janis. *They All Played Ragtime.*New York: Alfred A. Knopf, 1950; rpt. 4th ed. New York: Oak, 1971.

Bordman, Gerald. *American Musical Theatre: A Chronicle*. New York: Oxford University Press, 1978.

Bradford, Perry. *Born with the Blues*. New York: Oak Publications, 1965.

Brooks, Tim, and Earle Marsh. *The Complete Directory to Prime Time Network TV Shows, 1946–Present*. New York: Ballantine Books, 1979.

Brunn, H.O. *The Story of the Original Dixieland Jazz Band*. Baton Rouge: Louisiana State University Press, 1960.

Burns, George, with David Fisher. *All My Best Friends*. New York: G.P. Putnam's Sons, 1989.

Burton, Jack. *The Blue Book of Hollywood Musicals*. Watkins Glen, NY: Century House, 1953.

Cahn, William. *Good Night, Mrs. Calabash: The Secret of Jimmy Durante*. New York: Duell, Sloan and Pearce, 1963.

Castleman, Harry, and Walter J. Podrazik. *The TV Schedule Book: Four Decades of Network Programming From Sign-on to Sign-off*. New York: McGraw-Hill, 1984.

Chappell, George S. *The Restaurants of New York*. New York: Greenberg, 1925.

Charters, Samuel B., and Leonard Kunstadt. *Jazz: A History of the New York Scene*. Garden City, NY: Doubleday, 1962.

Cohn, Art. *The Joker is Wild: The Story of Joe E. Lewis*. New York: Random House, 1955.

Dardis, Tom. *Keaton: The Man Who Wouldn't Lie Down*. New York: Charles Scribner's Sons, 1979.

Delong, Thomas A. *Pops: Paul Whiteman, King of Jazz*. Piscataway, NJ: New Century Publishers, 1983.

Durante, Jimmy, and Jack Kofoed. *Night Clubs*. New York: Alfred A. Knopf, 1931.

Eames, John Douglas. *The MGM Story: The Complete History of Fifty Roaring Years.* New York: Crown, 1975.

Eells, George. *The Life That Late He Led: A Biography of Cole Porter.* New York: G.P. Putnam's Sons, 1967.

Federal writers' project. *New York City Guide.* New York: Random House, 1939.

Firestone, Ross, ed. *The Big Radio Comedy Program.* Chicago: Contemporary Books, 1978.

Fisher, John. *Call Them Irreplaceable.* Drawings by Hirschfeld. New York: Stein and Day, 1976.

Fowler, Gene. *Schnozzola: The Story of Jimmy Durante.* New York: Viking Press, 1951.

Friedrich, Otto. *City of Nets: A Portrait of Hollywood in the 1940's.* New York: Harper & Row, 1986.

Gabler, Neal. *An Empire of Their Own: How the Jews Invented Hollywood.* New York: Crown, 1988.

Gaver, Jack, and Dave Stanley. *There's Laughter in the Air!: Radio's Top Comedians and Their Best Shows.* New York: Greenberg, 1945.

Gil-Montero, Martha. *Brazilian Bombshell: The Biography of Carmen Miranda.* New York: Donald I. Fine, 1989.

Goldman, Herbert G. *Jolson: The Legend Comes to Life.* New York: Oxford University Press, 1988.

Gottlieb, Polly Rose. *The Nine Lives of Billy Rose.* New York: Crown, 1968.

Graham, Jefferson. *Vegas: Live and in Person.* New York: Abbeville Press, 1989.

Green, Abel, and Joe Laurie, Jr. *Show Biz: From Vaude to Video.* New York: Henry Holt, 1951.

Green, Stanley. *The Great Clowns of Broadway.* New York: Oxford University Press, 1984.

Halliwell, Leslie. *Halliwell's Filmgoer's Companion.* 9th ed. New York: Charles Scribner's Sons, 1988.

Halsman, Philippe, and others. *The Candidate: A Photographic Interview with the Honorable James Durante.* New York: Simon & Schuster, 1952.

Harmon, Jim. *The Great Radio Comedians.* Garden City, NY: Doubleday, 1970.

Hope, Bob, as told to Pete Martin. *Have Tux, Will Travel.* New York: Simon & Schuster, 1954.

Hotchner, A.E. *Choice People: The Greats, Near-Greats, and Ingrates I Have Known.* New York: William Morrow, 1984.

Hughes, Langston, and Milton Meltzer. *Black Magic: A Pictorial History of Black Entertainers in America.* Englewood Cliffs, NJ: Prentice-Hall, 1967; rpt., New York: Bonanza Books, 1967.

Inman, David. *The TV Encyclopedia.* New York: Perigee Books, 1991.

Isman, Felix. *Weber and Fields: Their Tribulations, Triumphs and Their Associates.* New York: Boni and Liveright, 1924.

Jasen, David A. *Tin Pan Alley: The Composers, the Songs, the Performers and Their Times.* New York: Donald I. Fine, 1988.

Jenkins, Henry. *What Made Pistachio Nuts?: Early Sound Comedy and the Vaudeville Aesthetic.* New York: Columbia University Press, 1992.

Kimball, Robert, ed. *The Complete Lyrics of Cole Porter.* New York: Alfred A. Knopf, 1983.

Kinkle, Roger D. *The Complete Encyclopedia of Popular Music and Jazz, 1900–1950.* 4 vols. New Rochelle, NY: Arlington House, 1974.

Laurie, Joe, Jr. *Vaudeville: From the Honky-tonks to the Palace.* New York: Henry Holt, 1953.

Lennon, Dianne, Peggy, Kathy, and Janet. *Same Song—Separate Voices: The Collective Memoirs of the Lennon Sisters.* Santa Monica, CA: Roundtable Publishing, 1985.

Macadams, William. *Ben Hecht: The Man Behind the Legend.* New York: Charles Scribner's Sons, 1990.

McBride, Joseph. *Frank Capra: The Catastrophe of Success.* New York: Simon & Schuster, 1992.

McCabe, John. *George M. Cohan: The Man Who Owned Broadway.* Garden City, NY: Doubleday, 1973.

Maltin, Leonard, ed. *Movie and Video Guide.* 1992 edition. New York: Signet, 1991.

Merman, Ethel, with George Eells. *Merman: An Autobiography.* New York: Simon & Schuster, 1978.

_____, as told to Pete Martin. *Who Could Ask for Anything More*. Garden City, NY: Doubleday, 1955.

Minsky, Morton, and Milt Machlin. *Minsky's Burlesque*. New York: Arbor House, 1986.

Morehouse, Ward. *George M. Cohan: Prince of the American Theater*. Philadelphia and New York: J.B. Lippincott, 1943.

On Stage: Selected Theater Reviews from The New York Times 1920–1970. Ed. Bernard Beckerman and Howard Siegman. New York: Arno Press/Quadrangle, 1973.

Parish, James Robert, and William T. Leonard. *The Funsters*. New Rochelle, NY: Arlington House, 1979.

Pilat, Oliver, and Jo Ranson. *Sodom by the Sea: An Affectionate History of Coney Island*. Garden City, NY: Doubleday, Doran, 1941.

Richard Rodgers Fact Book. New York: The Lynn Farnol Group, 1965.

Riis, Jacob. *The Battle with the Slum*. New York: Macmillan, 1902.

_____. *The Children of the Poor*. New York: Charles Scribner's Sons, 1923 [c. 1892].

_____. *How the Other Half Lives: Studies Among the Tenements of New York*. New York: Charles Scribner's Sons, 1890.

Robbins, Jhan. *Inka Dinka Doo: The Life of Jimmy Durante*. New York: Paragon House, 1991.

Rose, Al, and Edmond Souchon. *New Orleans Jazz: A Family Album*. Rev. ed. Baton Rouge: Louisiana State University Press, 1978 [original edition, 1967].

Rust, Brian. *Jazz Records 1897–1942*. 2 vols. 4th rev. enl. ed. New Rochelle, NY: Arlington House, 1978.

_____, with Allen G. Debus. *The Complete Entertainment Discography: From the Mid–1890s to 1942*. New Rochelle, NY: Arlington House, 1973.

Schuller, Gunther. *Early Jazz: Its Roots and Musical Development*. New York: Oxford University Press, 1968.

_____. *The Swing Era: The Development of Jazz*. New York: Oxford University Press, 1989.

Schuster, Mel, comp. *Motion Picture Performers: A Bibliography of Magazine and Periodical Articles, 1900–1969*. Metuchen, NJ: Scarecrow Press, 1971.

Seldes, Gilbert. *The Public Arts*. New York: Simon and Schuster, 1956.

Settel, Irving. *A Pictorial History of Radio*. New York: Citadel Press, 1960.

Smith, H. Allen. *The Life and Legend of Gene Fowler*. New York: William Morrow, 1977.

Sobel, Bernard. *A Pictorial History of Vaudeville*. New York: Citadel Press, 1961.

Stine, Whitney, with a running commentary by Bette Davis. *Mother Goddam: The Story of the Career of Bette Davis*. New York: Hawthorn Books, 1974.

Stoddart, Dayton. *Lord Broadway, Variety's Sime*. New York: Wilfred Funk, 1941.

Summers, Harrison B., comp. *A Thirty-Year History of Programs Carried on National Radio Networks in the United States, 1926–1956*. Columbus: Ohio State University, 1958; rpt. New York: Arno Press, 1971.

Taylor, Glenhall. *Before Television: The Radio Years*. South Brunswick and New York: A.S. Barnes, 1979.

Terrace, Vincent. *Encyclopedia of Television: Series, Pilots and Specials*. Vol. 1 (of 3): 1937–1973. New York: Zoetrope, 1986.

Thomas, Bob. *I Got Rhythm!: The Ethel Merman Story*. New York: G.P. Putnam's Sons, 1985.

_____. *Thalberg: Life and Legend*. Garden City, NY: Doubleday, 1969.

Thompson, Charles. *Bing: The Authorized Biography*. New York: David McKay, 1975.

Thompson, Craig, and Allen Raymond. *Gang Rule in New York: The Story of a Lawless Era*. New York: Dial Press, 1940.

Traubel, Helen, with Richard G. Hubler. *St. Louis Woman*. New York: Duell, Sloan and Pearce, 1959.

Whiteman, Paul, and Mary Margaret McBride. *Jazz*. New York: J.H. Sears, 1926.

Wilde, Larry. *The Great Comedians Talk About Comedy*. New York: Citadel Press, 1968.

Zeidman, Irving. *The American Burlesque Show*. New York: Hawthorn Books, 1967.

Zellers, Parker. *Tony Pastor: Dean of the Vaudeville Stage*. Ypsilanti, MI: Eastern Michigan University Press, 1971.

Zolotow, Maurice. *No People Like Show People*. New York: Random House, 1951. [The same chapter on Durante was included in a partially different version of this book, *It Takes All Kinds: Some Actors and Eccentrics*, London: W.H. Allen, 1953.]

INDEX

271